**DO NOT REMOVE
CARDS FROM POCKET**

POLITICAL
LEADERS OF
CONTEMPORARY
AFRICA
SOUTH OF THE
SAHARA

POLITICAL LEADERS OF CONTEMPORARY AFRICA SOUTH OF THE SAHARA

A Biographical Dictionary

EDITED BY
HARVEY GLICKMAN

Greenwood Press
WESTPORT, CONNECTICUT • LONDON

Library of Congress Cataloging-in-Publication Data

Political leaders of contemporary Africa south of the Sahara : a
 biographical dictionary / edited by Harvey Glickman.
     p.   cm.
   Includes bibliographical references and index.
   ISBN 0-313-26781-2 (alk. paper)
   1. Politicians—Africa, Sub-Saharan—Biography—Dictionaries.
 2. Statesmen—Africa, Sub-Saharan—Biography—Dictionaries.
 3. Africa, Sub-Saharan—Biography. 4. Africa, Sub-Saharan—Politics
 and government—1960- I. Glickman, Harvey.
 DT352.8.P63   1992
 967.03′2′0922—dc20   91-39641

British Library Cataloguing in Publication Data is available.

Library of Congress Catalog Card Number: 91–39641
ISBN: 0-313-26781-2

First published in 1992

Greenwood Press, 88 Post Road West, Westport, CT 06881
An imprint of Greenwood Publishing Group, Inc.

Printed in the United States of America

The paper used in this book complies with the
Permanent Paper Standard issued by the National
Information Standards Organization (Z39.48–1984).

10 9 8 7 6 5 4 3 2 1

Copyright Acknowledgment

Some of the material on Jomo Kenyatta by Carl G. Rosberg appeared in slightly different form in
the *Dictionary of National Biography 1971–1980*, edited by Lord Blake and C. S. Nicholls,
Oxford University Press, 1986. Reproduced with permission and gratefully acknowledged.

To Sylvia, partner and coadventurer

CONTENTS

CONTENTS   ix

PREFACE

The purpose of this volume is to provide a reference for persons seeking political and biographical profiles of the major political leaders of sub-Saharan Africa, leaders who have made important and often determinative contributions to politics and government in the states of Africa south of the Sahara since 1945. It serves as an introduction to the politics of Africa south of the Sahara via politics' major personalities. As such, it provides an analytical orientation, derived in part from the paradigm of "personal rule" but also from other research on political leadership in Africa, for the character of politics over much of the last half of the twentieth century in sub-Saharan Africa.

Every reference volume must make choices. In this volume the initial choice was which countries to include. Sub-Saharan Africa has served as a conventional classificatory category for some years, with the Sahara desert dividing black Africa from Arab North Africa. In common with all classifications, the Sahara dividing line does not wholly reflect actuality, as trans-Saharan contacts among Africa's inhabitants continue despite political and administrative changes of the past two hundred years. The classificatory separation responds to the need to account for the differing patterns of duration, intensity and type of European imperial impact on the two parts of geographical Africa. It reflects also the politics of Arab ethnic and cultural unity in North Africa and that relationship to a larger categorical coherence with the Middle East. An earlier Greenwood companion volume to this one included Sudan in North Africa and North Africa with the Middle East, thus determining the definition of the rest of Africa as the preserve of this volume.

Second, the period from the end of World War II represents an established historical watershed that ushered in the end of European colonialism and the rise and expansion of liberationist nationalism among the African populations in colonial territories. This was followed by the inauguration of new and independent governments, to be followed in turn by changes induced by military coups in many postcolonial states. By 1991 worldwide changes in the wake of the end of the Cold War and the collapse of world communism were being manifested in African states by the breakup of centralized and personal rule. This volume reflects the circumstances of the beginning of the 1990s and attempts to answer the question, who have been the major African political leaders since 1945? Space limitations account for the third factor, the actual number of leaders to be included, fifty-four in this instance, a number large enough to be able to illustrate the major political trends of anticolonialism and independent governance through almost half a century; large enough also to be able to include leaders from most of the African countries south of the Sahara, but small enough to serve as an effective reference without striving for the comprehensiveness of a *Who's Who* in every African country. Rather than attempting to present each country's entry in a roster of "top of the charts" in African leaders, the grouping here balances types of political leadership, such as the nature of authority and behavioral influence that is exercised, with geographical representation. We expect controversy: All lists of the "most outstanding" regularly enliven social science and popular debate. The choices here are meant to say something more than "who wins"; they should stimulate discussion of who and what have been important in African politics. Our study should be both useful for first-time investigators and a healthy challenge to veteran analysts.

Specifically whom to include in the end represents the final choice and responsibility of the editor, although certain criteria were employed to construct the list. A survey of the major works on political change in sub-Saharan Africa during the period resulted in a list of most mentioned figures. With the help of a number of experts, many of whom are contributors to this volume, this list was expanded, then refined and reduced via recommendations and advice.

In deciding who qualified as a leader for inclusion, we asked, "Who in the past half century have acted and written in ways to contribute most to shape events—political debate, political processes and political systems—for good or ill in Africa south of the Sahara?" We meant by "shape events" to focus on persons whom we believe that people in Africa would also agree have been in the vanguard of organizing, distributing and manipulating public power in the service of creating, maintaining, developing and drastically changing African states. More concretely, we were seeking persons who have made a noticeable mark in Africa's major political trends since 1945: nationalism and anticolonialism, state reorganization for economic development, and foreign policy toward international alignment or nonalignment. Since we were limited by our mandate of about fifty leaders and by the fact of centralized rule in African states for much of the period covered, it is no accident that most of the leaders included are or have been heads of governments. The categories of thinker, theorist, party leader and politician have run together in Africa, as party and government leaders in many cases wrote the major political tracts and documents of the nationalist and postindependence periods. Second, virtually all the states became single-party or no-party systems rather quickly, or the regimes were overthrown by military coups, thus reducing overt opportunities for leadership to only one channel for political acts and ideas. To put the point another way, potential political debaters and aspiring political leaders had their chances of making an impact severely reduced by the closed system of politics that has existed in most African countries over most of the period under review.

Within the confines of appropriate expertise and the constraint of availability, the editor has tried to transcend a purely American perspective by assembling an international roster of contributors, many of whom have written a biography of the person they were chosen to profile for this volume. All are specialists in the politics of the country they write about, and almost all are social scientists. Each biographical sketch reflects the personal vision of its author, addressing in common five elements: salient personal life details, especially with regard to entry into politics; the process of the individual's advancement and the evidence of leadership skills of the subject; the political mission assumed, accomplished or partially accomplished; the resources assembled and political means utilized; and an assessment of the impact on politics of the individual's career or the political legacy of the particular leader for one country, for the continent, and perhaps beyond. The profiles will facilitate further study of the role of personalities in politics in Africa and elsewhere. An introductory chapter extends the scope of the discussion of political leadership in Africa by treating several analytical themes.

For purposes of quick recognition, each profile subject is identified briefly by one or two—not all—major leadership distinctions. A short bibliography of works by (when appropriate) and about the subject profiled follows each entry. Limited largely but not exclusively to works in English, this bibliography will be helpful to persons beginning more extensive study of the leader or the politics of the country involved. A brief, more general bibliography near the end of the volume of works in English on elites and political change in Africa south of the Sahara permits comparative and contextual investigations. Spelling follows common English usage, accepted transliterations from Arabic and other African languages, and an internationally accepted order of first and last names of persons.

A list of subjects by country follows the profiles. To provide a historical and political context for the reader, a chronology of significant political events since 1945 has been compiled, within which the important dates in the lives and careers of the profiled figures are included. The index helps to cross-reference entries and provides information on persons not profiled as well as notable events in the biographical sketches, facilitating use with the chronology.

This book could not have been completed without the help of many people. Throughout the long and complicated gestation period it was sustained by the generous support of Haverford College. Provosts Jerry Gollub and Bruce Partridge did more than authorize; they were a regular source of encouragement. To all the contributors must go most of the credit for this volume. Among them, important assistance and guidance were provided by Richard Sklar, Mark DeLancey, William Tordoff, John Holm, Marina Ottaway, Elwood Dunn, Robert

Rotberg, Peter Ekeh and Carl Rosberg. Useful advice also came from Thomas
Karis, Gail Gerhart, Edmond Keller, Larry Diamond, Nelson Kasfir, Victor Le
Vine, John Cartwright, Allen Isaacman, Richard Joseph, Claude Ake, John
Marcum, Joel Barkan, Norman Miller, Annette Seegers and Crawford Young.
Student aide William Kropp helped with early investigations of leadership stan-
dards and Robert Hall helped with fact checking. Two outstanding successors,
Najel Klein and Jessica Lewis, also Haverford students, served as the equivalent
of managing coeditors as well as research and production assistants. Lisa Pearl-
man helped complete the chronology rapidly and efficiently. Scott Bomboy did
the index with care and dispatch. Patricia Lynn and Margaret Schaus of the
Haverford College Library were unfailingly helpful in all matters investigational.
Mildred Vasan of Greenwood Press recruited me for this volume and never
flagged in her confidence in the project despite my derailments of the schedule.
She is a model for editors at scholarly presses. Finally, this volume is dedicated
to my wife, Sylvia, whose ties to Africa go back four decades and are regularly
renewed in surprising ways.

INTRODUCTION: POLITICAL LEADERSHIP IN AFRICA SOUTH OF THE SAHARA

> Leaders induce followers to act for certain goals that represent
> the values and the motivation—the wants and needs, the values
> and aspirations—of both leaders and followers.
>
> *James MacGregor Burns, 1977*

What is political leadership? Political leadership is much explored but resists
systematic explanation. It remains necessarily subject to individual volition,
chance and circumstance, often in the midst of larger historical forces, which
the character and effectiveness of leadership itself may subsequently serve to
interpret. Political leadership has been defined as articulating and acting to overcome obstacles to the achievement of mass, often popular goals that are initially
often unpopular with governmental elites. It means also seeking, generating,
manipulating and—usually—capturing power.

Leadership manifests itself in different ways. Some leaders create or crystallize
the goals of followers. Some leaders begin a process of overcoming obstacles
to the achievement of community goals, leaving others to complete the task of
accomplishment. Some leaders bring a stalled project to fulfillment, taking up
goals that others have inspired. Some leaders are faced with the task of overthrowing and then building or rebuilding. All these manifestations of leadership
are illustrated in the Africa of the past half century and in this dictionary.

The spectrum of political leadership runs from "heroic" to "reconciliational"
or (in alternative terms occasionally utilized) from "transformational" to "trans-
actional." The most celebrated is the heroic, where leadership appears larger
than life in a person who articulates a mission for a community and draws others
to himself or herself for the pursuit of that mission (see Nelson Mandela or Steve
Biko of South Africa or Ahmadu Bello of Nigeria). But the reconciliational
leader can fashion the creative compromises that generate unity in addressing

challenges to the accomplishment of a political mission. There are innovative as well as conservative leaders, transformers as well as transactors (brokers). We often forget the contributions of the reconcilers and consensus builders (see Léopold Senghor of Senegal and Dawda Jawara of The Gambia).

In Africa we can also speak in economic terms of "accommodation/reconciliation" of postcolonial nationalist leaders with the former colonial regimes. The successful nationalist political leader does not necessarily attempt to uncouple all connections with the former metropole. With the exception of Sékou Touré and Guinea, this applies to the leaders of the former French colonies, despite varieties of leftist rhetoric (see Senghor, Félix Houphouët-Boigny of Côte d'Ivoire, Ahmadu Ahidjo of Cameroon, Modibo Keita of Mali, and even Thomas Sankara of Burkina Faso). While this policy was intended to accompany the Africanization of enterprise, these Francophone political leaders exchanged military protection and economic and financial regulation for a foreign partnership in domestic domination. In actuality, the putatively radical "transformationist" path, over time, did not differ greatly, in terms of the essentials of political and economic practices or achievements, from the path of "accommodation."

Many political leaders are admirable, but not all of them. Some accomplish major goals of political destruction (see Milton Obote and Idi Amin of Uganda or Hendrik Verwoerd of South Africa). Most political leaders utilize nonadmirable methods, at least some of the time. Memorable political leadership involves the capacity to act and the achievement of some important result, even if it is apparent later than the leader's lifetime (see Eduardo Mondlane of Mozambique, Robert Sobukwe and Albert Luthuli of South Africa and Amílcar Cabral of Guinea). Perhaps we admire most the leaders who give up their lives in a good cause, but some leaders must be seen as memorable simply because they preside over systems that are relatively admirable in their openness (see Seretse Khama and Quett Masire of Botswana, and Jawara.) Some are memorable because they try to move a system from closed to open (Olusegun Obasanjo of Nigeria, Senghor.)

Yet exactly what determines who leads? Historians, social scientists and journalists recognize the connection that emerges between one or a few persons and many others who are induced to follow, but other than attaching the quality of leader to a spokesperson or the holder of an institutional position, commentators usually describe the personal qualities of successful individuals, that is, the qualities of those who induce others to follow. Certainly personal qualities count: shrewdness, charm, oratorical skill, willpower, compulsion to succeed, ruthlessness. We speculate about the formative elements in the early years of persons who come to lead: authoritative parents or relatives, the social status of the "outsider," rootlessness, the favored education, and so on. (In Africa, it is interesting how many future leaders have come from smaller ethnic groups or have spent their youth being taken from town to town.) But in politics the modest qualities of later high achievers, or the failures of those groomed for the top, or the identically perceived personal qualities of later achievers and failures, all suggest that environment plays an equally or more important role, that leadership is a function of—although not determined by—the type of regime in which it emerges. That suggests two themes for Africa. One group of political leaders will emerge as protesters and mobilizers against oppressive governments; another overlapping and complementary group of leaders will be founding fathers and successor governors, establishing connections with their populations from the materials of charismatic and patrimonial authority.

The African political experience since 1945 nests within a global environment of anticolonialism and the emergence of new states in the former colonies in what came to be called the Third World. One phase of leadership emerged in the 1950s and 1960s to mobilize populations inside their colonial envelopes toward independence. Nationalist leadership, however, varied with the manner in which colonial rule ended: elections or rebellion. Félix Houphouët-Boigny of Côte d'Ivoire came to power via parliamentary politics in France and in Africa, while Samora Machel of Mozambique distinguished himself as a guerrilla general before assuming the presidency. The circumstances surrounding transition to independence (stability of inherited institutions, foreign intervention) help explain why nationalist leaders with apparently similar qualities—charisma perhaps, exemplified by both Sékou Touré in Guinea and Patrice Lumumba in Zaire—suffered quite different fates in the immediate postcolonial period.

To what extent do environment and type of regime explain specific differences in the exercise of the leadership that emerged in Africa? While most nationalist successor governments to colonial rule quickly established one-party regimes, some were more tyrannical and oppressive than others; some were relatively more successful in generating economic development and well-being than others. Leaders coming to power after guerilla victory or military coup can mistakenly assume a wartime unity of support and interpret opposition as subversion (see Yoweri Museveni of Uganda and Mengistu Haile Mariam of Ethiopia). They can interpret support for anticolonialism from Communist countries as an element of government worthy of imitation (see Robert Mugabe in Zimbabwe and Machel in Mozambique). African nationalist party leaders in an independence electoral competition did not have to build strong political organizations or intense commitment among all their followers in order to take over the institutions of the new state (see Ahidjo in Cameroon and Kenneth Kaunda in Zambia). Perhaps because of this they felt even more insecure and vulnerable. The political environment and type of regime established are not determinative of the type of leadership exercised. But whether they acceded to power via electioneering or soldiering, African national government leaders established centralized, statist economic policies (despite leftist and nonleftist rhetoric) and cemented their authority by varieties of clientelism, patronage and ethnic and factional favoritism. Within this essentially authoritarian paradigm personal and individual qualities play a role, for example, in differentiating the oligarchic leadership of Jomo Kenyatta in Kenya from the "prophetic" leadership of Julius Nyerere in Tanzania. That is where the personal experiences (upbringing, education, early challenges) of the individual can make a difference and why biographies can always illuminate.

Are personalities more important in African politics than elsewhere? Some observers argue that an attack on colonial policies unnecessarily sapped colonial institutions as well, thus reinforcing the vulnerability of postcolonial politics to excessively personal rule. Others argue that traditional Africa featured chiefly rule, drawing on accepted leadership roles of patriarch, sage and warrior, which was politically manipulated by nationalist leaders seeking validation. Kenyatta in Kenya and, more dramatically, Mobutu Sese Seko in Zaire illustrate this trend. Backed by guns and racist rage, Idi Amin in Uganda still fell back on the African warrior image to strengthen his popularity in the early days of his rule. Despite elements of assimilation, important differences in the establishment and maintenance of legal and bureaucratic institutions exist between sub-Saharan African governments and politics and the European governments from which they sprang—with the exception of South Africa, whose apartheid system perverted British-style parliamentary rule in a special way. In what has come to be the Western European tradition, power, exercised through law, is formally vested in the office and not dependent on the person, and the scope and jurisdiction of officials are limited by law. Favoritism and patronage influence governing, but political authority and processes do not rest on their exercise.

In practice a low degree of institutionalization of public or citizenship roles in favor of personal connection, coupled with the command of economic resources, reinforce in Africa the tendency to emphasize the importance of the "big man" in politics. The other side of the coin is not the lack of pluralism in politics, but rather the dominance of ethnic and client pluralism over functional associations. In addition, the influence over markets by government in African states and the small and weak private sector mean that there are few alternative channels of opportunity or checks on personal rule/government in the making of what becomes public policy.

How different is military leadership from civilian? Civilian party leaders were replaced in many instances after independence by military figures. In most cases their authority depended on a new hierarchy but came to rely on old forms of clientelism, with the inclination to coercion creating a more deadly mixture of consequences for political actions (e.g., Mengistu in Ethiopia). Like their civilian counterparts, military-political leaders featured left- or right-wing rhetoric (compare Jerry Rawlings in Ghana and Thomas Sankara in Burkina Faso with Samuel Doe in Liberia; Siyaad Barre in Somalia shifted from left to right while in power). The coup became the main leadership selection device in African politics for almost a quarter century after independence. A handful of military leaders have attempted to expand the base of their authority beyond the barracks (Rawlings, Mobutu, Sankara, Machel). A phenomenon of the 1990s is the guerila rebel successful in a claim against an independent African government (Jonas Savimbi in Angola and the several guerrilla leaders of the regional liberation fronts who overthrew Mengistu in Ethiopia). But military rulers have thus far been even less effective than civilians in Africa, not because generals can never make effective presidents, but because generals—particularly in the Third World— usually tackle financial and economic policies by abolishing politics, even when they espouse populism. Africa's political problems require a sustained effort at bargaining and consensus building, skills rarely rewarded in a military career. To some extent in Ghana and more comprehensively in Nigeria, there have been efforts by military leaders to formulate and reconstruct civilian political institutions and carry on a dialogue with the masses about an acceptable system for the country (see Rawlings and Obasanjo).

Is Africa likely to get a different brand of leadership in the future? Military-political leaders in African countries today can no longer rely on Cold War competition to inflate their positions into strategic assets in one view or another of global security, as witnessed by the collapse of Doe, Barre and Mengistu and their regimes. Africa's weak economies (except South Africa) are essentially wards of international financial and economic institutions. While a covey of intellectuals in almost every African country may still speak of "autonomic development" and "economic decoupling," the major freedom that challenges current political leaders has more to do with enterprise and speech than national liberation and self-determination.

Regimes are changing in Africa. Competitive elections are occurring in places where previously they were mere formalities. By no means a landslide yet, peaceful handovers of power are no longer a total rarity. Strengthening administrative capacity is a priority of assistance from international economic agencies. Respect for the paper rights in state constitutions is increasingly under foreign scrutiny. Leaders are emerging from previously silent or cowed institutions, such as the church or the bar or the press. The last decade of the twentieth century in Africa ought to see the emergence of political leaders less dependent on a personal following and more dependent on power gained through competition for institutional authority.

THE ROLE OF WOMEN

Unique in the world's regions, sub-Saharan African states have yet to promote women to the top political positions. No Benazir Bhutto, no Cory Aquino, no Evita Peron, no Golda Meir, no Indira Gandhi has appeared. This dictionary includes no profiles of women political leaders in Africa, no women exerting national political leadership equivalent to that of men in the territorial states in the period under review. This imbalance is a commentary on past processes of politics in Africa, on the nature of leadership in Africa and on prospects for the future.

Traditionally subordinate in precolonial African societies, women gained certain new opportunities but also new burdens under colonialism as an agency of modernization, which in effect reinforced and authorized male leadership in economics and in politics. In precolonial traditional African societies men were usually the leaders (heads) of households, but women retained relative autonomy in their own spheres. Men cleared land and fought to gain more, while the women farmed and took care of the family in a roughly unequal division of labor. The male heads of households owned or commanded the use of land and distributed its resources. They formed a council of elders, essentially the political authority of the community.

In many African societies polygamy was practiced, and each wife usually formed a separate economic subunit with her children. Most societies were patrilineal, although a few were matriarchal. In the patrilineal societies women could not inherit property from their husbands and were, in fact, part of the property that sons or family inherited. Even in matriarchal societies men controlled land, marriage, dependents and politics, although women could remain with their own families when they married, and they had rights to their children.

Islam, brought to Africa by traders and by conquest beginning in the seventh century A.D., merged in varying degrees with local traditional religions and customs and had a mixed (mostly negative) effect on the status of women. Formally, women gained a basic dignity, but their actual entitlements remained unequal to those of men. Strict interpretation of Islamic law permitted men to control women. Women were encouraged to stay at home and to dress and behave modestly; they retained a certain restricted access to the marketplace, and some women remained traders.

European slaving, commercial penetration, Christian missionizing and colonial conquest brought with them Western conceptions of gender relations of the times, which also accorded quite restricted public roles to women. Not unexpectedly, colonial administrators were predisposed to grant authority to African men. The extension of commerce and public finance into Africa brought with them the need for cash and created new relationships in African society. Men had to enter wage labor and migrated to the cities, while women remained on the farms to care for and feed their children. Plantation farming drew male labor away from peasant plots for cash wages, reinforcing the need for women to remain at home on the smallholdings. After independence, when the state could focus part of its agricultural subsidies on peasant smallholdings in addition to Africanizing the ownership or management of plantations, it transferred technology and credit largely to men for use on the land.

Christian missionaries reinforced the idea of separate and unequal spheres for men and women. The advent of Western education favored men, relegating women to home economics or elementary education, or seeing education as wasted altogether on women. These attitudes continue today. Only at the primary level is there equal participation for women and men in education. A decade ago about three-fourths of all African women were illiterate, while about half of the men were. Girls get taught the basic skills for low-paying jobs and not much about agriculture, despite the fact that most farmers in Africa are women. In the workplace, even educated women often receive less pay than men for the same type of work. Nevertheless, it is level and type of education that grant greater equality and status to women, in Africa as elsewhere.

Territorial national independence movements and the male leadership welcomed roles for women in the struggle. Women participated in party membership drives, electoral mobilization and guerrilla warfare. Just about every nationalist party had its women's section and a few women candidates for national assembly. Populist military leaders, such as Sankara in Burkina Faso, vaulted women into the cabinet as a manifestation of opposition to "feudal" traditions. More publicized were women prominent in the left-wing one-party states, such as Guinea, as well as in liberation movements and their military auxiliaries in Mozambique (Front for the Liberation of Mozambique [FRELIMO]), Angola (Popular Movement for the Liberation of Angola [MPLA]), Guinea-Bissau (Partido Africano da Independéncia da Guiné e Cabo Verde [PAIGC]), Zimbabwe (Zimbabwe African National Union [ZANU]) and South Africa (African National Congress [ANC]). When the guerrilla armies and their political counterparts won territory, they included women in the newly established local governments. The PAIGC, for example, mandated that at least two people in its five-member village councils be women. A number of women leaders emerged in this way. Some became ministers or regional governors, but none rose to durable national prominence. Yet most Africans still live as peasants in rural areas where children are not only social security, but essentially fulfill the meaning of both womanhood and manhood. The wife remains responsible for feeding and raising the children, including earning money for school fees and uniforms. Little time is left over for politics. Finally, as difficult as it has been for women to be taken seriously as rising political leaders in civilian regimes, it is doubly difficult in military regimes, for obvious reasons, and much of Africa has been governed by military leaders for many years.

Foreign-aided economic development efforts, despite the stated goal of attending to women's needs in agriculture, find plans difficult to implement, as agricultural extension workers are almost always men who ignore the roles of women. Women are expected to be farmers and nurturers but not innovators. The United Nations Decade for Women (1975–85) culminated in an international conference in Nairobi that created spillover effects in legislation and practices in many African states. Women's paragovernmental organizations found administrative counterparts in women's bureaus in ministries dealing with social services and the like. Legislation codifying property and marriage rights for women has been passed, although in several countries with large Muslim populations increased openness in politics has stirred a fundamentalist backlash.

On the other hand, since the 1970s a number of women have held ministerial and junior ministerial portfolios and headed state delegations to the UN and to international conferences in countries such as Tanzania, Guinea, Burkina Faso, Ethiopia, Zimbabwe, Uganda and Liberia. Women lawyers have become increasingly active in national organizations affecting civil rights and the environment. Wangari Mathaai, a Kenya lawyer, was recognized internationally for her struggle on behalf of environmental planning by the Africa Leadership Prize in 1990. The civilianization of politics and the breakup of authoritarian rule in Africa ought to provide greater opportunities for women in politics. Competitive politics will bid for women's votes, and one way is through promoting women political leaders.

BIBLIOGRAPHY

Bailey, F. G. *Humbuggery and Manipulation: The Art of Leadership*. Ithaca, N.Y. Cornell University Press, 1988.

Blondel, Jean. "Leadership." In Vernon Bogdanor (ed.), *The Blackwell Encyclopaedia of Political Institutions*. Oxford: Basil Blackwell, 1987, 321–22.

Burns, James MacGregor. *Leadership*. New York: Harper and Row, 1978.

Cartwright, John. *Political Leadership in Africa*. New York: St. Martin's Press, 1983.

Fieldhouse, D. K. *Black Africa, 1945–1980: Economic Decolonization and Arrested Development*. London: Allen and Unwin, 1986.

Glickman, Harvey, and Kathleen Staudt (eds.). "Beyond Nairobi: Women's Politics and Policies in Africa Revisited." *Issue: A Journal of Opinion* 17, no. 2 (Summer 1989): whole issue.

Hay, Margaret Jean, and Sharon B. Stichter (eds.). *African Women South of the Sahara*. New York: Longman Group, 1984.

Jackson, Robert H., and Carl G. Rosberg. *Personal Rule in Black Africa: Prince, Autocrat, Prophet, Tyrant*. Berkeley: University of California Press, 1982.

Mazrui, Ali A., and Michael Tidy. *Nationalism and New States in Africa*. London: Heinemann, 1984.

Njoku, John E. Eberegbulam. *The World of the African Woman*. Metuchen, N.J.: Scarecrow Press, 1980.

Paige, Glenn D. *The Scientific Study of Political Leadership*. New York: Free Press, 1977.

Parpart, Jane L., and Kathleen A. Staudt (eds.). *Women and the State in Africa*. Boulder, Colo.: Lynne Rienner Publishers, 1989.

Parpart, Jane L., and Sharon B. Stichter (eds.). *Patriarchy and Class: African Women in the Home and the Workforce*. Boulder, Colo.: Westview Press, 1988.

Rustow, Dankwart (ed.). *Philosophers and Kings: Studies in Leadership*. New York: Braziller, 1970.

Seligman, Lester G. "Leadership: Political Aspects." In David L. Sills (ed.), *International Encyclopedia of the Social Sciences*, Vol. 9. New York: Macmillan and The Free Press, 1968.

Wallerstein, Immanuel. *Africa, The Politics of Independence: An Interpretation of Modern African History*. New York: Vintage Books, 1961.

Wildavsky, Aaron. *The Nursing Father: Moses as a Political Leader*. University, Ala.: University of Alabama Press, 1984.

Wriggins, W. Howard. *The Ruler's Imperative*. New York: Columbia University Press, 1969.

HARVEY GLICKMAN
with the assistance of Najel Klein and Jessica Lewis

A

AHMADOU AHIDJO (1924–1989), Prime Minister, President, Republic of Cameroon, 1958–1982.

In the thirty-five years of his political career, Ahmadou Ahidjo—the first president of the Republic of Cameroon—brought independence to his country, established its political structures and national identity, and fostered economic growth and development within the confines of Cameroon's position in the world economy. In these respects, he was the father of his country.

Ahmadou Ahidjo was born in August 1924 (some reports claim 1922) in Garoua, a major city in the north of the then French mandate territory of Cameroon. According to some reports, his father was a chief and his mother of slave descent among the Fulani or Peuhl peoples, but it is clear that he was brought up by his mother in an essentially single-parent family. He was raised as a Moslem and attended Quranic school. In 1932 he entered the local government primary school, but he failed his first school certificate examination in 1938. After a brief stint in the veterinary service he returned to school and succeeded in his examination in 1939. Three years followed at the Ecole Primaire Superieure in Yaounde, the administrative capital of the mandate. During these school years he is reported to have been a soccer player and a cyclist; his interest in soccer was maintained throughout his life, and as president he provided significant support for the development of the sport in the country. In 1942 Ahidjo joined the civil service and, after a brief period of training, entered the postal service as a radio operator. His duties took him to assignments in several major towns and cities—Douala, Ngaoundere, Yaounde, Bertoua, Mokolo and Garoua. An official biographer claimed that Ahidjo was the first civil servant of northern birth ever to serve in the southern portions of the territory. Whether that is correct or not, Ahidjo's experiences as student and bureaucrat in various regions of the mandate were significant in the development of his sense of a Cameroon nation and identity and in later years provided him with considerable insight into the problems of governing a multiethnic state and constructing a Cameroon nation from this pluralistic society.

Ahidjo's interest in politics was apparent at an early age. At twenty-four he sought his first office, running successfully for delegate to the Representative Assembly (ARCAM) in 1946. This was the Trust Territory of Cameroon's first elected legislative body, but as France moved toward granting independence to its African territories almost continual constitutional change took place in Cameroon. In 1947 Ahidjo was defeated in an election for the Assembly of the French Union, but in 1952 he was re-elected to the Territorial Assembly (ATCAM, successor to ARCAM). In 1953 he was elected councillor to the Assembly of the French Union. During the four years he spent in this body he was associated with the Overseas Independents group, which included men such as Léopold Senghor[*] and Dr. Louis Aujolat, a Frenchman active in Cameroon politics. Ahidjo aligned his followers with Aujolat's Bloc Démocratique du Cameroun in the ATCAM, where Ahidjo retained his seat.

Originally Ahidjo based his electoral support on a group he founded, the Friendly Association of Benoue. At this time he also played a leading role in the Moslem Youths group. He opposed the traditional rulers of the northern areas, joining together with the younger and more Western-educated "modernizing" faction. In later years his opposition to the northern chiefs mellowed, and they were to become significant supporters of his long reign as president. His marriage to the daughter of the *lamido* (chief) of Garoua may have aided in this reconciliation.

In 1955 the delegates elected him vice president of the ATCAM, and in 1956 he won re-election to the Assembly. His supporters in the Benoue area were not sufficient to bring him victory in an attempt to win a seat in the French National Assembly that year; he lost to Jules Ninine, the candidate supported by the colonial administration. The loss was an important lesson, for it indicated to Ahidjo the need for a base of support broader than the Benoue district. In January 1957 he was elected president of the Legislative Assembly (ALCAM, successor to ATCAM) with the support of the northern delegates. In February he organized these supporters in the Union Camerounaise, which in 1958 became a recognized political party, eventually to become the predominant party and the parent of the Union Nationale Camerounaise (UNC), founded in 1966; the UNC became the sole political party of Cameroon.

This powerful base of support in the ALCAM led to Ahidjo's appointment as deputy prime minister in charge of the Ministry of the Interior when Cameroon received self-government in May 1957. This first government, led by André-Marie Mbida, a southerner, faced significant political problems. Most important of these was the open war in the territory between the French administration and the radical political party, the Union des Populations du Cameroun (UPC). Second was the question of reunification, the desire of many Cameroonians to rejoin those portions of the old German colony of Kamerun that had been placed under French and British mandate after World War I. Third was the timing and manner of independence from France. Mbida followed unpopular policies on each of these issues, and the more politically astute Ahidjo, sensing public attitudes, resigned from the government. A few days later Mbida resigned, to be replaced on February 18, 1958, by Ahidjo.

Ahidjo, a pragmatic political realist, now was in a powerful position to build a territorywide political constituency. He had developed personal relations from the Benoue district throughout the north, and now he was expanding these ties throughout the country. Cameroon gained independence from France on January 1, 1960, and, after a plebiscite, portions of the British trust territory joined the Republic of Cameroon on September 1, 1961, to form the Federal Republic of Cameroon. While strengthening his base of support in the ex-French territory (the East Cameroon), Ahidjo now began to develop a base in the ex-British territory (the West Cameroon).

Soon after independence and with the adoption of the first of several constitutions, Ahidjo became president of the republic. He won re-election in 1965, 1970, 1975 and 1980. On November 4, 1982, supposedly due to ill health, Ahidjo resigned from his post of president of the country and yielded power to his personally chosen, constitutional successor, Paul Biya.

In common with most African states, Cameroon at independence had severe political and economic problems. This multiethnic entity consisted of numerous language and cultural groups and large numbers of Muslims and Christians as well as followers of African religions; there were regional differences and—after the rejoining of the two trust territories—significantly different colonial inheritances. In addition, over seventy-five years of colonial rule had led to the construction of only the rudiments of a national political system. Weak institutions of government, a shortage of trained and experienced personnel and a still-to-be-built political process challenged the ingenuity of the new president and his advisors.

Complicating the political problems of nation and state building was the sad condition of the economy, a mere appendage of the French economic system. The majority of Cameroonians were involved in subsistence farming, with a few producing cash crops important for export. A small industrial sector existed, but its main activity was the production of aluminum for export. Industrial goods were imported at great expense, and infrastructure was grossly inadequate. France and French citizens played powerful roles as major customers of Cameroon produce, as major exporters to Cameroon, as the prime investors in the country and as the source of most professional, technical and high-level commercial personnel.

Faced with these critical issues and involved in a raging civil war with the followers of the UPC, Ahidjo undertook the establishment of a highly centralized state in which almost all power was concentrated in one man, the president. Borrowing from African political practice, the lessons of French colonial rule and his own creativity, Ahidjo built an authoritarian political system with himself at the center. With the power he accumulated Ahidjo forged the rudiments of a

Cameroon nation, constructed the institutions and political process of a national government, and promoted significant economic growth.

The major policies of Ahidjo were centralization, coalition building and repression. His control of the economic resources of the state—the country's largest employer and source of funds for economic development and the construction of infrastructure—provided him the wherewithal to proceed with these policies. The dissolution of all political parties except the Ahidjo-dominated UNC (1966), the dissolution of the federation to form the United Republic of Cameroon (1972), the linking of previously autonomous organizations (unions, women's and youth groups, and other voluntary organizations) to the UNC, the concentration of administration in the capital, and frequent revision of the constitution to provide the legal background for an ever-strengthening presidential power were the most important of Ahidjo's centralization tactics.

To gain the support necessary to enable him to enact these tactics, Ahidjo built a coalition of local and regional leaders (traditional and modern), which also included the bureaucracy, the military, urbanites and elements of the petite bourgeoisie, and his original northern and Benoué-based network. In building this coalition, the president relied on the economic power of the state, his total control of nominations and appointments, the state security apparatus, and a careful and adroit manipulation of ethnicity in the appointment process. He constructed a patron-client network that extended from his office to the smallest village through the granting of employment, contracts and development projects. Corruption, the use of state resources for individual gain, and smuggling were allowed to go unchecked for those favored by the president.

If support could not be gained through persuasion or financial means, the state would rely on repression and the suppression of human rights. Freedom of speech and press were denied. Political prisoners were common, and the population believed, correctly or not, that torture was frequently used on such prisoners. Public demonstrations, unless initiated by the government, were not tolerated and were usually met by shows of overwhelming force and violence.

Under Ahidjo's rule Cameroon's foreign policy, while ostensibly nonaligned, was generally based on a close relationship with France and the Western, capitalist countries. He successfully played a delicate balancing game in maintaining good relations with France and receiving the economic, military and diplomatic benefits of that relationship, while simultaneously developing economic and political ties to other Western powers in an effort to decrease dependency on France. Thus today France remains as the foremost external economic and political influence on Cameroon policy, but Cameroon now trades with and receives investment from a more diversified list of countries. Ahidjo's economic policies were looked upon with great favor by Western governments and investors. Planned liberalism, whereby a free-market society was linked to economic planning by a strong central government; self-reliant development, whereby the government welcomed foreign investment (but only if such investment was directed toward priorities established by the government) while trying to increase reliance on local capital, technology and personnel; and balanced development, whereby the government attempted to equalize the distribution of benefits of economic growth among the regions and the rural areas of the country, were the major rubrics under which the economy was promoted. Overall, the government followed conservative policies, international debt was kept low, and much attention was devoted to attracting investment.

One may debate the wisdom of various aspects of Ahidjo's economic policies; most certainly there were errors, waste and corruption. But in comparison to most African countries, the Cameroon economy grew considerably during the years of his rule. In this respect Ahidjo was assisted mightily by the discovery of exploitable petroleum resources. Petroleum came into production about the same time as oil prices increased rapidly. Thus Cameroon was able to garner substantial wealth from the export of oil while avoiding the balance-of-payments problems met by oil-importing countries. The rapid growth of oil revenues in the late 1970s provided Ahidjo with considerable funds to maintain support for his rule. However, the appearance of rapid growth masked the failure of the government to alter the dependent nature of its economy. In the end Cameroon remained dependent on the export of raw materials (petroleum, coffee, tea and timber) for income. Little industrial development had taken place; minimal funds were in reserve; infrastructural development was sorely needed; and Cameroon still relied on external capital for investment. It was left to Ahidjo's successor, Paul Biya, to face the economic crisis that was impending at the time of Ahidjo's resignation.

On November 4, 1982, Ahidjo resigned from the office of national president; his successor, Paul Biya, took office on November 6. At first glance, this resignation was quite unusual, for few African presidents have voluntarily given up power. But in fact, Ahidjo did not intend to surrender power in leaving this office; he remained in a second significant position, leader of the UNC. Ahidjo believed that President Biya would be under his control, in part because Ahidjo had personally groomed Biya for this position, in part because Ahidjo left behind a cabinet packed with his supporters, and in part because he believed that his position as head of the UNC would allow him to dominate the political process.

A power struggle between the two men broke out after a few months of apparent cooperation. Biya proved to be a stronger, more independent character than Ahidjo had envisaged. Biya used the financial resources of the president's office to take over the patron-client network established by Ahidjo: Ahidjo tried to assert the primacy of the party by proposing a constitutional change that would have given the party sole power to nominate presidential candidates. The effort failed; the party leaders stood behind Biya. Ahidjo left the country.

In August 1983 Ahidjo was implicated in an antigovernment plot. In April 1984 a major coup attempt was put down after considerable destruction and loss of life. Northerners and supporters of Ahidjo were predominant amongst the rebels, and it has been widely assumed that Ahidjo was involved. From this point until his death (November 30, 1989), Ahidjo apparently withdrew from political activity, living out his last days in southern France and Dakar, Senegal.

For a brief time after the plot and coup attempts Ahidjo's reputation in Cameroon was diminished. Those who had never liked his authoritarian, procapitalist and pro-Western politics were joined by those infuriated that he had been unable to give up power gracefully and that he had been willing, as it seemed, to bring the country to the brink of a north-south civil war in his desire to regain power. However, today a process of reinvigorating his reputation is under way. The Biya regime has been plagued by economic problems as well as political upheavals. For many Cameroonians, Biya is to blame for these conditions, and some look back to the Ahidjo years as a golden age of political stability and economic growth. Eventually, Ahidjo must be properly recognized for the significant contributions his leadership made to Cameroon. He established and institutionalized a Cameroon political process, a process so well entrenched that President Biya has maintained it almost intact. Ahidjo presided over Cameroon for twenty-two years, long enough to establish a pattern of human interaction that ties the country together in a national identity, a Cameroon nation. His economic policies carried the country through substantial progress within the limits of a dependent, export-oriented economy. For Ahidjo's successors there remain the daunting problems of democratizing the political system he established and finding the way to break out of the country's status as a dependent economy, still heavily dominated by external forces and still unable to satisfy many of the material needs of its people.

BIBLIOGRAPHY

Work by Ahidjo:

Fondements et perspectives du Cameroun nouveau. Aubagne-en-Provence: Saint Lambert, 1976.

Other Works:

Bayart, Jean-François. *L'Etat au Cameroun*. Paris: Presses de la Fondation Nationale des Sciences Politiques, 1979.
Beti, Mongo. *Main basse sur le Cameroun: Autopsie d'une décolonisation*. Paris: François Maspero, 1977.
Cameroon National Union. *The Political Philosophy of Ahmadou Ahidjo*. Monte Carlo: Paul Bory, 1968.
DeLancey, Mark. *Cameroon: Dependence and Independence*. Boulder, Colo.: Westview Press, 1989.
DeLancey, Mark, and H. Mbella Mokeba. *Historical Dictionary of Cameroon*. Metuchen, N.J.: Scarecrow Press, 1990.
Joseph, Richard (ed.). *Gaullist Africa: Cameroon under Ahmadou Ahidjo*. Enugu, Nigeria: Fourth Dimension, 1978.
LeVine, Victor. *The Cameroon Federal Republic*. Ithaca, N.Y.: Cornell University Press, 1971.
Ngayap, Pierre. *Cameroon, qui governe? De Ahidjo à Biya, l'heritage et l'enjeu*. Paris: Harmattan, 1983.

Njeuma, Martin (ed.). *Introduction to the History of the Cameroon in the 19th and 20th Centuries*. London: Macmillan, 1989.

MARK DELANCEY

IDI AMIN (1925–   ), Military dictator, President, Republic of Uganda, 1971–1979.

Possibly no other recent event catapulted Uganda, and with it Africa, into the global spotlight as did Idi Amin's January 25, 1971, coup d'état and his bloody eight-year reign in Kampala. To this day Amin's name is synonymous with personal dictatorship, senseless murder and brutality. The massive socioeconomic ravages and dislocations his regime exacted still plague and destabilize the current administration in Uganda.

Idi Amin was born in 1925 (according to some, in 1926) in Koboko County in the distant and remote northern West Nile District, itself the smallest in Uganda. His mother was a Lugbara, while his father was a common laborer of the small Kakwa ethnic sliver, both Sudanic ethnic groups largely outside the mainstream of Uganda's social and political evolution. Since Amin's rise to power there has been considerable, but unresolved, speculation about his possible Nubi origins, because many of his actions in office favored this unique but suspect itinerant Nilotic group that originated in the Equatoria Province of Sudan. However that may be, Amin's very humble origins in a marginal ethnic group in the distant and underdeveloped pastoral periphery of Uganda, where physical prowess, stamina and combative skills are valued (the West Nile District has the highest homicide statistics in Uganda) played a key role in his formative years and distinctly colored his perception of the world.

Shortly after Amin's birth his parents separated. His father returned to Sudan, where he had frequently resided, in search of work. Amin was raised by his mother, who, while migrating southward, became a military camp follower and practitioner of petty witchcraft and traditional medicine. Amin received no formal schooling whatsoever, though while assisting with the household income by peddling biscuits in the streets he picked up a smattering of English and several indigenous languages.

In 1946 Amin joined the King's African Rifles, originally as a cook and/or orderly. There he finally found his niche in life, since he was the ideal kind of soldier for Britain's colonial armies—rugged, powerful, uncomplicated, servile and gregarious. He was popular with the rank-and-file troops, where his barracks-style humor and antics, as well as his sexual proclivities, gained him respect and loyalty. His physical prowess also gave him an edge in sporting events, a fact that endeared him to his superior officers. He played on the army rugby team and later became the heavyweight boxing champion of Uganda. (He retained the crown for nine years and retired undefeated.)

Amin saw active military duty in helping suppress the Mau Mau rebellion in neighboring Kenya, where his callous brutality nearly brought his career to an end on two occasions. (Later, as president of Uganda, he was to gleefully recount one of his exploits, which involved stuffing handkerchiefs down prisoners' throats, to a shocked group of heads of state attending a conference of the Organization of African Unity.) Despite his acute personal limitations and streaks of brutality, he was viewed by his British military superiors as an able and reliable leader of men, and by 1960 he had risen to the highest NCO rank any African could attain in British East Africa, *effendi*.

By that time prospects of decolonization and eventual independence had created the necessity of promoting to commissioned officer at least a few African soldiers who would assume the mantle of leadership in the new national army. Due to his lengthy tenure and proven reliability as an NCO Idi Amin became one of the first two Ugandans to be commissioned. His lack of formal education was brushed under the carpet, and his practical experience was stressed. Once again, in 1962, this time as a lieutenant, he showed utter lack of regard for human life during a patrol of the unruly Karamojong District in the northeast. Yet once he had broken through the NCO barrier, there was no way his further promotion could be blocked, especially in light of the paramount nationalist goal in postindependence Kampala to Africanize the Ugandan officer corps and its highest echelons as fast as possible. By 1965 the unlettered Amin had been promoted to the rank of major and held the post of deputy commander of the armed forces.

In 1965 Amin was entrusted by Prime Minister Milton Obote[*] (behind the back of the chief of staff) with surreptitiously assisting the arming and financing of the Christophe Gbenye regime in Stanleyville (contending for power in the Congo, now Zaire). The parliamentary imbroglio that resulted when details of the affair surfaced (the ''gold and ivory affair'') brought demands for Amin's dismissal. Instead, Obote's cabinet opposition was arrested, and on February 22, 1966, Amin was promoted to commander of the armed forces. As the simmering tug of war between Obote and the *kabaka* (king) of Buganda (reflecting the north-south cleavage in Uganda) came to a head, Amin was ordered to disperse threatening demonstrations in Kampala, which he did in an unnecessarily brutal way. Though Amin was to continue to serve his political master well over the next few years, an estrangement between the two men developed that was to lead to the 1971 coup d'état.

The roots of Amin's seizure of power had to do with his perception that he was slowly being eased out of his monopoly of power in the armed forces. By the late 1960s there were numerous other officers in the Ugandan army. Many possessed formal education and had been promoted after attending military staff colleges overseas rather than by special promotion from the ranks, as with Amin. Among them were several of Obote's ethnicity who were clearly being groomed to replace Amin, whose tenure at the summit of the military had created internal factions. Moreover, Amin's personal administrative limitations had resulted in gross unauthorized military overexpenditures and the embezzlement of funds. Amin's attempts to staff his key regiment with Kakwa recruits from his home region (as opposed to Obote's directive to recruit Langi) had raised questions about his intrinsic loyalty; some of his undiplomatic actions while on missions abroad caused unrest at home; and finally, there was evidence that Amin was involved in the murder of a fellow senior officer who had cast aspersions on Amin's courage and/or loyalty in the aftermath of an assassination attempt on Obote. Leaving for a Commonwealth heads of state meeting, Obote gave the minister of defense and the chief of staff an ultimatum to resolve the embezzlement and murder issues before his return. Whether or not Obote later telephoned from Singapore to have Amin arrested for these crimes (the point is disputed), on January 25, 1971, Amin seized power in Kampala.

Given the motivations of his coup d'état—a pre-emptive personalist seizure of power stemming solely from fear of eclipse and arrest—and his unsocialized personality makeup, it is not surprising that once Amin was in power his reign proved to be rudderless, totally barren of policy, and resting on the utilization of brute force alone, leading Uganda into monumental socioeconomic dislocation and lawlessness. Although he published a white paper listing the flaws of the antecedent regime and was at the outset greeted with some popular acclaim in the south, very rapidly Amin was to alienate every segment and ethnic group in the country, including his own Kakwa. As his leadership led to deep economic decay and regression, there were not even adequate funds to keep the armed forces docile; this explains the unruliness of the only force that sustained Amin's dictatorship.

Amin's initial attempt to rule with the assistance of a largely civilian advisory cabinet was a fiasco. The purpose of cabinet meetings eluded him. He could not follow the discussion, nor was he willing to delegate authority or follow the recommendations of his ministers. Indeed, no one has ever seen Amin read or write any document, and his command of English or Luganda (the lingua franca of the south) was rudimentary. With limited ability to concentrate, a poor memory and little penchant for the niceties of detail, Amin rapidly became bored by cabinet deliberations, in which he invariably imposed his will through brute intimidation. By 1973 he had dismissed his cabinet and ruled with the aid of an ad hoc group of sycophants and/or unlettered military cronies that he promoted from the rank and file of the armed forces—his social and mental peers.

Virtually from the outset of his reign Amin initiated an ethnic bloodbath, as specially designated armed squads were sent out to isolate and physically liquidate Acholi and Langi soldiers and officers (supportive of Obote) in the various military camps of Uganda. Thousands died gruesome deaths, and many others escaped into exile to Kenya and Tanzania. Some of these troops were to participate in an ill-fated pro-Obote invasion of Uganda in 1972 and later in the successful invasion by Tanzania in 1979 that led to Amin's ousting. The ethnic massacres included indiscriminate punitive measures against civilians in districts regarded as inherently disloyal and random settling of old scores. Military discipline in the Ugandan armed forces all but disappeared. The country was transformed into a patchwork of autonomous military fiefdoms over which specific garrisons had power of life and death, living off the land and terrorizing and brutalizing the population. As early as 1973 the International Commission of Jurists was to refer to Uganda as "a lawless state."

The number of people who died under Amin's aegis has been estimated at 250,000. The swathe of destruction started with Acholi and Langi districts but rapidly encompassed the entire country, including Amin's own West Nile District. Individuals particularly targeted for liquidation (who simply "disappeared") included especially the former political leadership, intellectuals and Christians. Even the archbishop of Kampala was not immune (he was murdered in 1977); two American reporters investigating a pogrom in a military camp were likewise casually murdered. Some were personally murdered by Amin himself, and there have also been allegations of Amin's practice of ritual cannibalism.

To replace his decimated officer corps and to triple the size of the army, now his sole prop in power, Amin undertook a massive recruitment of northerners and foreigners, thereby completely transforming the ethnic composition and command hierarchy of the army. By 1977 the armed forces were largely non-national in origin: Some 50 percent were Nubi or Sudanese and 25 percent Zairians, united solely by motivations of self-interest and prospects of plunder. The officer corps was overwhelmingly Muslim, a 10 percent minority in Uganda. Fully seventeen of its twenty-two most senior officers were Muslim, thirteen originating from the West Nile District, the smallest in Uganda. Only three were of the ethnic groups comprising 98 percent of the rest of the population, and most had been orderlies, drivers (one a tractor driver) or NCOs before being tapped for command of entire regiments or divisions by Amin.

Notwithstanding the remodeling of the armed forces along Amin's own image, the unruliness of the military was a key characteristic of Amin's eight-year interregnum, which was punctuated by constant revolts and mutinies. His own regiment rebelled and was dismantled. Amin's motorcade convoys were ambushed numerous times, though he evaded injury through his innate deviousness; there were even two occasions when attempts were made to shoot down his plane as he returned from international visits.

Aided by a Ghanaian soothsayer, at times alluding to divine inspiration, Amin made public policy-making in Uganda little more than a function of his ad hoc gut biases, reactions and inclinations. Despite the utter ruthlessness of his regime, Amin relished giving rambling disconnected impromptu speeches to farmers and students alike of the necessity for hard work, providing his audiences with highly moralistic suggestions about public demeanor and behavior. He attained global notoriety, however, for his international antics, which included mocking presidents Nixon and Nyerere* and prime ministers Thatcher and Meir. Relations with Britain were ultimately ruptured, as were those with Israel in exchange for Arab (Libyan and Saudi) loans and military support. Amin offered numerous "master plans" for the liquidation of Israel, the defeat of South Africa and the resolution of the conflict in Northern Ireland, and he also declared his candidacy for the headship of the British Commonwealth. He gave his support to terrorists who brought a hijacked Air France plane to Kampala, lauded Hitler, applauded the Munich Olympic massacres, bullied neighbors like Rwanda, and taunted others like Kenya and Tanzania.

Despite the extreme centralization of power in Amin's hands and the brutality of his dictatorship, there was a total lack of leadership from the top and a massive administrative breakdown in Uganda. Bureaucratic chaos was the norm, especially after Amin's drastic expulsion of Uganda's long-resident Asian community. The latter's sixty thousand members constituted the country's commercial, entrepreneurial, industrial and professional backbone, and their ouster threw the economy (exports and domestic revenues in particular) into a tailspin from which it may never recover. Many fields of economic activity virtually disappeared; tourism, the country's second earner of foreign exchange, ground to a halt, while formerly vibrant Asian tea plantations grew wild after being plundered at the time of the Asian expulsions.

The state treasury was treated as Amin's private purse. There was no semblance of planning or accountable expenditures. When funds dried up, the Bank of Uganda was simply ordered to print more money, triggering a 1,000 percent inflation rate. Smuggling of crops across the Kenyan border became routine as producers moved into the underground economy, further contributing to the economic decay. By 1977, with many of Uganda's exports at levels of sixty years previous, international suppliers were unwilling to ship anything into the country except against prepayment. Amin's sole lifeline was the biweekly flight to Djibouti that evacuated Uganda's dwindling coffee exports and flew in luxury goods for Amin and his cohorts. By that time many farmers had shifted from producing cash crops to subsistence crops in order to physically survive in a country rife with shortages of all commodities. A massive brain drain accompanied economic decline as thousands of intellectuals, teachers and professionals fled the country.

The collapse of the Amin dictatorship occurred in 1979. Faced with a new series of revolts in his unruly armed forces, Amin announced that he had repulsed a fictitious Tanzanian incursion and ordered the invasion of part of Tanzania. The Tanzanian counterassault that followed was joined by an assortment of Ugandan armed forces that ultimately, and without too much actual fighting, secured the entire country. While continuing to exhort his troops to repel the invaders, Amin slipped into a jet together with several wives, concubines and twenty of his children and escaped to Libya and then to Saudi Arabia.

Since his ouster Amin has led a sedate life in a comfortable but secluded villa in Riyadh. In January 1989 he surprisingly flew into Kinshasa from Lagos, using a forged Zairian passport. He was recognized on arrival and not allowed to land. The purpose of this rare venture abroad is not known, although unsettled conditions in northern Uganda might have enticed him to consider a military comeback.

BIBLIOGRAPHY

Avirgan, Tony, and Martha Honey. *War in Uganda: The Legacy of Idi Amin.* London: Zed Press, 1982.
Decalo, Samuel. "Idi Amin: The Brutal Reign of the Iron Marshal." In Samuel Decalo

(ed.), *Psychoses of Power: African Personal Dictatorships*. Boulder, Colo.: West-view Press, 1989.
Listowel, Judith. *Amin*. London: Irish University Press, 1973.
Martin, David. *General Amin*. London: Faber and Faber, 1974.
Omara-Otunnu, Amii. *Politics and the Military in Uganda, 1890–1985*. London: Mac-millan, 1987.

SAMUEL DECALO

OBAFEMI AWOLOWO (1909–1987, Regional Premier and Minister; Federal Commissioner and Vice Chairman, Federal Executive Council; Opposition Party Leader, Federal Republic of Nigeria, 1960–1984.

The life and political career of Chief Obafemi Awolowo—teacher, clerk, journalist, businessman, lawyer, author and one of Nigeria's pre-eminent politicians of this century—spanned the period from the British colonial occupation of Nigeria and the emergence of a new generation of militant youth nationalist movements in the 1930s to the last phase of Nigeria's freedom struggle, the attainment of political independence in 1960 and the early postcolonial period of Nigerian history. This period saw advances in health and education, but also the sustenance of a neocolonial economy, the infusion of manipulative ethnicity and rabid regionalism into Nigerian politics, the collapse of colonial federalism, military rule from 1966 to 1979, the return to civilian rule between 1979 and 1983, and the return of military rule since 1984. During a long career spanning over four decades (from the 1940s to 1987), Awolowo was an active participant and major contributor to the political, social, educational, ideological and intellectual issues that affected the course and texture of Nigerian political life.

Obafemi Awolowo was born on March 6, 1909, at Ikenne in Ijebu Remo in the present Ogun state of Nigeria. His father, David Sopolu Awolowo, was a farmer, while his mother, Mary Efunyela Awolowo, was a trader. He had his primary education in St. Savior's School, Ikenne, and Wesleyan Primary School, Imo, and his secondary education at Baptist Boys' High School, Abeokuta, and Wesley (Teachers) College, Ibadan. Awolowo's family was plunged into poverty following his father's death in 1920. Through hard work they recovered.

Awolowo, like most ambitious youths of the colonial period, used whatever opportunities were available to advance his education. In the absence of university-level institutions in Nigeria before 1948, young Nigerians went abroad for higher education, sponsored by their parents, missionaries, the colonial state or their communities. The other option was enrollment as an external student of British universities or correspondence schools and work toward various diploma and degree certificates. Awolowo enrolled as an external student of the University of London and received his bachelor of commerce in 1944. But this correspondence degree did not satisfy the ambitious and determined young man. He sponsored himself to study law in London between 1944 and 1946. He qualified as a lawyer and was called to the bar at Inner Temple, London, in November 1946.

His professional career reflected the path of the most promising occupations of his time. Awolowo was a teacher in 1928–29, a stenographer in Lagos in

1930–32, a clerk in Wesley College in 1932, a reporter with the *Daily Times* in 1934–35 and a motor transporter and produce buyer between 1937 and 1944. Awolowo also organized the Nigerian Produce Traders Association and became secretary of the Nigerian Motor Transporters Union. On his return from London, he set up a legal practice in 1947. He established a newspaper, the *Nigerian Tribune,* in 1949.

Awolowo's political career effectively began in the late 1930s when he became general secretary of the Nigerian Youth Movement (NYM) branch in Ibadan, Western Nigeria. This movement had been formed in 1932–33 by the young Lagos intelligentsia to protest the establishment of the Yaba Higher College as a diploma-granting rather than a university-level degree-granting institution. The movement soon metamorphosed into Nigeria's pre-eminent nationalist organization of the 1930s, with branches across the country. It campaigned for self-government, an end to racial discrimination, and better wages and working conditions for workers and struggled to protect the interests of Nigerian farmers, traders and transporters against colonial commercial firms and the colonial railway corporation. Awolowo participated in these NYM struggles and other anticolonial protests. He led agitations for the reform of the Ibadan Native Authority Administrative Council that led to the formation of the Ibadan Native Authority Advisory Board in 1942. But Awolowo also criticized the movement and called for its reorganization and regionalization. After the disruptive leadership struggles in the Lagos NYM in 1941, Awolowo attempted unsuccessfully to revive the movement.

In 1943 Awolowo and other labor leaders founded Nigeria's first national trade union, the Trade Union Congress of Nigeria. He edited its paper, the *Nigerian Worker.* While in London, he and others formed the Egbe Omo Oduduwa, a Yoruba cultural association, in 1945. In 1947 he published his first book, *The Path to Nigerian Freedom*, where he propounded his early views on Nigerian federalism, which gave precedence to the various nationalities and ethnic groups over the emergent nation.

In 1950 Awolowo and others formed the Action Group (AG) party, based partly on the old NYM and the Egbe Omo Oduduwa. He won elections to the Western Regional Assembly and became leader of government business and minister of local government between 1951 and 1954. In this capacity he reformed the local government system of Western Region, making it elective with reserved seats for traditional rulers in the local councils. Awolowo became premier of Western Region during 1954–59 under the 1954 regionalist federal constitution.

A major aspect of his political career was his ambition to become prime minister or president of Nigeria. He attempted to extend his AG party's reach outside its regional and ethnic base in the late 1950s. He got support from minority nationalities in Benue, Plateau and Borno areas of the old Northern Region and in the Calabar, Ogoja and Rivers areas of the old Eastern Region. In spite of this effort and one of the most lavish and expensive electioneering campaigns during the general elections of 1959, he failed in his quest for the post of prime minister.

Between 1960 and 1962 he was leader of the opposition in the federal parliament. He continued to espouse his views on social welfarism, the nationalization of strategic enterprises, the abrogation of the compromising Anglo-Nigerian Defense Pact and the need for a radical continental African Union. During this period Awolowo disagreed with his deputy and premier of Western Region, Chief S. L. Akintola, on policy, personality and ideological grounds. Awolowo had moved to the left of the mainstream business constituency of the party. The party split and a crisis amidst violence ensued in the Western Region. The federal government intervened. Awolowo was detained in prison between May and November 1962 on allegations of an attempt to overthrow the federal government.

With several of his compatriots, he was charged with treasonable felony and conspiracy in one of the most protracted political trials in postcolonial Nigeria, lasting from November 1962 to September 1963. He was found guilty and sentenced to ten years in prison. His appeal to the Supreme Court was dismissed in August 1964. Awolowo spent just over three years in the Calabar Prison. While there he worked on several books: *Thoughts on the Nigerian Constitution* (1966), *The People's Republic* (1968), and *The Strategy and Tactics of the People's Republic of Nigeria* (1970), which articulated his political philosophy for a new constitution and an ideologically reconstructed Nigeria. Awolowo was released and granted full pardon in August 1966 by Gen. (then Lt. Col.) Yakubu Gowon,* who assured him that Nigeria needed his wealth of experience during a turbulent time.

The period from the mid–1960s to 1970 was a particularly difficult one in Nigeria's history. The country experienced its first military coup in January 1966. Thereafter, the misrule of the first postindependence regime (1960–66) manifested itself in political instability, communal violence, secessionist threats, the collapse of the colonial triregional federation, the emergence of a new Nigerian federalism with the creation of twelve states in May 1967, and the Nigerian civil war from June 1967 to January 1970, following the secession of Eastern Region in May 1967. During this trying period of Nigerian history, Awolowo initially went along with the secessionist current of thought and action of Nigeria's three big nationalities (Igbo, Yoruba and Hausa-Fulani). He proclaimed that if the Eastern Region seceded, the Yoruba Western Region would similarly secede from Nigeria.

The military government of General Gowon, struggling to maintain Nigeria's territorial integrity, co-opted Awolowo into the pan-Nigerian political current by appointing him federal commissioner of finance and vice chairman of the Federal Executive Council (the federal cabinet), where he served between June 1967 and June 1971. This was the only period of Awolowo's career when he served at the national level as a quasi-national leader. In June 1971 Awolowo resigned from his cabinet positions, arguing that with the end of the civil war in January 1970 the national emergency had also ended and that the military should work toward the speedy return to civilian rule. He returned to his private legal practice. Between 1967 and 1978 he also served as chancellor of the University of Ife, Ile-Ife (now Obafemi Awolowo University) (1967–75), and Ahmadu Bello University, Zaria (1975–78).

Between 1975 and 1979 the military government implemented programs of return to civilian rule that involved the formulation of a new presidential constitution. Awolowo declined to serve on the Constitution Drafting Committee (CDC) on the grounds that he first learned of his appointment over the radio. In September 1978 the military regime lifted the ban on partisan politics. Awolowo and his Committee of Friends immediately launched the Unity Party of Nigeria (UPN). The party's early followers embraced the spectrum of Nigerian liberals, social democrats, socialists and some of the old Action Group constituency of businessmen and women. The party's ideology was democratic socialism. This was expressed in the party's four-point campaign manifesto: free education, free health services, full employment and integrated rural development.

In 1979 Awolowo and his party ran one of the best-organized and most exhaustive electioneering campaigns among all the five parties of the Second Republic. In the event, the UPN won power in the five states that made up Awolowo's old Western Region base: Lagos, Oyo, Ogun, Ondo and Bendel states. His bid for the national presidency failed, as he was second to the National Party of Nigeria (NPN) candidate, Alhaji Shehu Shagari, who became Nigeria's president in October 1979. Awolowo's second attempt during the general elections of 1983 was also unsuccessful. The military returned to power in 1984 and ended party politics. Three years later, in May 1987, Awolowo died. His death marked the end of an era of Nigerian politics—a long period during which Awolowo's extraordinary leadership qualities in politics, education, economic management and literary, intellectual and ideological activism made a decisive impact on Nigerian affairs and indirectly on Africa as a whole.

As a leader, Awolowo was able to generate massive support among the Yoruba and to some extent among other Nigerian groups. This was partly because he developed politically during the colonial period when the colonial regime established a triregional federal system narrowly based on Nigeria's three big nationalities: the Hausa-Fulani, the Yoruba and the Igbo. Most politicians from these groups assumed the "naturalness" of their ethnic and regional domination of Nigerian affairs. Awolowo, however, acquired a more powerful stigma as a Yoruba nationalist and regionalist, partly because of his blunt advocacy of ethnic and linguistic nationalism and his formation of the Egbe Omo Oduduwa and of the Action Group as a regional party. But in fact, in his ethnic and regionalist orientation he was no different than his political peers, Nnamdi Azikiwe* and Ahmadu Bello,* all of whom contributed to the salience of manipulative ethnicity in Nigerian politics. However, by the time Awolowo formed the UPN in the 1970s and attempted to transcend his ethnic and regional base, the views of him as a Yoruba nationalist had solidified in the popular consciousness of other Nigerian groups to such an extent that they became an obstacle to his aspirations for national leadership. The ethnic nationalism that he helped to create had now become a prison from which he could not easily escape.

Awolowo as a political leader was extraordinarily self-disciplined and hard working. His style of governance was cautious, frugal and purposeful, boosting his image within the larger Nigerian polity. But his demand for near-absolute fidelity from followers bordered on the authoritarian. His followers tended to magnify his leadership skills and ideological prescriptions and almost deified Awolowo, his ideas and his leadership style, thereby projecting him as a messianic leader.

Awolowo demonstrated his organizational abilities, management skills and political and ideological orientations when he held important political positions. As premier of Western Region, he ran one of the most efficient administrations in Nigeria during the late colonial period. He also implemented policies and programs of free primary education and free health services for children eighteen and under. He increased the wages of laborers in the region. He attempted to improve agriculture through establishing farm settlements. He also established industrial estates to encourage industrialization. His programs in education and health services marked him as a social welfarist. Later in his political career he defined his political philosophy as democratic socialism. This philosophy embraced bourgeois politics, the rule of law, thorough economic planning, the careful management of the neocolonial capitalist economy, the provision of "free" social services and rural development. In mainstream Nigerian politics these ideas generated debates and influenced the choice of constitutional articles in Nigerian constitutional engineering of the 1970s and 1980s. In his capacity as wartime federal commissioner of finance, Awolowo demonstrated his economic and financial management prowess. Through countertrade and carefully devised budgets he was able to procure considerable foreign exchange. Consequently, Nigeria prosecuted the war practically entirely from national resources with virtually no external borrowings.

At the same time, Awolowo's personal discipline, abstemiousness and bureaucratic fact-gathering tendency, while extremely useful for a scholar or bureaucratic chief, may have become an obstacle to his ability to make the necessary deals with other politicians. He tended to approach rivals from a position of seeming intellectual superiority. Awolowo came across more as a tough and able administrator than a traditional politician, one who needs to combine administrative ability with a large dose of populist flair and horse-trading capacity to attain objectives. Still, Awolowo was a major Nigerian leader, with a legacy of administrative, economic and financial management, free primary education and health schemes and an extension of these social prescriptions to the national agenda. His intellectual activity, embodied in his several books, bequeathed an ideology of democratic socialism as well as the espousal of a radical if cautious Pan-Africanism. Within the nature of mainstream Nigerian national politics, which has thus far produced few able leaders, the testimonial of C. Odumegwu Ojukwu, the former Biafran leader, that Awolowo was the best president that Nigeria never had, is a fitting tribute.

BIBLIOGRAPHY

Works by Awolowo:

Path to Nigerian Freedom. London: Faber, 1947.
Awo: The Autobiography of Chief Obafemi Awolowo. Cambridge, Eng.: Cambridge University Press, 1960.
The People's Republic. Ibadan: Oxford University Press, 1968.
The Problems of Africa: The Need for Ideological Reappraisal. London: Macmillan, 1977.
Adventures in Power. Lagos: Macmillan, 1985, 1987.

Other Works:

"Awo, 1909–1987." *African Guardian* (May 21, 1987): Special Issue.
"The Awolowo Years: If Not Me, Who?" *This Week* (Nigeria) (June 15, 1987): whole issue, collector's edition.
Coleman, James Smoot. *Nigeria: Background to Nationalism*. Berkeley: University of California Press, 1958.
Diamond, Larry. *Class, Ethnicity and Democracy in Nigeria: The Failure of the First Republic*. Syracuse, N.Y.: Syracuse University Press, 1988.
Eleazu, Uma O. *Federalism and Nation-Building: The Nigerian Experience, 1954–1964*. Ilfracombe, Eng.: Stockwell, 1977.
Ezera, Kalu. *Constitutional Developments in Nigeria*. Cambridge, Eng.: Cambridge University Press, 1960.
Joseph, Richard. *Democracy and Prebendal Politics in Nigeria*. London: Cambridge University Press, 1987.
Post, K. W. J. *The Nigerian Federal Election of 1959*. London: Oxford University Press for the Nigerian Institute of Social and Economic Research, 1963.
Sklar, Richard L. *Nigerian Political Parties*. Princeton, N.J.: Princeton University Press, 1963, 1970; New York and Enugu: NOK Publishers International, 1983.

EHIEDU E. G. IWERIEBOR

NNAMDI AZIKIWE (1904–   ), Nationalist party leader; Regional Premier; Governor-General and Commander-in-Chief of the Federation of Nigeria; President, Federal Republic of Nigeria, 1944–1966.

In his classic study of nationalism in Nigeria, James Smoot Coleman offered this rationale for Nnamdi Azikiwe's eminent place in the pantheon of African political leaders: "During the fifteen-year period, 1934–1949, Nnamdi Azikiwe was undoubtedly the most important and celebrated nationalist leader on the West Coast of Africa, if not in all tropical Africa" (Coleman 1958:220). As the twentieth century draws to a close, Azikiwe's career may still be unsurpassed as the prototypical example of modern African nationalism in its pure, anticolonial and essentially bourgeois form. The nationalist career of Jomo Kenyatta* would be comparable to Azikiwe's, while that of Kwame Nkrumah,* who was inspired by Azikiwe, diverged drastically from the bourgeois ideological norm, as did that of Ahmed Sékou Touré.* The two giants of Francophone African nationalism, Félix Houphouët-Boigny* and Léopold Sédar Senghor,* were too metropolitan for prototypical status. The former was a minister in the French government; the latter was a champion of French civilization in Africa. On balance, Julius Nyerere[*] will be remembered for his socialist, rather than nationalist, thought; Amílcar Cabral[*] for his contribution to the theory and practice of peasant revolution. The South African "greats," Albert Luthuli,[*] Robert Sobukwe[*] and Nelson Mandela,[*] stand for the cause of equal rights rather than colonial freedom. Within these imprecise parameters, designed merely to situate the subject of this biography, the figures of Azikiwe and Kenyatta epitomize African nationalism in its strict sense.

Azikiwe was born in Zunguru, Nigeria, on November 16, 1904, into the family of a clerk in the Nigerian Regiment. His ethnic heritage is Onitsha Igbo. In his youth he was educated at a few of the finest schools of that time in various parts of Nigeria. As a student and, later, a junior clerk in the civil service, he imbibed the prevalent indignation of the racially sensitive, anticolonial intelligentsia. He was inspired by reports of the Black Zionist movement led by Marcus Garvey in the United States and by the teaching of an American-educated African minister and educator, Dr. Kwegyir Aggrey, whose observation, "Nothing but the best is good enough for the African," was taken to heart by the impressionable young man. Ambitiously, he resolved to seek higher education in the United States. At the age of twenty-one he enrolled in Storer College, a two-year preparatory school in Harper's Ferry, West Virginia, where the abolitionist, John Brown, had made his last stand. Fellow students there gave him the nickname "Zik" (pronounced *zeek*), by which he became widely known throughout Africa.

Azikiwe spent nine hard, but ultimately successful, years in the United States, laboring under the physical and emotional hardships of an impoverished "Negro" student in prewar America. He was an undergraduate at both Howard and Lincoln universities, earning an M.A. in political science at the latter institution. He pursued graduate studies at the University of Pennsylvania, where he earned an M.S. in anthropology, and at Columbia University, where he obtained a certificate in journalism and studied political science. He was also employed by Lincoln University as an instructor in political science. In 1934, choosing to pursue the vocation of journalism in Africa rather than professional scholarship in the United States, he returned to Africa as editor of a nationalistic daily newspaper in Accra, Gold Coast (now Ghana). Three years later, and wiser by one prosecution for the publication of a "seditious" article (resulting in his acquittal on appeal), he went home to Nigeria to found a daily newspaper, the *West African Pilot,* in the capital city, Lagos. In order to attract subscribers, he published an edited collection of his columns and other articles, entitled *Renascent Africa,* which soon became something of a bible for the nationalist intelligentsia of British West Africa. His personal column, "Inside Stuff" by "Zik," treated readers to pungent and informed commentaries on Nigerian and world affairs. During World War II he was foremost among leaders of thought in West Africa who argued that the issue of colonial freedom should be raised in conjunction with the war against fascism. To that end, he led a 1943 delegation of eight West African editors to London; their proposal, drafted by Azikiwe and endorsed by a majority of his companions, to initiate a fifteen-year program for West African independence was prophetic, but "evoked no response" (Coleman 1958: 197) from the British Colonial Office.

In 1944 Azikiwe joined with the venerable Herbert Macaulay, known as the "father of Nigerian nationalism," to found the National Council of Nigeria and the Cameroons (NCNC). After Macaulay's death in 1946, Azikiwe became president of the NCNC. Meanwhile, a large and representative group of his youthful followers from all parts of the country created the Zikist Movement to combat the British decision to establish three regional governments within Nigeria, each including one of the three largest cultural-linguistic nationalities, namely, the Hausa in the north, the Igbo in the east, and the Yoruba in the west. However, the extralegal "positive" actions taken by Zikists were not endorsed by Azikiwe, whose personal commitment to strictly constitutional methods of agitation would become a hallmark of his political career. Eventually, many of his ardent disciples, some of whom were imprisoned for planning and proposing illegal actions, became estranged from Azikiwe, whose revolutionary credentials were further tainted by his acceptance of office as president of the Ibo (later Igbo) State Union in 1948. His occupancy of that office, which had been thrust upon him by Igbo supporters, was impolitic for a national leader of the NCNC. Although he declined re-election in 1952, the trace of ethnic politics tainted his career no less indelibly than those of his principal rivals.

Despite Azikiwe's pre-eminence in the movement for independence from Great Britain, rival nationalists blocked his bid for political leadership in the Northern and Western regions of Nigeria. As a result, the NCNC decided to compromise on the issue of regionalism and install its leader in office as premier of Eastern Nigeria with a status equal to that of his main political rivals, Ahmadu Bello* and Obafemi Awolowo,* who held similar offices in the Northern and Western regions, respectively. Azikiwe's tenure as a regional premier was tempestuous. In 1956 the secretary of state for the colonies appointed a tribunal of inquiry to probe the investment of Eastern Region funds in a banking corporation that was largely owned by Azikiwe and members of his family. Years earlier, Azikiwe had acquired a bank to help finance his fledgling newspaper business. When he accepted ministerial office in the government of the Eastern Region, he resigned his directorships of the bank and related companies (the Zik Group, a consortium of companies formed to support his newspaper-publishing enterprise, e.g., printing, property, supplies, syndicated news services and transportation) in favor of a close business and political associate. The investment in question was consistent with three policies of the NCNC: to break the financial stranglehold of British banks in Nigeria; to create a Nigerian-controlled capacity to finance African businesses; and to establish a publicly owned banking system, financed by repatriated Nigerian public capital that had been invested abroad, mainly in British governmental securities. At length, the tribunal found that although the premier's primary motive—the liberalization of credit for Nigerians—was laudable, he ought to have relinquished his residual ownership interest in the bank when the proposal to invest funds controlled by the government that he headed was considered. His failure to do so was alleged to constitute ministerial misconduct. Thus challenged, Azikiwe's government resigned, and his party fought the ensuing general election in the Eastern Region primarily on the issue of conflict between foreign and indigenous banking. Its vindication by the voters of Eastern Nigeria was decisive.

During 1957 and 1958 Azikiwe and fellow nationalists, including his major political rivals, conducted negotiations with the British Colonial Office for a constitution under which Nigeria would become independent. In 1959 Azikiwe resigned his premiership of Eastern Nigeria and led his party in a three-cornered national election for the federal legislature. As expected, the dominant political party of the populous Northern Region, which contained approximately 54 percent of the national population, gained a strong plurality of seats in the House of Representatives, 142 out of 312; the NCNC and its allies ran second with 89; Awolowo's Western-based party came in third with 73. When leaders of the NCNC's Western wing threatened to bolt the party if Azikiwe were to attempt a coalition with Awolowo, he decided to support the appointment of a northerner, Alhaji Abubakar Tafawa Balewa, who was vice president of the Northern Peoples' Congress, as prime minister of the federation. Azikiwe resigned from the House of Representatives to assume the honorific position of president of the Nigerian Senate. Shortly after the attainment of independence on October 1, 1960, he was appointed by the queen to the ceremonial office of governor-general and commander-in-chief of the Federation of Nigeria, as recommended by the prime minister. Upon the proclamation of a federal republic on October 1, 1963, Azikiwe became its first president, but this change in his title as the ceremonial head of state did not increase his constitutional power or formal authority.

As president, Azikiwe warned his compatriots of an impending tragedy, but he could not forestall its occurrence. Shortly before the general legislative election of December 1964, he publicly advised the warring politicians to consider a peaceful division of "national assets" as an alternative to violent conflict; if Nigeria must "disintegrate," he declared, let it do so "in peace and not in pieces." When opponents of the prime minister's party decided to boycott the election on the ground that it would not be free and fair, Azikiwe vainly urged the prime minister to postpone it for six months and to ask the United Nations for assistance. Both before and after the disputed election, he consulted leaders of the armed forces. When he could not obtain assurances of their support (which would have been contrary to their constitutional obligations to the prime minister), Azikiwe reached an agreement with the prime minister on the formation of a national government that would be controlled substantially by the latter's party. However, the crisis of the First Republic culminated in the bloody coup d'état of January 1966, while Azikiwe was abroad, ending his presidency but destroying a regime controlled, in the main, by his political opponents.

Once constitutional government in Nigeria had been swept away, the cycle of violence could not be contained. Ethnic and regional animosities fused with the resentments of soldiers whose grievances were attributable to politicization of the army. Following a wave of systematic violence against easterners in Northern Nigeria, the Eastern Region declared its independence as the Republic of Biafra on May 27, 1967. At first, Azikiwe served Biafra in diplomatic capacities; during the spring of 1968 his entreaties influenced the governments of Côte d'Ivoire, Gabon, Tanzania and Zambia to recognize secessionist Biafra. Later that year, however, he settled in Britain, having despaired of persuading the Biafran leader, Lt. Col. Chukwuemeka Odumegwu Ojukwu, to negotiate an end to the war without preconditions. In August 1969 he returned to Nigeria for a meeting with the head of state, Maj. Gen. Yakubu Gowon; thereafter, he advocated reconciliation within a united Nigeria until, and beyond, the collapse of Biafran resistance in January 1970. His first and only appointment to an office by the military government occurred in 1972, when he was installed as chancellor of the University of Lagos. Soon afterward, he roused the ire of many Nigerians by proposing the formation of a "combined civil and military government" for a period of at least five years after the anticipated and widely desired withdrawal of the military from politics and the restoration of constitutional government.

When the ban on national party politics was rescinded in 1978, Azikiwe was nominated by the Nigerian People's Party to contest the office of president (chief executive) of the impending Second Republic. He ran third in a field of five with but 16.75 percent of the total vote, distributed as follows: more than 80 percent in the two Igbo states, nearly 50 percent in a third, non-Igbo state, but not more than 15 percent in any of the remaining sixteen states, and less than 5 percent in eleven of them. In the 1983 presidential election Azikiwe obtained a mere 14 percent of the vote—third-highest in a field of six—with well over 50 percent in the two Igbo states, 43 percent in a third state, but under 5 percent in nine of the sixteen others. In both elections his decision to be a candidate, rather than to step aside in favor of a potential ally, helped to ensure victory for the front-runner, Alhaji Shehu Shagari, a northerner. As Nigerian political analyst Billy Dudley observed with reference to the 1979 election, Azikiwe's strategy may have been designed "to ensure that the Igbos were not left out of the leadership stakes, a game that Azikiwe had played with consummate skill in 1959" (Dudley 1982:217). Assuming that premise, one might conclude that these "last hurrahs," in the seventy-fifth and seventy-ninth years of Azikiwe's life, did help to reintegrate the Igbo people firmly into the fabric of Nigerian politics. However, last hurrahs are customarily faint echoes of once-thundering political trumpets. Azikiwe's exit from the stage of electoral politics in Nigeria as a relatively minor presidential candidate has projected a misleading impression of his real stature in African history.

Azikiwe's ideas have been no less influential than his political actions. His early books (*Liberia in World Politics* and *Renascent Africa*) and newspaper columns strongly condemned colonial "miseducation" and espoused the cause of "mental emancipation" as a precondition for national liberation in Africa.

His career exemplifies the prototypical intellectual in politics; as premier of the Eastern Region he fulfilled the dream of his student years by founding a university, the University of Nigeria at Nsukka. Since 1946 he has been addressed and identified almost invariably as "Doctor" Azikiwe by virtue of the honorary LL.D. conferred by his alma mater, Lincoln University, followed, in 1947, by an honorary D.Litt. from Storer College and other honorary doctorates in later years. In 1976 he was appointed *owelle* of Onitsha by the *obi* (traditional king) of his ancestral city-state.

BIBLIOGRAPHY

Works by Azikiwe:

Liberia in World Politics. 2 vols. London: Stockwell, 1934.
Renascent Africa. Accra: privately printed, 1937.
Political Blueprint of Nigeria. Lagos: African Book Co., 1943.
The Development of Political Parties in Nigeria. London: Office of the Commissioner in the United Kingdom for the Eastern Region of Nigeria, 1957.
Zik: A Selection from the Speeches of Nnamdi Azikiwe. Ed. Philip Harris. London: Cambridge University Press, 1961.
Tribalism: A Pragmatic Instrument for National Unity. Enugu: Eastern Nigeria Printing Corporation, 1964.
My Odyssey: An Autobiography. New York: Praeger, 1970.

Other Works:

Abernathy, David B. *The Political Dilemma of Popular Education*. Stanford, Calif.: Stanford University Press, 1969.
Coleman, James Smoot. *Nigeria: Background to Nationalism*. Berkeley: University of California Press, 1958.
Diamond, Larry. *Class, Ethnicity and Democracy in Nigeria: The Failure of the First Republic*. London: Macmillan, 1988.
Dudley, Billy. *An Introduction to Nigerian Government and Politics*. Bloomington: Indiana University Press, 1982.
Ikeotuonye, Vincent O. *Zik of New Africa*. London: Macmillan, 1961.
Jones-Quartey, K. A. B. *A Life of Azikiwe*. Baltimore: Penguin Books, 1965.
Joseph, Richard A. *Democracy and Prebendal Politics in Nigeria*. London: Cambridge University Press, 1987.
Kirk-Greene, A. H. M. (ed.). *Crisis and Conflict in Nigeria: A Documentary Sourcebook, 1966–1969*. 2 vols. London: Oxford University Press, 1971.
Olisa, Michael S. O., and Odinchezo M. Ikejiani-Clark (eds.). *Azikiwe and the African Revolution*. Onitsha: Africana-FEP Publishers, 1989.
Olusanya, G. O. *The Second World War and Politics in Nigeria, 1939–1953*. Ibadan and London: Evans Brothers, 1973.
Orizu, A. A. Nwafor. *Without Bitterness*. New York: Creative Age Press, 1944.
Sklar, Richard L. *Nigerian Political Parties*. Princeton, N.J.: Princeton University Press, 1963, 1970; New York and Enugu: NOK Publishers International, 1983.
Whitaker, C. Sylvester, Jr. (ed.). *Perspectives on the Second Republic in Nigeria*. Waltham, Mass.: Crossroads Press, 1981.

RICHARD L. SKLAR

B

HASTINGS KAMUZU BANDA (1898?–   ), Prime Minister, President, Republic of Malawi, 1963–   .

Hastings Kamuzu Banda's claim to fame lies not merely in the length of time he has been prime minister and president of Malawi (since 1963) but also in the special style of authoritarian politics he practices, the relative success of his governments in terms of political and economic stability, and his relations with white-ruled South Africa. Unpopular in many quarters, especially among radicals and intellectuals, he has nevertheless survived for more than a quarter of a century at the helm of Malawian politics with recourse to less repressive measures of political control than most enduring leaders in Africa.

Kamuzu Banda was born in a small village near Kasungu in what is now central Malawi. According to his major biographer, the year was 1898; Banda himself has accepted 1902; officially, the year of his birth is 1906. Encouraged by his uncle, he was one of the small band of Cewa to go to European-style missionary schools, was baptized (taking the name Hastings), and became deeply committed to the pursuit of learning. In 1915 he left Malawi on foot for South Africa in search of further education. However, he spent the next two years in Southern Rhodesia (Zimbabwe) mainly as a sweeper in a hospital, thereby confirming his determination to become a doctor and experiencing for the first time the crude racism against which he fought throughout his life.

In 1917 his uncle joined him, and the two completed the journey to South Africa, where Banda worked in the mines. Here his fascination for politics originated, and he formed a distinctly more favorable evaluation of South Africa (where he could then enter shops on an equal footing with white people) than of Southern Rhodesia. Here, too, he became associated with the African Methodist Episcopal (AME) church, a black separatist church, through which he met Bishop W. T. Vernon of the American parent church. Vernon encouraged Banda to go to the United States to study. In July 1925 Banda, whose linguistic skills had elevated him to the relatively well paid post of clerk, raised the money for his steamship ticket and left Africa. He did not return until 1958.

Education dominated Banda's life for the next fifteen years. From 1925 to 1928 he studied at the AME's Wilberforce Institute in Ohio, from 1928 to 1930 at the University of Indiana on a premedical course, from 1930 to 1932 at the University of Chicago, first studying history and political science (and providing data for a study of the Ci-Cewa language) and then taking a postgraduate course in chemistry, and from 1932 to 1937 at the Meharry Medical College in Nashville, Tennessee, where he qualified as a doctor of medicine. Finally, from 1938 to 1941 he attended the University of Edinburgh, since he needed some specifically British qualifications if he was to practice, as he hoped, in colonial Nyasaland.

Banda's American experience impressed four things upon him: the generosity as well as the racism of white people (white philanthropists funded much of his education), the welfarism of Franklin D. Roosevelt's New Deal, the positive values of individualism and enterprise, and the importance of Garveyism, the black nationalist, return-to-Africa movement. When he entered politics in the 1960s, therefore, he differed from most African nationalists in his ideological orientation. While he shared a deep commitment to the dignity of black people and a profound antipathy to racial discrimination and welcomed an essentially British Fabian conception of the welfare state, he was unusual in favoring an individualist and entrepreneurial culture and acceptance of whites as friends and guides.

Banda's plans to return to Africa as a medical missionary were disrupted by World War II and the colonial service's unreadiness to incorporate an articulate black doctor into its all-white service. After the war Banda settled down as a family doctor, ministering to basically working-class patients in Harlesdon, a suburb of London, while he lived the life of a respectable family doctor in middle-class Brondesbury Park, complete with car, white receptionist and a standard of living that deeply impressed his African visitors. These were some of the happiest days of his life.

He was much revered by his patients, whom he looked after with his typical single-mindedness; he had a coterie of white friends, who were amused by his austere puritanism (perhaps internalized during his Edinburgh years) and his very formal attire; and he remained in regular touch with events in Nyasaland, sometimes "representing" the African position in London and financing the education of many young compatriots. His links with the Nyasaland African Congress were long and personal; indeed, both his money and his advice were critical from time to time.

The burning political issue of the early 1950s for him was the constitutional developments in central Africa. Banda was deeply opposed to any links with Southern Rhodesia, and he lobbied among his Labour Party friends and other contacts against any association. By the end of 1951, however, the Conservative government, building upon Labour foundations, affirmed the principle of federation despite almost universal African opposition. His response was an almost pathological opposition to what he called the "stupid" federation, and although he spoke from London, he was soon at the center of antifederation action. He then enjoyed an impeccable reputation as an African nationalist.

In 1953 his comfortable and self-confident life was rudely shattered. He was deeply hurt by the British government's apparent readiness to follow the white settlers' interests in central Africa rather than those of the congress, and he was further dismayed by the willingness of some senior congress members to participate in the Central African Federation. He withdrew from politics and departed for the Gold Coast (Ghana) with Margaret French, his former secretary. There he deliberately withdrew from political activity, established a private practice in Kumasi, and lived quietly.

The Ghanaian years were not happy ones. Banda's independence of mind, even with his diminished self-confidence, could not easily accommodate Kwame Nkrumah's* requirements of him. Furthermore, in December 1957 he was suspended from practice by the registrar of medical practitioners and dentists in the Ghanaian Ministry of Health. Although he was formally reinstated five months later, he had already decided to leave. An internal crisis in Nyasaland resulted in the congress's new young leadership pressuring him to return home to lead the nationalist movement. The call came at an opportune moment. On July 6, 1958, Hastings Banda flew into Chileka Airport to begin his active political career at the age of sixty.

The young leadership of the congress had already begun to build Banda into a major personality; Henry Chipembere had written to Banda in Ghana that he should not be frightened if he was "heralded as a political messiah." Banda's wounded self-esteem was more than healed. He was rejuvenated, and the old confidence of the doctor dealing with life and death and of the exiled sage to whom the congress had turned in times of trial returned. With the single-mindedness that had sustained him throughout his remarkable educational odyssey, he set about destroying the Central African Federation and creating a Malawi fashioned on his own preferences. The young leadership had helped to create a tiger they were not able to ride.

The facts of Banda's political life thereafter are relatively simple. His unremitting and articulate opposition to the federation established him as a hero among most black people in central Africa but a villain among whites. When violence erupted in Nyasaland and a state of emergency was declared, Banda was detained, with other young politicians, in Southern Rhodesia, where he planned the central features of the new Malawi. The British government's Devlin Commission exonerated Banda, and the ensuing Monckton Commission paved the way to the dissolution of the federation and the independence of Nyasaland as Malawi. His cordial relations with the governor, Sir Glyn Jones, and his reasonableness on all matters not related to the federation ensured a smooth path to independence.

His dominance of Malawian politics had begun with his demand in 1959 to fill senior posts within the Malawi Congress Party (MCP) with his chosen people. He was politically astute enough then to choose the young leaders who had recalled him from exile. A generation older than any other member of the cabinet, Banda treated them as children. When they challenged his pragmatic policies of slow Africanization in the civil service and amicable relations with white-ruled trading partners, they were ruthlessly purged from the cabinet.

The 1964 crisis colored the next quarter of a century as the dismissed ministers left the country to seek support for the overthrow of Banda (there was actually an incursion at Mangoche in 1965). Banda became obsessed by the political threat to his authority that they posed. Unrepentant, he pushed ahead with his policies of individual entrepreneurship, harmonious relations with whites and a curious mixture of emphasis on indigenous culture (he was concerned that Ci-Cewa should be spoken in the proper "traditional" way) and modern practices (he established an elitist boarding school called Kamuzu Academy).

The significance of his exile experiences is everywhere to be seen and often paradoxical. The European-baptized Hastings Banda was the scourge of white politicians in the early 1960s; the African Kamuzu Banda, who had revered Marcus Garvey and been a member of the AME church, established diplomatic relations with apartheid South Africa. The Fabian Dr. Banda increased governmental expenditure on health, education and welfare; the self-made Dr. Banda espoused a high level of free enterprise and meritocratically preferred qualified whites to less qualified blacks. Above all, the man made into a messiah came to see himself as the Malawian Messiah who had freed Nyasaland and whose conception of Malawian national interests could not be challenged. Nobody of political standing had such long and deep links with the congress, had entered the European world and proved himself the equal of Europeans, or had the same grasp of detail, intellectual security and personal self-confidence. Banda's dominance was thus primarily based upon his age, status and unflinching assurance.

Although free of factional support (his Cewa ethnic base was always strong) and therefore factional opposition, he established one important dynastic link. Cecilia Kadzamira, the official hostess and his confidante, was the niece of John Tembo, who was for many years head of the Reserve Bank and a member of the MCP's Executive Committee and whose brother ran the Agricultural Development and Marketing Corporation. But despite popular fears, Banda has carefully not elevated John Tembo to become secretary-general of the party.

President Banda's leadership is marked not only by its extraordinary length, but also by its style and his shrewd use of power. Obsessed by the response to his 1964 purge, Banda has permitted little opposition. He has been withering in his criticism of intellectual dissent and quick to dismiss or relegate any minister who is even mentioned in the media as a possible successor. Some who fell out of favor have been incarcerated, but none has been done to death (although some still believe that the car deaths of three ministers in 1983 were not accidental); indeed, occasionally he has reinstated the fallen, as he did with Aleke Banda.

He has usually been astute in his treatment of dissent, permitting some popular forms and focusing his antagonism on individual political figures or groups with little popular backing (such as the Jehovah's Witnesses). He has been quick to realize that poor peasants do not instinctively support intellectuals or socialists, especially when the even tenor of their lives is not upset. Above all, he is seen to listen often enough (at party conventions, for example) and to act often enough (over traditional courts, for instance) to establish a perceived link between popular wishes and presidential action.

The presidential structure of the Malawian state is a familiar one in Africa. But the MCP, of which Banda became life president in 1971 and which is the sole legal party, is not a hollow shell. Because it is subservient to government, its interests are primarily local, and on balance it has been less oppressive than monolithic parties in other single-party states. Furthermore, its annual conventions, although regimented where central matters of national economic or foreign policy are concerned, permit a considerable latitude for the expression of disquiet. Every five years electors are offered a choice of MCP candidates for election to the national Parliament. Although the final list of candidates results from close presidential scrutiny (and thus excludes avowed dissenters), it nevertheless offers Malawians a choice and some meaning to their participation. Although highly centralized, the system is not closed. By distinguishing between "high politics" (the president's prerogatives) and "low politics" (the popular arena), Banda has cleverly managed to legitimize his essentially authoritarian rule.

His leadership derives from six sources. First, his constitutional position and the number of central ministerial portfolios he himself holds (in 1989, those of external affairs, agriculture, justice and works and supplies) provide a strong legal base, of which his regular dismissals of whole cabinets are an eloquent sign. Second, as head of the MCP, he can use an institution that is far from moribund to favor his friends and punish his enemies. Third, his remarkable control over the details of policy until the late 1980s, his absolute certainty of broad policy goals, and his movement of other politicians from ministry to ministry have given him an overwhelming advantage in intragovernmental debates. Fourth, his generally good relations with the major economic powers have ensured, where necessary, their assistance in times of more than usual economic difficulty (although this has also made him subject to pressure from such outsiders on the prioritization of his programs). Fifth, his personality cult, epitomized by the media coverage given to him and the women's groups who sing and dance his praises, established and then confirmed him as the human symbol of Malawian nationality. Sixth, he has been happy, like General de Gaulle, to go over the heads of the intermediaries, often to their humiliation, shrewdly listening to popular demands on many local issues and punishing party officials who antagonize local populations.

While the structure of the political process and the style of rule are significant, the role of Malawi's economy should not be underestimated. Although still poor, Malawian farmers have generally found markets, acceptable prices and immediate payment for their surplus produce and cash crops. Additionally, there has been a much smaller growth of rich politician-entrepreneurs than in most other African countries. Although Banda himself has amassed considerable wealth through his own economic activities and state bounties, he has repaid much to "the people" through his highly publicized support of various development schemes. His preindependence emphasis on the watchwords "Unity, Loyalty, Obedience and Discipline" has been effectively carried over into the postindependence era.

Banda has been a remarkable figure by any standards. His life from peasant child to respected London doctor is itself an achievement; his central role in the dismantling of the Central African Federation is another; his maverick performance as president of Malawi, clearly explicable in terms of his personal history, has nevertheless had many successes. Although a committed friend of the West, he is not its lackey; nobody who has worked closely with him would argue that he has ever been anything other than his own man, quick to challenge Malawians and non-Malawians alike. His failure to institutionalize political discourse on national priorities and to establish a smooth succession will plunge the country into political uncertainties, and possibly turmoil, on his death. But his irritating self-certainty, intolerance and moments of irrationality in later life should not obscure his very real qualities and achievements as a man and as an African leader.

BIBLIOGRAPHY

Works by Banda:

John Kambalame, et al. *Our African Way of Life*. Translated and edited with a preface by Cullen Young and Hastings Banda. London and Redhill: United Society for Christian Literature, 1946.

Other Works:

Hodder-Williams, Richard. "Dr. Banda's Malawi." *Journal of Commonwealth and Comparative Politics* 12 (1974): 91–114.
McMaster, Carolyn. *Malawi: Foreign Policy and Development*. London: Julian Friedmann, 1974.
Rotberg, Robert I. *The Rise of Nationalism in Central Africa: The Making of Malawi and Zambia, 1873–1964*. Cambridge, Mass.: Harvard University Press, 1965.
Short, Philip. *Banda*. London and Boston: Routledge and Kegan Paul, 1974.
Williams, T. David. *Malawi: The Politics of Despair*. Ithaca, N.Y.: Cornell University Press, 1978.

RICHARD HODDER-WILLIAMS

MUHAMMAD SIYAAD BARRE (1919?–   ), Major-General, President of the Supreme Revolutionary Council, President of the Somali Democratic Republic, 1969–1991.

Muhammad Siyaad Barre rose to power through the Somali police and military in the 1950s and 1960s and took power as head of state following a military coup in 1969. He ruled Somalia until January 1991, enjoying one of the longest reigns in power of any contemporary African leader. Because of his lengthy tenure in office, Barre's name is intimately linked to the tumultuous changes, both positive and negative, that have shaken this East African country since the end of its first decade of independence. Initial successes in his government's revolutionary undertakings seemed to promise Barre near-heroic status in the annals of Somali history. Instead, however, his early initiatives foundered, and his rule became increasingly repressive, corrupt and unpopular. By 1988 Barre's government presided over an economy in shambles and faced a full-scale civil war that threatened to permanently divide the country. In January 1991 he and his supporters were ousted from power and were forced to flee into the countryside in southern Somalia, following a bloody and destructive battle with rebels in the capital city, Mogadishu. Popular in the early years of his rule for his efforts to abolish clanism and forge unity within the Somali nation, Barre by 1990 presided over the tragic disintegration of his country.

As befits his nomadic background, the precise year and location of Barre's birth are uncertain. It is generally agreed that he was born to pastoral parents in 1919 or 1921. His place of birth is officially said to have been at Garbahaarey in what is today the Gedo region, near the Somali border with Kenya and Ethiopia; other accounts, however, contend that he was actually born near Shilabo in Ethiopia. Barre was born into the Marehan clan, a relatively small lineage group with a fierce reputation earned through its chronic struggle to protect its grazing and watering rights from larger and more powerful neighboring groups. Barre's mother came from the very large Ogaadeen clan, a link Barre would later rely upon in forging clan alliances in office.

Throughout much of his life, Siyaad Barre devoted himself to both formal and self-styled education while steadily advancing his career. As a child, despite being orphaned by age ten, he was able to attend elementary school in the town of Lugh in the Upper Jubba region. In 1941, when Barre was about twenty years old, he joined the police force, then under the authority of the British military, which had occupied the Italian Somaliland colony in the course of World War II hostilities. This career in the police force took Barre to the capital city Mogadishu and afforded him the opportunity to pursue his education in public and private schools; he eventually gained the equivalent of a secondary-school education in the 1940s. By the last year of the British Military Administration, 1950, Barre had achieved the highest rank possible for a Somali, that of chief police inspector.

An Italian trusteeship was established in the former colony of Italian Somaliland for ten years prior to the territory's independence in 1960, and Barre worked closely with his new superiors. He attended the Military Academy in Italy in 1952, principally studying politics and administration. Throughout the 1950s he pursued studies in languages in Somalia, eventually becoming conversant in Arabic, English, Italian and Swahili. He was promoted to the rank of second lieutenant and by 1960 had achieved the rank of colonel and second-in-command of the newly formed Somali national army. Four years later his superior, General Da'ud, died in Moscow, enabling Barre to assume the role of commander-in-chief of the army. In 1966 his rank was promoted to major general. Barre was thereafter well positioned to take political power in the event of a military coup.

Following the assassination of the president of Somalia and the Parliament's inability to agree to a successor in October 1969, the Somali military and police did in fact step in to take power, an action that would retrospectively be recast as a "revolution." The coup, which was greeted enthusiastically by most Somali citizens, was initially justified as a move to clean up rampant corruption and abolish divisive clan politics that had paralyzed the civilian government. While Barre did not appear to have instigated the coup, he participated in the takeover. Following the dissolution of the National Assembly and the suspension of the constitution, Barre emerged as the president of the Supreme Revolutionary Council, the new ruling body of the Somali Democratic Republic, in November 1969.

Observers are not in full agreement in their assessment of Barre's early years of rule, but most acknowledge that both Barre and his government enjoyed widespread support and real success up to 1974. Certainly Barre's campaign against "tribalism," or clan-based politics, was a progressive, unifying and popular platform that kindled a sense of renewal in Somali social and political life. For a time, ministerial appointments appeared to be based solely on merit and competence, not on clan affiliation. Indeed, reference to one's lineage identity, and even the use of the common greeting "cousin," was outlawed in favor of the salutation *jaalle* (comrade). Because much of the corruption plaguing the civilian governments of the 1960s was linked to nepotism, Barre's campaign against "tribalism" went hand in hand with his promise to clean up corruption and mismanagement.

By the end of his first year in power, Barre announced that Somalia would henceforth be guided by the principles of "scientific socialism." Thereafter the country embarked on a foreign policy featuring close ties to the Soviet Union, economic planning that enhanced the state's role in production (although key sectors were left private), and political centralization of power. The swing toward socialism was not surprising: The Somali military had received training and aid from the USSR and was more predisposed toward the Eastern bloc than the civilian governments; Somalia's chief foreign policy objective, its irredentist claims to Somali-inhabited territory in Ethiopia and Kenya, had been frustrated by Western support for those states; and socialist principles of equality appealed to a historically egalitarian Somali society unsettled by the rapid process of economic stratification in the capital.

Barre himself, however, appeared to have little knowledge of Marxism and viewed socialist ideology pragmatically, as a vehicle with which to increase, consolidate and justify the power of the state and, by extension, his own authority. Indeed, he distrusted socialist intellectuals and excluded them from positions of influence, and his own articulation of scientific socialism in the Somali context was never coherent. He had little patience for those who questioned the compatibility of Islam and Marxism, and his intolerance culminated in the execution of ten dissident shiekhs in 1975. After his Soviet patrons deserted him in favor of Ethiopia in 1977, Barre had little difficulty abandoning socialist ideology in favor of rhetoric more palatable to his new, reluctant patrons in the West.

Whatever Barre's motives, his enunciation of a socialist development program sparked some significant successes in the 1970s. Perhaps most notable among these was the adoption of an official script, based on the Latin alphabet, for the Somali language, followed by a massive literacy campaign that ranks as one of the most successful in the world. Women's rights were significantly improved, at least legally, and primary health care and education facilities were extended throughout the country. Under the banner of self-reliance, Barre also spearheaded a drive to redirect development priorities to the country's ailing rural sector. Large-scale agricultural projects were established, which Barre hoped would bring Somalia closer to food self-sufficiency; ambitious cooperative programs in agriculture and fishing, often involving the resettlement of tens of thousands of drought victims, were initiated; and agricultural "crash programs" provided work to the urban unemployed. Volunteer programs, enlisting the participation of urban dwellers in sand-dune stabilization and other schemes, captured the spirit of participation and renewal that characterized Somali society in the first half of the 1970s.

Behind the scenes, Barre devoted himself to consolidating his own power. Real or perceived rivals were discredited, arrested and sometimes executed. An array of governmental structures was developed to institutionalize power around Barre. With the establishment of the Somali Revolutionary Socialist Party (SRSP) in 1976 and a new constitution in 1979, Barre garnered overwhelming organizational power. His titles by that time included president of the republic, commander-in-chief of the armed forces, secretary-general of the SRSP, president of the Politburo, chairman of the Council of Ministers, and chairman of the Higher Judiciary Council. There were few, if any, governmental authorities in a position to debate, let alone challenge, Barre's decisions.

Barre consolidated power outside the halls of government as well. A secret security police force was created to monitor and suppress dissent. It was a powerful and feared organization loyal to the president. The army was vastly increased in size, and a corps composed predominantly of adolescents, called "Victory Pioneers," was established with the primary task of surveilling towns and neighborhoods. A climate of fear, mistrust and repression grew. As it did, Barre came increasingly to rely on his own clan and its allies, frequently referred to as the "MOD" (Mareehaan-Ogaadeen-Dolbahante) alliance, further fueling dissident charges of "tribalism" and nepotism. Simultaneously, government propaganda portrayed Barre as a cult figure, the "father of the nation" and the "father of knowledge."

These trends indicate that Barre would have faced increasing internal opposition under any circumstances; but his decision to commit regular Somali troops into the Ogaden region of Ethiopia to assist the Western Somalia Liberation Front in its bid for autonomy from Ethiopia wrought devastating results for Somalia and severely damaged Barre's political support domestically and abroad. Had Barre succeeded in the Ogaden War of 1977–78, he would certainly have been remembered as the hero of Somali reunification. Instead, Barre's Soviet patrons abandoned him in favor of the Marxist Ethiopian regime, shifting massive military support to Ethiopia. In March 1978 Somali forces were routed. Tens of thousands of Somalis were killed or wounded, the army was in disarray, and Barre's government was left diplomatically isolated. It was a disaster for which Somalia would pay for years to come and that very nearly ended Barre's rule. Indeed, as accusations of incompetence and disloyalty flew, dissenting generals were executed, and members of opposition movements were exiled, few observers expected Barre to survive politically.

Yet Barre remained in power for thirteen years after the war, reigning over what has unquestionably been the most difficult and bitter period since independence. Whatever economic and social gains were accrued during the heyday of Barre's socialist initiatives were erased by a combination of economic crisis, drought, corruption and repression. In 1988, after years of sporadic armed opposition to Barre's regime, a major civil war in the north of the country broke out, pitting the government's troops, many of them forcibly conscripted, against the Somali National Movement, composed predominantly of the northern Isaaq clan. Government troops and airpower destroyed Somalia's second-largest city, Hargeisa, prompting the exodus of four hundred thousand refugees into Ethiopia. Subsequently, other armed opposition groups in the central portion of the country (the Somali United Congress [USC]) and in the south (the Somali Patriotic Movement) successfully reduced Barre's control of the country to the capital city and the surrounding countryside. As the international community froze foreign aid to the regime, following documentation of gross human-rights violations, and as USC forces closed in on the capital, Barre announced plans for a return to a multiparty system in Somalia in a desperate attempt to stave off defeat. The announcement was ignored, and by December 1990 USC forces were battling Barre's troops in Mogadishu. The capital was thrown into complete anarchy and suffered severe damage from the civil war and from looting by armed bandits. Barre and his family were forced to retreat to bunkers at the airport and then, on January 26, 1991, fled southward into the countryside, leaving Somalia shattered and ungovernable.

Barre, an old and, since a serious car accident in 1986, enfeebled man, survived in power during the 1980s through a variety of tactics. He successfully exploited fractious clan divisions among his opposition, fostering an atmosphere of mistrust so great that unified action against him by other clan groups never occurred. He relied increasingly on his own family members in positions of power and promoted his son, Maslah Muhammad Siyaad Barre, to a key position in the military in the hope of enabling him to succeed Barre upon his death. Repression of dissent reached alarming proportions; civilian massacres in the civil war, the shooting of over four hundred demonstrators outside a Mogadishu mosque in 1989, and widespread torture provoked outcries from human-rights organizations. In addition, the state was converted into a structure of political patronage, in which rapidly reshuffled civil servants accrued fortunes illicitly and through which Barre bought off potential rivals and divided adversarial clans. This patronage system was financed with large levels of foreign aid that Barre was able to secure from Western and Persian Gulf state donors by exploiting Cold War tensions and regional insecurity in the Middle East.

Barre bequeathed Somalia a tragic legacy, one of failed and unrealized visions of unity and self-reliance. Instead of forging unity among Somalis, he oversaw the society's disintegration into highly armed anarchy. By effectively playing clans off one another to weaken opposition, he created deep clan divisions and vendettas for which future generations will pay. Instead of rendering the country more self-reliant, Barre left Somalia more dependent than ever on foreign aid and remittances from migrant workers for its very survival. By allowing civil servants, including members of his own family, to abscond with millions of dollars from development projects, he squandered an entire generation of development efforts and left the country saddled with a crippling foreign debt.

Yet history may judge Barre too harshly, for not all of Somalia's woes were within his ability to control. Somalia's lineage-based society is at its very core unstable, subject to disunity and vulnerable to nepotism, which, in the context of clan affiliation, constitutes a familial duty rather than a form of corruption. Likewise, the disastrous decision to invade Ethiopia in 1977 was largely determined by events beyond his control, a dilemma from which Barre had no easy escape.

BIBLIOGRAPHY

Works by Barre:

My Country and My People: Speeches of Jaalle Siyad, 1969–1979. Mogadishu: Ministry of Information and National Guidance, 1979.

Other Works:

Concerned Somalis. "The Transfer of Power in Somalia." *Horn of Africa* 5 (January–March 1982): 35–61.
Laitin, David, and Said S. Samatar. *Somalia: Nation in Search of a State*. Boulder, Colo.: Westview, 1987.
Lewis, I. M. *A Modern History of Somalia: Nation and State in the Horn of Africa*. 2nd ed. New York: Longman, 1980.
Nelson, Harold D. (ed.). *Somalia: A Country Study*. 3rd ed. Washington, D.C.: American University, 1982.
Samatar, Ahmed I. *Socialist Somalia: Rhetoric and Reality*. London: Zed Press, 1988.

KENNETH MENKHAUS

AHMADU BELLO (1910–1966), Premier, Northern Region of the Federal Republic of Nigeria, 1954–1966.

Ahmadu Bello was the first premier of the Northern Region of Nigeria (1954–66); almost certainly he will also be the last. Although the least educated, in terms of formal Western qualifications, of Nigeria's three regional premiers in the decolonizing decade of the 1950s, he steadily raised the influence of his leadership until by independence (1960) he was unquestionably the most powerful of the premiers in the Federation of Nigeria and had consolidated his reputation, however grudgingly conceded by his peers or challenged by his constitutional superior, the prime minister of Nigeria, as both the Giant of the North and the Strong Man of Nigeria. For all his decorations and accolades, he resolutely preferred recognition by his traditional Fulani title of Sardauna to those of Alhaji, sir, doctor or premier.

Ahmadu Bello was born in 1910 at Rabah, a small town in the Sokoto emirate of the Northern Provinces of Nigeria. His father was a traditional fief holder, one of the forty-eight district heads in the emirate. This was only seven years after the British forces had, after a short engagement, occupied the caliphate capital of Sokoto on March 15, 1903—a significant date in the history of Northern Nigeria, which Ahmadu Bello made even more so by his deliberate choice, as premier in 1959, of March 15 as the day of the Northern Region's self-government. Of even greater importance than this parentage was the fact that Ahmadu was the grandson of Atiku na Rabah, the seventh sultan of Sokoto (1873–77); the great-grandson of Sultan Bello (1813–37), statesman and scholar, and arguably the outstanding ruler in the nineteenth-century Western Sudan; and great-great-grandson of Shehu Usman dan Fodio (1744–1817), the great reformer and revered founder of the Fulani empire of Sokoto in the opening years of the nineteenth century, whereby two-thirds of the subsequent Northern Region of Nigeria came under his sway. Ahmadu Bello's perception and manipulation of his genealogy was to prove a constant throughout his career, an asset that he never failed to exploit.

Opportunities for Western education were severely limited in the emirates between the two world wars, and Ahmadu Rabah (as he was then known) was one of the fortunate few when he went to the Sokoto Provincial School in 1915. He was to be one of the yet more fortunate and fewer when he was selected for training as a teacher at the elite Katsina College in 1926. Returning to Sokoto in 1931, he joined the Native Administration service that was, as the emirate local government bureaucracy under the British system of indirect rule, invested with considerable powers formalized in the hands of the sultan. Ahmadu was appointed a *mallam* (teacher) in the Middle School. However, three years later the sultan "turbanned" him district head of Rabah, a remarkable promotion at the age of twenty-four. In this capacity he was responsible for the complete administration of the district, three hundred square miles carrying a population of some thirty thousand. A yet bigger advance came in 1938, when the new sultan—Ahmadu's cousin Abubakar (1938–1988)—posted (exiled, in terms of Sokoto court politics) his kinsman to the cosmopolitan urban center of Gusau to oversee the work of no less than fourteen of the district heads in the prosperous and populous southern area of the emirate. At the same time he was made a member of the sultan's council. Yet for Ahmadu all this high-flier advancement paled before his installation as Sardauna of Sokoto in 1938. This traditional title, whose nearest rendering is "captain of the bodyguard," is restricted to scions of the ruling house. During his period at Gusau, Sardauna, as he was now known, Ahmadu successfully appealed to the Supreme Court against a sentence of one year's imprisonment for alleged peculation.

It was not until after World War II that Sardauna (for a Hausa/Fulani word, the definite article is better omitted), as he now liked to be called, first broke out of the traditional emirate and Native Administration cocoon in which he had been brought up for forty years. Unlike his subsequent copremiers, Nnamdi Azikiwe* and Obafemi Awolowo,* who had acquired a university education in the United States and Britain, respectively, Sardauna had never been out of the Northern Provinces until 1948, when the British Council awarded him a bursary to attend a short course on local government in Britain. The following year he paid his first visit to Lagos; his lasting impression, apart from a dislike of the city, was how far the north had to go before its people could catch up with the political sophistication of the south. By now he had been elected as the second Sokoto member for the new Northern House of Assembly: Sardauna had determined to make his career not in public administration but in party politics.

Consequent to the introduction of a new constitution for Nigeria in 1951, Sardauna moved to Kaduna, the northern capital, on his appointment as minister of works in the regional government. At the same time he joined the nascent political party, the Northern People's Congress (NPC), and quickly became its president. In 1953 he added local government and community development to his ministerial portfolio. The former gave him virtual responsibility over all the Native Administrations, and it is generally believed that the powerful emirs and chiefs would not have accepted the risk of seeing a politician in this sensitive position had he, too, not been of royal blood and so "one of us." Following the constitutional breakdown of 1953 in Lagos, when yet another constitution was introduced in 1954, this time recognizing Nigeria as the federation of three regions (four after 1963), Sardauna, visibly head and shoulders above any possible competition, was appointed premier of the Northern Region on October 1. He was to hold this position until his assassination on January 15, 1966.

On his elevation to a knighthood in the British honors system in 1959, he standardized the style of address as Alhaji Sir Ahmadu Bello, carefully reviving the name of his respected forebear, Sultan Bello. Once again in contrast to his counterpart premiers, Bello unswervingly refused to contemplate moving to the center of government in Lagos, preferring regional to federal politics. In the event, there was little need for any such move, for he gave the impression that he was quite ready and able from his base in Kaduna to exercise control over decision making in the capital. Such, indeed, were the contradictions and imbalance in the federation that the northern tail was often able to wag the federal dog, especially when it belonged to such an authoritarian, charismatic and strong-minded leader as Sardauna.

The political history of Nigeria, stormily competitive in the last five years of British rule (1955–60) and bitterly cutthroat in the first five of independence (1960–65), has been frequently told in the standard texts. Three events may be taken to illustrate the measure of Sardauna's leadership during this critical decade of Nigeria's emergence onto the international scene as the anticipated "Giant of Africa."

The first relates to his passionate perception, first sensed on his visit to Lagos in 1949 and then never to be forgotten or forgiven after the abusive reception encountered from the Lagos *canaille* (as Sardauna would happily have described the vulgar rabble had he known French) by the NPC delegation during the acrimonious "self-government in 1956" motion proposed by the southern members of the federal legislature, of how educationally backward (and hence politically disadvantaged) the north was. This explains his controversial implementation, from 1954, of a "northernization" program, whereby crash courses were progressively initiated for the training of northerners at every level of government employment, from clerks and artisans up to professional civil servants. This was done not only to northernize a still largely expatriate and southern Nigeria-dominated regional civil service, but also to ensure that in a future independent Nigeria the north could play its equal (at least) share in the staffing of the federal public service and armed forces. The concomitant ruling of this northernization campaign, as offensive to the south as it was critical to the north, was that in filling vacancies in the senior ranks of the northern civil service preference would be given, where there was no qualified northerner available, to hiring Europeans on contract, and only in the last instance would nonnorthern Nigerians be offered employment. If these measures can be said to have protected and preserved the north, as they undoubtedly did, they understandably generated much resentment in the south and contributed little toward any claim by Sardauna of fostering the unity of Nigeria, at least in so far as that was interpreted in Lagos, Enugu and Ibadan, in other words, in the other regions of Nigeria.

The second example was a regional and not a federal matter. This was Sardauna's decision, in the name of Islam, to promote and personally undertake a vigorous proselytization program among the millions of northerners who were neither Moslems nor Christians but were, for want of a better word, animists. His conversion campaign of 1963–65 brought Sardauna into further conflict with southern politicians and in the end proved to be counterproductive to his reputation as a statesman. Related to this is the third illustration. This was his brusque and totally unconstitutional foray into foreign affairs—exclusively the prerogative of the prime minister and the federal cabinet—by publicly denigrating Israel and refusing to accept Israeli development aid enjoyed and appreciated by other regional governments. Instead, he set about emphasizing his own links with, status in and marked preference for the geopolitical world of Islam. In this connection, too, he went so far as to publish a classical genealogy (*salsala*) proving his line of descent from the Prophet Mohammed.

In the twelve years of Sardauna's premiership, there could be no doubt in anybody's mind where power lay in Nigeria. His style of leadership, an effective blend of profound respect for traditional values and the procedural realities of modern government, was complemented by a personal exercise of patronage as vast and encompassing as his own monumental and splendid figure. If the north and Sardauna seemed to be synonymous to a chafing southern political class, they also appeared to be as immovable as the Jebba Rock. Inevitably, then, when the young southern army officers struck brutally in the early hours of January 15, 1966, the elimination of Sardauna, symbolic of northern hegemony and perpetual domination of the south, was priority number one. Led by a fanatic Igbo major, the soldiers stormed State House under the guise of night maneuvers. The officer gunned down Sardauna and his senior wife in cold blood.

The principal analysts of leadership in contemporary Africa have shied away from attempting to analyze the style of Sardauna. Yet, as his biographer John Paden has demonstrated, his is a supreme case of the link between values and leadership. To that accurate interpretation of Sardauna's leadership the present author has offered two extensions. One questions the extent to which Sardauna, at one time for millions the hero of twentieth-century Hausaland, might not be better looked on as epitomizing the values of Fulani leadership, leaving the prime minister, Abubakar Tafawa Balewa, to epitomize the continuing values, less flamboyant and more modest, of Ur-Hausa leadership. The second argues that one might go further yet and portray the Sardauna as representing a superb, albeit likely sole, example of the kind of African leadership that has so far eluded its classifiers, namely the leader as culture hero. His deliberate and skilled use of Hausa proverbs in his public speeches; his method of conducting cabinet meetings and the manipulation of his clients, his personal court and his favorites, so similar to the Fulani emir in action over the past two centuries; and his continuous reference to the achievements of his great-great-grandfather in creating the Sokoto Empire and how he looked on his role as the protector of the inviolability of that empire (by now the Northern Region of Nigeria) against threats from outside (by now the south) as sacred trust, all bring credence to such an argument of the culture hero as a fresh dimension to the study of leadership in contemporary Africa.

Sardauna's liquidation by the military rebels in 1966 was the hoped-for finale to remove once and for all the symbol and specter of northern domination. Yet his legacy survived right into the formation of the political parties of the Second Republic (1979–83); only with the banning of the old guard political class from the making of the putative Third Republic (1992–) and the military government's legislative cultivation of the ''new breeds'' can the Sardauna years of direct political influence be said to have come to an end.

His memory lives on in the subconscious of millions of Nigerians, many of whom never knew him; in the minds of countless northern Nigerians who would not be where they are today, or were yesterday, had Ahmadu Bello not given them—often obliged them to take—the opportunity; and in the memory of thousands of others upon whom he conferred his generosity and his humanity— for those were the days before Africa's heads of state executed their opponents and sometimes their predecessors. If, as seems possible in the unhappy and often mediocre procession of African leadership since independence, only Kwame

Nkrumah* and maybe Julius Nyerere* are likely to be readily recalled outside Africa by the turn of the century (and then not for their success but for their personality), inside the quondam Northern Nigeria Alhaji Sir Ahmadu Bello, Sardauna of Sokoto, is likely to be remembered as a lasting symbol of the old north, as the most powerful of modernizing traditionalistic leaders of the first generation of modern African leadership, and as an unparalleled example of the leader as culture hero. He was at once a leader impossible to separate from the values of his history and difficult to appreciate or fully understand outside the context of his time.

BIBLIOGRAPHY

Works by Bello:

My Life. London: Cambridge University Press, 1962.
Rayuwata. Zaria, Nigeria: Gaskiya Corporation, 1964.

Other Works:

Dudley, Billy J. Parties and Politics in Northern Nigeria. London: Frank Cass, 1968.
Kirk-Greene, A. H. M. Mutumin Kirki: The Concept of the Good Man in Hausa. Hans Wolff Memorial Lecture, African Studies Program, Indiana University, 1974.
Paden, John N. Ahmadu Bello, Sardauna of Sokoto: Values and Leadership in Nigeria. Zaria: Hudahuda Publishing Co., 1986.
Sharwood Smith, Sir Bryan. Recollections of British Administration in the Cameroons and Northern Nigeria, 1921–1957: "But always as Friends." Durham, N.C.: Duke University Press, 1969.
Whitaker, C. Sylvester, Jr. "Three Perspectives on Hierarchy: Political Thought and Leadership in Northern Nigeria." Journal of Commonwealth Political Studies 3 (1965): 1–19.
———. The Politics of Tradition: Continuity and Change in Northern Nigeria, 1946–1966. Princeton, N.J.: Princeton University Press, 1970.

A. H. M. KIRK-GREENE

STEPHEN BANTU BIKO (STEVE BIKO) (1946–1977), Leader of the black consciousness movement, South Africa, 1969–1977.

Steve Biko was born in Kingwilliamstown in the eastern Cape on December 18, 1946. He came from a family of very limited means. His mother worked as a domestic for white families, and his father was a clerk. On September 12, 1977, he died in detention as a result of brutal police beating. In less than fifteen years of political activity, Biko had established himself as the theoretical and organizational mastermind behind the black consciousness movement of South Africa. Under his brief leadership, the movement came to represent the unifying thread of black resistance to apartheid in the 1970s.

Biko's political life began at an early age. In 1963 he was expelled from Lovedale High School following a police interrogation about his older brother's suspected involvement in Poqo, the military wing of the Pan-Africanist Congress. This experience contributed to Biko's growing hatred of white supremacy and influenced his subsequent understanding of the black liberation struggle.

Upon his expulsion from Lovedale, Biko entered a Catholic boarding school for Africans in Mariannhill in Natal. There he began to articulate his uneasiness about white liberal principles of multiracialism, an uneasiness that would continue to grow after high school. In 1966 Biko was admitted to the "nonwhite" campus of the University of Natal to study medicine. He was soon drawn into student politics, and as an elected officer of the Students' Representative Council, Biko joined the liberal, white-dominated National Union of South African Students (NUSAS).

At the time NUSAS was one of the few remaining legal antiapartheid organizations. Yet precisely because legality required liberal-based, meliorist policies, Biko became increasingly convinced that NUSAS could not satisfy the growing demands of black students. Within the white-dominated NUSAS, blacks were, from his point of view, at best aliens and at worst token emblems of the organization's sanctimonious multiracialism. He argued that the weight of white hegemony had so distorted and compromised the initial goals of NUSAS that blacks ought to abandon the movement altogether. It was time for blacks to recognize that their future lay in their own black hands. As Biko put it: "Black man, you are on your own" (Biko 1986:91).

In December 1968 black students formed the South African Students' Organization (SASO) at Mariannhill, under Biko's leadership. SASO was officially inaugurated in July 1969 at Turfloop, the "tribal" University College of the North. At this stage Biko and SASO were concerned only with student matters; they had yet to drop the term "nonwhite" as their ethnic designation. As an exclusively nonwhite organization, SASO was frequently accused of succumbing to the divisive structures of apartheid and of espousing a form of black racism. Biko, who had been elected president of SASO, denied these charges vehemently. He supported the goal of racial integration, but was convinced that this goal would be futile, and even suicidal, if it respected the cultural, economic and moral norms of white liberalism. A meaningful integration could not be achieved, according to Biko, without a complete transformation of the existing white, racist capitalist system. In Biko's eyes, white liberals were responsible for arresting the black revolutionary élan and for filling the minds of black intellectuals with a mythical vision of nonracialism. Biko argued that the liberal notion of integration was in truth merely a pseudointegration, a vision that diverted blacks from focusing on themselves and their inferior material conditions. The liberals' proposals for integration would also mean the creation of a deformed culture— deformed in the sense that it could not be the result of a common experience but would be the imposition of an exclusively white paradigm. Biko observed that if by integration people understood a breakthrough into white society by blacks, an assimilation and acceptance of blacks into an already-established set of norms and code of behavior set up and maintained by whites, then he was against it. If, on the other hand, by integration people meant that there would be free participation by all members of a society, catering for the full expression of the self in a freely changing society as determined by the will of the people, then he was for it. Not surprisingly, in 1970 Biko led a drive within SASO to withdraw recognition of NUSAS as the national union. He firmly maintained that this organization of the white liberal establishment was irrelevant to the black struggle and that its multiracialism within apartheid society represented trickery and untruth.

The SASO policy manifesto adopted in 1971 under the strong influence of Biko formulated the dominant themes of the black consciousness movement. It stated:

> SASO is a Black Student Organization working for the liberation of the Black man first from psychological oppression by themselves through inferiority complex and secondly from physical oppression occurring out of living in a White racist society.
> ... We define Black people as those who are by law or tradition, politically, economically and socially discriminated against as a group in the South African society and identifying themselves as a unit in the struggle towards the realization of their aspirations.
> SASO believes: ... That ... because of the privileges accorded to them by legislation and because of their continual maintenance of an oppressive regime Whites have defined themselves as part of the problem. ... SASO upholds the concept of Black Consciousness and the drive towards Black awareness as the most logical and significant means of ridding ourselves of the shackles that bind us to perpetual servitude. ... SASO accepts the premise that before the Black people should join the open society, they should first close their ranks, to form themselves into a solid group to oppose the definite racism that is meted out by the White society, to work out their direction clearly and bargain from a position of strength. SASO believes that a truly open society can only be achieved by Blacks (SASO *Newsletter* August 1971:10–11).

Biko, however, was concerned that because SASO was comprised exclusively of students, it was not the proper organization to mobilize the black masses. He therefore played a major role in creating the Black Peoples Convention (BPC) and the Black Community Program in 1971. He hoped that these organizations would spread the message of black consciousness throughout South Africa.

Biko's powerful intellectual condemnation of both apartheid and white liberalism generated the growth of the black consciousness movement, a movement that by 1971 went far beyond university campuses to invigorate the intellectual renaissance of black South Africans. As envisaged by Biko, black consciousness was bent on forming a strong ethicopolitical ideology capable of liberating blacks from their own mental submissiveness to white cultural hegemony. As such, black consciousness was a radical critique of the pretensions and aims of white liberalism. It stressed the necessity of black solidarity as the means to emancipation and defined the category "black" as an exploited group of people. The pejorative term "nonwhite" came to define those Africans, Asians and "coloreds" who derived power, status and privileges from their collaboration with white authorities. Biko felt that black consciousness was an attitude of mind and a way of life. Based on self-examination, it led blacks to believe that by seeking to "run away from themselves and emulate the white man, they are insulting the intelligence of whoever created them black." As Biko observed, "At the heart of this kind of thinking is the realization by blacks that the most potent weapon in the hands of the oppressor is the mind of the oppressed" (Biko 1978:92).

From Biko's perspective, then, black consciousness and black morality meant the realization of an understanding that the emancipation of blacks and the liberation of society as a whole required the mental renaissance of the black intellect. This understanding also meant the development of a black political will that, if necessary, would generate a massive insurrection culminating in the overthrow of white supremacy and the ushering in of black hegemony. Biko's ultimate objective was the complete transformation of the existing socioeconomic system into a black creation. Thus black consciousness became a revolutionary theory. The immediate task was to contribute to the rise of black dignity, and Biko's definition of black consciousness recognized this: "Blacks are out to completely transform the system and to make of it what they wish. Such a major undertaking can only be realized in an atmosphere where people are convinced of the truth inherent in their stand" (Biko 1978:49).

Biko's vision of the free society of the future was profoundly dialectical. He recognized that no true sense of black dignity could be cultivated within the context of apartheid; a complete overhaul of socioeconomic structures was needed if blacks were to realize their full cultural and intellectual potential. In his view, however, such structural and material changes would not suffice. Thus for Biko, the black consciousness movement was to liberate blacks from both their enslavement to white values and from their existential misery. He argued that it was only when blacks understood their alienated and exploited condition that they would take upon themselves the responsibility of transforming their historical reality.

This is why Biko emphasized the necessity of spreading the ideology of black consciousness to all sections of the black community. To perform this task, SASO developed a strong following among African, Indian and "colored" students. Its internal organization and its means of communications were highly effective. While it is difficult to assess its total membership, SASO claimed four thousand subscribers to its regularly published newsletter. Moreover, SASO, the BPC and other affiliated groups organized many well-attended conferences and meetings where the black consciousness ideology was discussed and proselytized. In this sense, the movement achieved one of its central aims: It eroded and ultimately displaced the hegemony of white bourgeois culture. It created a new ethos rooted in a new system of black values.

The development of a new sense of black dignity contributed to a wave of popular protests in early 1973. The government responded to these challenges by banning Biko and many other black consciousness leaders in March of that year. Biko remained silent until he was called to testify in the 1976 trial of Sathasivan Cooper and eight other leaders of SASO and BPC. On this occasion he delivered one of the most eloquent defenses of the black consciousness movement. Biko's courtroom testimony further enhanced his status and popularity; he came to symbolize the resistance of black men and women. The black struggle culminated in the urban revolt of Soweto that engulfed South Africa in 1976 in an acute social and political crisis. The crisis reached its climax with Biko's tragic murder on September 12, 1977, at the age of thirty. While in police custody, he was fatally struck by the blows of one of apartheid's brutal security guards. The murder demonstrated the government's determination to crush an emergent black revolution, yet it also indicated clearly that black South Africans were prepared to pay the ultimate price for their emancipation. In Biko's words: "To stop us now they will have to kill us all first" (*Southern Africa* 10, no. 8 (October 1977): 10).

The killing in fact escalated after Biko's death. On October 19, 1977, the government imposed a massive crackdown on black resistance, and all black consciousness organizations were banned. The violence unleashed by the government was a sign of power, but it was a power that had lost whatever remnant of legitimacy it may have had. Biko's life and death contributed decisively to the erosion of white supremacy in South Africa. They cracked the walls of apartheid and opened the gates to the long road of black emancipation.

BIBLIOGRAPHY

Works by Biko:

I Write What I Like. Edited with a personal memoir and a new preface by Aelred Stubbs. San Francisco: Harper and Row, 1986.

Other Works:

Arnold, Millard (ed.). *Steve Biko: Black Consciousness in South Africa*. New York: Vintage Books, 1979.
Bernstein, Hilda. *No. 46—Steve Biko*. London: International Defence and Aid Fund, 1978.
Fatton, Robert, Jr. *Black Consciousness in South Africa: The Dialectics of Ideological Resistance to White Supremacy*. Albany: State University of New York Press, 1986.
Gerhart, Gail M. *Black Power in South Africa*. Berkeley: University of California Press, 1978.
Woods, Donald. *Biko*. New York: Vintage Books, 1979.

                                                                          ROBERT FATTON, JR.

PIETER WILLEM BOTHA (1916–   ), Prime Minister, State President, Republic of South Africa, 1978–1989.

P. W. Botha devoted his entire career to politics, first as a paid party organizer, then as a member of Parliament, and later as a member of successive cabinets, as prime minister and, finally, as state president. South African politics is only eighty years old, and P. W. Botha was an active participant for more than fifty.

Pieter Willem Botha was born on January 12, 1916, in the Orange Free State to politically aware parents. Indeed, his mother was interned in a concentration camp by the British during the Anglo-Boer War. His father too had strong political convictions. Botha briefly attended the local university but dropped out to enter full-time politics as an organizer of the National Party (NP). As a result of his enormous energy and strong personality, he was rewarded with a nomination to a parliamentary constituency in the George area of the Cape Province. In the 1948 elections he won the seat and was to remain the George representative until 1984.

In Parliament his progress was slow but steady. Ten years after he first entered, he became a deputy minister, and three years later he became a full minister. He was to make his mark in national politics from 1966 when he became the minister of defense, a post he was to hold for more than thirteen years. As the minister of defense, Botha presided over the massive expansion of South African armed might until it became the most powerful military establishment in Africa. During this period Botha refined his leadership style and developed the philosophy that was to guide his later career as the nation's chief executive.

During the 1970s few expected Botha to rise any further in the political establishment. He was never very popular with his colleagues, who regarded him as temperamentally unsuited for a top leadership position, given his notoriously short temper and erratic and impulsive leadership style. On policy issues too he was suspect: a confirmed hawk and militarist in foreign-policy matters and a suspected dove on racial matters. His biggest drawback, however, was his political base, which was in the minority Cape section of the National Party, which is organized on a federal basis. The provincial party leaders are very powerful, and the largest province at that time, Transvaal, was led by the young and charismatic Connie Mulder, who was generally viewed as the heir apparent.

Botha's opportunity to win the top leadership position came unexpectedly with the so-called Information Scandal that destroyed Connie Mulder's career. This scandal revolved around the abuse of power and financial corruption that surrounded the secret projects of the Department of Information. This department, nominally under Connie Mulder's control, embarked on a secret program of buying South Africa international respectability by, among other things, bribing journalists, establishing a government-controlled English-language newspaper in Johannesburg, and attempting to buy the *Washington Star* newspaper. In 1977, when reports of financial abuse and illegal projects began to surface, Mulder made the fatal mistake of lying to Parliament, and when this became public knowledge, his ultimate fate was sealed. Prime Minister Vorster, his health broken (in part because of the unfolding scandal), announced his resignation from the office in 1978.

Furious lobbying for support began immediately, and tension was high when the National Party caucus met eight days later to elect a new leader. There were three candidates: the popular foreign minister, Pik Botha, P. W. Botha himself, and Connie Mulder. The vote was close: In the first ballot, P. W. Botha received seventy-eight votes to Mulder's seventy-two and Pik Botha's twenty-two. In the second and final ballot, P. W. Botha obtained ninety-eight votes to Mulder's seventy-four.

The new prime minister set himself an ambitious agenda upon taking office. Botha's first move was to overhaul the machinery of government. In the past his greatest strength had been his talent as an organizer, and he immediately began to restructure the governmental system. He established for the first time an Office of the Prime Minister with a staff and planning capability, reduced to five the many ad hoc cabinet committees set up by his predecessor, and reorganized the bureaucracy.

Given his past experience in the defense portfolio, his management style and policy system tended to reflect the values of order, hierarchy and controls. Most at ease with committee government, he proceeded to eliminate the personalistic system of his predecessor. The most important cabinet committee was the State Security Council, which was not only chaired by the prime minister, but enjoyed statutory recognition and had its own staff of full-time officials. This committee, although nominally restricted to the examination and advice function in the security area, was to become Botha's chosen instrument of policy-making in a wide range of fields.

With control established over the machinery of government, Botha now turned his attention to control over the ruling National Party. The main problem here was represented by the Transvaal leader of the NP, A. P. Treurnicht, whose ultraconservatism threatened to undermine the credibility of Botha's policies. Because Treurnicht had an independent political base, he was not beholden to Botha and was therefore more difficult to control. Treurnicht represented old-style apartheid in terms of which all South Africans who were not white would, at best, be second-class citizens (''colored'' people and Indians); at worst, they would not even be regarded as citizens at all (the African majority). Crude racism and segregation would be the policies of the government.

Botha, in contrast, recognized that if white domination did not become modernized, its very survival would be endangered. He therefore believed it necessary to find some way of meeting the political aspirations of colored people and Asians in a way that did not endanger basic white hegemony. Botha did not believe it possible to grant the African population genuine political rights, but he did believe that if their socioeconomic conditions could be improved, the prospects for a revolutionary challenge would be reduced.

Botha recognized that the conflict with Treurnicht was irreconcilable and planned to drive his opponent from the NP. This he proceeded to do with consummate skill. In 1982 Treurnicht and a handful of parliamentary supporters were driven out of the NP. In March 1982 Treurnicht established an ultraconservative party, the Conservative Party, to challenge Botha from within the Afrikaner community.

With relatively free hands, Botha began in earnest to implement his reform program. In the socioeconomic sphere the guiding philosophy was based upon a belief in a ''total onslaught'' by radicals and Communists against South Africa, which could only be deflected if black people could be persuaded to support the white-ruled state. This support, it was believed, could only be secured if the material position of blacks was improved. Under Botha the state began to spend increased resources on black education, housing, salaries, pensions and infrastructure.

Simultaneously, Botha began to deracialize many other aspects of South African society and to reverse many of the old-style apartheid measures. The laws that prevented interracial marriages and sexual relations were repealed, while public facilities such as parks, libraries and beaches gradually became open to all. In the labor field African workers were for the first time granted rights to unionize, strike and bargain in officially sanctioned institutions with employees.

In the political field Botha sought to build an anti-African coalition of whites, colored people and Indians. A new constitution was introduced in 1984 that created a tricameral legislature with a chamber for whites, another for colored people, and yet a third for Indians. Africans were totally excluded. The machinery of government, however, remained firmly under white control. The key to continuing white control lay in a new institution, the President's Council, which contained a built-in white majority. This body served a critical function in that if the three racially based chambers of Parliament did not agree about legislation, the President's Council could decide which version of the legislation would become the law. The white chamber of Parliament could thus, with President's Council support, overrule legislation passed by the other two chambers.

White control was also ensured by a powerful executive system under the control of a president. The executive president was elected by an electoral college of Parliament with a built-in white majority. Thus, while the 1984 constitution made power sharing between whites, coloreds and Indians possible, it did not make it mandatory.

In the realm of foreign policy, Botha acted ruthlessly to safeguard the interests of his constituents. He launched a vigorous program of destabilization against the neighboring black states to force them to seek an accommodation with the apartheid regime. Aid given to black resistance groups such as the African National Congress (ANC) provoked powerful military retaliation from South Africa. For a brief period during 1984 and 1985, however, it seemed that diplomacy would replace the military in regional relations. The Nkomati Accord and the Lusaka Agreement with Mozambique and Angola, respectively, both seemed to place South Africa on the road to peace with its neighbors with agreements to avoid violence in the resolution of conflicts.

The new constitution and the Nkomati Accord were for Botha the high points of his administration, and had he retired at that point, his reputation would have been that of a successful, if cautious, reformer. Botha, however, decided to remain in politics and become South Africa's first executive president.

Decline set in with remarkable speed. Violence began to increase throughout the country. The African majority, which had been explicitly excluded from the new system of government, organized and agitated against this exclusion. Many members of the colored and Indian communities objected to being co-opted against Africans; they also opposed a system that still granted them only second-class citizenship. New organizations such as the United Democratic Front (UDF) came into existence to organize opposition to the new constitution. Political awareness and activism spread rapidly throughout the country.

Botha became progressively more enraged by what he perceived to be ingratitude from blacks for his reform measures. The turning point was the so-called Rubicon speech in August 1985, in which Botha disappointed the world by failing to announce bold changes in the apartheid system. As a result, the currency fell dramatically in value, and foreign banks began the process of withdrawing from South Africa. In 1985 Botha declared a partial state of emergency to contain the violence, and in June 1986 he declared a national state of emergency that was to continue in effect throughout the remaining years of Botha's rule.

Under the emergency the state responded to black violence with considerable force. Civil liberties were largely suspended, stringent media restrictions were adopted to control the press and television, and state-sponsored vigilante groups assassinated apartheid opponents. The government campaign was led by Botha himself, supported by a team of "securocrats," that is, security-oriented advisors, and an elaborate organizational structure known as the National Security Management System. During this period more than four thousand people died in political violence, while about forty-five thousand more were detained by the authorities.

By the end of 1986 the state had largely succeeded in crushing the uprisings. Botha, however, had no new political initiatives up his sleeve. His remaining years were characterized by stagnation in which reforms were placed on the back burner. Futile attempts were made to begin a political debate with blacks, but the continuing state of emergency, the banning of the ANC and other organizations, and the continued incarceration of ANC leader Nelson Mandela[*] made success impossible.

In the foreign-policy field relations also deteriorated. The high hopes for peace embodied in the Nkomati Accord were soon dashed as Botha resumed his destabilization campaign. The Commonwealth Heads of State peace-brokering mission, known as the Eminent Persons Group, returned from South Africa prematurely and in failure in 1988 after Botha scuttled the exercise by attacking targets in Mozambique, Zambia and Zimbabwe.

In early 1989 Botha suffered a stroke and, in a major miscalculation, resigned as NP leader while seeking to remain as state president. In the power struggle with his successor as party leader, F. W. de Klerk,[*] Botha became increasingly isolated and was forced to resign the presidency in August 1989.

The tragedy of the Botha era was that the promising beginning of 1978–83 ended eventually in stagnation and disillusionment. Botha himself was never able to transcend the blinkers of Afrikaner nationalism and National Party interests. Yet he was the first reform-oriented NP leader. He demolished much of the structure of social apartheid. He openly acknowledged the need to treat black people with fairness, even if his actions often contradicted his rhetoric. He removed two of the major African grievances: the industrial relations legislation that had formerly prevented African workers from participating in legal trade unions and the negotiation process, and the influx control system that prevented Africans from moving freely throughout the country. Botha thus finally acknowledged the permanence of urban Africans in the common area of South Africa.

The major failure was in the political sphere. The 1984 tricameral parliamentary system failed to give even the minority colored and Indian population full citizenship. Although Botha was eventually to recognize the moral claim of the African majority to political rights, he was never able to act boldly in this area. At the end of the Botha era in 1989, South Africa was a land divided and held together by a brutal state of emergency. Both blacks and whites were deeply polarized on many of the key issues. The rise of the racist Conservative Party in white parliamentary politics and of extraparliamentary white vigilante groups, like the Afrikaner Resistance Movement, was a direct response to the Botha policies. Similarly, black politics was divided by regional, ethnic and ideological conflicts.

Botha thus suffered the fate of the half-hearted reformer. While many of his traditional white supporters cried out against his "treachery to his people," the so-called black beneficiaries of reform maintained that it was all "too little and too late." Botha must thus be judged a political failure despite his not-insignificant reforms. However, in his failures lay the dynamic for future reforms. By destroying the apartheid dream, by weakening white confidence, by contributing to the globalization of the South African issue, and by further politicizing black South Africans, Botha made inevitable a further process of deracialization. Ironically, the unintended consequences of the Botha era hold out more hope for a resolution of the conflicts than the intended consequences of his own more limited reforms.

BIBLIOGRAPHY

Davenport, Trevor. *South Africa: A Modern History*. Johannesburg: Macmillan, 1987.
De Villiers, Dirk, and Johanna de Villiers. *P. W.* Cape Town: Tafelberg, 1984.
Giliomee, Hermann, and Lawrence Schlemmer. *From Apartheid to Nation-Building*. Cape Town: Oxford University Press, 1989.
Johnson, Shaun. *South Africa: No Turning Back*. London: Macmillan, 1988.
Lemon, Anthony. *Apartheid in Transition*. Aldershot, Eng.: Gower, 1987.
Pottinger, Brian. *The Imperial Presidency*. Johannesburg: Southern Books, 1988.
Rhoodie, Eschel. *P. W. Botha: The Last Betrayal*. Melville, South Africa: S. A. Politics Publishers, 1989.
Schrire, Robert. *The Botha Era and the End of White Politics*. New York: Ford Foundation, 1990.

ROBERT SCHRIRE

MANGOSUTHU GATSHA BUTHELEZI (1928–) Chief Minister of KwaZulu; President, Inkatha yeNkulukeko yeSizwe (Freedom of the Nation), Republic of South Africa, 1976– .

In a country where from its inception in 1910 no black African has ever been allowed to participate directly in any of the central political institutions of the state (other than until 1960 as parliamentary voters, under highly restrictive conditions), Chief Gatsha Buthelezi has become a nationally prominent political figure with whom other leaders, both black and white, must reckon. Among the African majority, however, he is a singularly controversial individual, as a "homeland" leader who has opposed both international sanctions against South Africa and the strategy of "armed struggle" against apartheid that the African National Congress (ANC), the best known of several liberation groups, has followed since the early 1960s shortly after it was banned.

M. Gatsha Buthelezi was born August 27, 1928, at Mahlabathini in Zululand, a village about 120 miles north-northeast of Durban. His father was Chief Mathole of the Buthelezi tribe, and his mother was Princess Constance Magogo Zulu. Through his mother's side he is descended from King Cetshwayo, a nephew of the legendary Shaka (1787–1828), putative founder of the Zulu nation. His paternal great-grandfather, Chief Mnyamana Buthelezi, was political advisor ("prime minister") to Cetshwayo at the time of the Anglo-Zulu War in 1879, whose outcome cost the Zulu their independence. Buthelezi is also a nephew of Pixley Seme, a founder in 1912 of the ANC and later the organization's president-general from 1930 to 1937. On July 2, 1951, Buthelezi married Irene Audrey Thandekile Mzilla; they have three sons and four daughters.

After a traditional early childhood spent in part as a herdboy, Buthelezi attended Impumalanga primary school in Mahashini for nine years. In 1944 he enrolled at Adams College, a Congregational teacher-training institution in Amanzimtoti, whose principal, Dr. Edgar Brookes, was well known as a spokesman for African interests in the Senate, the upper house of the Union's Parliament at the time. Four years later Buthelezi was admitted to Fort Hare University College in the eastern Cape Province. Here he joined the company of other African students who would later become politically prominent throughout the subcontinent. These included Robert Sobukwe,* founder in 1959 of the Pan-Africanist Congress, and Robert Mugabe,* the first prime minister of independent Zimbabwe.

At Fort Hare, where he studied history and "native administration," Buthelezi came under the influence of Professor Z. K. Matthews, already a respected national leader of the African National Congress. Buthelezi joined the Fort Hare branch of the ANC Youth League, but political activities soon got him into trouble with the university authorities, and he was expelled from Fort Hare in 1950. This made it necessary for him to complete his B.A. degree through the University of Natal, where he was able to write his Fort Hare examinations in absentia.

In 1951–52 Buthelezi worked briefly as an interpreter in the Durban office of the Department of Native Administration. He left to become a clerk in a firm of Durban attorneys, Crowley and Crowley. In 1953, however, Buthelezi left this position too and with the reported blessings of senior ANC leaders returned to Mahlabathini to assume at age twenty-five the duties of chief of the 30,000 members of the Buthelezi tribe. Technically his position at first was only that of acting chief until September 1957, when the central government finally confirmed him.

When a "territorial authority" made up of hereditary chiefs was established for KwaZulu in 1970 under terms of the Bantu Authorities Act of 1951, Buthelezi automatically became a member of this new body and was elected its chief executive officer. Three years later, when the KwaZulu territorial authority was reconstituted as a partially elective legislative assembly, Buthelezi became its chief executive councillor, though still owing his own membership in that assembly to an ex officio appointment. At the time the KwaZulu "homeland" government was granted enhanced executive responsibilities in 1976, Buthelezi was elevated to the new post of chief minister.

In 1928 Buthelezi's uncle, King Solomon ka Zulu, founded a cultural organization for the Zulu people, which he named Inkatha ka Zulu. It lasted only a few years before disappearing in the early 1930s. Four decades later, however, his nephew revived the body, changing its name to Inkatha yeNkululeko yeSizwe (Freedom of the Nation). As Inkatha's president, Buthelezi gradually transformed the organization's earlier character until he could represent the modern Inkatha as a nonviolent, antiapartheid, mass liberation movement.

Buthelezi has claimed a role for Inkatha in South African domestic affairs as the "custodian" of the political ideals of the proscribed African National Congress. Indeed, in 1975 Inkatha adopted for itself the flag and uniform of the ANC, although both were also banned at the time. However, Inkatha's frequent, unabashed Zulu ethnic chauvinism is at odds with the long-standing supraethnic and nonracial principles of the ANC. By 1988 Inkatha claimed a signed-up membership of nearly 1,300,000 persons, understandably mainly Zulus. Independent observers, however, usually credit the body with a following perhaps half this size, and some believe that a significant number of Inkatha's members were pressured into joining. Until 1990 Inkatha was clearly the largest legal black political organization in South African history. How large the ANC will become now that the ban against it has been lifted remains to be seen.

In 1978 Buthelezi led Inkatha into a loose political coalition—the South African Black Alliance—with both the ("colored") Labour Party of South Africa and the miniscule Indian Reform Party. Later these three organizations were joined by the Inyandza National Movement of KaNgwana. (KaNgwana is the Swazi "homeland" within South Africa on the northern border of independent Swaziland.) Five years later the Black Alliance was fatally weakened by a major split on the issue of participation in the republic's new tricameral parliament established in consequence of the government's 1983–84 revision of the national constitution. Such participation was not, of course, an option open to Inkatha, as Africans continued to be excluded from any involvement in the national Parliament. But for the first time in South African history so-called coloreds and Indians were entitled to enter Parliament, albeit in separate, racially segregated chambers. The Labour Party chose to try to capitalize on this new opportunity, notwithstanding the predictable cost of its suspension from the Black Alliance.

For his part, Buthelezi campaigned actively around the country against accepting the new Parliament, while concurrently declining to sanction local elections of Africans to so-called urban community councils. These elections, he said, were being used by Pretoria to justify the continued exclusion of Africans from critical roles at the center of South African national life. Thus, unlike Chief Kaiser Matanzima in Transkei and the "homeland" leaders of similarly "independent" Ciskei, Venda and Bophuthatswana, Buthelezi has steadfastly refused to appear to barter away long-standing African claims to political representation "at the center" and at all political levels by accepting legal sovereignty for KwaZulu and its inhabitants on the periphery of South African society. Nor would Buthelezi agree to a proposal of Pretoria early in the 1980s that the Ingwavuma region of northern Zululand be ceded to Swaziland. This would have given landlocked Swaziland a much-desired outlet to the Indian Ocean, but it would have stripped the inhabitants of the region of any future claims as South Africans. In 1982, as KwaZulu chief minister, Buthelezi was instrumental in appealing successfully to the South African courts to block implementation of the proposal on grounds that the necessary consent of the KwaZulu cabinet had not been obtained.

Despite repeated entreaties from Pretoria, Buthelezi consistently refused to become a party to direct negotiations with the central government over the country's future so long as the ANC's Nelson Mandela* was in prison. But in 1980 Buthelezi did endorse the establishment of a multiracial commission of experts for the purpose of developing a form of "consociational" power sharing for Natal between the KwaZulu government and the existing all-white provincial administration. In time the recommendations of the Buthelezi Commission (as this body came to be known), further advanced in 1986 by an *indaba* (meeting) of representatives of both KwaZulu and Natal, resulted in Pretoria's acceptance of a joint KwaZulu/Natal executive authority within the province. This body began functioning in November 1987. However, the central government failed to act on the *indaba's* more far-reaching suggestion of a legislative union within Natal.

Tom Lodge has written that Buthelezi "is one of the more enigmatic and attractive figures to have emerged from the milieu of homeland politics" (Lodge 1983:350). By all accounts the chief minister is articulate, intelligent and forceful. In public he is often a flamboyant figure who shrewdly and effectively manipulates political symbols, depending upon the immediate circumstances. In small groups, it is said, he can be quite charming. Those who have met him speak easily of the chief's personal "charisma," but also recall his "hypersensitivity" and quick temper when faced with personal criticism. Clearly he possesses the prestige of high traditional status among the Zulu people. As these number slightly more than six million persons and are South Africa's largest ethnic group, Buthelezi's political base is an important one. It is especially strong in the rural areas of Natal province.

Buthelezi's domination of Inkatha, together with that organization's thorough-going penetration of the state structures of KwaZulu, including especially the "homeland's" educational establishment, gives him significant patronage to dispense and a mass following organized, at least in part, along conventional patron-client lines. On the other hand, it would be wrong to discount Inkatha's antiapartheid ideology as an important source of the political allegiance of the organization's many thousands of followers.

Buthelezi's popularity among Africans in South Africa must therefore be counted considerable, though it probably diminished in the 1980s. In 1984 a study at the University of Natal found that 54 percent of black workers in Durban favored Buthelezi/Inkatha. This compared with only 11 percent who preferred Nelson Mandela[*] and the ANC and 23 percent who preferred the United Democratic Front (UDF). The greater Durban area is ethnically a Zulu stronghold among African groups, but an earlier national survey by a West German polling group produced essentially similar results. However, in 1988 scholars reviewing subsequent polling data surmised that the relative positions of Buthelezi and Mandela in the esteem of black South Africans had probably been reversed. But by any reckoning Buthelezi remains a major figure in South African national politics.

It is not surprising, therefore, that as the years have passed Buthelezi has been openly courted by leaders of diverse political viewpoints and from all racial groups within South Africa, although there are other individuals and organizations who pointedly shun him. Buthelezi is frequently sought out by prominent visitors to the country from abroad, while in the course of his frequent travels overseas he has been received by innumerable world figures—popes, presidents, prime ministers and foreign ministers—as well as by the ANC leadership-in-exile itself, in a well-publicized meeting in London in October 1979. In Africa the chief minister has had interviews with several heads of state. In 1975, at one of these, the late President Tolbert of Liberia made Buthelezi a knight commander of the star of Africa in recognition of his "outstanding leadership." Buthelezi received the AFL-CIO's human-rights award in 1983, and later he received honorary degrees from two American universities. The University of Cape Town granted him an honorary doctor of laws in 1978. He is the ceremonial chancellor of the University of Zululand, though student opposition to him on that campus is also present.

Buthelezi elicits from some blacks in South Africa intense hostility, possibly more than anyone else in politics there. Doubtless some of this hostility can be seen as part of the inevitable struggle for power among organizations and individuals within the collective ranks of the overall liberation movement. Traditional African interethnic rivalry—for example, Xhosa versus Zulu—may play a part also, though some argue that this rivalry is exaggerated. In a country where abject poverty among Africans is common, some doubtless resent the relatively glamorous and comfortable life-style Buthelezi manages to follow. But in addition to all of this there are five substantive objections to Buthelezi and/or his Inkatha organization that are commonly encountered—objections that are more modern than traditional interethnic antagonisms and more principled than sheer opportunism or personal envy.

As an individual who has clearly traded upon his own high traditional status and exploited the one-time grandeur and independent power of the Zulu people, Buthelezi is called by some a "tribalist," "unprogressive" and possibly a danger to other African ethnic groups or even to the Indians of Natal. Because of his role as chief minister of KwaZulu, he is bitterly accused of having become a willing collaborator and agent of the hated apartheid regime. Buthelezi responds to this latter charge by saying that he is only using the leverage his statutory position gives him to hasten the destruction of apartheid, and that the weapons Africans possess for use against the white government in this battle are not so numerous or so powerful that any available ones should be abandoned.

His critics further contend that Buthelezi's willingness to embrace the idea of a black/white "consociationalism" in South Africa, if only for Natal Province, constitutes a "selling out" of the liberation movements' hallowed principles of political equality for blacks (and all other individuals) throughout the country and majority rule. His refusal to support the ANC's "armed struggle" or the international campaign for the economic isolation of South Africa puts him in further opposition to many other prominent leaders within the antiapartheid movement, both in the country and outside it. On the other hand, survey findings suggest that there are many ordinary blacks in South Africa who in fact agree with the chief minister's positions on these matters, especially sanctions. Buthelezi argues that working through Inkatha, he is following a careful, long-term strategy of mobilizing African workers and consumers politically for an eventual showdown with the white authorities, a strategy that in the end will be both more successful and less damaging to the interests of the Africans than premature or ill-advised political activism and "posturing." Finally, Buthelezi is condemned for the periodic political excesses of his organization, Inkatha. These, neutral observers agree, have ranged from coercing some persons into joining the body to political thuggery and violence against its organizational opponents, such as the ANC, the UDF and the Congress of South African Trade Unions (COSATU). Eyewitnesses suggest that all sides carry some of the blame for these violent encounters, but many commentators believe that Inkatha's responsibility in this regard is greater. In July 1991 newspaper reports in South Africa revealed secret government funding of more than $500,000 for political rallies of Inkatha and probably violence in order to destabilize the ANC. Two government ministers were transferred, and an Inkatha official resigned. Buthelezi denied any knowledge of the funds or the contacts.

The criticisms of Buthelezi arising especially from his role as KwaZulu chief minister underscore the special difficulties in South Africa that African incumbents of statutory positions have encountered within an overall legal and constitutional system that lacks legitimacy for nearly all blacks in the country. For many onlookers the mere willingness of an individual to serve in such a position, be it as policeman or "homeland" chief minister, constitutes politically fatal self-incrimination. It may not be accidental, therefore, that Buthelezi's principal rivals for prominence from among the African population were an Anglican archbishop and the formerly imprisoned leader of a formerly banned organization, Desmond Tutu* and Nelson Mandela, respectively, whose reputations clearly owed nothing at all to official incumbency. Indeed, it is in a way a tribute to Buthelezi's inherent political resources and skills that his influence within the country and overseas has survived—and in earlier times, at least, even prospered—during nearly two decades of prominent officeholding within the structures of the apartheid state.

BIBLIOGRAPHY

Works by Buthelezi:

Power Is Ours. New York: Books in Focus, 1979.
South Africa: My Vision of the Future. New York: St. Martin's Press, 1990.

Other Works:

Lodge, Tom. *Black Politics in South Africa since 1945*. London: Longman, 1983.
Mare, Gerhard, and Georgina Hamilton. *An Appetite for Power: Buthelezi's Inkatha and South Africa*. Bloomington: Indiana University Press, 1987.
Mzala. *Gatsha Buthelezi: Chief with a Double Agenda*. London: Zed Press, 1988.
Smith, Jack Shepherd. *Buthelezi: The Biography*. Melville, South Africa: Hans Strydom Publishers, 1988.
Temkin, Ben. *Gatsha Buthelezi: Zulu Statesman*. Cape Town: Purnell, 1976.

NEWELL M. STULTZ

C

AMILCAR CABRAL (1924–1973), Founder and leader of the Partido Africano da Independéncia da Guiné e Cabo Verde (PAIGC), Portuguese colonies of Guinea and Cape Verde, 1945–1973.

Amílcar Cabral founded and led the PAIGC, the nationalist movement that achieved independence for the two West African Portuguese colonies of Cape Verde and Guinea. His reputation as one of Africa's greatest nationalist leaders rests both on the success of the war of national liberation that the PAIGC waged against the Portuguese in Guinea and on the political acuteness of his writings.

His influence extended not only to the other Portuguese colonies (Angola, Mozambique and São Tomé and Príncipe), where the "Guinea model" of nationalist war soon imposed itself, but also to African countries where Africans were seeking an inspiration to challenge white minority rule or simply to resist political oppression. His writings have now become classics in twentieth-century Marxist/nationalist texts along with those of Gramsci, Lenin, Mao, Che Guevara and Franz Fanon.

Although Cabral was born in the Portuguese Guinean town of Bafatá, his parents were Cape Verdean, and he spent his formative years in Cape Verde. Portuguese Guinea (now Guinea-Bissau) was a small Portuguese enclave surrounded by the French colonies of Senegal and Guinea (Conakry) in which Cape Verdeans had also settled as traders, planters and civil servants. Cabral's father was a teacher in Guinea, while his mother ran a shop and a small hotel (pensão).

Cabral returned to Cape Verde before he was five and was brought up by his mother, by then no longer living with his father. There he went to school, completed his secondary education at the age of twenty and, as one of the best students of his generation, gained a scholarship to go to university in Portugal. He chose to study agronomy at Lisbon's Instituto de Agronomia.

Cape Verde, a ten-island archipelago lying some three to four hundred miles off the coast of Senegal, was a privileged part of the Portuguese empire in that its inhabitants, perhaps because they were descendants of Europeans who had mixed with the African slave population (thus creating a Creole society not unlike those found in the Caribbean), were automatically classified as *assimilados*, that is, legally Portuguese subjects. This entitled them, inter alia, to state education. As a result, the proportion of educated Cape Verdeans was significantly higher than that in the other Portuguese colonies, and this explains why so many worked in the colonial civil service, particularly in Guinea.

Cape Verde was, however, a land of desolation. Unlike the islands of Madeira and the Azores, the archipelago was not well suited to cultivation because of perennial rain shortage and recurring droughts. Once an important slave depot in the Atlantic slave trade, Cape Verde had declined steadily until in the nineteenth century the land could no longer support the population. Large-scale famine and emigration followed.

Portugal's indifference to the archipelago and its failure to address the ecological and agricultural problems of Cape Verde eventually led to the great famines of the 1940s, in which possibly a quarter of the population perished. It was in this environment that Cabral came of age, and it is not altogether surprising that he should have chosen to become an agronomist. Agriculture remained his lifelong interest.

His seven years in Lisbon (1945–52) were, paradoxically, to transform him from a Cape Verdean intellectual into an African nationalist. While excelling in his studies and graduating with a thorough professional grounding in agronomy, he was also involved in political and cultural activities that brought him into contacts with Africans from the other Portuguese colonies and exposed him to Marxist thought.

Postwar Portugal was firmly in the grip of the Salazar dictatorship, but despite political repression and censorship, there was much semilegal and underground political activity in which Cabral and his African colleagues participated. Opposition to Salazar was dominated by the Communist Party, which, although banned, managed to continue to influence generations of Portuguese and Africans. Cabral, like the other politically inclined African students of his generation, was thus well versed in Marxist thought and, though not a Communist, was certainly socialist in his outlook.

Even more importantly for him, it was in Lisbon that he, along with a nucleus of African students who were eventually to lead the nationalist movements in Portuguese colonies, underwent what they later dubbed ''the re-Africanization of the mind.'' By this they meant a cultural process similar to Negritude, the process undergone by French-speaking black colonial subjects in Paris, through which they, acculturated and assimilated colonial subjects, transcended the ideology of assimilation and returned to their African roots.

In Lisbon Cabral and his colleagues came to reject their privileged position in the Portuguese system of assimilation and to think of themselves as African nationalists and socialists. This was a determinant experience for Cabral. Although the Cape Verdean elite had traditionally dissociated itself from Africa,

Cabral was determined to cast his lot with Africa and to work eventually to join an independent Cape Verde to the African continent. It was to this end that he took a job as a colonial agronomist in Guinea.

Although between 1952 and 1959 he continued to work as a professional agronomist in Guinea, Angola and Portugal, his life was now devoted to the construction of a nationalist movement in Guinea and Cape Verde. In 1956 he founded the PAIGC and laid down its two objectives: the independence and the eventual integration of Guinea and Cape Verde. Following the failure to develop a legal nationalist movement in Bissau and suffering from increasing repression, the PAIGC moved in 1959 to Conakry, capital of the newly independent neighboring country of French-speaking Guinea, and prepared to launch a nationalist guerrilla war. At that date Cabral left Portugal for good and became a full-time leader of the party.

Insofar as it can ever be said that an individual political leader is responsible for the creation and success of a political movement, it has to be said that Cabral virtually single-handedly constructed PAIGC as a political and military force and led it to victory. Starting with a handful of supporters trained in his house in Conakry, Cabral went on to develop an organization capable of converting the majority of Guineans and Cape Verdeans to the nationalist cause and of driving a PAIGC-armed movement to the verge of military victory over the Portuguese.

Between 1963, when the armed action against the Portuguese began, and 1973, when the PAIGC unilaterally declared independence from Portugal, the nationalist movement evolved from a band of isolated activists to a fully developed political party with several thousand guerrillas operating inside Guinea. By 1973 the PAIGC controlled most of the countryside of Guinea and had pushed the Portuguese to retreat to the cities and to other fortified military positions. The Portuguese had already initiated secret negotiations with the PAIGC with a view to finding a political solution to the conflict.

Cabral was assassinated in January 1973 by a party member working for the Portuguese secret service in a futile attempt to drive a wedge within the party between Cape Verdeans and Guineans. Discontented Guinean party members had been promised "autonomy" for Guinea if they rid PAIGC of its Cape Verdean leadership. This action, whether it was sanctioned by the Portuguese government or not, was part of a last-ditch attempt by Portugal to keep control of Cape Verde, even if it meant making concessions in Guinea. Since at that time the military stalemate in Angola and Mozambique was perceived by Portugal to be favorable to it, there was a belief in Lisbon that a solution to "the Guinea problem" would leave it secure in Africa.

Despite Cabral's death, the PAIGC maintained its unity between Guineans and Cape Verdeans. It went on to intensify the war—using newly acquired ground-to-air missiles, it largely neutralized the Portuguese air force—and successfully to declare independence in 1973. Largely because of the success of Cabral's diplomatic efforts, the independence of the new Guinea-Bissau was immediately recognized by a majority of UN member states, and pressure was put on Lisbon to grant Bissau formal sovereignty.

The April 1974 revolution in Lisbon, in which radicalized army officers overthrew the Salazar-Caetano dictatorship, restored democracy in Portugal and brought about the decolonization of the African empire. The Portuguese revolution was a vindication of Cabral's belief that the colonial wars would eventually undermine the Lisbon regime and of his policy of reaching out to the Portuguese opposition so as to establish the basis of relations of cooperation with a democratic Portugal after independence. It also revealed the deep influence that his writings and political methods had had on some of the key Portuguese officers who were responsible for organizing and carrying out the April revolution.

Following an orderly withdrawal of Portuguese troops from Guinea, Lisbon formally recognized Guinea-Bissau's independence in September 1974. In Cape Verde an interim government was set up to prepare elections for independence. The PAIGC won an overwhelming popular mandate and, after independence was formally granted in July 1975, went on to form the postcolonial government. Cabral was dead, but the party that he had created had achieved his most cherished ambition, linking independent Guinea and Cape Verde in a single biterritorial political entity.

Despite the success of the PAIGC, however, Cabral's disappearance was a crippling loss to the party. Although it is impossible to know how successful he would have been had he lived, it is reasonable to assume that his presence would have been an asset to the PAIGC. As it was, the unity between Guinea-Bissau and Cape Verde did not survive the 1980 military coup in Bissau. Inevitably, perhaps, the Guineans came to resent the presence of Cape Verdeans in their government. Following the coup, most Cape Verdeans were removed from positions of authority, and all "federal" links between the two countries were severed.

In fact, Guinea-Bissau had begun to suffer economic collapse and political deliquescence as early as 1977. The post-1980 government, though it has stopped the economic rot, has presided over an increasingly rigid and coercive political system. Whether Cabral's legacy ever could have prevented Guinea-Bissau's descent into economic chaos and political repression is still debated and is today largely a moot point.

What is not in question, however, is that Cape Verde's history since independence has been one of relative success. Cabral's successors have transformed one of the poorest and economically least viable countries in the world into a well-managed nation-state in which people no longer starve, where social services and the economy have improved (even if they are still inadequate) and where a one-party state survived until 1991 through a careful balance between control and consent. Cape Verde's record of aid management and the efficiency of its government and administration are among the highest in the Third World and have earned the country sustained financial support from multilateral and bilateral aid organizations. In Cape Verde, certainly, Cabral's legacy is widely regarded as having provided the foundations on which a relatively successful nation-state has been constructed against overwhelmingly unfavorable odds.

Cabral's prominence in the nationalist history of Africa derives from his qualities as political leader and political analyst. Whatever the specific circumstances that facilitated the task of the PAIGC—among which the most frequently mentioned is that Guinea was a small country surrounded by friendly neighbors— it is undoubtedly the case that the PAIGC's nationalist campaign was the most successful in the history of colonial black Africa. By any criterion, it achieved its goal at considerably less cost than the wars that took place in Algeria, Cameroon, Kenya, Angola, Mozambique, Rhodesia and Namibia. In this respect, it ranks with the great nationalist campaigns of the twentieth century.

That this success was essentially Cabral's doing is clear, even if it is equally clear that the nationalist success was not necessarily a key to success after independence. The PAIGC's achievements were largely the result of Cabral's strategy and policies. The intimate knowledge of Guinea's socioeconomic structure that he had gained during his work as an agronomist led him to define accurately the nature of the nationalist struggle that the PAIGC ought to undertake. His greatest strength in this respect, as is the case with all guerrilla commanders, was his ability to devise strategy and tactics to suit the conditions at hand. The PAIGC strategy was predicated on the principles that (1) political mobilization must precede and at all times take priority over military action; (2) political action must be determined by internal and local rather than external or ideological factors; (3) consolidation and protection of the "liberated areas" must precede and take priority over further military objectives; (4) armed action must always be determined by political considerations; (5) the paramount political consideration must be the internal and international recognition of the PAIGC as the sole nationalist representative of the peoples of Guinea and Cape Verde; and (6) nationalist success was to be achieved through negotiations, that is, by diplomatic rather than military means.

A good example of Cabral's political acumen was the organization in 1972 of elections in Guinea's liberated areas. Following his success in arranging for a UN Commission of Enquiry to visit the liberated areas in 1972—the report of which vindicated the PAIGC's claim to control and administer large areas of the country—Cabral calculated that the holding of elections would help convince the West that Guinea-Bissau's forthcoming unilateral declaration of independence should be recognized in international law. Although the elections were no more, but no less, democratic than any elections in one-party states, they confirmed the PAIGC's standing inside the country and enhanced its legitimacy abroad. They also convinced many Portuguese officers of the futility of their task.

Cabral's writings are impressive not, as has usually been claimed, because of their theoretical contribution to Marxism, but because of their analytical clarity. Although Cabral wrote within a Marxist perspective and did indeed contribute to the theoretical debate about the relevance of Marxist thought to Africa, it is not these writings that most accurately reflect the incisiveness of his thinking. Indeed, his widely cited theoretical articles are more accurately seen as part of his diplomatic efforts to placate the socialist countries that gave him support than as an attempt to reinterpret Marx and Lenin for Africa.

It is in the analysis of the socioeconomic conditions of Guinea and Cape Verde and, above all, in his speeches to party members and villagers that Cabral displayed a subtle and sophisticated understanding of African realities rarely found among African leaders. These speeches are still enlightening today. While Cabral, like all modernizers, tended vastly to exaggerate the extent to which political agency could transform existing socioeconomic conditions in Africa, he remained more lucid than most about the difficulties the party faced and the limited success it had achieved in the "liberated areas." Despite the claims to the contrary, he was not optimistic about the success of socialism after independence.

In the end it is the combination of political intelligence and political skills that marks Cabral as one of the great leaders in Africa. For this reason, his early death at the age of forty-nine was a tragic loss, not just to Guinea-Bissau and Cape Verde but to the continent as a whole. The achievements of Cape Verde since independence are one possible indication of what Cabral might have contributed to the continent to which he had dedicated his life. As it is, he will be remembered for his role in the history of African decolonization, as widely admired in Portugal as he is in Cape Verde, Guinea-Bissau and throughout Africa.

BIBLIOGRAPHY

Works by Cabral:

Revolution in Guinea: Selected Texts by Amilcar Cabral. Ed. Richard Handyside. New York: Monthly Review Press, 1969.
Return to the Source: Selected Speeches by Amilcar Cabral. Ed. Africa Information Service. New York: Monthly Review Press, 1973.
Unity and Struggle. London: Heinemann, 1980.

Other Works:

Andrade, Mario de. *Amílcar Cabral: Essai de biographie politique*. Paris: Maspéro, 1980.
Chabal, Patrick. *Amílcar Cabral: Revolutionary Leadership and People's War*. Cambridge, Eng.: Cambridge University Press, 1983.
Chaliand, Gérard. *Armed Struggle in Africa*. New York: Monthly Review Press, 1969.
Chilcote, Ronald H. *Amilcar Cabral's Revolutionary Theory and Practice: A Critical Guide*. Boulder, Colo.: Lynne Rienner Publishers, 1991.
Davidson, Basil. *The Liberation of Guiné: Aspects of an African Revolution*. Baltimore: Penguin Books, 1969.
————. *No Fist Is Big Enough to Hide the Sky: The Liberation of Guiné and Cape Verde*. London: Zed Press, 1981.
Ignatiev, Oleg. *Amílcar Cabral: Filho de Africa*. Lisbon: Prelo, 1974.
McCulloch, Jock. *In the Twilight of Revolution: The Political Theory of Amílcar Cabral*. London: Routledge and Kegan Paul, 1983.

Rudebeck, Lars. *Guinea-Bissau: A Study of Political Mobilization.* Uppsala, Sweden:
    Scandinavian Institute of African Studies, 1974.

PATRICK CHABAL

D

FREDERIK WILLEM DE KLERK (1936–   ), State President of South Africa, 1989–

Frederik Willem de Klerk is likely to be South Africa's last white president. This fact in itself is likely to ensure de Klerk a place in history. But what is perhaps even more remarkable is that de Klerk will reform himself and his ruling National Party out of power—and will be doing so from a position of considerable power. This seems to be the inevitable consequence of the systematic dismantling of legislative apartheid and de Klerk's commitment to negotiate a new nonracial democratic political order. The period of transition from white rule to a black-led government under a postapartheid constitution may well last to the end of 1994, when the life of the current Parliament expires. During this phase de Klerk is likely to retain the presidency, and in this capacity he is bound to play a decisive role in shaping a "new South Africa," as it is commonly referred to.

President de Klerk's bold reforms have taken many observers by surprise because his earlier political track record gave the impression of a man deeply committed to the apartheid ideology in both its "grand" (Bantustan) and "petty" (socioeconomic discrimination) dimensions. Add to this his family background, and de Klerk was a true-blue Nationalist. But despite his impeccable National Party credentials, de Klerk has broken fundamentally with party orthodoxy. Yesterday's advocate of apartheid has become today's defender of democratic values.

F. W. de Klerk was born into a staunch Afrikaner-Nationalist family on March 18, 1936. Both his grandfathers had been actively involved in politics, and one of his uncles was Prime Minister J. G. Strijdom (1954–58). F. W.'s father, Jan de Klerk, became a National Party functionary in the late 1940s and was subsequently elected to the Transvaal Provincial Council. He was appointed to the Strijdom cabinet in 1954 and served as a government minister for the next fifteen years, a period that also spanned the premierships of H. F. Verwoerd[*] and B.

J. Vorster. This, then, was the house in which "FW" (as he became known from an early age) and his elder brother Willem (today a noted liberal political commentator) grew up.

The political values of his family were no doubt further inculcated in the young de Klerk during his years at Potchefstroom University. Steeped in the Calvinist tradition, the relatively small Afrikaans university was a self-proclaimed center for Christian higher education. There de Klerk in 1958 obtained the LL.B. degree cum laude. He played a leading role in student affairs, serving as vice chairman of the students' representative council, editor of the campus newspaper and an executive member of a national Afrikaans student association. His academic and leadership qualities earned de Klerk a travel bursary, which enabled him to spend some months abroad upon completing his studies.

Newly graduated, and incidentally also newly married, de Klerk became an articled clerk with a Pretoria firm of attorneys. In 1962 he bought his own law firm in the town of Vereeniging. There he took an active part in community affairs, occupying leadership positions in the local National Party branch, an Afrikaans cultural organization, the regional law society and the council of a technical college. In due course he became restless, not attracted to the prospect of spending the rest of his days as a small-town lawyer. An opportunity to broaden his horizons arose in 1972 when his alma mater, Potchefstroom University, offered De Klerk a chair in the law faculty, which he accepted. But before he actually took up the appointment, a more enticing opening arose when the parliamentary seat of Vereeniging became vacant. Choosing politics above academia, de Klerk made himself available as a candidate for the safe National Party seat and was duly elected to Parliament in a by-election in November 1972.

De Klerk's rise in the ruling party was rapid. In 1978, shortly after his forty-second birthday, Prime Minister Vorster appointed him to the cabinet as minister responsible for the dual portfolios of posts and telecommunications and of social welfare and pensions. Not only was de Klerk one of the youngest appointees ever to a Nationalist cabinet, but his promotion from the back benches to the cabinet was also among the swiftest in South African politics. Vorster, who saw in his new minister a future head of government, had indeed made a long-term political investment.

Over the next eleven years de Klerk held a variety of other ministerial portfolios in the Vorster and P. W. Botha* (1978–89) cabinets. He served successively as minister of sport and recreation, mining and the environment, mineral and energy affairs, and finally national education. In July 1985 de Klerk was appointed chairman of the Ministers' Council of the House of Assembly (the all-white executive of the white chamber of Parliament), and he became leader of the assembly in December 1986.

Parallel to his ascendancy in government, de Klerk was a rising star in the National Party. Early in his parliamentary career, de Klerk was appointed to the National Party's Federal Information Service, making him one of its chief propagandists. He was also entrusted with devising a new party youth strategy, which remains in operation to this day. In March 1982 he was elected Transvaal leader of the National Party after the right-wing revolt that led to the formation of the Conservative Party. As one of its four provincial leaders, de Klerk was now in the top hierarchy of the National Party. Seven years later, in February 1989, he reached the top rung on the party ladder when he became leader-in-chief of the National Party. But unlike his predecessors in the position of leader of the majority party in Parliament, de Klerk was not automatically elevated to the presidency of South Africa: P. W. Botha had relinquished his leadership of the National Party after suffering a stroke but had retained his position as state president. This local version of cohabitation did not work well at all, and Botha was virtually forced to resign as president in August 1989. De Klerk was immediately appointed acting president. Following a general election in early September, he was sworn in as executive state president. After eleven years in the cabinet and at the relatively young age of fifty-three, de Klerk had reached the ultimate position of power in South Africa.

In his years in office President de Klerk has brought about profound changes in the style, structures and substance of politics in South Africa. His presidency, however long it may last, already represents a watershed in South African political history. None of his predecessors since the formation of the Union of South Africa in 1910 has presided over domestic political changes of such consequence.

De Klerk's leadership style is very different from that of any of his Nationalist predecessors, but the contrast is perhaps the sharpest when de Klerk is compared with his immediate predecessor, P. W. Botha. A seasoned political observer, Ken Owen, neatly summed up the differences: "Where President Botha is rough, he [De Klerk] is smooth; where President Botha smashes, he bends; where President Botha confronts and rages, he yields and mollifies. His career is a tale of compromises, making the best of bad situations, of smoothing over difficulties" (*Leadership South Africa*, 9, no. 6 [July 1990]: 22).

A number of more specific features of de Klerk's style can be identified. It is in the first place a consultative one, based on an "open-door" approach that makes the president remarkably accessible to political allies and adversaries alike; a high premium is placed on building consensus through consultation. As a team player, de Klerk is committed to cabinet government and has built his team of ministers into a tightly knit and politically united forum for decision making. He approximates a textbook-type rational decision maker with his widely acknowledged ability to calmly and clinically analyze issues and draw out the implications of alternative courses of action. He has a strong preference for informality as opposed to the pomp and ceremony that characterized P. W. Botha's "imperial presidency," as it has been labelled. Specific mention should also be made of de Klerk's commitment to negotiation as the only way of resolving South Africa's politico-racial conflict; this is a technique of which de Klerk has already proved his mastery. His leadership style is, finally, built on such personality traits as common courtesy, humility, courage and also deeply held Christian convictions.

Given de Klerk's new style of leadership, it was only to be expected that he would change some of the formal structures of government inherited from his predecessor. Also, changed conditions in South Africa called for a reappraisal of Botha's state security apparatus. The war in Namibia was over, the near-universal retreat of communism virtually cured Pretoria of its obsessive fear of communism, and the status of the previously banned liberation movements was changed from violent enemies to political opponents. The State Security Council (SSC), the centerpiece of Botha's officially styled National Security Management System, has seen its role and influence sharply curtailed. Whereas the SSC had previously functioned as the principal decision-making body on many critical issues, the cabinet has been restored to its traditional role as the pre-eminent decision-making forum in the executive branch of government. The SSC's vast network of military-dominated subsidiary bodies has also been overhauled by de Klerk: They have been brought under civilian control and charged with development functions instead of combating a "revolutionary onslaught" as in the past. A similar scaling down has also occurred in the state president's office, which, under Botha, began to resemble a White House–type miniature civil service. De Klerk has reduced his office to much more modest proportions by transferring several units to relevant government departments.

It is the substantive changes to government policies that have really set de Klerk apart from his predecessors, changed the face of South African politics and placed the country on the road back to international respectability. In his inaugural speech as state president in September 1989, de Klerk committed his government to tackle the major obstacles in the road to negotiations on a new constitutional order. In a celebrated address to Parliament in February 1990, de Klerk announced a package of measures to help clear the way for negotiations. Among other things, the ban on the African National Congress (ANC), Pan-Africanist Congress (PAC) and the South African Communist Party (SACP), in force since 1960, was lifted, and people jailed for belonging to any of these organizations would be set free. Within a fortnight ANC leader Nelson Mandela* was released from prison, having been incarcerated for over twenty-five years. In the course of the next six months, the government and the ANC reached two important accords: In the Groote Schuur Minute of May, the two sides undertook to end the existing climate of violence and committed themselves to a peaceful process of negotiation, while the Pretoria Minute of August embodied an agreement on the definition of political offenses and the release of political prisoners. In November 1990 the state of emergency (in effect since 1985) was finally lifted.

De Klerk produced a further set of major reformist measures on February 1, 1991. Again choosing Parliament as his forum, he announced that three legislative pillars of apartheid—the Land Acts of 1913 and 1936, the Population Registration Act of 1950 and the Group Areas Act of 1966—would be repealed. By mid-1991 Parliament had acted accordingly, thereby cleansing the statute book of all major pieces of apartheid legislation save the constitution itself.

Enacted in 1983, the constitution restricts the franchise to whites, "coloreds" and Indians. De Klerk's National Party accepts that a new constitution should not contain any racially discriminatory provisions; color-blind universal franchise would therefore be one of the principal features of a postapartheid constitution.

Through these various measures, de Klerk has unshackled the political process and has begun to build trust between whites and blacks, both vital preparatory steps for eventual all-party negotiations on a new constitution. It is safe to say that the process of moving away from apartheid is already irreversible in the sense that it is entirely inconceivable that the ruling National Party could restore the status quo ante. If the road back to the past has been blocked, de Klerk can only move forward toward a new constitutional arrangement that will politically empower the black majority.

De Klerk's domestic political reforms have already led to a material improvement in South Africa's international fortunes. The tide of enforced isolation, which had steadily risen over some four decades, has been turned. The international community has been rewarding de Klerk's reforms by restoring or establishing ties with South Africa in the diplomatic, economic and cultural fields. A clear illustration of foreign recognition of de Klerk's role can be found in the frequency of his official visits abroad. Since his election as state president, he has been received by his counterparts in Nigeria, the United States, Britain, France, Germany, Denmark, Ireland, Italy, Spain, Portugal, Morocco, Côte d'Ivoire, Kenya, Madagascar and Namibia. No other Nationalist leader since 1948 has travelled so widely, since apartheid had made such leaders unwelcome guests in most foreign chancelleries.

Understandably, de Klerk as head of government has had all the praise (and indeed also the blame from white right-wingers at home) for the profound political changes heaped upon him. That, however, does not mean that he actually initiated all the reforms. The release of Nelson Mandela, for instance, can be traced to contacts P. W. Botha had established with the jailed ANC leader. De Klerk himself likes to portray the National Party's dismantling of apartheid and its commitment to a new nonracial constitution as logical steps in a process of political evolution begun under his predecessor. Be that as it may, the fact remains that under de Klerk's stewardship South Africa has broken fundamentally and irrevocably with centuries of white power and privilege.

Since the political reforms are identified with de Klerk, many observers have tried to determine the motivating forces behind his actions. Not surprisingly, there is little consensus on the matter. Some commentators attribute the changes almost exclusively to the damaging effects of sanctions on the South African economy. Others emphasize mounting black resistance within South Africa to apartheid, coupled with the ANC's armed struggle. Another perspective highlights the sheer unworkability of apartheid in South Africa's integrated society. There are also those who portray recent changes as the results of a government-initiated process of political evolution going back some years. In actual fact, the political reforms probably flow from the interplay between all these and other factors. In the end it was de Klerk who correctly read the signs that apartheid had landed South Africa in a dead end both domestically and internationally, and he has taken decisive action to steer South Africa away from what he saw as impending disaster.

De Klerk seems confident that as president he will lead South Africa into a postapartheid era. He also maintains that the National Party (perhaps under a different name) will retain a prominent political role in a future political system; de Klerk believes that the National Party could put together a coalition that could beat the ANC in South Africa's first truly general election. While few informed observers would rate the chances of de Klerk's party that high, the prospects seem quite good that there may be political life after apartheid for the white South African leader who finally buried apartheid.

BIBLIOGRAPHY

De Klerk, Willem. *F. W. de Klerk: The Man in His Time*. Johannesburg: Jonathan Pall Publishers, 1991.
Kamsteeg, Aad, and Evert Van Dijk. *F. W. de Klerk: Man of the Moment*. Cape Town: Vlaeberg, 1990.
Kotzé, Hennie, and Deon Geldenhuys. "Damascus Road." *Leadership South Africa 9*, no. 6 (July 1990): 12–28.
Kotzé, Hennie, and Anneke Greyling. *Political Organizations in South Africa*. Cape Town: Tafelberg Publishers, 1991.
Van Vuuren, D. J., et al. *South Africa in the Nineties*. Pretoria: HSRC Publishers, 1991.
                                                    DEON GELDENHUYS AND HENNIE KOTZE

SAMUEL KANYON DOE (1950–1990), General; Chairman, People's Redemption Council; President, Interim National Assembly; President, Republic of Liberia, 1980–1990.

For a decade beginning April 12, 1980, a once-obscure master sergeant in the Liberian army, Samuel K. Doe, presided over one of the bloodiest and most corrupt regimes in his country's history and perhaps in all of contemporary sub-Saharan Africa. Catapulted to power by way of a military coup, Doe ended the long reign of the True Whig Party, an oligarchy of Americo-Liberians. Yet in the years that followed, not only did Doe fail to establish a government that represented the hinterland population, but he proceeded to undermine the foundations of the state itself. His regime collapsed in the midst of a gory civil war, which as of 1992 has yet to yield a firm agreement on a successor government.

Doe was the first Liberian head of state of pure indigenous origin. Since its independence in 1847, Liberia had been ruled by a minority settler group, who, at the time of the coup, consisted of about 2 percent of the population of two million people. The form of government in Liberia before the coup was a de facto one-party oligarchy. The central government and the True Whig Party ran the country on a patronage system. Certain Americo-Liberian surnames and membership in the Ancient Free and Accepted Masons were the basic criteria for upward mobility in government. Thus most Liberians saw the coup as the first opportunity for the majority of the population to take control of their destiny.

Samuel Doe claimed that he was born on May 6, 1950, in the town of Tuzon, Grand Gedeh County, in the southeastern part of Liberia, a member of the minority Khran (Wee) tribe. His father, Private (retired) Matthew K. Doe, was a career soldier, and Samuel followed in his father's footsteps. Doe's formal education began in his home town. He finished elementary school in 1967. At the time of the coup, he had just been forced to drop out of the eleventh grade in Marcus Garvey School due to reassignment to a military training camp outside Monrovia, the capital.

It is not clear exactly when Doe enlisted in the Liberian army. In 1970 he completed courses in basic military training at the Tubman Military Academy in Todee, Montserrado County. Afterwards he was posted to Camp Schieffelin, a military base a few miles from Monrovia. In 1975 he became a corporal. Doe was selected for training under the American Special Forces (Green Beret) training program in Liberia from January to June 1979. While in training, he developed a reputation as a sharpshooter and an agile hand-to-hand fighter. His first major responsibility was that of first sergeant in charge of the Armed Forces of Liberia (AFL) arsenal. He was promoted to master sergeant on October 11, 1979, and made adjutant of the third battalion. One year after he seized power, on April 12, 1981, he assumed the rank of a five-star general. In May 1982 Doe received the degree of doctor of philosophy, honoris causa, in political science from the Seoul National University during a state visit to South Korea. After that, official government protocol required that he be addressed as Dr. Doe. He received a B.A. (summa cum laude) in political science from the University of Liberia amidst controversy that he was the beneficiary of a watered-down curriculum.

Doe was married to a former petty trader, Nancy, and officially had six children. However, it was common knowledge that he married a second and younger wife, Hawa, in a secret traditional ceremony in 1989. Doe's appetite for numerous extramarital affairs reached its peak in 1989 when he created a Ministry of Transportation for the purpose of appointing one of his female companions as minister.

The eleventh-grade dropout did not seem to possess the capacity to plan and implement the type of smooth military operation that toppled the 110-year-old True Whig Party oligarchy. It was rumored that Doe came to power through an American-backed coup d'état, although this report was never confirmed or denied by the U.S. State Department.

President William R. Tolbert had succeeded William V. S. Tubman,* the "grand old man" of modern Liberia, who ruled the country for twenty-seven years until 1971. During and before Tubman, Liberia could be counted on as a traditional friend of the West. When Tolbert came to power, things changed. Tolbert established diplomatic relations with the Soviet Union. He began sending Liberian students to Romania on scholarship. He broke off diplomatic relations with Taiwan and opted for Communist China. He went along with most of the members of the Organization of African Unity (OAU) and broke off relations with Israel. Despite American opposition he joined the majority of the United Nations General Assembly in condemning Zionism as racism.

At home, the Progressive People's Party (PPP) led by Gabriel Baccus Matthews, an avowed socialist, had succeeded in registering as an opposition party. The PPP constituents were mostly the urban poor and the rural peasants who had been mere spectators in Liberia's "growth without development." The Movement for Justice in Africa (MOJA) had become a powerful political force, comprising a portion of the intelligentsia, workers and university students. It appeared that if free and fair elections were held in Liberia, Tolbert and his party would lose. The platforms of the alternatives to Tolbert suggested that they considered the United States and the capitalist world coconspirators in Liberia's state of economic and political dependence. On April 14, 1979, citizens took to the streets in defiance of a government order not to demonstrate against a proposed increase in the price of rice, Liberia's main staple.

On coming to power, Doe's popularity was high among students, workers, the poor and the press. Despite the murder of Tolbert during the coup d'état and the summary execution of thirteen high officials in the Tolbert administration, young technocrats returned home from abroad, and many professionals at home threw their collective weight behind the new administration. But among well-meaning professionals were also zealots, sycophants, quacks and self-proclaimed philosophers who saw the inexperience and political naivete of the People's Redemption Council (PRC) government as an opportunity for personal gain.

The enlisted men who comprised Doe's seventeen-person People's Redemption Council were victims of the system they replaced. Inexperienced and semiliterate, these young men continually interfered with cabinet-level officials who were charged with the responsibility of overseeing the day-to-day administrative functions of government. At one point, the entire governmental structure was in danger of a collapse. In consolidating power, Doe eliminated all political forces with the potential to challenge him. He killed most of his PRC colleagues after accusing them of countercoup attempts, and he forced potential civilian rivals into exile. The most serious attempt to overthrow Doe before 1990 was the November 12, 1985, "invasion" led by Brigadier General Thomas Quiwonkpa. However, Doe fabricated several coups and then used the occasions to round up and kill his rivals. Doe's own claim that he survived thirty-six coup attempts is clearly exaggerated.

Doe promised to bring economic relief to the masses of Liberians in 1980. During his regime, basic health care, nutrition, education and infrastructural development steadily declined. While Doe and his cronies engaged in conspicuous consumption, the nation's public health facilities closed down for lack of medicine and staff. A "Green Revolution," launched a few years after he came to power, was wholly rhetorical, as prices of basic commodities rose, farmers abandoned their plots, and teachers in public schools fled their classrooms as salaries were delayed months at a time. Several private and parochial schools that had provided quality education for decades closed their doors when the government withdrew subsidies.

By Doe's own admission, corruption proliferated in his government, but he did nothing to stop it. He promised to reduce unemployment, but instead it rose as foreign concessions divested due to excessive taxation and demands for bribes made by the regime. The U.S. dollar, which was Liberia's medium of exchange prior to 1980, was replaced with a "Doe dollar," printed to meet domestic needs with little regard for inflation. Amidst the economic chaos, Doe himself stashed away in foreign banks and real estate holdings an estimated $200 million. In February 1987, following U.S. criticism of Liberian economic management and allegations that American aid had been diverted for unauthorized use, seventeen financial experts were sent to Monrovia for two years to help salvage the economy. After less than a year, the experts, frustrated by Doe and his bureaucrats, left the country.

Journalists who dared to question the regime were imprisoned or disappeared under mysterious circumstances, and their bodies were never recovered. Newspapers and radio stations considered critical of the government were routinely closed by security officers, their editors were put in prison, and their presses were destroyed. Workers who were in the vanguard of the struggle that led to the 1980 change in government were barred from exercising their rights to strike. Rural-to-urban migration increased with the decay of infrastructure and institutions in the countryside. Religious leaders who dared speak on behalf of their flocks were summoned to Doe's office, verbally castigated and threatened with death if they continued preaching against the abuses of the regime. Students were almost immediately subjected to repression, climaxing in an invasion of the University of Liberia by Doe's soldiers in August 1984, in which students and professors were beaten, raped and stripped of their clothing.

Perhaps the greatest scandal of Doe's regime was the subversion of the October 1985 general election, which was designed to return Liberia to democratic civilian rule. On the first anniversary of his accession to power, Doe promised to return the country to civilian rule on April 12, 1985. He appointed a twenty-five–person National Constitutional Commission, chaired by Amos Sawyer, a renowed political scientist, dean of Liberia College at the university, and a former high-school teacher of Doe. Sawyer later went into exile but returned in 1990 to claim leadership of the government after Doe's death.

Midway into the transition to democratic civilian rule, it appeared that Doe was having second thoughts. He announced that recovery of Liberia's battered economy was a criterion for returning the country to civilian rule. According to Doe, this recovery would require direct capital assistance of $2.5 billion. This request was apparently directed at those friends of Liberia, particularly the United States and the European Economic Community, who had indicated an interest in seeing a democratically elected government. When the strategy failed, Doe reluctantly abandoned it.

Doe received the draft constitution in late March 1983. He shocked the nation by announcing that all government officials who wanted to run for office under the new constitution should resign by April 30, 1983. Few persons resigned. It soon became obvious that this statement was designed by Doe to identify potential rivals, as persons who joined Doe's political party were exempt from the April 30 rule.

Under the submitted draft constitution, military personnel were barred from participating in politics and from voting. Doe changed this clause with the collaboration of a fifty-nine–person Constitution Advisory Assembly selected by electoral college to review the draft constitution. This move, coupled with his alleged age increase, paved the way for Doe to run for office in future elections.

The principal body with responsibility for supervising the return to democratic rule was the Special Elections Commission (SECOM), headed by Emmett Harmon. Doe, in collaboration with Harmon, manipulated the commission and the transitional process in a manner that made it clear that Doe was running for president. This threw a monkey wrench into the transition because it was an open secret that no incumbent sub-Saharan African leader up to that time had ever lost an election. Doe dismissed two members of the commission who were not cooperating with his plans. One member resigned. The three vacant seats were filled by persons who were executives of Doe's National Democratic Party of Liberia (NDPL), a clear violation of the election laws, which mandated that SECOM be nonpartisan. With this move Doe had assured majority support on the commission.

On July 21, 1984, Doe dissolved the PRC, replaced it with an Interim National Assembly (INA), and named himself president of the INA. He brought in as vice president Harry F. Moniba, Liberia's ambassador to Great Britain. On July 26, 1984, Doe lifted the ban on politics and political activities. Almost immediately, political parties proliferated. Six political parties met the SECOM requirements: Doe's National Democratic Party of Liberia (NDPL), the Liberia Action Party (LAP) headed by Jackson F. Doe (no kin to Samuel Doe), the United People's Party (UPP) of Gabriel Baccus Matthews, the Liberia's People Party (LPP) of Amos Sawyer, the Unity Party (UP) of Edward B. Kesselly and the Liberian Unification Party (LUP) of William Gabriel Kpolleh. However, the two political parties with the largest proven political base, the UPP and LPP, were arbitrarily denied the right to participate in the process.

The elections were held on October 15, 1985. Neither local nor international observers were permitted. Despite this, over 600,000 registered Liberian voters went to the polls. Many agree that this was the largest turnout ever in an election in Liberia. By the time the polls closed it was clear that Doe and his NDPL had lost the election. The Liberia Action Party claimed victory. Many observers agree that LAP had indeed won the presidency and vice presidency, with the legislative seats spread among all four parties.

Chairman Harmon of SECOM and Doe had not anticipated such a massive turnout against the regime. For four days Doe was silent; then Harmon hand-picked fifty persons to perform a recount, charging that opposition parties had tampered with the voting. On October 29, 1985, Doe was declared the winner of the presidential election with a 51 percent majority. On November 12, 1985, just before his inauguration, the most serious coup attempt against Doe occurred; nevertheless, Doe was sworn in as the first president of the Second Republic on January 6, 1986, and Liberia's twenty-first president.

Doe's brand of civilian rule did not differ much from the military regime he had headed. The bicameral legislature quickly became a rubber stamp. Under Doe, Liberia's formerly independent judiciary became a mockery. Leaders of opposition parties fled into exile. Those who dared to remain at home did so at great risk.

One would be hard pressed to identify any contribution Doe made to the domestic politics of Liberia. It is even harder to point out any positive impact he had on the regional and continental politics of Africa. If Doe had left office in 1985, historians might have credited him with overthrowing the True Whig Party settler oligarchy and expanding the political base for more mass partici-pation in domestic politics through free and fair elections. On the spectrum of leaders, Doe was an authoritarian dictator who, like many contemporary sub-Saharan African leaders, came to power by the barrel of a gun. He tried to use a rigged ballot process to legitimize himself.

Yet legitimacy continued to elude Doe. On Christmas Eve, 1989, Charles Taylor formed a National Patriotic Front (NPFL) and began a guerrilla action, which led to a civil war that culminated in removing Doe. Taylor derived the bulk of his army from the Mano and Gio tribes. A splinter group of the NPFL, led by Prince Johnson (the "Independent" NPFL) actually brought the decade of Doe's bloody regime to an end by killing Doe on September 10, 1990. Doe was wounded and captured in Monrovia in a gunfight during an unscheduled visit to the headquarters of Ecowas Monitoring Group (ECOMOG), a "mediation army" of five members of the seventeen-nation Economic Community of West African States (ECOWAS), which had intervened in the war to bring a stop to the bloodshed. Doe's mutilated body was placed on display at a local hospital. The man whose obsession with witchcraft had led him to publicly proclaim, "No bullet can touch me, no knife can scratch me" was put to death by the same weapons that had catapulted him to power ten years before—the barrel of a gun and the blade of a bayonet.

In 1992 two groups claimed to be in control of the country. Charles Taylor had declared himself president and ruled 95 percent of the country from his capital, Gbarnga, near the Guinea border. An interim president, Amos Sawyer, had been elected by Liberians in exile and had taken up residence in Monrovia. Prince Johnson's position was unclear. Remnants of Doe's bodyguard remained in action. In the midst of it all, the ECOMOG troops still battled the forces of Charles Taylor for control of the countryside. Liberia's future is still uncertain, unclear and undecided.

BIBLIOGRAPHY

Works by Doe:

Liberia: The Road to Democracy under the Leadership of Samuel Kanyon Doe. (A
    collection of speeches.) Ed. Willie A. Givens. Bourne End, Eng.: Kensal Press,
    1986.
"A Survey of Liberian - U.S. Relations." Unpublished B.A. thesis, University of Liberia,
    1988.

Other Works:

Berkeley, Bill. *Liberia, A Promise Betrayed: A Report on Human Rights.* New York:
    Lawyers Committee for Human Rights, 1986.
Bienen, Henry. "Populist Military Regimes in West Africa." *Armed Forces and Society*
    II (Spring 1985): 357–70.
Dunn, D. Elwood, and Svend E. Holsoe. *Historical Dictionary of Liberia.* Metuchen,
    N.J.: Scarecrow Press, 1985.
Dunn, D. Elwood, and S. Byron Tarr. *Liberia: A National Polity in Transition.* Metuchen,
    N.J.: Scarecrow Press, 1988.
Liebenow, J. Gus. "Liberia, 'Dr. Doe' and the Demise of Democracy." 2 parts. *University Field Staff International Reports, Africa,* nos. 17–18 (1984).
Sawyer, Amos. *Effective Immediately: Dictatorship in Liberia, 1980–1986: A Personal
    Perspective.* The Hague, Netherlands: Africa Center, 1988.
Wonkeryor, Edward Lama. *Liberia Military Dictatorship: A Fiasco Revolution.* Chicago:
    Strugglers' Community Press, 1985.

C. WILLIAM ALLEN

E

GNASSINGBE EYADEMA (1936-   ) President of the Togolese Republic, 1967– ; General of the Army.

Staff Sergeant Etienne Eyadema entered the history of Togo with a bang in the early hours of January 13, 1963. He was the trigger man who assassinated President Sylvanus Olympio in an event that is often seen as the first of a rash of military coups d'etat that have profoundly shaped the politics of sub-Saharan Africa. The reality is more complex, of course.

The Togolese Army in the third year of independence consisted of one company of about 150 soldiers. Due to French recruitment policies and popular attitudes in the more developed south of Togo, most of the Togolese who had served France and made up the bulk of the single company came from the north. Sergeant Eyadema, who had been released from the French colonial forces in the previous summer with severance pay after nine years of service, was part of a group of perhaps twenty former NCOs that had been urging President Olympio to create a second company in the national army so that there would be employment for them. Olympio resisted this demand adamantly for budgetary reasons and because he saw no reason to put more guns in the hands of people from the north of Togo, who generally were excluded from influence in his authoritarian government.

On the night of January 12–13, 1963, the unemployed NCOs broke into the military camp in Lomé, Togo's capital, with the complicity of friends, and commandeered weapons and vehicles. What happened next is unclear. By dawn Olympio was dead, shot just outside the United States Embassy compound which abuts his private residence.

In the confusion of the next few days Master Sergeant Emmanuel Bodjolle emerged as the first among equals of the former French NCOs. With their assent, a provisional government was formed under the leadership of Nicholas Grunitzsky and Antoine Meatchi, two of Olympio's bitter political rivals who had been in exile in neighboring countries. The Togolese Army was immediately expanded to absorb the excess veterans of France's colonial army and a period of grade inflation started that reached its culmination in 1976 when Eyadema became a four-star general. On February 1, 1963, Bodjolle was promoted to major and Etienne Eyadema became a second lieutenant. The next day Eyadema took personal responsibility for having eliminated the "tyrant," Sylvanus Olympio. The group of NCOs that assassinated Olympio had no plan to seize power and did not do so. They hoped either to coerce the president to give them military employment, or find someone who would. If the latter was their goal, however, the confusion of the days immediately after the murder suggests that they had no precise plan.

Little is known of Eyadema's life until 1963. The official story is that he was born in 1936, of poor peasants in the village of Pya in the Kabye region of north Togo. His father, Gnassingbe, is alleged to have died in 1940 as the result of a beating while doing forced labor. Eyadema received some primary schooling from Protestant missionaries. He was a good student, but he had to give up because of lack of money. He was the best of his age group in wrestling, a sport which is the centerpiece of the rite of passage ceremony among the Kabye. In 1953 he was recruited into the French Army and served in Indochina, Algeria, and Niger in the colonial infantry. In September 1962 he was discharged with the rank of staff sergeant and returned to Togo. None of this is improbable, nor does it give much indication that he would go on to dominate Togo.

The four years following Olympio's assassination were crucial to Eyadema's development. He was promoted to captain in September 1963, major in November 1964 and became a lieutenant colonel and chief of staff of the Togolese Armed Forces in January 1965. In 1966 the army intervened in the continuing political maneuvering between President Grunitzsky and Vice President Meatchi, to support the former and remove the latter from his post. On the anniversary of Olympio's murder in 1967, the army bloodlessly replaced President Grunitzsky with a Committee of National Reconciliation headed by Colonel Kleber Dadjo. Eyadema dismissed the committee three months later on April 14, and became President of Togo. In these four years Eyadema had forged a Togolese army loyal to himself personally, and forced Major Bodjolle and other potential rivals from positions of power. He also allowed the political class to prove its incompetence and thus create a vacuum into which the Army could easily move. Perhaps most significantly, he had used those years to identify individuals of sufficient obsequiousness, opportunism and talent to form a ruling clique which could help fill the void of his own ignorance of modern governance.

The more than twenty years of Eyadema's personal rule produced a welcomed haven of continuity, order, and control in a region of Africa that was politically and economically stressed. But those years also produced a mixed record and have not been entirely happy ones for the Togolese people. Eyadema's government has done a creditable job extending a road network to most of the country and paving the north-south axis. The port of Lomé has been modernized and contributes importantly to the infrastructure of the country. In the 1970s the government took a majority position in the company which mines the country's substantial phosphate deposits, and this has proved an important source of revenue and foreign exchange.

Phosphate revenue, however, whetted the appetite for development. The government embarked on numerous projects and contracted a large foreign debt. In consequence, Togo has been operating in recent years under an austerity program supervised by the International Monetary Fund and the World Bank. An important reason for Togo's economic stagnation is the major government investments that have been marred by waste and poor planning, and many of them appear to have been undertaken primarily for the kickbacks they generated. Examples include an unprofitable steel mill and oil refinery, an unused modern airport in the north and several luxurious tourist hotels that stand practically vacant. With over 25 years in power, the Eyadema government has not led Togo to any noticeable increase in the living standard of the average Togolese, while waste, corruption and the huge personal fortunes of the politically favored are evident to any visitor. The *per capita* domestic product in 1990 was under $400.

It would be unfair to judge Eyadema's rule by economic measurements alone. The political goal of personal power has always had higher priority. The basic instrument has been the army and the other security services. But the instruments of hard power have been buttressed, and to some extent obscured, by other devices. The universal party, the Rassemblement du Peuple Togolese (RPT), to which all Togolese belong, had the role of organizing the *animation*, or dances of praise which accompanied Eyadema's every public act. It also ran the neighborhood watch committees and kept an eye on all private associations. It provided patronage and was a safety valve by creating a path for the advancement of the ambitious and unscrupulous. The RPT was also the keeper of the cult of personality. It supplied the wrist watches that flashed Eyadema's portrait every 15 seconds. It commissioned the comic book *Histoire du Togo: Il était une fois . . . EYADEMA*, which in 1976 presented the Eyadema myth in comprehensive form. It hosted the continual round of rallies at which the myth was developed and polished. According to the myth, Eyadema is invulnerable. By implied divine protection he has survived military ambush, political assassination, and the crash of his airplane as the result of a colonialist plot. Every evening for years in the closing sequence on national television he rose into the sky above a map on which Togo was the center of the world. Eyadema thrilled in the flattery and apparent adulation with which he arranged to surround himself. He also fancied the role of admired African statesman and hosted numerous international and regional conferences, and engaged in innumerable, mainly pointless, state visits in its pursuit.

Eyadema's regime was extremely intrusive in the lives of its citizens. The government decided which religions could be practiced. In the pursuit of African authenticity, Eyadema replaced his given name of Etienne with Gnassingbe, and insisted that all Togolese give up European first names. Attendance at political meetings was obligatory and closely monitored. There has always been a dark side to Eyadema's rule. People were imprisoned without trial for "crimes," like lack of respect for the president. Major Paul Comlan was beaten to death for imagined subversive contacts with the American government in 1975. There have been mysteriously convenient auto accidents and unpunished murders of possible rivals. In 1984 former Vice President Meatchi died in prison of starvation. In 1985 fourteen people were arrested for possessing anti-government pamphlets. After investigation, Amnesty International concluded that "some or all" had been tortured.

While there has been a steady incidence of arbitrary arrests, quiet liquidations of undesirables, cases of torture and other official crimes, Eyadema's regime has never, or at least until 1991, produced the bloody scale of human rights abuses that can be attributed to Amin's* Uganda, Sékou Touré's* Guinea, Bokassa's Central African Empire or Mobutu's* Zaire, to name a few examples. Repression in Togo has aimed at producing fear, political apathy, and hence order and political control, but not a bloodbath. The clear threats to Eyadema's rule prior to 1990 were limited to mercenary incursions in 1978 and 1986 that were sponsored by political exiles from the Olympio era.

In 1990 the political calm was shattered. The rise of democracy in Eastern Europe caused a sea change in the political climate of francophone Africa. Purely African trends were also at work. The number of educated and politically sophisticated Togolese had grown to the point where it was no longer feasible to co-opt them or intimidate them on an individual basis using the old methods. In late 1989, for example, the Togolese bar association defended a member, Djove Gally, when RPT officials threatened to disbar him for advocating a more independent judiciary. Anti-government tracts circulated more openly. There was unrest among students. In June 1990 at the Franco-African Summit at La Baule, France, President Mitterrand of France called for movement toward democracy in francophone Africa.

In an apparent attempt to pre-empt the tide of events, Eyadema in May 1990 called for the separation of the RPT from the government. In July the government acquiesced in the creation of a Togolese League of the Rights of Man. In August Eyadema declared that Togo would seek democracy within the framework of a one-party state.

Then things came apart. On October 5, 1990, over 5,000 people demonstrated in favor of students who were arrested and tortured for distributing anti-government tracts. Five people were killed when the police opened fire and mass arrests were made. Efforts at reconciliation followed. The students were pardoned. The chief of the security police was transferred. The government announced a process aimed at constitutional reform. Before the end of 1990, Eyadema specifically proposed that the question of multi-party democracy be studied. The pressures continued to build for democracy. More human rights groups were formed and calls for an amnesty to allow exiles to return became more insistent. An independent press led by Forum Hebdo began to attack the government on a regular basis. In January 1991 Eyadema decreed a partial amnesty and ended the obligatory payment of dues to the RPT.

Following the violent suppression of student demonstrations, on March 14, 1991, Attorney Yawo Agboyibor founded the Front des Associations de Renouveau (FAR), an umbrella group of opposition forces. On the next evening his house was burned to the ground and his wife beaten. Sporadic riots broke out in Lomé and other southern towns, and eight people were killed. A general strike followed on March 17, and on March 18 President Eyadema met with the leaders of FAR. Negotiations continued, punctuated by confrontations with the police in which scores died. At times riots took on an ethnic cast pitting the Ewe population of Lomé against northerners, who were generically connected with the Eyadema regime in the mind of the ''street.''

On June 12 Eyadema consented to the convening of a National Conference, and calm returned. The conference opened on July 10 and immediately voted itself plenary powers. In turbulent sessions the conference accused Eyadema of specific human rights violations, set up a commission to inquire into the personal fortunes of government ministers, dissolved the presidential guard and placed the army under civilian control. At times government participants in the conference boycotted proceedings for days, and on August 27 General Eyadema ordered the conference dissolved and had troops surround the meeting hall. That evening the conference chose as prime minister Kokou Koffigoh, the head of the Togolese League of the Rights of Man, and directed him to establish a transitional government and organize elections. Eyadema remained president, but stripped of his army command and executive powers.

Under pressure from France, Germany and the United States, President Eyadema publicly acquiesced in these decisions, but the army refused to accept civilian control, resulting in a bloody struggle for power. In November the army occupied Lomé and besieged Koffigoh in the prime minister's official residence. On December 3, 1991, the troops assaulted the residence, seized Koffigoh, turned him over to President Eyadema and put him in virtual house arrest, but did not remove him from office. More than 100 people were killed in random clashes between troops and anti-Eyadema demonstrators in Lomé. The national army became an army of occupation. Most members of the National Conference went into hiding. The Koffigoh government was unable to meet or conduct business although Prime Minister Koffigoh was holding regular interviews with the international press.

In early 1992 no political solution was in sight. President Eyadema's power to restrain the army was unknown. A solution, Eyadema insisted, must protect him and the political and military cliques through which he has governed for 25 years from payment for their crimes. The prospect loomed of economic chaos, civil war between the supporters of the old tyranny and the new democracy, and violent ethnic conflict.

BIBLIOGRAPHY

Afrique Biblio Club. *Histoire du Togo: Il était une fois . . . EYADEMA.* Tournai (Belgium): Casterman, 1976.
Amnesty International. *Togo: Report of a Government Commission of Inquiry into Torture.* New York: National Office, 1986
Bonin, Andoch Nutepe. *Le Togo du sergent en général.* Paris: Lescaret, 1983.
Feuillet, Claude. *Le Togo "en general."* Paris: ABC, 1973.
Toulabor, Comi M. *Le Togo sous Eyadema.* Paris: Karthala, 1986.

WILLIAM B. YOUNG

G

YAKUBU GOWON (1934–), Head of State, Supreme Commander of the Armed Forces, Federal Republic of Nigeria, 1966–1975.

There are points in the histories of nations at which the tide of their fate could turn in the direction of either dismemberment or integration, at which momentous decisions by strong individuals could maim them or heal their wounds. It is such periods and such personages to which the privilege of historic counterfactual questions apply: What would have happened to these nations if some historically pivotal individuals had chosen to act otherwise? Whether this question is asked of William the Conqueror's decision not to invade Scotland, or of Abraham Lincoln's decision to fight southern secession from the United States of America, or of some other major actor who took a decision at a critical point of time that has affected the course and direction of his nation's history, it is to be understood that by their nature historic counterfactual questions can be asked of only a few individuals and events in any country's history.

In Nigerian history there have been two such momentous occasions. One was the initial act by the imperial government in Britain to bring together the two separate colonial territories of Northern Nigeria and Southern Nigeria. The man entrusted with the task of effecting what in Nigerian history is called the amalgamation began his work in 1914 and enthroned himself as a major figure in Nigeria's colonial history. But Frederick Lugard's work was an imperfect act and was subject to strains right through the British colonial rule of Nigeria. Even so, it has made of Nigeria an important nation where similar experiments in East Africa (to amalgamate Kenya, Uganda and Tanganyika) and in the Federation of Rhodesia and Nyasaland (which has yielded the separate nations of Malawi, Zambia and Zimbabwe) failed.

A more agonizing decision about the fate of Nigeria was made six years after colonial rule, in 1966. In the series of military putsches that followed the coup d'état of January 15, 1966, in which major politicians were killed, the sinews of the amalgamation were stretched to their limits. There was an active campaign to abort this colonial arrangement and allow the south and the north to go their separate ways. The burden of this onerous decision rested on the shoulders of a young lieutenant colonel, Yakubu Gowon, who, more by fate than by design, had assumed the leadership of the armed forces and had thereby become the head of state of Africa's most populous nation at the improbable age of thirty-two. If he decided to allow the country to drift apart, that would be final. This was the easier option. If he decided that Nigeria must stay together, then he had the additional responsibility of staving off the secession that was posed from one part of the south, then the Eastern Region. He vacillated, but finally decided in favor of the more difficult task of fighting for the integrity and unity of Nigeria. It is this decision and his success in pursuing it that will enable Yakubu Gowon to stand apart from all others in the history of postcolonial Nigeria.

Yakubu Gowon's decision and his tactics in fighting for what he fondly called the "oneness" of Nigeria were not as whimsical as they may appear on their face. In fact, his inclinations and acts fully echoed the history of Nigeria from his specialized perspective. Colonial Northern Nigeria, into which he was born, was made of two cultural and political areas. By far the more important—and clearly the most revered territory in all of British colonial Africa—was Emirate Northern Nigeria, consisting of the old Sokoto Caliphate and Borno. This was the darling of colonial administrators. The rest of Northern Nigeria was covered by what it pleased colonial administrators, geographers and anthropologists to call the "pagan" north. It was less favored because it was unruly and its pre-dominantly stateless, segmental social organization proved troublesome to the dream of Pax Britannica. Whereas, by the special terms of the understanding of the indirect rule arrangements between the British and the ruling Fulani aristoc-racy, Christian missionaries were barred from the emirate north, they were fully allowed in the "pagan" north. By the fateful year of 1966—when Gowon had to decide what to do with Frederick Lugard's amalgamation—the anthropolo-gist's pagan north had virtually become Christian north. While the Christian north shared administrative bonds with the emirate north, including the use of Hausa as a lingua franca of administration in the north as a region, it could act freely with the south, which had experienced similar changes in religion and education.

Yakubu Gowon was born on October 19, 1934, in the Christian north. Al-though his minority ethnic group of Anga is situated in the Christian Middle Belt, he grew up with his evangelist father in the village of Wusasa, a Christian enclave perilously perched on the outskirts of Zaria, the Moslem headquarters of one of the more important Fulani emirates. This background—along with his subsequent secondary-school education at Government College, Zaria (1949–53), military training in Ghana and at Sandhurst and elsewhere in England (1954–57), and spells of duty with the Nigerian forces patrolling the difficult Nigeria-Cameroon border, as well as with the Nigerian contingent in the United Nations peacekeeping force during the Congo crisis (1960–62)—was important preparation for dealing at once with the north and the south and for showing sensitivities to the needs of minorities and the underprivileged in Nigeria's complex political terrain.

Although Yakubu Gowon led an army that defeated the Biafran secession in a thirty-month civil war, his temperament was that of a fox rather than a lion, to employ Machiavelli's metaphor of leadership. His proverbial "moderation" enabled him to listen to all sides. His initial historic declaration in 1966 that there was no basis for the unity of the north and south—in all probability prompted by the Fulani ruling aristocracy in the Northern Region—was fully reversed when a cross-pressure group of "minority" Nigerians from the midwest analyzed the situation differently. He was able to work with Christians and Moslems because he understood both religions. While fighting Biafran secession, he preached tolerance toward the rebel Igbos and was mainly instrumental in their unusually rapid resettlement back into Nigeria at the end of the civil war in 1970. But there is more than a grain of truth in the nagging allegation in the 1970s that Gowon surrounded himself with "minorities." He clearly seemed to have been far more trusting of ethnic minority Nigerians who dominated the top echelons of his administration.

Yakubu Gowon and his team who ruled Nigeria from 1966 to 1975 must be credited with substantial decolonization of Nigeria, marked by the introduction of a series of policies that heralded qualitative changes in the country. The catalog is impressive: the change from colonial British-style left-hand roads; the switch to the international metric system of weights and measures; the change from British sterling currency and the creation of the Nigerian *naira*; the pioneering creation of states that broke down the political inequities of the colonial arrangements that had favored three ethnic groups (Fulani, Yoruba and Igbo); the establishment of the Nigerian Youth Corps; and the expansion of interstate road networks that have tremendously enhanced mobility in Nigeria. The civil service attained its height of excellence in this period. In spite of the civil war, these years of benevolent military rule saw more evidence of the rule of law than any other time since Nigeria's independence in 1960. It seems fair to say that these are the foundation on which modern Nigeria rests. Succeeding administrations have made quantitative amendments to these achievements, but the pioneering character of Gowon's regime is undeniable.

On the international scene, Gowon's personal character seemed to have been so reassuring, in a world awash with Cold War jealousies, that Nigeria was able to obtain military equipment and arms from the Soviet Union without provoking the United States and the West into taking sides with secessionist Biafra in the course of the civil war. In addition, Gowon was the architect of the Economic Organization of West African States (ECOWAS), perhaps Nigeria's most important long-term foreign-policy venture. Gowon invested a great deal of his foreign-policy capital in the Organization of African Unity and benefited enormously from it. Without its support, the Nigerian efforts in the civil war would have been imperilled.

By the time Yakubu Gowon (now major general) was overthrown in a military putsch in 1975, his nine-year rule had begun to be questioned on various counts. His failure to set a firm date for the return of Nigeria to civilian rule was by far the most serious of the complaints against him. While he was respected for his personal honesty, he was accused of not controlling members of his government and his military state governors, many of whom were corrupt. He was unpopular with university teachers for threatening their tenure during a strike—although in hindsight, and ironically, the universities attained their highest point of funding and freedom in his years of rulership. In retrospect, there are Nigerians who cast a longing look backwards and regret that on almost all of these counts the ills of the Gowon years pale into insignificance in comparison with the depravity of mismanagement and misgovernment that successor military and civilian regimes wrought in the 1980s.

Given his policies and achievements, Yakubu Gowon and his rulership of Nigeria are liable to be both prominent and controversial in Nigerian history. Perhaps a measure of the varied views about him and his exercise of power may be gained from the following proposition: If Yakubu Gowon were to contest fair and free elections on the same slate with all former military rulers of Nigeria (including his old rival C. Odumegwu Ojukwu, the Biafran ruler), he would decisively lead them all in Christian Northern Nigeria and possibly also in Muslim Borno, but not in the rest of the emirate north, which is politically controlled by the Fulani aristocracy. In the south he would probably beat anyone else in the ethnic minority states of Bendel, Rivers, Cross River and Akwa Ibom; he would also have an excellent chance of leading in the Igbo (that is, the former Biafran) states. But he would probably lose decisively in the Yoruba states.

Herein lies the historic significance of Yakubu Gowon's exercise of power. The preparations for Nigeria's political independence from colonial rule had been marred by the emergence of an unfortunate political arrangement that introduced invidious distinctions of inequalities during the process of decolonization. With the so-called regionalization of Nigeria in 1954 into the three political units of the north, the east and the west, the political map of Nigeria changed dramatically—in many cases defying precolonial regional histories. In the north the Fulani aristocracy easily captured overall power, even in areas that it had been unable to control in its ambitious bid to rule this region (which historians call the Western Sudan) a century before the British conquered Northern Nigeria: that is, Muslim Borno and the extensive groups that made up non-Muslim Northern Nigeria. In the west non-Yoruba ethnic groups were unhappy as it became clear that given the emerging ethnic inclinations in Nigerian politics, only the Yoruba could control power in the region. In the east a brash Igbo leadership had continuing problems with the numerous small, but historically well-endowed, ethnic groups in that region. At independence in 1960 Nigerians had thus been grouped into the so-called majority ethnic groups, which controlled power, and minority ethnic groups, which by the nature of political arrangements were denied the privilege of ruling. In large part, of course, the crisis from which Yakubu

Gowon rose to prominence was induced by the struggle for overall national power by the three groups that had been so unduly favored by the 1954 regionalization arrangements.

It was Gowon's rulership that destroyed this colonial legacy and thus erased the invidious distinction between powerful majority ethnic groups and powerless minority ethnic groups. In the process he was able to bring together the north and the south in a manner that British colonial rule had been unable, and most probably unwilling, to undertake and in the face of the dangers and fears that had threatened the country with dismemberment. By carefully balancing the participation in his government of persons from the areas that had been deprived of power and those that had controlled it, he allayed fears that the so-called minority ethnic groups would take revenge against those who had oppressed them—a formula that enabled the defeated secessionists to be integrated into the Nigerian political fold. Ultimately, since he came from a tiny ethnic group, which by itself would be of little political consequence, Gowon's greatest political achievement was to give a sense of citizenship and equality to all grades of Nigerians—a legacy that continues to be threatened, but which may well survive, because it has become part of Nigeria's political culture.

Perhaps Yakubu Gowon would prefer to be judged by his personal and private character rather than through his public image. It says something of the man that when he was overthrown in 1975, he humbly repaired to Warwick University in England, where he earned a first degree and then a doctorate in political science in 1984. In a country where soldiers have poor reputations with respect to women and family, Gowon stands out among Nigerian soldiers as a disciplined family man. Now living in England, from which he visits Nigeria frequently, Yakubu Gowon may still have something more to contribute to Nigeria's public life, while he awaits the final verdict of history.

BIBLIOGRAPHY

Elaigwu, Isawa. *Gowon: The Biography of a Soldier-Statesman*. New York: Humanities Press, 1985.

Odetola, T. O. *Military Politics in Nigeria: Economic Development and Political Stability*. New Brunswick, N.J.: Transaction Books, 1978.

Olorunsola, Victor O. *Soldiers and Power: The Development Performance of the Nigerian Military Regime*. Stanford, Calif.: Hoover Institution Press, 1977.

Oyediran, Oyeleye (ed.). *Nigerian Government and Politics under Military Rule, 1966–79*. New York: St. Martin's Press, 1979.

Panter-Brick, Keith (ed.). *Soldiers and Oil: The Political Transformation of Nigeria*. Totowa, N.J.: Frank Cass, 1978.

PETER P. EKEH

H

FELIX HOUPHOUET-BOIGNY (1905?–   ), President, Republique Côte d'Ivoire, 1960–   .

President of Côte d'Ivoire (Ivory Coast) from national independence in 1960 to the present, Félix Houphouët-Boigny has dominated Ivoirian politics since colonial reforms in 1944 permitted Ivoirians a political voice. His paternalistic and patrimonial rule was buttressed by remarkable economic growth until the 1980s; the "Ivoirian miracle" attracted considerable foreign capital, which accelerated economic growth and increasing economic inequality among Ivoirians. Côte d'Ivoire was badly hit by the falling commodity prices of the 1980s and the enormous debt accumulated during the free-spending 1970s. But with characteristic ability to turn situations to his political advantage, President Houphouët-Boigny recaptured much political power by initiating implementation of International Monetary Fund (IMF) economic reforms and even won a competitive election in 1990. While his leadership style has been pre-eminently successful in maintaining personal power and national stability, it leaves the country facing the succession question without a leader or the political institutions likely to ease the transition.

Houphouët-Boigny, born in 1905 in central Côte d'Ivoire, is a Baule. He reached the highest level of achievement among African subjects in that time, winning entry to the Ecole Ponty in Senegal, which trained Africans for the top jobs available to them in teaching, administration and medicine. Houphouët-Boigny was trained as an "African doctor." He was assigned to work in the Ivoirian southeast, the most developed region in the country with the most numerous and the richest African cocoa and coffee planters. His initiation to politics was an unsuccessful effort to organize African planters in 1933; this same avenue led him to national prominence in the postwar period.

In 1940 he inherited considerable coffee and cocoa land in his region of origin and returned home to manage these lands and accept an appointment as chief of canton. He created a national network of contacts through the Association of Customary Chiefs. When the collaborationist Vichy government was overturned in France in 1944, political liberalization resulted in a wave of political demands sweeping French West Africa. Houphouët-Boigny's status as doctor and chief, educated man and wealthy farmer positioned him well for political leadership. He emerged as a leader of the Syndicat Agricole Africain, an association of African coffee and cocoa farmers seeking to remove discriminatory price policies favoring French planters. Although one of several contenders, he was the sole leader from the Baule region, while the rest were from the Anyi southeast. Houphouët-Boigny became president of the African Planters' Association, next headed the winning all-African ticket to the Abidjan Council, and then represented Côte d'Ivoire in the First and Second Constituent Assemblies of the Fourth French Republic.

African radicals received vital support from the French left that dominated French politics in the immediate postwar period; Houphouët-Boigny and other Africans in the transterritorial RDA (African Democratic Assembly) were elected to the French National Assembly and formed a parliamentary alliance with the French Communist Party, which became an increasing liability as the Cold War sharpened and the French Communist Party was ostracized from the ruling coalition in France. The new anti-Communist colonial administration, pushed by the community of white planters and merchants in Côte d'Ivoire, set out to destroy the Ivoirian branch of the RDA in 1949–50. Houphouët-Boigny finally negotiated an agreement with a French Foreign Office representative, the young François Mitterand, in which the RDA broke with the French Communist Party in return for acceptance in the French governing coalition. Houphouët-Boigny's break with the Communists earned him the lasting opprobrium of radicals, while his recognition of shared Ivoirian and French colonial interests became the core of a prosperous alliance until the 1980s. The Soviet press attacked Houphouët-Boigny in 1950, calling him, with perfect accuracy, "a bourgeois nationalist." As an Ivoirian deputy in the French parliament for the decade preceding independence, and French government minister from 1956 until Ivoirian independence, Houphouët-Boigny proved himself indispensable to many in Abidjan, both French and Ivoirians, securing funds for infrastructure and education and fighting for French price supports when Ivoirian exports faced a slump in international markets.

At independence, as president of Côte d'Ivoire, Houphouët-Boigny made clear with a generous foreign investment code and the retention of many French administrators that foreign capital was welcome. Open opposition to Ghanaian and Guinean radicalism and to any talk of nationalizing foreign holdings, and continuity regarding the primacy of agricultural exports, underlined Houphouët-Boigny's determined gradualism. This did not sit well with some younger nationalists and radicals, while others resented the president's determination to monopolize the distribution of political access. To consolidate his political control, Houphouët-Boigny declared a one-party state and co-opted leaders of dissident regional, ethnic and ideological factions. Having removed at least one young potential challenger from office, in 1963 Houphouët-Boigny's government abruptly announced the discovery of a coup plot and arrested many Ivoirians, most occupants of government posts; a second similar announcement followed by more arrests occurred in 1964. Closed trials, replete with lurid confessions signed by the accused, followed by beneficent pardons from the president himself, sent a clear message to the ambitious and the idealistic in Côte d'Ivoire. Grateful loyalty to Houphouët-Boigny and unquestioning acceptance of his national policy was the *mot d'ordre;* cautious and tentative maneuvering to advance personal or group interests prevailed. But economic prosperity—fueled by rapidly expanding timber and cocoa exports, plus production of coffee and other crops promoted to diversify export earnings—ensured the regime's stability. By the 1970s Côte d'Ivoire had gained international visibility as one of Africa's "success stories."

The year 1970 marked a new confident stage in Houphouët-Boigny's rule, one punctuated by occasional "dialogues" presided over by the president himself. These were large "palavers," at which "representatives of every walk of life" drawn from the National Council, a kind of Ivoirian estates general, spoke freely, voicing complaints about government performance and policy. The dialogues were enthusiastically and sincerely acclaimed as transforming a climate of anxiety into one of security under the president's sharp and benevolent eye. The dialogues were a catharsis; men and women spoke frankly of widely recognized economic and political wrongs and problems, and the president reprimanded the guilty and rewarded the meritorious. Thus Houphouët-Boigny placed himself above the government, hearing complaints in person in an Ivoirian rendition of the *cahiers de doléances* of French kings. He assumed the role of teacher as well as student, lecturing his subjects on the need for dedication to work, to family and to country. The dialogues were usually occasioned by some disturbance—a labor incident, a xenophobic clash of Ivoirians with foreigners, parental outrage at Ivoirian failure rates on the secondary-school baccalaureate exams. These dialogues provided relief from the routine distance and formality of Ivoirian administrative authoritarianism.

The dialogues were also the precipitants of changed policy in response to selected middle-class and subelite grievances. The regime launched programs to encourage Ivoirianization, including increased technical and vocational education, and created a vast range of parastatal enterprises, fueled in large part by commercial petrodollar loans through Western banks. During the consolidation of his power in the 1960s, Houphouët-Boigny had relied heavily on European personnel to promote international confidence and maintain orderly and efficient administrative hierarchy. Houphouët-Boigny repeatedly warned his subjects that in Côte d'Ivoire there would be "no cut-rate Ivoirianization." By the 1970s the number of French in Abidjan had more than tripled, while the number and impatience of highly educated young Ivoirians grew apace. In response to one of the clearest messages of the dialogues, the regime promised to promote to positions of national responsibility those whose education equalled that of French managers and technocrats serving in the Ivoirian administration. The new generation of Ivoirian technocrats was promoted in the legislature, the civil service and particularly the emerging parastatal sector, giving rise to the characterization of Côte d'Ivoire as the "republic of good students."

The rationale for the parastatal boom—that foreign capital was not ensuring the development of priority regions and sectors—was put forth by a new generation of young Ivoirian ministers in 1970. But the pressure to act and the financial means emerged after the first oil shock of 1973: Côte d'Ivoire's remarkable 12 percent per annum growth rate for the 1960s, its political stability and the successful pragmatism of its president made Côte d'Ivoire a prime candidate for private petrodollar loans. The numerous parastatal companies formed, often with European partners, to promote agricultural diversification, especially in the underdeveloped north, to process agricultural products and to produce diverse manufactures, did not, the president insisted, indicate a departure from Ivoirian commitment to the liberal model of growth. Indeed, parastatals were necessary because of the dearth of private Ivoirian capital. As a strong Ivoirian bourgeoisie emerged, it was hoped that Ivoirian capitalists would buy out the state share in Ivoirian parastatals. Certainly the parastatal salaries, often three times those in the civil service, and the absence of governmental oversight of parastatal debts contracted from international banks were modelled on private capitalist growth.

The galloping increase in the Ivoirian public debts due to the parastatal boom, the personal fortunes obtained by those controlling international contracting and the substantial political empires some of the boom's beneficiaries were constructing drew a sharp response from the president in 1977. Houphouët-Boigny fired the four most powerful ministers (Usher of foreign affairs, Diawara of plan, Bedie of finances and Sawadogo of agriculture), making clear that he knew what they had been up to, but chose not to prosecute them. The president appointed an old political faithful to head a commission of reform for the parastatals. The commission's report and a presidential response did not come for three years, during which time the international prices of Côte d'Ivoire's primary exports, coffee and cocoa, dropped precipitously from an all-time high, while the national debt rose still further. By 1980 the pressure for reform from international creditors and the deterioration of national finances forced the government to seek assistance from the World Bank and the IMF. Houphouët-Boigny used this situation to reassert his political control, halting parastatal spending and clipping the wings of those parastatal managers who had built large clienteles during the parastatal boom.

Houphouët-Boigny announced a tough austerity program following IMF guidelines in 1980 and started a process of reorganizing, closing and privatizing various Ivoirian parastatals. The process was lengthy: Parastatal employees' salaries were finally reduced to civil-servant levels. The president appointed a Frenchman with wide discretionary powers to run a new powerful office overseeing all government contracts, which reduced costs and curbed corruption markedly. While acting to control the "hemorrhage of public money," Houphouët-Boigny made clear in 1980 that he would not seek to indict Ivoirian parastatal officials for embezzlement; rather, he upbraided this elite only for faulty judgment. The president himself shared the blame for one of the biggest debt items, the group of "state-of-the-art" sugar complexes in the north that had been Houphouët-Boigny's pet project and that, in retrospect, had clearly been adopted on the basis of unrealistic cost and profit projections.

The 1980s brought democratization of elections to lower governmental posts, but no clarification regarding the presidential succession. Houphouët-Boigny also initiated competitive elections for town mayors and councils, secretary-generals of the (then) sole national party and the members of parliament sitting in the National Assembly. Since Houphouët-Boigny had stifled his opposition in the early 1960s, each election had been a noncompetitive validation of party leaders' choices until 1990. In the national elections of 1980 and 1985, long slates of opponents who had received clearance from the party competed, and over half of parliamentary incumbents standing for re-election were voted out of office. But this relaxation of central control of political recruitment has not altered executive dominance of the legislature, and elected municipal authorities are limited by austerity budgets. The reforms served the president by permitting the electorate to remove from office many politicians who were of little use and were even embarrassments to the regime.

Although Houphouët-Boigny is at least eighty-six years old, the Ivoirian election reforms and the 1990 multiparty elections have not been accompanied by any resolution of the presidential succession problem. Over the past two decades presidential favorites have periodically amassed considerable power, only to be removed from contention by the president and then occasionally re-elevated to prominence: Konan Bedie, fired as minister of finance in 1977, returned to preside over the National Assembly in the post designated as president ad interim before the 1990 national elections. In the 1980s Houphouët-Boigny's advanced age and the economic crisis made the succession question pressing. The president's announcement that he would select a vice president for the 1985 elections produced explosive infighting among the ambitious "young wolves," contributing to unprecedented public financial scandals that have confirmed many suspicions regarding the regime. This infighting may have underlain Houphouët-Boigny's announcement in 1985 that he would not name a successor, a development that has neither lowered tensions nor increased international confidence in the future of Côte d'Ivoire.

In a surprise reversal of policy in May 1990 Houphouët-Boigny legalized opposition parties and announced a competitive presidential election for October 29 and parliamentary elections in November and December. In a short and restricted campaign Houphouët-Boigny garnered 81.7 percent of the vote against the "democratic left" coalition candidate, Laurent Gbagbo, who received 18.3 percent of the official tally. Turnout was just over 61 percent. Unofficial estimates

by outside observers gave Gbagbo 30 to 40 percent of the vote, but it was a
clear victory for Houphouët-Boigny nevertheless. The Parti Démocratique Côte
d'Ivoire (PDCI) faced twenty-six opposition parties, most of whom fielded candidates in the legislative elections. The results gave the governing party 163 of
185 seats, with the Ivoirian Popular Front (FPI), Gbagbo's party, gaining 9 of
the remaining 22. Although turnout was about 40 percent, and allowances must
be made for many irregularities, it was still a solid victory.

Although he remains close to the French government, Houphouët-Boigny's
rapport with other Western leaders has declined since his unsuccessful appeal,
as a faithful anti-Communist and economic liberal, for support to Thatcher and
Reagan in 1983, when debt, recession and a disastrous drought threatened to
destabilize Côte d'Ivoire. Houphouët-Boigny continues to point to the devastating
effect of the commodity price crash on Côte d'Ivoire and other Third World
nations, belatedly arguing the New International Economic Order position that
commodity producers deserve a fair price from the industrialized nations and
that only then could Côte d'Ivoire meet its enormous debt obligations. His
argument unheeded, Houphouët-Boigny has subsequently turned to posterity by
building in his home town, Yamassoukro, a fabulous basilica, taller than St.
Peter's in Rome and made entirely of Italian marble. Houphouët-Boigny's claim
that the basilica, Notre Dame de la Paix, Yamassoukro, is funded entirely from
his personal fortune has left many incredulous; its cost, between two hundred
million and over a half a billion dollars, reduces the president's credibility as
government austerity measures become ever more stringent.

The grim economic prospects for West Africa, which Côte d'Ivoire no longer
escapes, and the recurrent scandals regarding the intimate ties between money
and Ivoirian politics have placed the patrimonial character of Houphouët-
Boigny's regime in sharp relief. He is the wealthiest man in the country, and
his use of the levers of state power to tie all emerging power brokers to him has
been crucial to his longevity in office. This merging of political and economic
purposes weakened the Ivoirian bid for industrialization in the 1970s, when
numerous uncompetitive firms obtained state subsidies or protective tariffs and
patronage marred many parastatals. Houphouët-Boigny has earned praise for
moving faster in the 1980s to privatize parastatals than other African leaders,
but all Ivoirian buyers have made their purchases in closed bidding with his
approval.

After the 1990 elections, the new prime minister, Allasane Ouattara, a possible
successor now to Houphouët-Boigny, acted to reinforce and extend the economic
reforms of the past five years by cutting salaries in the civil service, putting up
for sale seventy-nine public enterprises, reducing the cabinet from the previous
thirty to forty to nineteen members, and sacking several directors of public
financial and fiscal agencies and heads of parastatal organizations. Speculation
continued over the identity of an actual successor to Houphouët-Boigny. In any
case a successor is unlikely to have the personal leverage over the Ivoirian elite
that Houphouët-Boigny has enjoyed due to his personal authority, his wealth

and national economic growth. The new conditions in international financial markets and the end of easy revenue sources due to the exhaustion of precious Ivoirian timber and to glutted world cocoa markets will make Houphouët-Boigny's presidency appear as a golden age. Even if it was tarnished by the structural crises of the 1980s, Houphouët-Boigny's influence and rule over more than four decades has been characterized by prosperity and stability remarkably free of violence.

BIBLIOGRAPHY

Works by Houphouët-Boigny:

"Black Africa and the French Union." *Foreign Affairs* 35, no. 4 (July 1957): 593–99.
Anthologie des discours, 1946–1978. Abidjan, Côte d'Ivoire: Centre d'Edition et de Diffusion Africaines, 1978

Other Works:

Alalade, F. O. "President Felix Houphouët-Boigny, the Ivory Coast and France." *Journal of African Studies* 6 (Autumn 1975): 122–31.
Amondji, Marcel. *Félix Houphouët Boigny et la Côte d'Ivoire: L'Envers d'une legende.* Paris: Karthala, 1984.
Baulin, Jacques. *La Politique inferieure d'Houphouët-Boigny.* Paris: Eurafor Press, 1982.
Faure, Y.-A., and Jean-François Medard. *Hommage à Houphouët-Boigny, homme de la terre.* Paris: Présence Africaine, 1982.
Jackson, Robert H., and Carl G. Rosberg. *Personal Rule in Black Africa: Prince, Autocrat, Prophet, Tyrant.* Berkeley: University of California Press, 1982.
Siriex, P. H. *Félix Houphouët-Boigny: L'Homme de la paix.* Paris: Seghers, 1975.
Zartman, I. William, and Christopher Delgado (eds.). *The Political Economy of the Ivory Coast.* New York: Praeger, 1984.

BARBARA LEWIS

J

SIR DAWDA KAIRABA JAWARA (1924–   ), Prime Minister, President, Republic of The Gambia, 1962–   .

In examining the political career of Sir Dawda Kairaba Jawara, one is struck by how quickly he rose to prominence in Gambian politics, and how effectively he managed to hold power without abandoning the democratic multiparty system he inherited from the departing British on February 18, 1965. Under his leadership the tiny pencil-shaped state of The Gambia moved from a colonial territory to an independent republic within the Commonwealth of Nations. Sir Dawda, as he is called by many of his fellow Gambians, has earned a reputation as an early and durable democratic leader, as evidenced by his unflagging support for a democratic society in The Gambia, which was recognized by the unanimous decision of the Organization of African Unity (OAU) to establish the headquarters of its Human Rights Commission in Banjul, the capital of The Gambia.

Born to Mandinka parents in the village of Barajali, Jarra District, Dawda Jawara spent the first decade of his life under the watchful eyes of his father and mother, who raised him in a strongly Islamic home. He went to Quranic school at age five and grew familiar with the chapters that young Gambian Muslims master by age ten. His life was destined to change as a result of an agreement between his father, Almani Jawara, and a Banjul-based friend and trader, Yorma Jallow, who offered to take the young Jawara to Banjul for a Western education. This decision helped pave the way for the future evolution of the Gambian political system.

Following his relocation from his home town, young Jawara soon developed into a perseverant scholar at school and a responsible youth at the mosque in Half-Die, the district in Banjul where his benefactor lived. Jawara was one of the few young people who occasionally performed the duties of *muezzin* (summoner to prayer) at the Half-Die mosque. He attended Muhammadan (elementary) School and the Methodist Boys High School. After passing his Cambridge matriculation examination, he went to Achimota College in Ghana. Upon his return he won a scholarship to study veterinary science at the University of Glasgow in Scotland. He obtained his doctorate degree in 1953 and returned home the following year. By 1958 he had risen to the position of a chief veterinary officer. The same year he converted to Christianity, adopting the name David Kwesi Jawara. David was the Christian equivalent of the Muslim Dawda; Kwesi was a Ghanaian nickname acquired at Achimota College.

In 1959 Dawda Jawara found himself in the midst of Gambia's political changes. The leaders of the Protectorate Peoples Society had decided to reconstitute their organization into a political party. Called the Protectorate Peoples Party, this organization had begun to mobilize rural Gambians in a bid to capture power from the urban politicians. The leaders of this party of the old protectorate asked Jawara to assume the post of secretary-general and party leader; at a meeting in the same year Jawara changed the name of the party from the Protectorate Peoples Party to the People's Progressive Party (PPP). The rationale he offered was that the party should become a national organization open to all Gambians regardless of tribe, religion or regional origin.

At the 1960 general election, which was called by the British colonial government, following the extension of the franchise to the protectorate people, the PPP won twelve of nineteen seats in the House of Representatives. Elected unopposed in his Brikama constituency, Jawara was appointed by the colonial governor to the position of minister of education. Less than nine months later, Jawara ran into difficulties over the publication and distribution of a pamphlet calling for self-government and independence. With the publication as a pretext, the governor decided to bypass Jawara for the post of chief minister. Jawara and his deputy in the PPP, Sheriff Sisay, resigned their positions in the cabinet and returned to the campaign trail.

Following the adoption of a new constitution in 1961, a new governor called an election for May 1962. The PPP swept in, winning eighteen of thirty-two seats, and was able to add one more later. Jawara was called to form a new government, and he assumed the title of premier. Later he became the first prime minister of The Gambia; in 1965 he led his country to independence. In 1970 he became the first president of the newly created Republic of The Gambia.

When The Gambia became independent, Dawda Jawara told his people that their postcolonial situation called for hard work and commitment to national development. Never a flamboyant leader, Jawara made it categorically clear to his countrymen that independence was not going to turn their peanuts into diamonds. He urged them to learn to live together as one people and adopt the philosophy of *tesito* (a Mandinka word for belt-tightening). The rationale for this policy was to organize the Gambians so that they would make sacrifices for national development. Unlike his contemporary African leaders, who spent much of their time philosophizing, Jawara went about the business of creating a political order that maintained one of the few democracies in Africa.

Jawara's commitment to the democratic process is evident in the move to republic status in independent Gambia. After the country attained independence, leading members of the PPP pressed for a referendum on a republican constitution. When the results were in and the ruling party had failed to poll the required number of votes to declare a republic, several PPP stalwarts urged Jawara to go ahead anyway. He refused, but waited for an opportune time to try again. He got the chance in 1970. Two developments were significant. The first was Jawara's decision to marry Chilel Njie, daughter of Gambia's richest businessman, Alhaji Modou Musa Njie, who had been the major financial backer of the main opposition, the United Party. The marriage of Jawara led to the defection of a large number of opposition-party members.

The second development affecting events leading to the passage of the 1970 republican constitution was the greater ability of the PPP government to use government power and largesse to build support in areas that had previously been opposition territory. The municipality of Banjul, the greatest source of opposition to Jawara in the early days of the PPP, gradually succumbed to government blandishments.

Throughout the postindependence period Jawara faced opposition from former colleagues. Although he had the opportunity to employ coercion, Jawara avoided any violent or authoritarian solutions to oppositional politics. Even in the heat of the debates over the republic, he refused to act unconstitutionally. When colleagues argued for a single-party system, he overruled them by saying that not everything tried elsewhere in Africa was good for The Gambia. Jawara's strong commitment to democracy is reflected in the record of the last twenty-five years, in which he has gone through four major crises of confidence.

The first crisis was in 1968 when Sheriff Sisay, number two man in the PPP, decided to challenge Jawara's leadership. Sisay and several younger leaders of the PPP felt that Jawara was compromising too much with the Banjul elite when a Banjulian was appointed to the post of commissioner of police. Sisay and his supporters argued that the decision to place the security of the PPP government in the hands of a Banjulian officer of dubious loyalty was dangerous. Sisay gathered support among party elders. Jawara reacted quickly at the general meeting of the party. He stunned his opponents by offering to resign from the PPP, but not from his post of prime minister, and he repudiated those saying that the Banjulians would stage a coup d' état against his government. Jawara was vindicated in this view some thirteen years later when an attempted coup originated with a socialist leader and paramilitary forces but not from among Banjulian opponents. Sisay and his supporters formed the People's Progressive Association (PPA), but it failed to materialize as a viable alternative to Jawara. In 1972 Sisay returned to the PPP fold. In time he was rehabilitated by Jawara and given a position of prominence in the cabinet. He died in 1989 after serving as minister of finance for several years.

In the second crisis the successor to Sheriff Sisay as the number two man in the ruling party, Sheriff Mustaphe Dibba, was considered by certain elements in the PPP as an heir apparent and therefore a threat to their careers. After a smuggling scandal and then his return in the position of minister of economic planning and industrial development, Dibba clashed with Jawara. But Dibba proved to be more enduring and more widely supported than any other opposition leader. His clash with Jawara led to his forced resignation in 1975. Dibba formed the National Convention Party in the same year. Except for a period of incarceration following the 1981 coup attempt and the ensuing trial of suspects, Dibba has been able to operate freely as an opposition leader. His party was never banned, and he unsuccessfully contested the presidency in 1977, 1982 and 1987.

The third crisis was the most serious challenge. It came from Kukoi Samba Sanyang, a socialist politician helped by elements of the Gambian paramilitary forces. While Jawara was abroad, Sanyang, a former member of Dibba's National Convention Party, shot his way into the Gambian State House. With his supporters in the Field Force, a paramilitary outfit, Sanyang seized control of the state for a few days. A Senegalese military response to Jawara's call for aid violently suppressed the coup attempt. Sanyang and his closest confederates fled abroad by way of Guinea-Bissau. Jawara instituted a series of trials of the suspected rebels. The government invited a number of foreign lawyers and legal experts to guarantee fairness. In the end two other opposition leaders were apprehended and jailed.

The fourth challenge was in 1987 when former Vice President Assan Musa Camara and other former leaders of the PPP decided to form an opposition party, the Gambia Peoples Party (GPP), which contested the 1987 elections without success. The GPP leaders were unable to mount a campaign around the country that could convince the electorate about their viability as alternatives to the PPP leaders. The GPP leaders were not seen as rivals but rather as opportunistic politicians seeking political vengeance against a former boss. In addition, the GPP was doomed without financial backers in the country. In The Gambia politics means not only the casting of ballots by the electorate, but also the distribution of gains by those who aspire to political posts. As in other contests, Jawara and his party emerged victorious.

Jawara's leadership is distinguished in three major areas. The first is the field of national integration. Although Jawara came to power amidst ethnic strife between Banjulians and provincials, during the past twenty-five years he has succeeded in building bridges between elements in the old colony and their counterparts in the old protectorate. He created a national party out of the original Mandinka Protectorate Peoples Party and set a precedent by appointing a vice president from among the three largest ethnic groups. He formed several cabinets that reflected the ethnic diversity of the country and avoided arbitrary tampering with the bureaucracy or the judiciary for the political or ethnic advantage of one group or another. Yet the climate of opinion in The Gambia today may be potentially detrimental to his lifetime work. The bureaucracy, which since colonial days has provided prestige and livelihood to the Western-educated, has become the battleground for the two most influential ethnic groups, the Mandinka and the Wolof. Thus far Jawara has resisted non-merit-based appointments to the senior civil service.

The second area of assessment is agricultural development in The Gambia. Under Jawara's administration the agricultural sector has made significant strides. Much money has been spent in diversification and in the attempt to be self-sufficient in rice. Cotton production, for example, which almost disappeared in the final days of colonial rule, has reappeared. Other agricultural products receive attention, and the government no longer pays tribute to peanuts as the preeminent commodity. Under the guidance of the World Bank's Structural Adjustment Program (SAP), entitled the Economic Recovery Program (ERP), agricultural progress is primary in the current development program of Gambia. The quality of life of some members of the rural population has improved through the "oxenization" program. Yet this program has strengthened the hand of the tiny fraction that dominates the local cooperative societies and the local wings of the ruling party. The Gambia has yet to achieve self-sufficiency in rice. As in other areas on the West African coast, rice consumption in The Gambia has become a national phenomenon. Hard-earned foreign exchange is spent on rice imports from Southeast Asia. Since the launching of The Gambia as an African tourist site in the mid-1960s, millions of dalasis, which could have been spent in agricultural development, have gone to build infrastructure for the European tourist trade. Tourist earnings have not overcome problems, such as rural exodus, ineffective agricultural extension services, mismanagement and corruption among certain officers in the cooperative movement and an urban bias in past development expenditure.

The Jawara regime will also be judged in educational and cultural development. Over the last quarter century the number of schools in the country increased through government expenditure and private efforts to build and run schools. As a result of this education policy the Catholic and the Muslim communities enrolled more school-age children. However, mass illiteracy is still a major problem in The Gambia. Added to this is the massive problem of joblessness among school leavers. The urban population does not understand or appreciate farm work, and the possibility of jobs brings rural people to the cities.

Education has also suffered major setbacks. It has failed to attract the brightest and the most committed in the country; it has lost to the civil service most of the bright young graduates who entered the teaching profession upon completion of their studies; it has produced a large number of young people who are either not sufficiently educated to study abroad or who are ill equipped mentally and attitudinally to contribute successfully to the country's development efforts. Education under Jawara has been devalued because the products of the school system do not perform at the same standard as the previous generation. The cutbacks forced by the SAP have created some resentment, and President Jawara's regime will be measured for its policies or lack of policies on education and culture.

President Jawara is a man of outstanding achievements, but his twenty-five years of leadership in The Gambia have yielded mixed results. He created a multiparty democracy in a continent where civilian and military dictatorships are still the rule. He forged a sense of Gambian nationalism among The Gambia's variegated ethnic groups, although much remains to be done. Jawara has attempted to diversify the economy, although his long-standing dreams of self-sufficiency in rice and diversification in other crops have continued to recede further into the future. Yet he has institutionalized the politics of bargaining and compromise, despite challenges to his personal and political safety, a matter of no small consequence.

BIBLIOGRAPHY

Gailey, Harry A. *A History of the Gambia*. London: Routledge and Kegan Paul, 1964.
———. "From Colonialism to Confederation: The Gambian Experience of Independence, 1966 to 1982." In Robin Cohen (ed.), *African Islands and Enclaves*. London: Sage, 1983.
Gamble, David P. *The Wolof of Senegambia*. London: International African Institute, 1958.
Nyang, Sulayman S. "The Historical Development of Political Parties in the Gambia." *Africana Research Bulletin* 5, no. 4 (July 1973): 3–38.
Sonko-Godwin, Patience. *Ethnic Groups of the Senegambia*. Banjul, The Gambia: Book Production and Material Resources Unit, 1985.
Wiseman, John A. "The Gambian Presidential and Parliamentary Elections of 1987." *Electoral Studies*, 27, no. 3 (December 1987): 286–288.
———. *Democracy in Black Africa*. New York: Paragon House Publishers, 1990.

SULAYMAN S. NYANG

K

KENNETH KAUNDA (1924–   ), Prime Minister, President, Republic of Zambia, 1964–1991).

Kenneth Kaunda is the political father of his country Zambia (formerly Northern Rhodesia); he was the first president of Zambia and retained office for 27 years. His political life reflects the ideals he set for his country: national self-government, political integration and national independence. His career reflects the struggle to overcome the harsh realities of independence: the problems of ethnic differences, dependence on the fluctuating earnings of a single resource (copper) and vulnerability to the political and economic power of a regional neighbor, South Africa.

Kenneth Kaunda was born in 1924 at Lubwa near Chinsali in the Northern Province of what was then the British Protectorate of Northern Rhodesia. He was the eighth child of David Kaunda, the first African missionary to be sent (in 1904) by the Church of Scotland Mission at Livingstonia in Nyasaland (now Malawi) to teach and spread the Christian gospel among the Bemba people; his mother was one of the first African women teachers in Northern Rhodesia. His non-Zambian parentage was to prove a political advantage to him as president. Although he was Zambian born and brought up among the Bemba, his tribal origin was Tonga Tumbuka of Malawi. He was therefore able to avoid that close identification with Bemba political aspirations that was to prove at first a strength, but ultimately a weakness, for his boyhood friend, fellow teacher at Lubwa, and future party and national vice president, Simon Kapwepwe.

Kaunda was educated at Lubwa Mission School, where he became a pupil-teacher. At the age of seventeen he enrolled at Munali Secondary School, Lusaka; he was on the school football team, ran for his house and played the guitar. After passing the Form II examination, he was recalled by the Lubwa Mission and made boarding master of the Lubwa school for boys. In August 1946 he married Betty Banda, a trained teacher.

After four years at Lubwa, Kaunda made fruitless visits to Tanganyika and Rhodesia in search of teaching posts. He then became a welfare assistant at the Nchanga Mine on the Copperbelt before resuming his teaching career at Mufulira, where he served on the Urban Advisory Council; he subsequently became a member of the Provincial Council. He returned to Chinsali in late 1948, founded the Chinsali Youngmen's Farming Association, and supplemented a precarious living as a small farmer by dealing in secondhand clothes. He joined the Northern Rhodesia African Congress and formed a branch in Chinsali, becoming secretary early in 1950. His meteoric rise in the party, which became known as the African National Congress (ANC) and was led by Harry Nkumbula from 1951, was a tribute to his organizing ability and boundless energy. He was appointed northern provincial organizing secretary of the congress in 1951 and secretary-general of the party as a whole in 1953; he edited the *Congress News Circular* and vigorously but unsuccessfully opposed the establishment of a Central African Federation the same year.

Kaunda was sentenced to three months' imprisonment in January 1955 for possessing banned literature. Following his release, his life-style became almost ascetic; he was a confirmed nonsmoker and teetotaller. In 1957 he spent six months in Britain as a guest of the Labour Party; the next year he visited Tanganyika and India.

Disillusioned by Nkumbula's indecisive, yet authoritarian leadership, Kaunda broke with the ANC and formed the Zambia African National Congress (ZANC) in October 1958. However, in March 1959, three months after his return from the first All-African People's Conference in Accra, ZANC was banned for its resistance to the "Benson constitution"; its leaders were rusticated, Kaunda himself being sent to Kabompo in the North Western Province. In June 1959 he was sentenced to nine months' imprisonment for holding an illegal meeting. On his release the following January, he was made president of the newly formed United National Independence Party (UNIP), which he represented at the Federal Review Conference and the Northern Rhodesian Constitutional Conference held in London in December 1960. The British constitutional proposals of June 1961 provoked angry disturbances in Northern Rhodesia, but the promise of amendments enabled Kaunda to restore calm. He pronounced the resultant 1962 constitution as unworkable. However, both UNIP and the ANC contested the elections held under it and together won a majority of the seats. Kaunda became minister of local government in Northern Rhodesia's first African administration. In the preindependence elections under a new constitution in January 1964, UNIP won an easy victory and Kaunda was appointed prime minister. He led his country to independence on October 24, 1964, and was sworn in as executive president. In successive elections in 1968 and at five-year intervals thereafter Kaunda was re-elected president; he gained 95 percent of the votes cast in the election in 1988. Yet in 1991, submitting to a contested presidential election, he was defeated, drawing less than 20 percent of the vote.

Kaunda is a strong family man and a Christian of great personal integrity. In 1967 he first formulated humanism, an eclectic ideology that combines capitalist, socialist and populist strands and seeks to create a just, equitable and human-centered society. Today, humanism has little appeal for young people; perhaps it always was too idealistic for a society in which the materialist ethic is strongly entrenched.

A gentle and humane person, Kaunda looks for nonviolent solutions to problems. But it is a mistake to overstress his gentleness. He is also a tough, skillful and sometimes authoritarian politician who is, at the same time, a highly emotional man, not ashamed of shedding tears in public. He is capable of outbursts of anger, as he admitted in his autobiography, to demonstrating during his restriction at Kapombo; there are stories of cabinet ministers quaking in their shoes when summoned to appear before him. Zambia's former president is an idealist who cares deeply for his country and people. If he was sometimes naive, for example, in failing to realize the risks to which his 1968–71 correspondence with John Vorster, the South African prime minister, exposed him, and if he cannot match ex-president Julius Nyerere[*] of Tanzania in the incisiveness of his thought, he is nevertheless an intelligent man whose writings and speeches, though often diffuse, show a clear understanding of the problems that Zambia faces. If we accept that Kaunda is a man of very considerable personal stature, we need to assess his performance as president.

On the political front, he has given his country political stability. In a continent where the military coup has become endemic, Zambia has not experienced any serious coup attempts; the plot of 1980 was discovered before it had become a real threat. The sectional tensions within UNIP and society, however, were potentially destabilizing during the First Republic. In 1967 the party was almost torn apart by the intense rivalry of its leaders (other than Kaunda himself) and their followers during the course of the bitter campaign that preceded the elections to its central committee. The rift within UNIP had not healed by February 1968, when the national council held a stormy meeting in Lusaka. On February 5 a disgruntled Kaunda announced his resignation as president, but the next day he was prevailed upon by all sections of the party to remain in office. However, tensions within UNIP continued; they came to crisis point in August 1969 and led Kaunda to dissolve the central committee and assume direct control over the party. He initiated a review of the party constitution.

Some of the key provisions of the new constitution, which was eventually approved by the UNIP general conference in May 1971, were a setback for Kapwepwe's Bemba-speaking group within UNIP; they were a further indication that the political pendulum was swinging away from it. In August Kapwepwe and his lieutenants left UNIP and formed a new sectionally based party, the United Progressive Party (UPP). Afraid that the UPP might detach from UNIP the Bemba-speaking Northern, Luapula and Copperbelt provinces, which had provided the core of UNIP support in the preindependence period, Kaunda and the ruling party overreacted: UPP leaders and organizers were detained, and in

February 1972 the party was banned. Intense factionalism, said Kaunda, was impeding development; the way to stop it was to give UNIP the legal monopoly of power. This was done in December of the same year.

Under the independence constitution, elements of the British Westminster system of government were retained. However, from 1968 especially, President Kaunda used his constitutional powers to the full: He initiated major economic reforms, notably the takeover by the state of a 51 percent capital share of the copper mines; he also politicized the provincial and district administration. Against the advice of the broadly based Chona Commission, which reported in 1972, the powers of the president were increased under the one-party state constitution. The latter established the central committee on a full-time basis and, unrealistically, assigned to it the overall direction of policy, with the cabinet relegated to the subordinate role of policy implementation and administrative decision making. Kaunda himself continued to preside over both bodies and to act at his own discretion on a wide range of issues, both at home and abroad. From 1973 these included the sensitive Angolan, Rhodesian and Namibian issues; though his own preference was for moderate liberation movements, such as Joshua Nkomo's* Zimbabwe African People's Union (ZAPU) in Rhodesia, he gave early backing to the Popular Movement for the Liberation of Angola (MPLA) and strongly supported the South West Africa People's Organization (SWAPO). The former president shares credit for the formation in 1979 of the nine-member Southern African Development Coordination Conference (SADCC) and has been in the forefront of moves to effect peaceful change in South Africa. He lost no time in holding discussions with F. W. de Klerk following the latter's election as state president in 1989. He is a strong supporter of the Organization of African Unity (OAU) and has served twice as its chairman.

In the domestic sphere, his intervention on a wide range of issues has sometimes had adverse consequences for the conduct of government and administration. For example, it has led to abrupt and unsuccessful changes in Zambia's rural development strategy, ranging from the introduction of Intensive Development Zones in 1971–72 and the Rural Reconstruction Program in 1975 to the huge state-run farms, which were established in 1980 with massive loans from twenty countries.

Policy proposals stemming from the president's office did not receive the critical examination that they deserved, particularly from civil servants. The National Assembly, however, did become a more critical forum following the general elections of 1973, when many able backbenchers with professional or business backgrounds were returned. They criticized government policy, particularly in the economic sphere and over South Africa, and called into question the government's overall development strategy. Members of the assembly were sharply rebuked by the president in June 1975, when he told them to desist from their "anti-party and anti-government mouthings." Nevertheless, periodic criticism of the government continued to be ventilated in the National Assembly, as well as in the press and in trade-union circles. The 1980 coup attempt apart,

Kaunda's own position as president was not seriously challenged until 1990, despite the troubled events of December 1986 and 1988. Kapwepwe died in 1980. But in 1990 a new contest for the presidency emerged.

The country's economy turned downward in 1974, when the price of copper (which, with cobalt, provides 95 percent of the country's foreign exchange earnings) fell dramatically; unemployment increased and living standards fell sharply. Members of the Mineworkers' Union of Zambia deeply resented the proposal, under the Local Administration Act of 1980, to integrate the Copperbelt mine townships into new district councils; they were convinced that there would be a sharp fall in the level of public services. Their resentment was augmented by the government's reduction of the subsidy on maize meal, the staple diet, causing a steep price rise. There were wildcat mineworkers' strikes when the government temporarily withdrew UNIP membership from seventeen leading trade unionists and further strikes following the detention for three months of Frederick Chiluba, then chairman of the Zambia Congress of Trade Unions (ZCTU).

The depressed state of the economy forced the Kaunda government to seek foreign help, especially from the IMF. The latter provided standby loans on condition that the government introduce austerity measures, including the withdrawal of subsidies on basic foodstuffs. When the government announced in December 1986 that the price of maize meal was to be more than doubled, violent disturbances took place on the Copperbelt, resulting in many deaths. The president hastily cancelled the price rise. In May of the next year Kaunda announced that his government could no longer accept the IMF's conditions and that debt repayments would in future be limited to 10 percent of export earnings. The World Bank and Western governments reacted by holding back funds for aid projects. In 1988 there was an acute shortage of foreign exchange, rising inflation and a growing black market. As criticism of the president mounted, Kaunda downgraded the position of members of Parliament. Despite adverse economic and international conditions, President Kaunda showed character and skill in surmounting a succession of domestic political crises and in maintaining political stability in Zambia.

The years 1989 and 1990, however, saw measures by Kaunda's government backfiring in attempts to meet international demands in order to deal with Zambia's economic problems, revealing the extensive unpopularity of the UNIP regime. In mid-June 1990 a price rise imposed on maize meal brought out students from the University of Zambia in Lusaka in a protest march into a nearby township, Kalingalinga. Riots and looting ensued. On June 30, a lone soldier took over the main radio station in Lusaka, and announced the ouster of President Kaunda, which brought hundreds of dancing, shouting people into the streets until security forces restored order a few hours later. Reacting, Kaunda first declared that he would hold a referendum on the continuation of one-party rule, then he decided to postpone and finally to cancel the referendum, announcing in September 1990 that all obstacles to multi-party government would be eliminated. He called for a new constitution, for the creation of an office of vice-president and new presidential and parliamentary elections, scheduled for a year later.

The most prominent opposition to emerge was the Movement for Multiparty Democracy, founded in December 1989, and led by Frederick Chiluba, who was backed by ZCTU, an organization of 300,000 members. The MMD put together a coalition across a broad spectrum of political, professional and class groupings. It pressed for popular involvement in the electoral process through local education meetings in addition to mounting a widespread advertising and door-to-door campaign. In a major strategic move, MMD also stressed independent monitoring and oversight of the electoral process. The campaign and the election itself was monitored by internal ad hoc groups, such as the Zambian Election Monitoring Co-ordinating Committee (ZEMCC), as well as the government's Electoral Commission and teams of observers from the Commonwealth and the Carter Center (which on election day included former president of the United States Jimmy Carter).

Election day(s), October 31 and November 1, 1991, saw a turn-out of 48 percent of the electorate and a smashing victory for the MMD, which swept nearly 90 percent of the votes in the parliamentary polling, taking 126 seats to 24 for UNIP. Chiluba trounced Kaunda for the presidency, receiving nearly 81 percent of the votes cast. On November 2, in a significant and gracious gesture, Kaunda appeared on national television to congratulate the victor. Before he took the oath of office, Chiluba responded, acknowledging his admiration for Kaunda and calling him the "father of Zambia," although in his post-inauguration remarks he observed that "the era of dictators, hypocrisy and lies is over." On the other hand, President Chiluba underlined what could be Kaunda's major legacy for his country and his continent when the new president also noted that "Zambia has shown the way forward for peaceful change in Africa" (*Washington Post*, November 3, 1991).

BIBLIOGRAPHY

Works by Kaunda:

Zambia Shall Be Free: An Autobiography. London: Heinemann, 1962.
Zambia, Independence and Beyond: The Speeches of Kenneth A. Kaunda. Legum, Colin
    (ed.). London: Nelson, 1966.

Other Works:

Anglin, Douglas G., and Timothy M. Shaw. *Zambia's Foreign Policy: Studies in Di-
    plomacy and Dependence*. Boulder, Colo.: Westview Press, 1979.
Gertzel, Cherry, C. Baylies and M. Szeftel (eds.). *The Dynamics of the One-Party State
    in Zambia*. Manchester, Eng.: Manchester University Press, 1984.
Macpherson, Fergus. *Kenneth Kaunda of Zambia: The Times and the Man*. Lusaka:
    Oxford University Press, 1974.

Tordoff, William (ed.). *Administration in Zambia*. Madison: University of Wisconsin
    Press, 1980.

                                                                        WILLIAM TORDOFF

MODIBO KEITA (1915–1977), President, Republic of Mali, 1960–1968.

Modibo Keita was a charismatic leader with a Marxist-Leninist outlook who
transformed the French colony of Soudan into the socialist Republic of Mali.
Although he generally worked through a collective leadership, he was clearly a
primus inter pares who, as president of the republic and as secretary-general of
the ruling Union-Soudanaise Rassemblement Démocratique Africain (US-RDA),
was able to forge political and economic policies according to his Marxist
theories.

Keita was born in Bamako on May 15, 1915. Although his patronym was that
of the rulers of the ancient empire of Mali, it is an extremely common one
among the Malinke people. The claims that he was a descendant of Mali's ancient
emperors are purely speculative, based only on a coincidence of patronym and
stories elaborated by his political supporters. He came from a family of modest
means and attended local schools in Bamako. He was later sent to the Ecole
Normale William Ponty in Dakar, Senegal, which was then the leading institution
of higher learning in French West Africa. He was trained as a schoolteacher
there and after graduation was assigned to a succession of teaching posts, eventually becoming a school inspector.

During the 1930s he showed an increasing interest in politics and became
active in a number of Bamako-based voluntary associations whose aims were
clearly political but whose stated purposes were social, cultural and sportive.
These voluntary associations, the forerunners of political parties, included the
Association des Lettres founded by Mamby Sidibe (1891–1977), a political
activist, schoolteacher and writer, and Art et Travail. They brought together the
colony's educated elites, consisting of schoolteachers, clerks and technicians,
cut across ethnic boundaries, and focused on the immediate and future concerns
of urban dwellers and less on traditional ethnic priorities. Through these associations Keita was kept in touch with Ponty alumni and was able to cultivate
contacts with most of the colony's elite.

The French, wary of the hidden objectives of the voluntary associations, sought
to control them by establishing the Maison du Peuple, both an organization and
actual building. Aided by the Amis du Rassemblement Populaire du Soudan
Français (ARP), an organization of French colonial officials who supported the
Popular Front in France, the French were able to keep the voluntary associations
in check for a while. They also exiled prominent leaders of the associations to
provincial posts, including Keita, who was sent to Sikasso in the late 1930s.

The liberal policies of the Popular Front made possible the development of
trade unions in the French Soudan. The first one of these was a teachers union,
organized by Mamadou Konate and his coalumni from the Soudan's secondary
school, the Lycée Terrasson de Fougeres. While the voluntary associations linked

the educated elite together, the trade unions served as a bridge of communication between them and the urban masses.

With the advent of World War II, political activity in the French Soudan was suppressed. In 1944, upon liberation in France, it started again with the formation of political groupings. The two leading political figures were Mamadou Konate, who enjoyed trade-union support, and Fily Dabo Sissoko, a schoolteacher and *chef de canton* who occupied an important place in traditional society in the western part of the colony and who also enjoyed the support of the French colonial administration. Keita was clearly in third place, supported by the Groupes d'Etudes Communistes (GEC), which founded the short-lived Communist Parti Démocratique Soudanais (PDS). Sissoko, who won election to the First Constituent Assembly of the Fourth Republic, and his supporters founded the Parti Progressiste Soudanais (PPS). In 1945 Keita joined forces with Mamadou Konate in founding the Bloc Soudanais, which merged with the RDA in 1946 to become the US-RDA, a political party with strong ties to the French Socialist Party and the French Communist Party. Ever the pragmatist, Keita was willing to subordinate his political views and take second place to Konate in the US-RDA in order to remain politically viable. However, he and his followers came to represent the radical wing of the party.

Between 1946 and 1956 the political struggle in the Soudan was between two political parties, the PPS, headed by Sissoko, and the US-RDA, headed by Konate. Although Keita was elected to the territorial assembly of the Soudan in 1948, he remained in Konate's shadow. Konate's death in 1956 opened the way for Keita's rise to power and the ascendancy of his radical political views. That same year, the PPS lost in the territorial elections to the US-RDA, in effect making Keita the dominant political leader in the colony.

Keita was consistently perceived by the colonial administration as a radical revolutionary. He was imprisoned in Paris for a month in 1950 and was exiled to the north of the colony to organize schools for nomads. His political ascendancy in the Soudan after 1956 was viewed with concern by the colonial administration. He was elected a deputy to the French National Assembly in 1956 and later became its first African vice president. Resigning this latter post, he became secretary of state for France overseas and later secretary of state to the council.

In 1958 General de Gaulle initiated a referendum on the future status of France's African territories under the Fifth Republic. The Soudan opted for political autonomy within the French Community and became the Republique Soudanaise. Keita became head of government and joined Léopold Sédar Senghor* of Senegal in championing a united and independent federation of former territories of French West Africa. In 1959 the US-RDA routed the PPS in territorial elections, and the latter merged with it. Keita became president and along with Senghor tried to induce the Ivory Coast and other states to join in a federation whose proposed name was the Mali Federation. Under pressure from the Ivory Coast, Upper Volta (now Burkina Faso) and Dahomey withdrew their interest from the proposed federation, leaving only Mali and Senegal.

The Mali Federation obtained its independence from France on June 20, 1960, with Keita becoming premier and head of state. Keita's advocacy of a unitary government versus Senghor's of a federal arrangement became the focus of conflict. Eventually, compromises from both sides allowed the federation to move forward. The understanding reached was that Senghor would be president, Keita premier, and Mamadou Dia of Senegal the vice president. However, at the eleventh hour Keita precipitated a crisis when he backed Lamine Guèye, the mayor of Dakar, for president and sought to place a Soudanese colonel as chief-of-staff over Dia, who was minister of defense. Keita tried to mobilize the federal army, but Dia and Senghor got the upper hand by mustering the gendarmerie led by a French commander. The latter trapped the Soudanese commander and sent Keita and the Soudanese leaders out of Dakar to Bamako on a sealed train on August 22, 1960. Despite the breakup of the Mali Federation, Keita tried to revive it during the following weeks, resorting to both diplomacy and threats of breaking relations with any country recognizing Senegal. Keita declared a state of siege in the Soudan, closed the border with Senegal and suspended train service between the two countries for what would prove to be a three-year period. On September 22, 1960, an extraordinary congress of the US-RDA declared the country independent as the Republic of Mali.

As undisputed leader of the Republic of Mali, Keita set about to eliminate the psychological, intellectual and economic legacies of colonialism. Guided by a Marxist-Leninist outlook, he forged a highly centralized form of government and galvanized the US-RDA into a mass party that had supremacy over the administration. He rapidly Africanized the civil service, even when it meant replacing colonials with less qualified Malians, and reaffirmed the "socialist options," which he had first elaborated during the brief life of the Mali Federation. The US-RDA rapidly absorbed all opposition groups and most voluntary organizations such as labor unions, women's groups, youth groups and the veterans' organization. This move effectively eliminated all potential organized political dissent outside the party structure.

Keita's chief domestic policies dealt with the economy, which was rapidly transformed into a state-run one. Although he alienated Mali's small but important merchant class with these moves, he had the support of the urban masses, who greatly benefited from employment opportunities in a spectrum of newly developed parastatals and an inflated government bureaucracy. An ever-expanding bureaucracy and steady growth in the number and size of parastatals virtually guaranteed the graduates of Mali's technical schools and institutions of higher learning government employment. In time, such employment, along with government educational stipends, came to be viewed by students as entitlements.

Keita inherited from the French a large cadre of wage-earning civil servants living in an artificially supported consumer economy, but he did not inherit the subsidies that had once been given to the Soudan through the federal budget of French West Africa nor those that had come from the metropole. True to his Marxist-Leninist views, he sought assistance from the Communist world of the time, especially from the Soviet Union, Eastern Europe and the People's Republic of China. Technicians and aid programs from Communist countries became prominent in Mali's economic life. Keita sent large numbers of Malian students to Communist countries for both technical training and political indoctrination.

Keita's special alignment with Communist countries on the economic front was paralleled by close political ties with them that gained for Keita the Lenin Peace Prize in 1963. Yet the moderates within the government served as a force to maintain lines of cooperation with France. Keita cast a wide net to set up relations not only with regional states, but also with other countries in Africa, Europe and America. In 1961 he, Sékou Touré* of Guinea and Kwame Nkrumah* of Ghana established the Guinea-Ghana-Mali union, which never evolved into a practical political entity. He also aligned Mali with the Casablanca States—Guinea, Ghana, United Arab Republic and Algeria—which denounced neocolonialism and supported Patrice Lumumba* in the Congo (Zaire). Under Keita Mali became active in the nonaligned movement and established special political ties with North Vietnam and North Korea, which in turn provided modest assistance in light industry development. Keita directed much of Mali's official anti-imperialist rhetoric against the United States and the war in Vietnam while benefiting from substantial U.S. aid programs. The latter were a bonus of the East-West rivalry then being played out in Africa.

In 1962 Keita withdrew Mali from the West African Monetary Union and issued the Mali franc, a nonconvertible currency. When merchants in Bamako protested the new currency because their regional trade was effectively destroyed by it, Keita's government ordered the arrest of old US-RDA rivals from the now-defunct PPS, charging them with inciting the riot. They were later tried before a "popular tribunal" outside the established judicial system and condemned to death, a sentence that was later changed to life in prison at hard labor. In imprisoning Sissoko and his supporters, Keita eliminated the major source of political dissension in the country. The prisoners were sent north to Kidal, where a Tuareg rebellion was in progress. It was soon rumored that Sissoko and two others had been shot. Two years later the Political Bureau of the US-RDA announced that they had been shot in a Tuareg ambush. However, it is widely held that Keita and his close associates ordered the executions.

Although Keita's state-run economy provided almost unlimited employment opportunities to urban elites, the nonconvertible currency, dwindling hard currency reserves, and production disincentives to farmers created by a state marketing board and collectivization led to serious food shortages and scarcities of consumer products. Keita's socialist options soon grew unpopular with vast segments of the public.

While Keita's orations exhorted people to self-sacrifice for the sake of socialism, many Malians resorted to smuggling and the black market in order to survive. Popular discontent, which steadily grew from 1963 through the time of Keita's ouster in 1968, was never galvanized into a political revolt. However, it served as a backdrop against which a military coup d'état could be successfully launched.

Keita's unpopular domestic policies were formulated through consensus within the Political Bureau of the US-RDA, the party congresses, and the National Assembly. Yet Keita was adept at manipulating these bodies, stacking them with supporters who shared his hard-line Marxist-Leninist views, and in swaying the public with charismatic orations. At the same time, he effectively foreclosed ethnic and regional rivalries by accommodating regional leaders in these power structures.

As popular unrest with Keita's policies grew, he resorted to extraordinary means both to defuse it and to preserve his hold on power. In March 1965 he established the National Committee for the Defense of the Revolution, comprised of a number of hard-liners, while at the same time he entered into monetary negotiations with France. These negotiations led to monetary accords signed in 1967 in which France agreed to support the Mali franc after it was devalued by 50 percent. The implementation of these accords in May 1967 was denounced by the hard-line radicals as a betrayal of Mali's basic socialist principles. In order to appease them and remain true to his own Marxist-Leninist views while benefiting from French help, Keita launched a number of radical initiatives. These initiatives also served to provide scapegoats who could be blamed for popularly perceived government failures.

Keita had the National Assembly and the Political Bureau of the US-RDA dissolve themselves. The party and the government were placed under the authority of the National Committee for the Defense of the Revolution. The committee and Keita launched a political and economic cleansing operation and reactivated the Popular Militia, a paramilitary body of three thousand men, to help carry it out. Local committees for the defense of the revolution were established in neighborhoods in the capitals and in all the country's administrative units. Moderates were pushed from the center of consensus policy-making and replaced by radical hard-liners.

During late 1967 and most of 1968 Keita's cultural revolution gripped the country. Members of the Popular Militia manned roadblocks, searched people and their homes at will, detained many on flimsy pretexts, and engaged in torture. These excesses rapidly alienated popular sentiment for Keita. Yet the public took satisfaction in the show trials of allegedly corrupt and dismissed party and government officials. Keita was deified in slogans, the newspapers, official pronouncements, and over Radio Mali as "le Guide Eclaire" and supreme guide of the revolution.

With moderates removed from power and most of the major institutions of state power dismantled, Keita and his relatively small nucleus of hard-liners became isolated within the National Committee for the Defense of the Revolution. Although this body continued to formulate policies through consensus, that consensus now emerged from a very narrow base compared to before.

The strains between the army and the Popular Militia steadily grew as members of the latter frequently harassed young army officers. A group of young officers asked Keita to disband the Popular Militia or else put it under army control. He refused to do either, and it was widely believed within the army that he planned to arrest a number of army officers on November 20, 1968. These conditions, intense popular dislike for Keita's policies and the ambitions of a group of young army officers to seize power for themselves led to Keita's overthrow on November 19, 1968, in a relatively bloodless coup d'état. Keita was arrested but never tried and was held in a number of places, including the capital, Bamako, where he died on June 6, 1977.

Keita's military successors gained immediate and widespread popularity by disbanding the Popular Militia and the US-RDA and by making small moves toward a free-market economy. Yet the presence of over fifty thousand wage earners in the civil service and the parastatals and Mali's close political and economic ties with the Communist bloc dictated pragmatic caution. Keita's legacy of a state-run economy and close political ties with Communist countries remained relatively intact for two decades after his ouster. While his immediate successors chipped away at the periphery of these, they did not radically alter them. Rather, they attempted to dilute them with add-on free-market initiatives and friendlier relations with countries of the West, including the United States. Keita's downfall came about largely because he lost control of balancing the radicals who conducted the revolution and the moderates who handled the rapprochement with France. In the end, the long-term economic benefits gained by the moderates were submerged out of popular view by the harsh and immediate activities of the radicals.

BIBLIOGRAPHY

Diarrah, Cheik Oumar. *Le Mali de Modibo Keita*. Paris: Harmattan, 1986.
Foltz, William J. *From French West Africa to the Mali Federation*. New Haven, Conn.: Yale University Press, 1965.
Imperato, Pascal James. *Mali: A Search for Direction*. Boulder, Colo.: Westview Press, 1989.
Snyder, Frank Gregory. *One-Party Government in Mali: Transition toward Control*. New Haven, Conn.: Yale University Press, 1965.
———. "The Political Thought of Modibo Keita." *Journal of Modern African Studies* 5 (1967): 79–106.

PASCAL JAMES IMPERATO

JOMO KENYATTA (1897–98?–1978), Prime Minister, President, Republic of Kenya, 1963–1978.

Jomo Kenyatta, one of Africa's most outstanding and astute leaders, led Kenya to independence in 1963, having been at the center of African nationalist politics for three decades. He was a charismatic orator, a person of great presence and ability and secure in his own values and culture. He was cautious and steadfast in achieving the goals of unity and freedom for his people and remained true to the ideals of African nationalism and racial dignity. After June 1963 he ruled Kenya for a year and a half as prime minister and then as president until he died at about eighty years of age in 1978.

Kenyatta was born Kamau wa Ngengi at Ngenda in the Gatundu area in Kiambu District. It is believed that he was born around 1897 or 1898 (although the exact date is unknown) on the eve of European colonization. His father, Mungai, and his mother, Wambui, were traditional Kikuyu cultivators. His parents died when he was quite young, and Kenyatta went to live as a herdsboy with his uncle and then his grandfather, a "seer" or wise man. In 1909 he enrolled in the newly established Church of Scotland mission school at Thogoto, a few miles west of Nairobi, where he gained a very rudimentary education, which provided entry into the world of the colonial state. A product of two cultures, he was baptized Johnstone Kamau in 1914. The year before, according to Kikuyu custom, he was circumcised and entered into his age grade of *Mubengi*.

Much of his life after leaving the mission was spent in and about Nairobi, which was rapidly becoming the center of colonial administration and European colonization. In 1919 he married his first wife, Grace Wahu. In 1920 they had a son, Peter Mungai, and in 1928 a second child, a daughter, Wambui, who was christened Margaret. After independence she was to become the mayor of Nairobi in 1970. Kenyatta's most successful position in the 1920s was in employment by the Nairobi Municipal Council. This provided him with a regular salary for himself and his family.

Kenyatta was aware of the early expressions of African nationalism, the political violence of 1922 in Nairobi, and the exile of Harry Thuku, the Kikuyu leader of the East African Association. By 1924 another voice of protest was heard—the Kikuyu Central Association (KCA), which established itself to represent Kikuyu political and social grievances. Of paramount concern was the security of their land. In 1928 Kenyatta became the secretary-general of the Kikuyu Central Association and the editor of their new publication *Muigwithania* (The reconciler) and took an active part in building up the organization.

In 1929 Kenyatta went to the United Kingdom on behalf of the KCA, whose leaders believed that it was imperative to make known directly to the imperial power in Whitehall their grievances concerning land policy and the need for elected African representation to the colonial legislature. This initial eighteen-month sojourn introduced Kenyatta to metropolitan politics and the world of anticolonial protest and provided an opportunity of seeing something of the continent, including the Soviet Union. Kenyatta returned to Kenya in 1930. Six months later he went to London with Parmenas Mukeri (later a chief) to represent the KCA concerns, particularly that of land, to the Joint Parliamentary Committee on Closer Union in East Africa. They were not received by the parliamentary committee, but in June 1932 they gave evidence before the recently established Carter Land Commission before it departed for Kenya. Land policy had become the key political issue of the 1930s. Kenyatta attended the Quaker College of Woodbrooke at Selly Oak, Birmingham, in 1931–32. In the winter of 1931 he sent to the Colonial Office a lengthy memorandum on Kikuyu land and other KCA grievances.

Among Kenyatta's contacts was his association with George Padmore,* with whom he apparently made his second visit to the Soviet Union in the winter of 1932–33. In addition to voicing African political protest for Kenya in England, writing letters to newspapers and lecturing, he attended London University from 1935 to 1937. In 1938 he published *Facing Mount Kenya,* a study of the Kikuyu people developed from papers presented in Professor Bronislaw Malinowski's seminar. For Kenyatta, anthropology was a means to advance the causes of African equality and human dignity. He wrote of order and cohesion in Kikuyu traditional society. Moreover, Africa had its own culture and was not a tabula rasa upon which a new civilization had to be created, as so many Europeans believed. After the appearance of *Facing Mount Kenya,* he replaced his baptismal name of Johnstone with Jomo.

In the late 1930s Kenyatta was part of the Pan-African movement, which created in 1937 the International Africa Service Bureau to foster and spread the message of African freedom. Its central achievement was the holding of the Sixth Pan-African Conference in Manchester at the end of World War II in October 1945, which was attended by Kenyatta and other Pan-Africanists, such as George Padmore, C. L. R. James, Wallace Johnson, Kwame Nkrumah[*] and the American pioneer, W. E. B. du Bois. During much of World War II Kenyatta was in Storrington, a village in West Sussex, where he worked on a farm as well as lecturing to soldiers. On May 11, 1942, Kenyatta was married a second time, to Edna Grace Clarke. Their son, Peter Magana, was born on August 11, 1943.

By war's end Kenyatta had grown into a sophisticated, mature and striking leader. In 1945 he published a pamphlet, *Kenya: The Land of Conflict,* setting forth the crucial need for economic and social reform and eventual self-government for Kenyan Africans. When he returned to Kenya in September 1946, he forged strong links with the influential Koinanges at Banana Hill in Kiambu. He married the daughter of Senior Chief Koinange, Grace, who bore him a daughter, Jane Wambui. He established himself at Kenya's Teachers' College at Githunguri, founded in 1939 by the American-university-educated Peter Mbiyu Koinange, whom he had come to know in London. After Grace died in childbirth, he took as a fourth wife Ngina, the daughter of Chief Muhoho, in 1951. They were to have five children: Wambui, Uhuru, Nyokadi, Mahaho and Christina.

On June 1, 1947, Kenyatta was elected president of the Kenya African Union (KAU), originally founded in 1944 to support Eliud Mathu, the first appointed African member to the colonial legislature. Leaders of the banned KCA, who originally had not supported this new territorial body, now gave it their strong and substantial support. Having secured the support of the KCA leaders, Kenyatta faced a deeper problem in making KAU into an effective vehicle for the advancement of territorywide African nationalism. There were formidable problems of social communication because of the uneven patterns of social change across the country, the limited numbers of educated Africans, and ethnic parochialism and antagonism, which permitted only limited mass mobilization among the

Kikuyu of central Kenya. Therefore, while Kenyatta articulated the concept of a Kenyan African people, the organizational base of KAU was fundamentally ethnic, although a few areas of support could be found in various other parts of the country.

Other factors were also hardly propitious for a program of African political reform. Foremost was the fact that the colony's economy was mortgaged to European agricultural settlement, with an agrarian color bar that legally regulated the use and ownership of land and even the growing of high-value crops, such as coffee. Kenya had become a "white man's country," with some thirty thousand Europeans occupying a privileged position who were determined to maintain and expand their economic and political control. Moreover, British colonial policy was concerned not with the creation of an African state, but rather a Western one, in which a new multinational community would take several generations to evolve. Policy emphasized economic production, in which increased postwar European settlement was essential for rapid development. At best, African political advancement was seen as gradual and the activism of African nationalists as destructive and self-serving. Seldom did the administration see Kenyatta's leadership as constructive, no matter how moderate his views were.

In this postwar period, as Kenyatta's politics of petition had no impact on bringing forth fundamental political and social change, thousands of Kikuyu bound themselves together by an oath of unity in opposition to colonial rule. By 1950 militant and radical leaders, mainly centered in Nairobi, gained increasing political influence and control. Their politics, rooted in a profound rural and urban poverty, fostered by neglected and overcrowded Kikuyu land areas and a low-wage economy, came to accept the employment of political violence in their quest for political and social reforms. This conspiratorial movement and the ensuing violence, which was identified as Mau Mau, was an integral part of Kenya African nationalism.

On October 20, 1952, Kenya's governor declared an emergency, and Kenyatta and other nationalists were arrested. While violence spread and intensified in central Kenya, Kenyatta and five colleagues were found guilty, in a controversial trial, of membership in and managing Mau Mau, though later a key witness against Kenyatta acknowledged that he had committed perjury. In June 1953 KAU was banned. To defeat Mau Mau, the colonial government used overwhelming force, and thousands of Africans were killed or detained.

During the emergency in the 1950s and the nearly nine years that Kenyatta spent in prison and detention in the remote northwest, a new political situation unfolded. It was fostered by a nationalism led by an educated leadership drawn from different ethnic groups and a British policy recognizing the need for political reforms. The achievement of African elected representation to the legislature in 1957 gave a legitimacy to African nationalism and made the legislature the arena for the struggle for African majority rule. However, because the colonial government prevented the creation of a territorywide political organization, factionalism among the leadership and ethnic parochialism undermined African unity.

The rally to Kenyatta, the imprisoned nationalist, provided some sense of unity among the new African leaders. Although the colonial government hoped that Kenyatta would be forgotten, the link of the new nationalism with his leadership could not be ignored.

In 1960 Britain recognized that Kenya would become an African state, and African national parties were permitted to take part in politics. In Kenya's first general election in February 1961, the dominant party, the Kenya African National Union (KANU), campaigned with the slogan of *uhuru na Kenyatta* (Freedom and Kenyatta). KANU, the winning party, refused to form a government with Kenyatta still detained, and the Kenya African Democratic Union (KADU) formed a government with the support of liberal Europeans and the colonial civil servants. Despite the fact that the British governor had maintained that Kenyatta was a leader into "darkness and death," he was finally released from detention on August 14, 1961. In October he became president of KANU; he became a member of Parliament in January 1962 and headed the KANU delegation in February–March 1962 to new constitutional talks in London for self-government leading to independence. In April he joined with KADU in a coalition government as minister of constitutional affairs and economic planning. His party, KANU, having reluctantly agreed to KADU's concept of a regionally based constitution, went on to win the May 1963 elections that brought Kenyatta into power as prime minister in June 1963. On December 12, 1963, Kenya became an independent state. Within a year Kenya became a republic (December 1964), with Kenyatta as executive president. KADU voluntarily joined KANU to form a de facto one-party state with regionalism abolished.

Kenyatta governed Kenya for fifteen years and made the presidency the commanding locus of political power and national politics. With unrivaled personal authority he presided over a political oligarchy and administration as Kenya's patriarch. As the focus of state power, allegiance to him was tantamount to loyalty to the state. Although factionalism was pervasive in the struggle for control of KANU leadership at the local and national levels, these conflicts seldom encroached on Kenyatta's paramount position. His ministers served at his pleasure, and cabinet membership reflected the multiethnic character of the country, with the Kikuyu having a predominant role. Moreover, leadership in administration, commerce and the armed services, as well as the inner cabinet, was also predominantly Kikuyu. Patron-client ties linking the national and local arenas were a distinctive feature of Kenya's factional politics. In 1974 Kenyatta became the president for life of KANU. While Parliament was democratically elected at regular intervals with a large number of incumbents going down in defeat, there were limits to its deliberations, for it was clearly subordinate to the presidency. Nonetheless, Kenyatta was very conscious of public opinion in asserting his authority.

To assure control across the country, he governed through the administration, whose capability had been greatly enhanced during the emergency in the 1950s. The provincial commissioners in each of the seven provinces were directly responsible to him. They and their staffs maintained law and order and were his personal representatives and links to the people. Much in the tradition of colonial rule, they were "political officers," Kenyatta's loyal prefects in whom he had confidence and trust.

Reconciliation and unity underlay Kenyatta's policies of moving the country from a colonial, racially stratified society to a more balanced multiracial one. Kenyatta consolidated changes introduced in the 1950s to dramatically improve African agriculture and oversaw an impressive expansion during the first decade of his rule in all sectors of the economy. In agriculture the achievements included remarkable advances by African smallholders in tea and coffee production. Further, land in the former "white highlands" was transferred to Africans by means of various schemes, and some progress took place in the Africanization of commerce. Manufacturing remained largely in non-African hands. However, the push for economic growth was offset by disparities in regional development and dramatic inequalities in income distribution in which a majority of people had a relatively low standard of living. Kenyatta's government responded to the demand for education, but the high birth rate of about 4 percent contributed to unemployment as a major feature of the economy.

While political stability marked Kenyatta's reign, it was not without severe tensions and violence. From 1966 to 1969 one-party rule gave way to a two-party system as the Kenya People's Union (KPU), led by the former vice president, Oginga Odinga, posed a radical alternative to development in contrast to KANU's laissez-faire ideology. KPU was banned by Kenyatta prior to the 1969 national election following the assassination of Tom Mboya[*] in July 1969 and a violent encounter with KPU supporters at the time of the presidential visit to Kisumu in October. A Luo and potential successor to the president, Mboya was KANU's general secretary and the minister of economic planning and development. In the aftermath of the political murder of this brilliant young national leader and the detention and elimination of a major Luo leader, Odinga, from national leadership following the clash at Kisumu, there was a withdrawal of Luo support for the Kenyatta regime. Perhaps the most serious crisis was the assassination of J. M. Kariuki, a populist Kikuyu member of Parliament, who was seen as the champion of the poor and a critic of the government. This crisis evoked the specter of class politics and hostility toward the government. A parliamentary investigation placed the responsibility for the killing on high-ranking government officials.

President Jomo Kenyatta died in Mombasa on August 22, 1978, and was constitutionally succeeded by his vice president of eleven years, Daniel Torotich arap Moi,[*] a Tugen from western Kenya. Kenyatta chose not to name a successor or ensure that the presidency would remain among the Kikuyu, as some politicians had hoped. Although very much a Kikuyu, he was also a nationalist whose policies fostered an elite with a stake in the development of the country. He was a conservative, pragmatic leader whose legacy was the shaping of a strong state and national government. While a signatory of the Charter of the Organization of African Unity and a supporter of the OAU Liberation Committee for southern Africa, he was a firm believer that achievement of African unity or Pan-Africanism depended on the critical development of strong and viable states. In 1977, in an environment of disunity among East African states, he witnessed the termination of the East African Community. His role in African interstate affairs was limited, although Kenyatta twice agreed to be an arbiter—without success—in the Congo (Zaire) crisis of 1974 and in Angola in 1976.

BIBLIOGRAPHY

Works by Kenyatta:

Facing Mount Kenya. London: Secker and Warburg, 1938.
Kenya: The Land of Conflict. London: International African Service Bureau, 1945.
Harambee! The Prime Minister of Kenya's Speeches, 1963–1964. Nairobi: Oxford University Press, 1964.
Suffering without Bitterness: The Founding of the Kenya Nation. Nairobi: East African Publishing House, 1968.

Other Works:

Bennett, George, and Carl G. Rosberg. *The Kenyatta Election: Kenya, 1960–1961.* London: Oxford University Press, 1961.
Delf, George. *Jomo Kenyatta: Towards Truth about "The Light of Kenya."* London: V. Gollancz, 1961.
Gertzel, Cherry. *Government and Politics in Kenya: A Nation Building Text.* Ed. Maure Goldschmidt and Don Rothchild. Nairobi: East African Publishing House, 1969.
——— Gertzel, Cherry. *The Politics of Independent Kenya, 1963–68.* London: Heinemann, 1970.
Karimi, Joseph, and Philip Ochieng. *The Kenyatta Succession.* Nairobi: Transafrica, 1980.
Murray-Brown, Jeremy. *Kenyatta.* New York: E. P. Dutton, 1973.
Rosberg, Carl G., and John Nottingham. *The Myth of "Mau Mau": Nationalism in Kenya.* New York: Praeger, 1966.
Throup, David L. *Economic and Social Origins of Mau Mau, 1945–53.* London: James Currey, 1987.

CARL G. ROSBERG

SIR SERETSE KHAMA (1921–1980), Heir to the Bangwato Chieftaincy, President of the Botswana Democratic Party, President, Republic of Botswana, 1962–1980.

Seretse Khama was born to a chieftaincy that was eventually denied to him by successive British governments beginning in 1948 and that propelled him into nationalist politics leading to the achievement of independence for the Republic of Botswana on September 30, 1966. As president of the Republic of Botswana from 1966 to 1980, Seretse Khama presided over a rapidly expanding, mineral-led economy, which supported a one-party-dominant but freely competitive democratic political system. At the time of his death from cancer in July 1980, Seretse Khama left a lasting imprint on the life of the nation and region.

Seretse Khama was born on July 21, 1921, in Serowe, capital of the Bangwato state, then a tribal reserve in the east central portion of Britain's Bechuanaland Protectorate in southern Africa. He was the first-born son of Sekgoma II, *kgosi* (king) of the Bangwato, by his recognized *mohumagadi* (queen) and as such was heir to the throne under the succession rule of male primogeniture. He was never to assume that office.

Sekgoma II died in 1925. His younger brother, Tshekedi Khama, Seretse's uncle, returned from studying in South Africa to be the regent during Seretse's minority. Seretse was educated in Serowe and South Africa before proceeding to England to study law in Oxford and in London. It was in London that Seretse met, fell in love with and, in 1948, married Ruth Williams, a young Englishwoman.

Tshekedi Khama opposed the marriage on the grounds that the tribe would never accept a white queen or accept their son as *kgosi* and that the marriage was contracted without the advice of the royal uncles, which contradicted tribal practice. There were those who believed that Tshekedi was using the marriage issue to retain the chieftaincy for himself, though this was never proved. In a series of *kgotla* meetings (a traditional assembly of all adult males offering, in public, advice to the *kgosi* on matters of national policy) in Serowe, Seretse Khama turned public opinion in his favor and was acclaimed chief with his wife in June 1949.

The British government in public proclaimed its interest to be that of the welfare of the Bangwato, but in private it kowtowed to the white supremacists in South Africa and believed that the recognition of Seretse and his wife would give the new nationalist government in South Africa an excuse to leave the Commonwealth. Seretse was therefore summoned to London only to be informed that he had been banned from the Bangwato Tribal Reserve and the protectorate. He would be forced to live in exile in England on allowance provided by the British government. The issue was a public sensation in England, southern Africa and around the world.

Seretse and Ruth Khama were reconciled with Tshekedi and were allowed to return to Bechuanaland in 1956, but on condition that neither he nor his children would claim the chieftaincy. He became vice chairman of the Bangwato Tribal Council and a member of the African Advisory Council, but he showed no signs of personal political ambition until after the death of Tshekedi, a dominating personality, in 1959.

Increasingly concerned about white racism in South Africa and the radical political direction taken internally with the formation of the Bechuanaland Peoples' Party in 1960, Seretse led a group that, with the tacit support of progressives in the colonial administration, formed the Bechuanaland Democratic Party (BDP) in January 1962 with Seretse as its founding president. It was an instant success, due in no small part to Seretse's position in Bechuanaland society. He combined traditional legitimacy and the patron-client economic relations that lay behind it in the rural areas with a Western education and modern nonracial outlook. This attracted popular support as well as the support of moderate traditional leaders

and the new social strata of the colonial-era teachers, civil servants and progressive farmers, whose future lay in the national, not the tribal, context.

This coalition under Seretse's leadership in the BDP swept the 1965 Legislative
Assembly elections, winning twenty-eight of thirty-one seats with an average of
80 percent of the votes. Seretse became the first prime minister and led the
negotiations for independence, which was achieved in 1966. He became the first
president and was re-elected to office following National Assembly elections in
1969, 1974 and 1979, in which the BDP (Botswana Democratic Party) returned
large majorities.

Few presidents have come to power in less auspicious economic circumstances.
The economy of Botswana was dependent on South Africa and, to a lesser
extent, on Southern Rhodesia for the employment of Botswana labor, the transportation of people and goods and the supply of essential commodities. Besides
an old railroad, an abattoir and a tiny new capital city, there was no modern
infrastructure nor an inch of metaled highway outside the main streets of three
railroad towns. The human resources required to plan and execute development
projects were absent. Cattle production led the agricultural economy, but after
several years of drought was unproductive. Botswana was at the bottom of world
development tables, with a gross domestic product estimated below fifty dollars
per capita. Government revenue, which was insufficient to cover even recurrent
expenditure and required a subvention from the British Treasury, depended
heavily on receipts from the Southern African Customs Union, controlled by
South Africa. Politically, the nation-building problem was the need to reduce
and marginalize the power of chiefs without undermining the legitimacy of the
national government. The problems were daunting.

The president and the BDP government adopted an incrementalist and technocratic approach to economic problems. The government would develop and
maintain an infrastructure and support services in rural areas with revenue from
a partnership with foreign (as it turned out, mainly South African) capital in
mining projects, leaving agricultural, commercial and other industrial activities
in private hands. The resulting "trickle-down," it was hoped, would produce
employment and a livelihood for a growing population. Issues of inequality in
income and access to productive resources were secondary. Expatriates were
recruited, grants and loans from mainly Western sources were secured, and the
Rhodesian Selection Trust and South Africa's De Beers Diamond Mining Company were granted wide latitude to prospect for minerals. A relatively efficient
and uncorrupt civil service oversaw the process with much success. The customs
union agreement was renegotiated in 1969, which enhanced revenue from that
source. Copper and nickel, and especially diamonds, were discovered and mining
begun. Budgetary self-sufficiency was achieved in 1972. Schools and roads were
built, and water resources—critical to development in the semiarid conditions
of the country—were developed.

In the rural economy cattle production continued to be the main preoccupation.
The commercialization of beef production found expression in the Tribal Grazing

Lands Policy in the mid-1970s, working to the advantage of the largest cattle owners, among whose number were Seretse Khama and a significant component of the cabinet and leadership in the party. In 1974, 45 percent of rural dwellers owned no cattle at all.

The political power of the chiefs to allocate land use and collect and spend revenue was greatly reduced in the early years of independence as the elected district councils (whose jurisdiction more or less coincided with tribal boundaries) and the national government asserted themselves. The chiefs, however, were not eliminated. Seretse Khama, himself born to be a chief, understood the significance of the chieftaincy in retaining the loyalty of the rural, semiproletarianized majority. His combination of traditional legitimacy with the elected legitimacy of the presidency created a unique ability to deal with this problem.

Not all the chiefs gracefully accepted the suzerainty of the national government under Seretse's leadership. Bathoen Gaseitsiwe, chief of the Bangwaketse, resigned his chieftaincy and stood as a candidate in the National Assembly election in 1969 for the Botswana National Front (BNF), a political party formed shortly after the 1965 elections. Bathoen defeated Quett K. J. Masire,* then vice president and minister of finance and development planning and a founder of the BDP, one of the rising generation to join Seretse in 1962. Chief Linchwe II Kgafela of the Bakgatla, less dramatically but with equal effectiveness, kept the debate about chieftaincy on the national political agenda.

A commitment to an open and competitive party system was persistent during Seretse's presidency. This was put to the test, though not a very difficult one, with the formation of the BNF by Kenneth Koma, who articulated a socialist critique of what he considered to be the neocolonial character of the BDP. Koma's party encompassed a variety of disgruntled elements, including the feudalist ex-chief Bathoen, and it did not achieve great success during Seretse's presidency. Still, Seretse seems to have defended the multiparty principle, even though some members of the BDP and the cabinet were not convinced that parties like the BNF should be completely unfettered in their activities.

Throughout his presidency Seretse maintained a relatively cohesive governing coalition, centered around large cattle owners and local notables. A unifying interest in developing an infrastructure and the resources to do so aided this process. But he also responded to the need to accommodate new strata emerging as the political economy changed. Co-optation of younger backbenchers into the cabinet, the accommodation of professional elites and the recruitment of senior civil servants into the National Assembly on their retirement are examples. Through these means Seretse was able for the most part to maintain the legitimacy of the BDP in the eyes of most of the rural, semiproletarianized majority and of much of the growing middle class in urban areas.

As a matter of principle and personal example, Seretse Khama vigorously promoted a policy of nonracialism. Botswana of European descent were welcome in the BDP, the National Assembly and the cabinet. Seretse was quick to respond to criticism of the large number of civil servants of European descent, some of whom were citizens, often occupying quite senior positions; but he was equally quick to point out that European descent of itself bestowed no particular privilege.

Nonracialism was also a key to Botswana foreign policy during the period from 1966 to 1980. The country was increasingly drawn into the struggle against white minority rule in Namibia, Angola, Mozambique, Southern Rhodesia and South Africa. Botswana's economic and military vulnerability prevented a high-profile role, such as allowing its territory to be used by liberation movements, for example. But Seretse and the government took what steps they could. Botswana did not establish diplomatic relations with Pretoria and refused to recognized the ''independent'' homelands of the Transkei and Bophuthatswana. Refugees from South Africa and Rhodesia found a welcome in Botswana, although for many only as a transit point. Botswana supported economic sanctions against South Africa even though it could not impose them, and it argued that the impact of sanctions on other countries in the region, like Botswana, should not be used as an argument against sanctions.

While promising to be a good neighbor to South Africa, Seretse made it clear that his government was committed to the dismantling of minority regimes. Botswana was a Front Line State (along with Angola, Mozambique, Zambia and Tanzania) in the struggle for Zimbabwe. Out of the Front Line States came the Southern African Development Coordination Conference (SADCC), designed to create complementary economies among the nine member states and to achieve greater economic independence from South Africa. In the Front Line States Seretse Khama played a lesser role in the liberation of southern Africa than the two other chief executives with whom he was closest—Kenneth Kaunda[*] of Zambia and Julius Nyerere[*] of Tanzania—but he was the main instigator of SADCC as a body looking to the regional future beyond liberation.

Viewed from the baseline of British colonial neglect and resulting deep economic dependence on South Africa, Botswana's independence era was one of dramatic achievement, internally and in the international arena. Economic growth, based on the good luck of discovering diamonds, was sustained. Politically, Botswana was nearly unique in maintaining an open competitive political process characterized by regular multiparty elections and the observance of freedom of speech and association in a nonracial setting. It was a dramatic contrast with the apartheid system next door in South Africa.

Some of the reason for these achievements must be found in the life, career and contribution of Seretse Khama. He did not, of course, act alone. The Central District, the Bangwato territory, contributed a disproportionate share of nationalist politicians to the national scene. There was also a growing educated elite in Bechuanaland in the late 1950s and early 1960s ready to work for a broadly based and moderate nationalist movement. Moreover, Seretse's career was often driven externally by events and circumstances, as the crisis surrounding his marriage and the process of forming the BDP show. From this perspective Seretse Khama was as much thrust into the forefront of the movement for independence and into the leadership of the nation as anything else. But it is equally important to conclude that having been placed in these circumstances, Seretse Khama rose to the occasion, put together a broadly based national party, and then quickly led it to independence in 1966. His leadership instincts were strong, as were his abilities to select and act on cogent advice. After independence he was able to maintain a cohesive governing coalition and a relatively popular mass base, no small achievement and one that was rare on the continent.

There were limits to Seretse's leadership in independent Botswana. He could not, for example, completely overcome the perception that his presidency was simply the Bangwato chieftaincy writ large. This limitation was underlined for some when in 1979 Seretse's life came full circle, as it were; his son, Seretse Khama Ian Khama, brigadier of the Botswana Defence Force, was installed as chief of the Bangwato by popular demand. This made it particularly difficult for Seretse to handle the minorities question in the national context. Nor could he ignore his position in the economic system. For a large cattle owner, the natural choice was an agricultural strategy that facilitated the commercialization of cattle production. Conflict over the resulting inequality of incomes and access to assets for agricultural production could be papered over, but not resolved. The government refused to accept, for example, a minimum wage for agricultural workers and concern for the plight of remote-area dwellers, who often worked for little remuneration for large cattle owners almost entirely limited to expatriates.

Internationally there can be little doubt that Seretse Khama contributed substantially to the good reputation of Botswana and its ability to generate foreign aid as well as political support. Seretse Khama's cultivation of international recognition and support for Botswana's place in the region and the world assured a favorable international press and some degree of insulation for the country from South African political pressures.

BIBLIOGRAPHY

Works by Khama:

From the Frontline: Speeches of Sir Seretse Khama. Ed. Gwendolen Carter and E. Philip
    Morgan. London: Rex Collings, 1980.

Other Works:

Colclough, Christopher, and Steven McCarthy. The Political Economy of Botswana: A
    Study of Growth and Distribution. Oxford: Oxford University Press, 1980.
Holm, John, and Patrick Molutsi (eds.). Democracy in Botswana. Athens, Ohio: Ohio
    University Press, 1989.
Morton, Fred, and Jeff Ramsay (eds.). The Birth of Botswana: A History of the Be-
    chuanaland Protectorate from 1910–1966. Gaborone, Botswana: Longman Bot-
    swana, 1987.
Parson, Jack. Botswana: Liberal Democracy and the Labor Reserve in Southern Africa.
    Boulder, Colo.: Westview Press, 1984.
——— (ed.). Succession to High Office in Botswana. Athens, Ohio: Ohio University
    Center for International Studies Monographs in International Studies, 1990.

Picard, Louis. *The Politics of Development in Botswana: A Model for Success?* Boulder, Colo.: Lynne Rienner Publishers, 1987.

JACK PARSON AND NEIL PARSONS

L

PATRICE LUMUMBA (1925–1961), Prime Minister, Republic of Zaire, 1960.

The meteoric career of Patrice Lumumba—he led his country for only its first two months of independence—symbolizes the tragedy of African nationalism: A fledgling government is submerged in internal conflict that triggers international competition of truly global significance; the process, which transits civil war and international intervention, culminates in internal military authoritarianism, thwarting the original aims of nationalism for decades. Lumumba himself achieved perhaps greater fame in his martyrdom than he might have for his achievements, through the university named for him in the USSR and through the use of his name by various radical African groups for some years.

Patrice Lumumba was born on July 2, 1925, in the village of Onalua in Kasai Province. He belonged to the Tetela ethnic group, and his family were poor peasants in an essentially poor area of the Belgian Congo. Many Tetela left their home area in order to seek their fortune in other parts of the colony. Earlier they had cooperated with the Arabized trading empires centered in the Maniema area, which were in turn connected to the Indian Ocean coastal markets. The Tetela were also used as soldiers by the Congo Free State and were at the heart of two major mutinies in the last decade of the nineteenth century.

Lumumba had an eclectic educational history. He was expelled several times and migrated between different Catholic and Protestant Methodist mission schools in northern Kasai Province. Eventually, at age sixteen, he returned to his home village without a school certificate. He had failed at his first attempt at upward mobility. At that time this would have involved moving from a Catholic mission school to a seminary and then into the priesthood or a white-collar job.

After two years back in the village, Lumumba changed his name (he was originally called Elias Okit'Asombo) and followed the path of many other ambitious and energetic Zairians: He left the rural milieu to seek his fortune in industrial and urban centers. First, he became a clerk in a mining center in Maniema and then, a few months later, he ventured further to the provincial capital of Stanleyville (now Kisangani). In Kisangani Lumumba was able to get a job as a postal clerk and also attended evening school in order to finally get his school certificate. He did well in the post office, gaining promotion as well as admission to a course given to postal employees in Leopoldville (now Kinshasa), the colony's capital. Soon Lumumba became an active member and leader of several voluntary associations. He began to write newspaper articles and—most unusual for this time and place—became an active collaborator of a French sociologist who was conducting research on urban problems in the Belgian Congo.

Lumumba's urge for upward mobility in Belgian colonial society led him to apply for ''immatriculation'' status, a legal classification that attested to the fact that a ''native'' had attained a high degree of ''assimilation'' and ''civilization.'' It conferred certain rights that other Zairians did not have, such as the ability to buy alcoholic drinks, the freedom to move about after night curfews and better conditions if one was hospitalized or imprisoned. It was similar to the *assimilado* status in Portuguese colonies; however, few Congolese applied for it. Significantly, the most educated Congolese, for example, the Catholic clergy, refused to have anything to do with it. Lumumba's endeavor failed; the examining board refused Lumumba ''immatriculation'' status, although later he did manage to obtain it.

Despite this early disappointment, Lumumba achieved a position that was virtually unique for a member of the modernized elite in the 1950s under Belgian rule. He established personal links to the minister for colonial affairs and the governor of Orientale Province, and he managed to have two personal discussions with the king of the Belgians, Baudouin I, while the latter was visiting the Congo. Although these connections ruffled the feathers of many local Belgians, Lumumba gained prestige from these contacts. He was also able to translate them into concrete advantages for members of the modernized elite in Kisangani in the area of housing.

Lumumba was one of the first Zairians in the 1950s to speak in the name of the Zairian masses, going beyond the self-interest of the modernized elite or a specific ethnic group. In 1956 Lumumba was chosen to be a member of one of the first groups of Zairians allowed to go to Belgium on a study tour. However, on his return to Kisangani his rising star collapsed: He was arrested by the colonial authorities for having stolen 126,000 Belgian francs from the post office. He admitted his guilt, and attempts were made to collect enough money to reimburse the post office. But in the end nothing could prevent the imposition of an eighteen-month prison sentence. Wide differences of opinion existed then, and later, as to why he took the money, to what use he put it, and why his friends were not permitted to pay it back in order to prevent his going to prison. Yet his prestige among the modernized elite did not suffer appreciably, as some local Belgians and some of his Zairian competitors no doubt hoped it would.

On the contrary, to some, Lumumba's imprisonment made him into rather a hero.

In this period Lumumba finished writing a book about Belgian colonial policy and the future development of the colony. *Le Congo, terre d'avenir, est-il menacé?* was a moderate statement, formulated in terms of giving assimilated Zairians the opportunity of participating in a nonracist society. During his lifetime Lumumba found no publisher for the manuscript, although after his assassination, it was published in Belgium, presumably without his permission.

In June 1957 Lumumba was freed from prison, six months before the end of his term. Dismissed from the post office, he moved to Kinshasa, where he found a job as a public relations representative of an important brewery. This position put him in contact with social circles in the colonial capital. Soon he became the leader of two organizations, a politically oriented discussion group, the Liberal Circle, with ties to the conservative, anticlerical Belgian Liberal Party, and an ethnic mutual help association, the Federation of Batetela.

At this moment in history, internal and external forces accelerated the speed of political developments in the Belgian Congo. By 1958 political party activities were tolerated by the colonial administration. Lumumba joined the Mouvement National Congolais (MNC), which, at the time, was a loose association with moderate goals under considerable Catholic influence. Within a short time Lumumba once again moved into a leadership position, although one that was disputed by several of the founding members.

Lumumba's name was beginning to be known abroad as well as in Zaire. In December 1958 he was invited—along with two other Zairian leaders—to the major Pan-African conference in Accra. Significantly, Joseph Kasavubu, the leader of the ABAKO (an ethnic party representing the Bakongo group), was prevented from attending by the Belgian authorities. The Accra meeting was a turning point in Lumumba's life, especially because of his talk with Kwame Nkrumah.* Thereafter, he not only adopted Pan-Africanism, but he also perceptibly radicalized his demands for independence. On returning to Kinshasa, Lumumba made a speech to several thousand listeners that established him as an effective mass orator. He began also to devote himself to organizing the MNC on a colonywide basis.

Apart from the Belgian administration, Lumumba faced several major difficulties. First, the MNC split, and Lumumba's faction (soon to become a separate party) failed to attract most of the well-known founding members of the party. Since political mobilization tended to follow ethnic lines, this meant that the ethnic groups led by his internal opponents were for the most part beyond his reach. Second, the ABAKO party had not only obtained the virtually unanimous adherence of the Bakongo ethnic group, which was dominant in the capital, but it had also achieved levels of organization and party discipline that far surpassed those of the MNC, and specifically the MNC/Lumumba (MNC/L). Indeed, the ABAKO was, up to this point, seen by the Belgian administration as the most radical and dangerous nationalist force. This rivalry led to one of the few ideological divisions in the Zairian independence struggle; the ABAKO opted for federalism, having earlier flirted with the idea of a separate Bakongo state. Lumumba became a strong advocate of "unitarism," that is, a powerful centralized state encompassing the entire Belgian Congo. This division reflected differences of "poor" and "rich" regions, with the richer regions opting for federalism.

During most of 1959 Lumumba scurried around the country attempting to organize first the unified MNC and later, after the split, the MNC/L. His declarations and speeches alternated between appeals for militancy and efforts to hold back the spontaneous anti-Belgian, antiwhite sentiments released among the Zairian masses by the newly acquired freedom of expression. In October 1959, during an MNC/L congress in Kisangani, Lumumba called for a boycott of scheduled local elections, due to take place in December, and demanded immediate negotiations with the Belgian government. The demand for such negotiations was viewed as outlandish, as it would scrap an elaborate Belgian plan for consulting the Zairian population, but three months later, this is exactly what occurred. At the Kisangani congress, Lumumba ignored the absence of a permit and held public meetings in which he called for civil disobedience. A confrontation between MNC/L partisans and a substantial military presence resulted in a number of deaths and the decision by the administration to imprison Lumumba for inciting violence. This second imprisonment had the advantage of making Lumumba a persecuted hero of the independence struggle. At the same time, it forced him out of the political arena at a most crucial moment. The MNC/L without Lumumba was a shadow of itself.

The collapse of Belgium's ability to administer certain rural areas caused its government to accept the idea of a round table conference with Zairian politicians, at which the future of the colony was to be decided. The alternative was the substantial use of military force. Moreover, early and easy acquiescence to Zairian demands, coupled with support for moderate political parties, nurtured the hope that pro-Belgian, easy-to-get-along-with leaders would take over at the end of colonial rule. In the first weeks of 1960 the leaders of all Zairian political parties migrated to Brussels. One of the first things they did was to demand the release of Lumumba, which occurred four days after Lumumba was condemned to six months confinement by a Kisangani court.

Lumumba joined the other politicians in Brussels and soon became a leading figure in a surprisingly united Zairian "delegation." Caught off guard, the Belgian government agreed to most of the Zairian demands, including the proposition that there would be no reserve clauses limiting independence and that the date for independence would be set for June 30, 1960, only a few months away.

Lumumba returned from the round table conference believing himself to be destined to lead the country after independence. To do so, he had to win the scheduled May elections and establish himself as the pre-eminent nationalist leader. He was the head of the only party with some support in all the provinces, but it had not as yet established a strong organizational base at the grass-roots level. All other strong nationalist or radical parties had ethnic or regional bases. The only exception was a loose, administration-backed party.

Lumumba devised an eminently empirical strategy to emphasize nationalist unity. Party cadres were sent from village to village to mobilize support and to collect party dues. They worked on a commission basis. In areas such as the Batetela homeland, where ethnic solidarity produced automatic support, the MNC/L courted traditional leaders. Where direct support for the party seemed impossible to achieve on short notice, Lumumba created alliances with small parties, most of which were ethnic.

During this period Lumumba became increasingly suspicious of Belgian intentions and actions, although he was careful to avoid legitimizing anti-Belgian or antiwhite racism. He always had close Belgian advisors and managed to obtain financial and moral support from diverse Belgian sources, such as the Belgian Communist Party on the left and major corporations on the right. Nevertheless, many Belgians were angered by his tone and accusations, and Belgian families living in some MNC/L-controlled areas began to escape from Zaire.

The electoral campaign was a great victory for Lumumba as well as for the MNC/L, its allies and the more radical nationalist parties. The MNC/L won more than twice as many votes as any other party, although that amounted to no more than about 26 percent of the total seats in the Chamber of Representatives. Lumumba became prime minister, and with his support Kasavubu became president. But the result was far from giving Lumumba the type of power he had imagined he would achieve, the type of power a Nkrumah in Ghana or a Sékou Touré* in Guinea had gained. He headed a cabinet half-filled with opponents, and his archrival was head of state.

The incredibly short terminal colonial period meant that the new state was destined to be far more dependent on the former colonial power than was the case elsewhere. Virtually the entire middle and upper levels of the administration were staffed by Belgians, not a single Zairian military officer had been commissioned, and the first generation of university graduates was just beginning to appear. Only the church had been Africanized.

Four days after independence, on July 5, 1960, the army mutinied, creating a situation of virtual anarchy. Belgians fled by the thousands, vacating virtually every executive and technical function. Several days later Belgian troops intervened, initially to protect Belgian lives and property. Eleven days after independence Katanga (now Shaba) Province, the rich copper-producing region of Zaire, seceded with Belgian military protection. Lumumba and Kasavubu together travelled around the country attempting to calm the situation and at the same time appealed for help from the United Nations.

Although, at the time of these events, Lumumba was portrayed as having lost his grip on reality, being drugged and hysterical, and shortly afterwards as having become a Communist stooge, his response to these challenges was, on the whole, reasonable, although consistent with his personality and past successes. Regarding the mutiny, which was essentially caused by the lack of Africanization in the army's ranks, he proclaimed a program of Africanization and expelled some Belgian officers who were disliked by the troops or had proven themselves disloyal to his leadership. When Belgian troops intervened, he at first accepted their presence but turned radically against this "interference" when among other nonhumanitarian acts they protected Shaba secession. He fully expected that the United Nations would use military forces to maintain the state's unity, that is, to force the end of the Shaba secession. When he encountered resistance to this goal, indeed when it was argued that the reintegration of Shaba would be achieved without force, he organized a two-pronged invasion of Shaba by units of the Zairian army whose loyalty he had been able to regain. The campaign was a disastrous failure and allowed some to accuse him of conducting "genocide" against the Baluba in Kasai Province. Yet two years later and after his assassination, he was proven correct in the view that Shaba secession would not end without the use of force. In the end the UN did organize a military campaign to achieve this goal.

Perhaps the most fateful decision was to appeal for Soviet aid when the West and the Western-dominated UN operation failed to meet his demand that Belgian troops be ejected and Shaba forcibly reintegrated. The Soviet Union gave Zaire and Lumumba much moral support but relatively little material help (essentially limited to some transport planes and trucks). However, this act resulted in Lumumba being perceived, especially by the United States, as a dangerous Soviet tool and also helped to antagonize Dag Hammarskjold, the UN secretary-general, who took the view that bilateral aid undermined the UN and was inadmissible. Finally, this act severed Lumumba's relationship with Kasavubu and resulted in the president dismissing the prime minister.

With hindsight, Lumumba's decisions were consistent with the methods he had used with success earlier in his career. He had brilliantly played opponents against each other to his own advantage, first with different Belgian political parties and then with different Zairian politicians and ethnic groups. New in the international arena, Lumumba sought to balance Soviet aid by visiting Washington and by signing a contract with an American financier to give the United States a fifty-year monopoly for the extraction of Zaire's mineral resources. But the Cold War game was different and harsher than colonial politics. The U.S. government was unimpressed. It organized a plan to assassinate Lumumba.

On September 5, 1960, only a little more than two months after taking office, Lumumba was dismissed by President Kasavubu. Since Lumumba possessed a parliamentary majority, this act under normal circumstances would have had a short-lived effect. Lumumba tried to get the upper hand by "dismissing" the president and tried to rally popular support. The head of ONUC (the now-substantial UN military and administrative presence in the Congo) intervened to deny Lumumba the airwaves for broadcasting and the airport for travel. The population in the capital was on the whole ethnically linked to Kasavubu, not Lumumba. A few days later Mobutu Sese Seko,* at the time a colonel, who was chief of the General Staff of the Zaire army, announced a coup with the goal of "neutralizing" both Lumumba and Kasavubu. Not only had Lumumba lost political power, but Mobutu's army sought to arrest him while troops from the UN force protected his isolated prime minister's residence. At the UN head-quarters in New York a battle ensued as to who was the legitimate representative of Zaire, Lumumba or Kasavubu, another battle that Lumumba lost.

In the meantime, the Shaba secession was increasingly taking root, and in Kisangani allies of Lumumba set up their own "central" government, claiming that the government in Kinshasa was illegal. In a journey illustrative of Lu-mumba's assertive, optimistic, courageous and yet imprudent personality, he fled by car toward Kisangani, making speeches to enthusiastic crowds along the way, and was finally arrested at a river crossing by an army unit.

Brought back to Kinshasa, a bound Lumumba was beaten by Zairian soldiers as foreign correspondents watched. On news that a new mutiny might be brewing in the camp in which he was held, the Kinshasa authorities sent him to Lub-umbashi in a secessionist province, where there would be no doubt as to his fate. Severely beaten in the airplane, Lumumba and a companion were killed on or about January 17, 1961. He was thirty-five years old.

Lumumba's assassination was far more than a personal tragedy. His exclusion from Zairian politics contributed heavily to the explosion of revolutionary forces three years later, costing the lives of hundreds of thousands of Zairians. The distrust created for the UN meant that the international organization was pre-vented from having a role in later African crises, such as Rhodesia/Zimbabwe and Angola. During the two months of his premiership Lumumba had tried to dominate events without the necessary unity and support among his own people. Externally, his attempt to gain advantage by balancing Western and Soviet aid was a casualty of the growing Cold War in postcolonial Africa. What would have happened if he had reached Kisangani and if he had lived long enough to deal with the Kennedy rather than the Eisenhower administration in United States remain tantalizing questions.

BIBLIOGRAPHY

Works by Lumumba:

Le Congo, terre d'avenir, est-il menacé? Brussels: Office de Publicité, S.A., 1961.
Congo, My Country. Introduction by Colin Legum. New York: Praeger, 1962.
Lumumba Speaks: The Speeches and Writings of Patrice Lumumba, 1958–1961. Ed. Jean Van Lierde. Boston: Little, Brown, 1972.

Other Works:

Blouin, Andree. *My Country, Africa: Autobiography of the Black Pasionara.* New York: Praeger, 1983.
Gerard-Libois, Jules, and Benoit Verhaegen. *Congo 1959 & Congo 1960.* Brussels: CRISP, 1960, 1961.
Heinz, G., and H. Donnay. *Lumumba: The Last Fifty Days.* New York: Grove Press, 1969.

Kalb, Madeleine G. *The Congo Cables*. New York: Macmillan, 1982.

Kamitatu, Cleophas. *La Grande mystification du Congo-Kinshasa: Les Crimes de Mobutu.* Paris: Maspero, 1971.

Kanza, Thomas. *The Rise and Fall of Patrice Lumumba: Conflict in the Congo.* Cambridge, Mass.: Schenkman Publishing, 1977.

Weiss, Herbert F. *Political Protest in the Congo*. Princeton, N.J.: Princeton University Press, 1967.

Weissman, Stephen R. *American Foreign Policy in the Congo, 1960–1964*. Ithaca, N.Y.: Cornell University Press, 1974.

Willame, Jean-Claude. *Patrice Lumumba: La Crise congolaise revisitée*. Paris: Editions Karthala, 1990.

Young, Crawford. *Politics in the Congo: Decolonization and Independence*. Princeton, N.J.: Princeton University Press, 1965.

HERBERT F. WEISS

ALBERT JOHN LUTHULI (1898–1967), President, African National Congress, Republic of South Africa, 1952–1967; Nobel Peace Prize, 1960.

Albert Luthuli, described as a man of dignified and noble bearing, first a schoolteacher, then a chief, was catapulted by nationalist politics in 1952 to the leadership of the African National Congress (ANC), the largest antiapartheid movement in South Africa. The climax of his career was the Nobel Peace Prize in 1960.

Chief Luthuli, as he was commonly addressed, was descended from Zulu royalty, his mother having grown up at the royal court of Cetshwayo, the third in the line of Zulu kings since Shaka, the founder of the Zulu empire, who ruled much of South Africa in the second quarter of the nineteenth century. Of Christian parents, Luthuli was born on an undetermined date in 1898 in Southern Rhodesia (Zimbabwe) at a Seventh-Day Adventist mission near Bulawayo, where his father had moved from Groutville in Natal.

His father died when Luthuli was a little boy, and his mother, Mtonya, returned to South Africa, where she became a vegetable farmer to support her son. She sent him to attend primary school at Groutville, where he stayed with his uncle Martin, who was the local chief. After finishing high school at Ohlange Institute, Luthuli went to teacher-training school at Adams College, from which he graduated in 1921. As a small institution run by American missionaries, Adams was insulated from the full reality of race discrimination. As Luthuli was to say later, Adams College students knew of racism only in theory.

It was not until 1936, when Luthuli was elected chief of the mission reserve near Groutville, that he became fully aware of the economics of discrimination. He was exposed to the problem of the poverty of his people, inflicted by racist laws that restricted African access to land, reserving the best land (87 percent) for whites and the remaining land (13 percent), often poor and infertile, for Africans. The pain and humiliation was perhaps more graphic to the Zulu, a people steeped in heroic and proud traditions who had been reduced to a miserable existence in overcrowded reserves. He found the task of distributing land a perpetual nightmare. To defend his people against repeated police raids, ostensibly in search of "illicit beer brewing," whose main cause was poverty, he developed an effective administration to try to reduce the practice. His sense of fair play and justice earned him his people's respect and confidence.

The year 1936 saw the passage of "the Hertzog bills," a landmark legislative onslaught on the rights of the African people. The Land Trust Act reinforced the 1913 Native Land Act in barring Africans from owning land outside the reserves. A second act removed Africans from the common voters' roll in the Cape Province.

Luthuli had been politically active since he was chief, but he formally joined the ANC only in 1945 when, in an effort to resurrect the ANC Natal branch following the death of the chairman, Luthuli found himself elected provincial executive secretary. In 1951 he became the Natal provincial president. He also joined the Native Representative Council, which had been set up in 1936 to replace the Cape Franchise, but which remained an impotent organ for African representation. The ANC refused to participate, but allowed individuals to join, largely to prevent stooges from claiming to represent Africans.

In 1949 the ANC adopted a Program of Action to oppose the Nationalist government's proclaimed apartheid policy. Together with the Indian Congress, the ANC launched the Campaign for the Defiance against Unjust Laws in 1952, attracting thousands of new members. The government reacted by ordering Luthuli to resign as chief of the Groutville reserve or quit membership in the ANC. He refused both, making a strong speech in defense of his views and actions after the government deposed him from the chieftainship.

Of strong liberal inclinations, Luthuli was opposed to violence and supported a strategy of active nonviolent opposition. Rising in stature in the nationalist movement and regarded as a voice of reason and moral leadership, he was elected to the national presidency of the ANC in 1952. It was from this point that he began to experience repeated restrictions and bannings that left him little scope for the exercise of his leadership. He remained uncompromising and continued to release statements when possible and to attend meetings each time his bans expired. However, his leadership remained largely moral and symbolic as real power shifted to the young militants of the youth wing, such as Nelson Mandela* and Oliver Tambo. The Freedom Charter was adopted in June 1955 by a multiracial Congress of the People that included the ANC and all major parties. As an organization the ANC did not formally adopt it until 1956. Luthuli was not consulted, and this offended him, as he felt that he would have taken issue with a number of clauses.

Luthuli was one of the 156 original defendants in the treason trial of the late 1950s. A man committed to nonviolence and Christian principles, he was charged with plotting violent overthrow of the government through a Communist-inspired conspiracy. The trial showed how the Cold War mania of the 1950s could be rabidly orchestrated in South Africa: A Polish "expert" on communism was imported to prove that the ANC's Freedom Charter was a Communist-inspired document. Charges were dropped against Luthuli and sixty others in 1957 after a preliminary stage of the trial. In 1961 the trial ended in acquittal of all the remaining accused, thus vindicating Luthuli and the ANC.

In the mass protests and strikes after the Sharpeville riots in March 1960 Luthuli publicly destroyed his pass, leading thousands to follow his example. The government declared a state of emergency followed by the banning of the ANC. An underground opposition emerged under Mandela, and a call to armed struggle was issued at precisely the same time Luthuli was being feted with the Nobel Peace Prize in December 1961. Luthuli died under suspicious circumstances in 1967, reportedly hit by a train while taking a walk near his Natal home.

Luthuli acquired a stature in life and later in death larger than that of most men. He was dedicated to the cause of freedom for his people and his country. The love for his country transcended the bounds of race and color. He always prayed for a free, democratic and nonracial South Africa. Not of literary bent or scholarly, he did not have the luxury of the time to read as widely as he would have wished. But he had great presence of mind and a broad political and intellectual outlook. He also had a sense of history, especially the history of his own people. Because he was deeply religious, he perhaps tended to overemphasize the role of Christianity in the development of his people. A modern African observer might chastise him for his seemingly unqualified support of Christian missionary influence in South Africa. Enthralled by the etiquette of the Zulu royal court, which he often visited, he could remark, "I suppose I am not a black Englishman." His use of terms like tribe, tribal law and custom, terms invented by colonial historiography, reflect his ideological instruction based on colonial missionary education.

In the political spectrum of South African antiapartheid resistance, he belonged to the liberal and social democratic wing. His political goal was a South Africa transformed through peaceful reform, adopting a British Labour Party type of socialism. As a nonviolent activist, he was influenced by Gandhi's approach. During his presidency of the ANC, the organization took a confrontational approach marked by strikes, demonstrations and active civil disobedience. He was not naive, however, about the near-fascist government policies and always feared that these would eventually force the masses into open revolt. He warned that no people acquiesces forever in the face of oppression, and he condemned what he regarded as the uncivilized behavior of a regime that spoiled the prospects for racial harmony.

In spite of the repeated banning orders, which kept him away from running the daily affairs of the ANC, Luthuli worked to unite broad sections of the people against the regime. He addressed many audiences of workers, youths, students, peasants and whites. During an address to one white audience, he was attacked and knocked to the ground by young white vigilantes. In dignified fashion typical of his character, he got up and continued his speech as if nothing had happened. This moderation won him praise from liberal whites and even from opponents as a voice of reason and hope.

His political views are inseparable from those of the ANC, which above all else emphasized that South Africa belongs to all who live in it, black or white. However, his leadership was largely symbolic, as he was not effectively in control of the ANC. If South Africa had had a more reasonable and reform-minded government, Luthuli would have been pivotal in the creation of interracial harmony. His efforts to develop interparty cooperation reflected a strong non-doctrinal approach to politics. He was committed to forming broad alliances. Unity of the people and all political groups was his overriding and burning concern. He tempered moderation with an uncompromising challenge of injustice. He was as critical of apartheid as he was of those compromisers who sought accommodation with the system. He attacked black middle-class elements apologetic to apartheid, charging them with wishful thinking and creating a perverted sense of values.

Luthuli tried to stand above ideological partisanship, which partly explains his appeal. He once remarked, "Our primary concern is liberation, and we are not going to be side-tracked by ideological clashes and witch hunts" (Harcourt 1966: 165). Sternly opposed to "red baiting," he deflected charges of Communist influence in the ANC by arguing that the ANC represented and reflected all political tendencies. One of his closest associates, in spite of their ideological differences, was Moses Kotane, the general secretary of the South African Communist Party. Luthuli's personal respect for Kotane was so deep that he once confessed that he was not a Communist but if Kotane asked him to join the Party, he wondered what he would do.

Luthuli's concerns were not limited to South Africa alone. He was actively interested in world peace and justice, as his Nobel Prize speech testifies. He supported the total liberation of the African continent from colonial domination, condemning the British military campaign against Kenya's Mau Mau uprising, the French colonial war in Algeria and the establishment of American bases on African soil.

Luthuli lived long enough to see the emergence of armed struggle in 1961, an option he eschewed. On the other hand, he was a practical man. He regretted armed struggle, but blamed it on the government. Armed sabotage by the ANC in 1961 commenced at precisely the time Luthuli was receiving the Nobel Prize in Oslo, possibly with his tacit approval. Chief Albert Luthuli will go down in history as a contributor in no small measure to the liberation of his country. Nelson Mandela's release in 1990 vindicated the struggle, ninety-two years after Luthuli was born and twenty-three years after he died.

BIBLIOGRAPHY

Works by Luthuli:

Let My People Go. London: Fontana, 1962.
"Africa and Freedom." In *Africa's Freedom*. London: Unwin Books, 1964.

Other Works:

Benson, Mary. *Chief Albert Luthuli of South Africa*. London: Oxford University Press, 1963.

Callan, Edward. *Albert John Luthuli and the South African Race Conflict*. Kalamazoo: Western Michigan University Press, 1962.

Carter, Gwendolen M. *The Politics of Inequality: South Africa since 1948*. New York: Praeger, 1958.

Feit, Edward. *African Opposition in South Africa: The Failure of Passive Resistance*. Stanford, Calif.: Hoover Institution Press, 1967.

Gerhart, Gail M. *Black Power in South Africa: The Evolution of an Ideology*. Berkeley: University of California Press, 1978.

Harcourt, Melville. *Portraits of Destiny*. New York: Sheed and Ward, 1966.

Karis, Thomas, and Gwendolen M. Carter (eds.). *From Protest to Challenge: A Documentary History of African Politics in South Africa, 1882–1964*. Volumes 1–4. Stanford, Calif.: Hoover Institution Press, 1972–1977.

Woodson, Dorothy. *The Speeches of Albert J. Luthuli*. Buffalo: State University of New York at Buffalo, 1982.

CHOOLWE BEYANI

M

SAMORA MACHEL (1933–1986), President, People's Republic of Mozambique, 1975–1986.

Samora Machel, a charismatic and forceful personality, commanded the guerrilla army of the Front for the Liberation of Mozambique (FRELIMO), the national liberation movement that spearheaded the overthrow of Portuguese rule in Mozambique. The first president of independent Mozambique in 1975, Machel headed the state, the Politburo and the Central Committee of the ruling party in an ill-fated attempt to implement a Leninist model of socialist transformation in one of the poorest countries in Africa. In global and regional policy Machel found himself thwarted and victimized by his country's dependence on South Africa and deserted by his Communist supporters elsewhere in the world. His untimely death in a plane crash cut short what might have become broader policy shifts and trends toward political pluralism, private enterprise and reconciliation with internal political enemies.

The military liberator and president for the first eleven years of independent Mozambique, Samora Machel, was born on September 29, 1933, in Xilimbene (Chilimbene) in the Chokwe District of Gaza Province. His parents belonged to the Shangaan subgroup of the Tsonga, the second largest of Mozambique's ten ethnic groups. His political education came, he said, "not from reading Marx or Engels but from seeing my father and mother forced to grow cotton for the Portuguese and going with them to the market where they received prices which were appreciably lower than those paid to the Europeans. . . . As I read [Marx], I realized I was 'reading' it for the second time" (Christie 1988:123). Machel's grandparents and great-grandparents had fought against the Portuguese in the 1800s. In the 1950s the Portuguese expropriated land of the Machels and numerous other Mozambicans in order to settle recently arrived Portuguese immigrants.

Although raised Presbyterian, Machel received Catholic baptism in order to enter the Catholic-monopolized education system. School officials regarded him as a rebel, yet offered him entrance into a seminary. Machel declined the offer; instead, he became a male nurse and then a medical assistant in the capital city of Lourenço Marques (now Maputo). He financed his training by working as a contract laborer in South Africa.

Machel's work in South Africa and in medical institutions furthered his anticolonialism, causing him to reject his *assimilado* status. The trying mine conditions had killed his older brother and other relatives. While in Mozambican hospitals, Machel reflected that the rich man's dog gets more in the way of vaccinations, medicine and medical care than do the workers upon whom the rich man's wealth is built.

In June 1962 three Mozambican exile groups formed the Front for the Liberation of Mozambique (FRELIMO). Fleeing the Portuguese secret police (PIDE) to Tanzania in 1963, Machel joined FRELIMO. He quickly impressed FRELIMO organizers, who selected him as one of FRELIMO's earliest military trainees in Algeria. Returning to Tanzania, Machel established FRELIMO's first training base. He subsequently commanded FRELIMO's first assault on Portuguese positions in September 1964. Machel headed FRELIMO's Niassa command, established the Nachingwea Center for Political and Military Training in Tanzania, and became FRELIMO's secretary of defense in October 1966 and a member of the party's Central Committee. Later he took over as commander in chief of FRELIMO's armed forces.

To lessen FRELIMO's military limitations, Machel employed Maoist, guerrilla, protracted war tactics, which drained the Portuguese capabilities while building up FRELIMO's political infrastructure. Machel waged a two-pronged political and military struggle to minimize the loss of soldiers and equipment. He established a strong political base among peasants to gain the military advantages of sanctuary, food, intelligence and recruits. In 1966 Machel abolished the division between FRELIMO's political and military wings.

Machel actively politicized the rural areas not only for immediate military advantage but also to create a new, nontribal Mozambique society. FRELIMO became a revolutionary, rather than solely a nationalist, organization. Against the desires of many Mozambican males, including most *regulos* (chiefs), FRELIMO raised women's status in 1967 by integrating them into the army. Increasingly FRELIMO opposed polygamy and initiation rites. Machel and FRELIMO replaced feudal authority with peoples' committees and clustered peasants together for protection and food production in prototypes of future collective villages.

FRELIMO's growing radicalism gained numerous recruits but divided the organization. Machel admitted that the ideological as well as the internecine and personal splits, which resulted in the murders of several FRELIMO militants, "paralyzed" FRELIMO between 1967 and 1969. The February 1969 assassination of Eduardo Mondlane,* FRELIMO's first president, was probably a joint operation by the Portuguese and party dissidents. It capped a moderate-radical struggle inside FRELIMO that saw Machel elected president in 1970.

Machel's units did not succeed in occupying a town until 1974, but the frustrations of junior officers in a conventionally trained European infantry, fighting a counterinsurgency campaign in Africa, helped trigger the Portuguese officers' coup of April 1974 in Lisbon. On September 7, 1974, Machel and Mario Soares, Portugal's foreign minister, signed a peace accord in Lusaka, Zambia, that established a cease-fire and a FRELIMO-dominated transitional government. On June 25, 1975, Mozambique received full independence with Machel as president.

FRELIMO was not prepared for its own success. It had a small number of activists (perhaps ten thousand) and was based in the north with only a token presence in Maputo. Machel, Mozambique's military liberator, governed with unquestioned authority from the outset. He quickly tried to bolster his southern organization with Dynamizing Groups (Grupos Dinamizadores), a form of participatory democracy. FRELIMO had not fully planned for a postindependence government and therefore had to improvise quickly with a bare minimum of bureaucratic expertise. It quickly antagonized the already-fearful Portuguese settlers by nationalizing land as well as the fields of law, medicine, education and funeral services. About half the Portuguese (some 110,000) had left at independence; most of the remainder departed within the next year, taking with them much of Mozambique's foreign exchange and technical knowledge.

Faced with an imminent collapse of the administration, a mutiny in December 1975 by several FRELIMO military units and the growing independence of a number of Dynamizing Groups, Machel and the Central Committee of the party invested the state with strong centralized authority to implement party decisions. The Party Congress established the means for socialistic transformation by converting FRELIMO from a mass movement into a Leninist vanguard party. Several purges of party ranks lessened the general quality of debate. In 1977 the Third Party Congress declared that "all the strategic sectors of the economy must be under state control: the state-owned sector of the economy will tend to be the principal source of state finance."

Machel's personal style of governing helped legitimate the new state to its citizens. Paradoxically, he gained popularity by serving as his government's most prominent critic. He removed unpopular administrators and instituted "legality offensives" against bullying security personnel. In front of large audiences Machel sometimes hectored leading officials to their faces. By listening and by sometimes acceding to public frustrations, Machel gained time and political maneuverability. Machel's humor when joking with his mass audiences or when criticizing his government ("We don't know how to rule. We just do a critique.")

added to his charismatic and quasi-ombudsman image. Yet Machel kept FRE-LIMO together—the Politburo remained unchanged between 1969 and 1983—by reshuffling, rather than purging, his administrators.

This contributed to the paradox of Mozambique in the 1980s: having a strong state but an increasingly weak nation. While maintaining political loyalty, it lessened efficiency by retaining incompetent officials. Machel's engaging personality proved important, especially with hard-liners, in retaining loyalty following the basic policy changes after 1983, which began undoing centralized authoritarian development.

Machel's early foreign policy surprised few observers. He viewed as interlinked the futures of independence struggles and existing black states: White minority rule in Rhodesia or South Africa would undermine neighboring black governments. The Rhodesian government continued its anti-ZANU military operations into Mozambique after FRELIMO's installation, and in March 1976 Machel cut economic ties with Rhodesia. A year later, during a visit of Soviet president Podgorny, Machel signed a twenty-year Treaty of Friendship and Cooperation with the Soviet Union. Machel had borrowed extensively from the Chinese revolutionary experience and had received most of his weapons from the People's Republic of China. Yet pragmatism—the Soviet Union could give more assistance (especially military) to independent Mozambique—as well as ideology—the Soviet Union's industrialization of a previously rural economy—appealed to the Mozambican leadership.

Economic difficulties, attributable to both happenstance and FRELIMO policies, increasingly plagued Machel's leadership. The late 1970s saw a drop in worldwide commodity prices. Inside Mozambique damaging droughts and floods reduced food production. The drought of 1981 to 1984 was the worst in southern Africa for half a century. FRELIMO's statist economic policies exacerbated Mozambique's circumstances: colonial underdevelopment, a continuing lack of skills and capital, Rhodesia's military destabilization, low commodity prices and poor weather. FRELIMO's vanguardism and "large-project mentality" excluded peasants from decision making and helped prompt major economic distortions. The favored state farms swallowed scarce foreign exchange. By 1981 the government admitted that not one state farm had turned a profit. Family farms produced 80 percent of Mozambique's produce even in 1983.

Machel's decision to support Zimbabwe's liberation struggle incurred substantial domestic costs. Increasing Rhodesian cross-border operations caused over $100 million in damage; and closure of Rhodesian trade in March 1976 cost Mozambique $400 million in foreign exchange. In 1976 South Africa cut the number of Mozambican miners from 115,000 to 40,000 and a year later stopped paying their wages at the old fixed official gold prices. In 1983 Mozambique declined to publish a national budget; by 1984 the country's GNP was half of that in 1973; by 1986 industrial and agricultural production had dropped 50 percent from 1981.

FRELIMO's centralization also hampered operations against the rebelling Mozambique National Resistance Movement (RENAMO). The South African military was employing RENAMO (formed inside Rhodesia following Mozambique's independence) as a terrorist group to destabilize Mozambique's economy. FRELIMO's economic policies, including forced collectivization, undercut traditional leaders, convincing some peasants to support RENAMO. The military transformation of FRELIMO's previously small-unit, locally tied guerrilla units into a conventionally trained and equipped force in central garrisons divorced the military from the peasantry.

More than foreign-educated FRELIMO members, notably Marcellino dos Santos, Machel based his policies largely upon experience, and Mozambique's difficulties belatedly forced policy changes. In 1982 Mozambique explored possibilities of membership in the Council for Mutual Economic Assistance (COMECON), the Soviet bloc's trade cooperation organization, overtures that were later rebuffed. The Fourth Party Congress in 1983 opted for decentralization of planning and a larger role for the private sector in order to boost food production and reduce inroads made by RENAMO. Seeing the shortcomings of his Marxist-inspired economy ("We have erroneously developed a hostile attitude to private enterprise that must be changed") and receiving inadequate aid from ideological allies, Machel turned to the West. By the end of 1984 Mozambique had joined the World Bank and the International Monetary Fund (IMF), had signed the Lomé Accords for trade with the European Community and had unveiled an attractive investment code.

The Nkomati Accord of March 16, 1984, capped Machel's controversial policy changes. The nonaggression pact with the hated apartheid regime in South Africa drew wide and often bitter criticism from previous allies in Africa. While Mozambique recognized the South African government de facto, the accord forced Machel to expel 800 South Africans, African National Congress (ANC) members, often at gunpoint. Machel countered that the Nkomati Accord was necessary to provide breathing room for economic recovery and that RENAMO's "bandits" could not survive without foreign assistance. But as RENAMO still grew after the accord, Machel drew increasing criticism for gambling on an international agreement that Mozambique followed but that, by many accounts, South Africa violated. RENAMO's continued growth also prompted questioning of Machel's contention that RENAMO had no indigenous political appeal.

Tensions between Mozambique and South Africa as well as Malawi had escalated in autumn 1986. On October 9, 1986, President Machel left Zambia after consulting with presidents dos Santos of Angola, Mobutu* of Zaire, Kaunda* of Zambia and Mugabe* of Zimbabwe. His Soviet-piloted night flight crashed inside South Africa, close to the Mozambique border. Machel and thirty-four others were killed. In July 1987 a commission composed of international aviation experts blamed the crash on the Soviet crew, but failed to convince numerous skeptics of South African innocence.

Machel's greatest domestic legacies were his leadership against Portuguese colonialism and his subsequent preservation of FRELIMO and Mozambique against tremendous odds. More than simply a nationalist seeking political independence from a colonial power, Machel campaigned continually for a new and more egalitarian Mozambican society. Economic and military damage amounting to $4 billion dollars between 1975 and 1985 kept much of his program from implementation. Yet Mozambique's social services improved, at least until the improvements were cancelled by RENAMO's destructiveness. Literacy rose from 5 to 20 percent, and rural health care aided millions of previously unreached Mozambicans. Although often depicted as an irrevocable ideologue, Machel contributed—by increasingly favoring limited democracy and decentralization and the introduction of private property—to a sense of political pragmatism that by 1991 had prompted FRELIMO to approve a multiparty system and a market economy.

Machel relied on personal charisma and his military experiences. In a country that lacked political institutions, Machel's personality gained significant support for the new state. As one writer observed, Machel exuded "an electric charge, a strength of personality, a kind of royal African experience" (Christie 1988:91). Upon his death, the institutions he had created and largely legitimated passed successfully to his successor, Mozambique's current ruler, Joaquim Chissano.

Regionally, Machel's own experiences led him to seek peaceful negotiations, even at the cost of ideological purity. Machel convinced Zimbabwe's Robert Mugabe at a crucial point to continue talks that led to independence and, later, to embrace the economically productive white population. Machel also served as a moderating influence upon Angola's José Eduardo dos Santos in the Namibian independence negotiations. Finally, Machel was a catalyst and then a constant supporter of the Southern African Development Coordination Conference (SADCC), which sought greater regional economic independence from South Africa.

BIBLIOGRAPHY

Works by Machel:

Mozambique: Sowing the Seeds of Revolution. London: Committee for Freedom in Mozambique, 1974.
The Tasks Ahead: Selected Speeches. New York: Afro-American Information Service, 1975.

Other Works:

American University, Foreign Area Studies. *Area Handbook for Mozambique*. 3d ed. Washington, D.C.: United States Government Printing Office, 1985.
Christie, Iain. *Machel of Mozambique*. Harare, Zimbabwe: Zimbabwe Publishing House, 1988.
Hanlon, Joseph. *Mozambique: The Revolution under Fire*. London: Zed Press, 1984.

Isaacman, Allen, and Barbara Isaacman. *Mozambique: From Colonialism to Revolution, 1900–1982*. Boulder, Colo.: Westview Press, 1983.

Munslow, Barry. *Mozambique: The Revolution and Its Origins*. London: Longman, 1983.

———. *Samora Machel, An African Revolutionary: Selected Speeches and Writings*. London: Zed Press, 1985.

HERBERT M. HOWE

NELSON ROLIHLAHLA MANDELA (1918–   ), Leader, African National Congress, Political Prisoner, 1962–1990; President, African National Congress, Republic of South Africa, 1991–

Africa's most famous living "prison graduate," Nelson Mandela, walked to freedom before the television cameras of the world on February 11, 1990. After serving twenty-seven and a half years, Mandela, at an age when most politicians have retired, is at the peak of a political career spanning almost five decades. The most prominent black South African leader of the continent's oldest political body, the African National Congress (ANC), founded in 1912, Mandela is in the forefront of the negotiations with the National Party government of South Africa for the end of apartheid and the establishment of a new nonracial South African political system. Mandela has passed through five stages of leadership— "young Turk," mobilizer and organizer, underground strategist, courtroom publicist and internationally recognized political prisoner—and is now in a sixth stage even more in the public eye as the active senior statesman of the black resistance in South Africa.

Nelson Mandela was born in 1918 in Umtata in the Transkei, a member of the royal Tembu family. Educated at missionary schools in the Transkei, he enrolled at Fort Hare University College, South Africa's first higher educational institution for Africans, in 1938, but was suspended in 1940 for participation in student protest. Moving to Johannesburg, he completed a B.A. degree through the University of South Africa in 1942. A year later he began work on a law degree at the University of the Witwatersrand, embarking upon a professional career in which legal representation and ANC politics increasingly fused.

While he was a part-time law student, Mandela was already deeply immersed in efforts to revitalize the ANC. A founding member of the Youth League of the ANC in early 1944, he participated in its lively debates about the nature and appropriate role of African nationalism in South Africa. He supported the push of the Youth League to galvanize the senior ANC into greater assertiveness. He also endorsed its emphasis upon African self-reliance, keeping distance from not only white liberals, but also Communist and Indian nationalist sympathizers. At first he did not take a prominent role, but in 1948 he was elected national secretary of the Youth League, and in 1950 he was elected national president.

With the passage of the Youth Leaque's Program of Action by the ANC in 1949, mandating greater militancy, Mandela also took responsibilities in the senior organization, achieving election to the ANC National Executive Committee. Reflecting the views of the Youth League, he remained distrustful of collaboration with Communists and Indians. But in response to the relentless post-1948 implementation of apartheid and the determined opposition to it by Communist and Indian activists, Mandela shifted his views in favor of united action against government policy. By the start of the Defiance Campaign in mid-1952 Mandela, as volunteer-in-chief, was at the center of the ANC-led civil disobedience actions, uniting Africans and antiapartheid volunteers of all races and ideological persuasions. With nineteen other leaders he stood trial in December 1952 under the Suppression of Communism Act and was given a suspended nine-month sentence, his first conviction for political activity.

In the words of his longtime friend and political associate, Oliver Tambo (retired ANC president), with whom he formed a law partnership in 1952, Mandela was "the born mass leader." Tambo's assessment was shared by both the ANC and the government. In the second half of 1952 Mandela was elected president of the Transvaal provincial ANC, and in December he was chosen deputy national president of the ANC. The government responded by banning Mandela from gatherings and travel outside of Johannesburg; denying the legitimacy of the bans, Mandela chose to keep his positions but to work beyond the public eye. In September 1953 new government restrictions required him to resign officially and not to attend meetings for five years. For the remainder of the decade Mandela concentrated upon organizational activity behind the scenes, devising the M-plan, named for himself, a scheme designed to build a grass-roots network of local ANC cells, linked through middle-level leaders, that could function efficiently without public meetings. Only during the long-running treason trial, from 1956 to 1961, in which 156 ANC members and their allies were charged but ultimately found not guilty, was Mandela highly visible as lawyer, witness and spokesman from the dock.

With the proscription of the ANC in 1960 Mandela and the ANC were confronted with a radically changed situation in which all legal political activity was foreclosed. Rallying supporters at the All-In African Conference in March 1961, Mandela then went underground to organize mass protest for a national convention of all races and against the declaration of an independent Republic of South Africa. When the three-day stay-at-home of May 29–31, 1961, met massive police repression and failed completely to deflect government policy, Mandela joined other leaders of the ANC and its allied organizations to rethink whether the strategy of nonviolence, in place since the inception of the ANC, should be changed. In mid-1961, with other leaders of the banned ANC and its ally, the Communist Party, Mandela formed Umkhonto we Sizwe to conduct sabotage and prepare for eventual guerrilla warfare. Popularly dubbed the "Black Pimpernel," he evaded arrest for incitement, slipping out of the country in late 1961 to travel to independent African states and England. He dramatically surfaced in January 1962 at the conference of the Pan-African Freedom Movement of East, Central and Southern Africa in Addis Ababa, offering arguments for the ANC's acceptance of the necessity of the use of violence. Returning to South Africa, he was apprehended eight months later and charged with incitement and leaving the country illegally.

Brought to trial in October 1962, Mandela conducted his own defense, articulating African grievances and aspirations as he challenged the right of the court to try him. Sentenced to five years, he was transported to Robben Island, off Cape Town. In late 1963, after the Rivonia raid of July, in which the authorities captured nine leaders at the underground headquarters of Umkhonto we Sizwe, Mandela was brought from prison to stand trial as a member of the high command. In a final statement from the dock, which received worldwide publicity, Mandela accepted the charge of sabotage and preparation for guerrilla warfare. Detailing his political philosophy, he labelled himself "an African patriot" and "a socialist" who had been influenced by Marxism, but in contrast to Communists, he was "an admirer" of the parliamentary systems of the West, regarding the British Parliament as "the most democratic institution in the world." He expressed similar admiration for "the American Congress, that country's doctrine of separation of powers, as well as the independence of its judiciary." In closing, he stated, "I have cherished the ideal of a democratic and free society in which all persons live together in harmony and with equal opportunities. It is an ideal which I hope to live for and to achieve. But if needs be, it is an ideal for which I am prepared to die." Receiving a life sentence (as did the other seven found guilty), instead of the death sentences that could have been passed, Mandela was returned to Robben Island with his six black codefendants.

For the next eighteen years Mandela lived in a single cell in a special section with other more prominent black political prisoners, sharing prison labor duties (which initially included a brutal routine of rock breaking) with all types of prisoners. Assertively demanding that the government adhere to prison regulations and that the prisoners be accorded political prisoner status, Mandela was in the forefront of successful efforts to represent the interests of all prisoners, regardless of their political affiliation. As an individual he reached out to prisoners whether or not they were ANC members, while simultaneously spearheading the organization of ANC discussion groups. Through his conduct he gained almost universal respect across the political spectrum, particularly in the period after the Soweto riots of 1976, when he and other ANC leaders succeeded in persuading many young black consciousness prisoners to adopt the nonracial stance of the ANC.

Placed at the center of the stage by a rising chorus of demands inside and outside South Africa for his release, Mandela and four companions were shifted in 1982 from Robben Island to Pollsmoor on the mainland, and then after a bout with tuberculosis in 1987, Mandela was placed in a cottage in Victor Verster Prison. Steadfastly refusing government offers of conditional release, Mandela deftly kept the government on the defensive through reports by visitors and statements smuggled to supporters. In 1986 government ministers began discussions with him, leading in 1988 to interviews with President Botha* and President de Klerk,* ultimately resulting in the unconditional release of Mandela's fellow Rivonia trialists and then Mandela himself.

Reiterating the closing words of his Rivonia trial statement hours after his release, Mandela threw himself immediately into the hectic politics of heightened expectations engendered by his release and the willingness of the new South African government under President de Klerk to lift the ban on the ANC and to enter into negotiations about a changed South African political system. By his achievements before his imprisonment on Robben Island he had moved to the front ranks of the leadership of the antiapartheid struggle. His conduct in prison, both as an individual and as a leader of the ANC, guaranteed that upon his release he would become the major black political leader in South Africa. Explicitly seeking to assuage white fears of majority rule, yet still fully committed to the ANC as a lifetime member, Mandela is uniquely placed at the culmination of his political career to facilitate the transition to the open, democratic and nonracial South Africa that he has sought through almost fifty years of political activity.

In 1990 Mandela conducted a triumphal tour of major cities in Europe and the United States, which included talks with prime ministers and presidents. Many supporters outside South Africa saw him as his country's president-in-waiting. But the difficult task of constructing the institutions of a postapartheid democratic state lay ahead. In mid-1991, at the first open convention of the ANC inside South Africa in over thirty years, Mandela was elected its president, replacing the crippled Oliver Tambo, who led the organization in the years of exile. At seventy-three years of age, Mandela faces what are probably his final challenges—building a national party and a state constitution that thrive on toleration, competition and consent, and building a party that not only wins free elections but acquires the capacity to govern a contentious society.

BIBLIOGRAPHY

Works by Mandela:

No Easy Walk to Freedom: Articles, Speeches and Trial Addresses. Ed. Ruth First. London: Heinemann Educational Books, 1965.
The Struggle Is My Life. Ed. International Defence and Aid Fund. New York: Pathfinder Press, 1986.

Other Works:

Benson, Mary. *Nelson Mandela: The Man and the Movement.* New York: W. W. Norton, 1986.
Johns, Sheridan, and R. Hunt Davis, Jr. (eds.). *Mandela, Tambo and the African National Congress: Forty-One Years of Struggle against Apartheid, 1948–1989.* New York: Oxford University Press, 1991.
Mandela, Winnie. *Part of My Soul Went with Him.* New York: W. W. Norton, 1984.
Meer, Fatima. *Higher Than Hope: Rolihlahla We Love You.* Johannesburg: Skotaville Publishers, 1988.

SHERIDAN JOHNS

QUETT KETUMILE JOHNNY MASIRE (1925–   ), President, Republic of Botswana, 1980–   .

Quett Masire began his political career in 1958 with his election to the Ngwaketse Tribal Council. In 1961 he became a member of the newly created Bechuanaland Legislative Council. When political parties emerged in the protectorate in the early 1960s, Masire joined with Seretse Khama,* the future first president of Botswana, and others to found the Bechuanaland (later Botswana) Democratic Party (BDP). As the party's principal organization man, Masire played a major role in building it into the effective vote-getting machine it has been for the last twenty-five years. From independence in 1965 to 1980, he was also vice president and minister of finance and development planning. More than any other politician, he gave political direction to the country's economic growth. When Khama died in July 1980, Quett Masire became the second president of Botswana. He has won re-election twice since then. The expectation is that he will serve as president until the end of his current term in 1994.

President Masire was born in Kanye, the capital of the Ngwaketse tribe (the second-largest tribe in the country). His father was a headman of low status in that the family came from Hurutshe (another Tswana tribe) rather than Ngwaketse stock. Masire was the oldest of six children. He spent his childhood as a herdsboy, entering primary school in Kanye at the age of thirteen. In 1944 he began his secondary education at Tiger Kloof in South Africa, finishing with a primary higher certificate and matriculation. Almost all the nationalist politicians of his generation attended the same institution shortly before or while Masire was there. Once back in Kanye in 1949 Masire took up teaching in a primary school. He also became active in various progressive causes. Most prominent was an association to establish the first secondary school in Kanye. He was selected to be its first headmaster, a duty he assumed while still teaching in primary school.

As a community activist, Masire was part of a group of educated young adults, sometimes referred to as "new men," who sought to modernize Ngwaketse society in ways that would be independent of the then very powerful chief, Bathoen II. Beginning with this period Masire found himself both clashing and cooperating with traditional authority. While Masire has recognized the need to allow chiefs to play a symbolic role in Botswana politics because of their prestige in the public mind, at the same time he has worked to strip them of as much political influence as possible. Even in the late 1980s he continued to pursue this point of view, as he transferred supervision of the major chiefs out of the Office of the President to the Ministry of Local Government and Lands to reduce the chiefs' status in the politics of the state.

Masire took up journalism as a career in 1957, working as the southern Bechuanaland correspondent for *African Echo,* a newspaper based in South Africa. However, when the BDP was established in 1962, he became a full-time organizer for the party, not only serving as its general secretary but also as editor of *Therisanyo,* the party newspaper. Contacts with colonial government officials at the highest levels, developed previously as a newspaper reporter, provided covert and critical information and ideas at important junctures in the development of the BDP. Many in the colonial government were so sympathetic to

Masire that they preferred him to Khama as the future head of the independent government.

Observers in the nationalist period give him primary credit for the BDP's growth as a political organization. It was the only party to field candidates in every constituency in the country in the 1965 elections. More important, it won 80 percent of the vote and twenty-eight of thirty-one seats in the Legislative Assembly. Masire was particularly renowned for organizing remote-area dwellers, who were among the poorest in the country.

Masire continued after independence to be general secretary of the party until he became president in 1980. The party won the 1969, 1974 and 1979 elections by commanding majorities. However, his personal abilities as a politician were dramatically tarnished when in 1969 the Ngwaketse chief, Bathoen, resigned as chief and beat Masire in the Kanye South Constituency with 71 percent of the vote. Masire continued as vice president by accepting a nominated position in the National Assembly. Fearing another drubbing from Bathoen in 1974, Masire ran in a safe BDP constituency.

Masire's reputation as a politician has suffered from the fact that he could not win election in his home area of Kanye. He is thus viewed as lacking the personality to campaign effectively. In the 1989 elections Masire made only a few last-minute appearances at political rallies, preferring to leave most of the speech making to his more dynamic ministers.

In his long tenure as minister of finance and development planning, Masire presided over the government ministry that designed and directed the rapid development of the Botswana economy. In spite of his completion of only a secondary education, his ability to absorb and debate complicated policy issues such as the advisability of changes in Botswana's exchange rate is much respected. His strategic plans as minister for the overall growth of the economy have succeeded to an extent that far exceeds any other such attempts in Africa.

The basic strategy was to invest available government resources during the 1970s in a mineral economy based on diamonds, copper and nickel, with profits distributed to other sectors in the 1980s. Real growth in the GNP averaged around 10 percent per annum between 1966 and 1980, and formal-sector employment increased by a similar margin during this period. In the 1980s an increasing portion of the total government budget, about one-third, was devoted to social-welfare expenditures, including a school system at both the primary and secondary levels. The most significant criticism of Masire's record of economic leadership, however, is that the country's income distribution is more skewed against the poor in 1990 than it was at independence.

Masire relied heavily on a cadre of expatriate economists to direct the government's massive investments. He also protected the power of the ministry staff to supervise all government expenditures so that corruption was minimized. While the BDP claims to be a capitalist party, the Botswana government is heavily involved in all sectors of the economy. It not only funds most development projects out of its profits from the mining sector, but it has formulated extensive regulations that constrict both foreign and domestic entrepreneurs. The civil servants view themselves, very much as the colonial government did, as protectors of the people against capitalism's ills. In recent years President Masire has responded to increasing demands from local entrepreneurs for less government regulation by some expansion of economic freedom and government support where locals are in competition with foreign capital.

Since 1980 Masire as president has concentrated on Botswana's foreign policy. His main concern is white-dominated South Africa and the problem of bringing about majority rule. He has refrained from having any formal political relations with either Pretoria or the African National Congress (ANC). However, informally and quietly, Botswana allowed ANC freedom fighters to move through the country. While eschewing formal political relations with his neighbor to the south, Masire has supported Botswana's membership in the South African Customs Union and has allowed, if not encouraged, extensive private South African investment in most sectors of the Botswana economy. To counter this form of white domination, Masire has taken a leadership role in the Southern African Development Coordination Conference (SADCC), which seeks to promote the economic development and integration of black-ruled states north of South Africa. In sum, while Masire has not often confronted the South African regime on the immorality of its apartheid system, he has sought to take practical steps, so long as Botswana's economy is not jeopardized, to show support for majority rule.

In domestic politics Masire follows executive tradition in leaving policy-making to civil servants until a political furor arises. New programs emerge from conflict and cooperation among the various ministries. Elected politicians (members of Parliament and local councilors) are largely relegated to petitioning for the interests of their local communities about programs already in place.

The heart of the BDP's overwhelming electoral majorities lies in the rural areas. Particularly important are two tribes, the Bakwena and the Bangwato, who see the BDP as representing their interests. The Masire government has sought to expand this constituency with a series of rural development programs. The government has not neglected other parts of the rural community. There are two programs to provide free or low-cost agricultural inputs of various kinds to small and medium-size farmers. In addition, during the drought of 1982 to 1987 the government waived repayment of short-term crop loans and interest on agricultural capital investments. Many farmers thus see the BDP government as their benefactor.

President Masire's record on political rights is impressive. He has shown little concern with public criticism by opposition politicians in Parliament or at political rallies. No members of the opposition have been put in jail or have gone into exile. None have even had their passports revoked, as did happen under President Khama. During Masire's rule the first private newspapers have emerged. Despite the distress they have caused the president with their occasional exposés, he has not closed one down, although two BDP supporters did buy one of the newspapers when it became particularly troublesome. In 1987 the University of Botswana was closed when students demonstrated peacefully. The cabinet, with Masire's support, took this action more because such behavior contradicts the norm of silent obedience expected of youth in Botswana society than because the regime was threatened.

Masire's rule as president has been characterized by rapid economic growth, massive expansion of government social services and the emergence of a significant African business class. But the urban population is growing much faster than available housing (the population of the capital is expected to triple by the year 2000), resulting in severe overcrowding among lower-income groups. Much of the rural population, despite the many agricultural and welfare programs, increasingly feels excluded from the rapid economic development. Growing numbers of youths are unemployed, or if employed, are disillusioned with the incompetence of their less educated seniors and the continuing presence of a sizeable expatriate technician class. Trade unions in the fast-growing wage sector are frustrated by the government's refusal to free them from regulations constraining their ability to organize and bargain for their members.

Many question whether President Masire will be able to deal with these problems when they lead to open discontent. In recent years he has preferred to rely on civil servants rather than politicians for advice. After the 1989 election he appointed his senior permanent secretary minister of finance and development planning and the top army general to the post of minister of presidential affairs. In effect, the most powerful ministerial appointments went to persons who had never been active in politics. The president appears to prefer to solve problems by dealing with skilled bureaucrats rather than allowing the disorder of politics to intrude on his choices. It is possible that Masire's government will not have the ability at the highest levels to listen and react to the discontent generated by the massive social and economic change taking place. The struggle for succession could become politically destabilizing, and the image of Masire's regime and party could be considerably tarnished.

BIBLIOGRAPHY

Harvey, Charles, and Stephen R. Lewis, Jr. *Policy Choice and Development Performance in Botswana.* London: Macmillan, 1990.
Holm, John D. "Botswana: A Paternalistic Democracy." In Larry Diamond, Juan J. Linz and Seymour Martin Lipset (eds.), *Democracy in Developing Countries,* vol. 2, *Africa.* Boulder, Colo.: Lynne Rienner Publishers, 1988, 179–216.
Holm, John D., and Patrick P. Molutsi (eds.). *Democracy in Botswana.* Athens, Ohio: Ohio University Press, 1989.
Morton, Fred, and Jeff Ramsay (eds.). *The Birth of Botswana: A History of the Bechuanaland Protectorate from 1910–1966.* Gaborone: Longman Botswana, 1987.
                                         JOHN D. HOLM AND NEIL PARSONS

TOM MBOYA (1930–1969), Trade Union and Party Secretary-General, Government Minister, Republic of Kenya, 1953–1969.

In a public career spanning nearly two decades, Tom Mboya occupied the center stage in the labor movement and nationalist politics of Kenya. The combination of intellectual brilliance and political vision made him an outstanding Kenyan and African. His public career was launched at the height of Mau Mau, the anticolonial rebellion. In the subsequent years Mboya lent his organizational ability and political brilliance to the creation and leadership in 1955 of the Kenya Federation of Labor as its secretary-general; the founding and steering of the Kenya African National Union (KANU) in 1960, again as its secretary-general; and the consolidation of the postindependence state as the most illustrious cabinet minister, as well as chief ideologist and strategist.

The politics of decolonization in Kenya had a strong Pan-Africanist dimension, and Mboya was the linkman with the political leadership, regionally in the Pan-African Freedom Movement for the East and Central Africa (PAFMECA) and continentally in the All-African People's Conference and its labor constituency, the All-African Trade Union Confederation. Postindependence politics, immediately after the event in 1963, were about direction; here Mboya steered economic policy into the pro-Western capitalist camp. They were also about giving the new state a voice in the corridors of power in the United States and at the organs of the United Nations, such as the Economic Commission for Africa (ECA) and the General Agreement on Tariffs and Trade (GATT), as well as in the International Confederation of Free Trade Unions (ICFTU). Mboya's was that voice. In the decade of the 1960s Mboya signified the youth and ambition of Africa's newly won independence.

Thomas Joseph Odhiambo Mboya ("Tom") was born on August 15, 1930, on a European-owned sisal estate at Kilimambogo in Central Kenya to Luo-AbaSuba parents from Rusinga Island in Western Kenya. He was situated from childhood to be a Kenyan, as his surroundings were inhabited by Luo, Kikuyu and Akamba laborers. Mboya received a Roman Catholic education at elementary and high schools before training as a sanitary inspector and later taking a job in Nairobi.

His public career began at age twenty, when he joined the Nairobi African Local Government Servants' Association. The outbreak of Mau Mau was a crucial event in his life: Older political and trade-union leaders were arrested by the British, and a leadership vacuum was created amidst Nairobi's urban Africans. Mboya rose to the occasion. He resigned his employment in 1953 and became a full-time labor leader as secretary-general to the Kenya Federation of Registered Trade Unions, which in 1955 became the Kenya Federation of Labor (KFL). This umbrella organization pursued the popular mass goals of the time: It advocated the right of the workers to form unions, agitated for a raise in pay from a "boy's wage" to a "family wage," and urged employers to provide housing and contracts. Its political demands included lifting of the emergency that the British had imposed on the country. The federation insisted on the rights of the Africans to assembly, freedom of expression and a free press. At the same time it urged the ending of racial apartheid—"color bar," as it was called in public places—and of the harassment of the Kikuyu, Embu and Meru ethnic nationalities on the arbitrary assumption that they were fomenting Mau Mau, and it proclaimed the rights of the Africans to elective representation in the colonial legislature. The KFL in effect advocated an economic and political solution as opposed to a military solution to the colonial crisis in Kenya. Mboya wrote numerous petitions and memoranda to the local administration and commissions of enquiry and represented the Africans generally at the various rendezvous with the local authorities and visiting British parliamentary and humanist groups.

The year 1955 catapulated him into countrywide prominence as a skillful negotiator between the Mombasa dockworkers and their employer. Mboya successfully talked the workers off a strike and achieved for them a 30 percent pay raise. For the next two years he extended his trade-union and political horizons internationally through travel, study and writing. He affiliated his KFL with the ICFTU and with the AFL-CIO trade-union organization in the United States. He traveled in Belgium, Germany and the United States, making powerful linkages with workers' leaders. He also did this in Britain, where he studied at Ruskin College, Oxford, in the 1955–56 academic year, making useful allies with the British Trade Union Congress (TUC) and with humanist intellectuals, such as Fenner Brockway and Margery Perham.

His return to Kenya at the end of 1956 launched the next stage of his growth. For the next seven years the consuming agenda in Kenya was the constitutional struggle for independence. Mboya was thrice elected to the legislature by an urban constituency in Nairobi, a placement that centered him in the thick of this struggle. He played the orator in the legislature and became a spokesperson for freedom for all of colonial Africa. The political platform was his stage, and he played the politics of the hero and the crowd to its fullest extent at political rallies in his capacity as an elected member and as leader of the African Caucus in the Legislative Council. He also gained regional stature as a leading member of PAFMECA, as well as an active participant in Kwame Nkrumah's* Pan-African solidarity conferences. At the age of twenty-eight Mboya chaired the All-African People's Conference in Accra in December 1958. But the basic constituency remained Kenya where, once Jomo Kenyatta* was proclaimed the genuine leader of all Africans, the call for freedom and Kenyatta—*uhuru na Kenyatta*—rose to frenzy pitch. The political struggle also called for political organization. Mboya's Nairobi People's Convention Party, founded in 1957, became his launching pad. A milestone in this endeavor was the formation of KANU in 1960. KANU became the premier nationalist organization. Mboya was its mobilizational secretary-general and articulate negotiator at the constitutional conferences at Lancaster House, London, in 1960 and 1962, which culminated in the attainment of African self-government in Kenya in December 1963.

Independence launched Mboya into perhaps the most innovative phase of his life. For the next six years he was the architect of key institutions of the postcolonial state in Kenya and the most innovative formulator of its future. In addition, Mboya was the most formidable practitioner of competitive party politics, while he was also the most sophisticated intellectual debater in President Kenyatta's cabinet.

Mboya's contribution to Kenyan governance lay in institution building. His first ministerial innovation appropriately had been as minister of labor in the immediate preindependence cabinet of 1962. In a season heady with workers' strikes Mboya negotiated and got approved the Industrial Relations Charter, an instrument outlining the parameters of industrial relations and the machinery for settling industrial disputes from the shop floor all the way to the Industrial Court, set up in 1964. Industrial relations were thus stabilized, routinized and, in Mboya's view, modernized in Kenya for the first time.

His second assignment, as minister for justice and constitutional affairs in 1964, involved the drawing up and setting up of a unitary and republican constitution to replace the regionalist and cumbersome constitution that the British had bequeathed. By the end of 1964 this was achieved both instrumentally and legislatively: The postcolonial state thus acquired political legitimacy, imbued with a constitution that entrenched democratic freedoms, the Bill of Rights, the supremacy of Parliament, multiparty democracy and the independence of the judiciary and the public, police and army commissions. The foundations of democratic institutions were thus laid.

Thereafter, Mboya became minister for economic planning and development, a post he held until 1969. This was a crucial assignment in terms of theoretical conceptualization, policy formulation and practical implementation. Mboya's vision was pragmatic: He opted for a capitalist, mixed economy, in part because the framework was already in place, but also as a matter of preference. Mboya envisaged a society where economic development would take place as a result of a concert of local investment and labor, driven by capital investment or borrowing from the West. This developmental paradigm was in vogue in the modernization era of the 1960s and was embraced both by local economic planners and their advisors from Western universities and institutions, such as the World Bank. But Mboya sold the package as the logical path of progress, given Kenya's endogenous development to that point. He reified the discussion into the ideological plane by positioning himself against the "socialist" option advocated by his populist opponents and by stealing their rhetorical thunder in his claim that his strategy embodied the communocratic values of traditional Africa.

African Socialism and Its Application to Planning in Kenya, Parliamentary Sessional Paper no. 10 of 1965, encapsulated Mboya's outlook. This seminal document provided protection for foreign investment and argued against nationalization strategies. Formulated under the prosperous commodity trade setting of that decade, it stabilized the policy climate and laid the foundation for the economic prosperity of the 1960s. The often-applauded "Kenya miracle" that carried through to the end of Kenyatta's regime in 1978 was thus Mboya's miracle.

These policy choices were of course disputed with regard to their theoretical soundness, their practicality, their political expediency and their impact on national sovereignty vis-à-vis the enunciated foreign-policy goals of nonalignment and anti-imperialism. It was a measure of his ability—and a mark of the practice of his leadership—that Mboya debated his position with all and sundry who took him on. He embodied the politics of intellect. In his praxis he thus institutionalized open, public debate on policy issues as a significant feature of Kenya's political culture. His catchment area for debate ranged from the parliamentary oppositions posed by the right-wing Kenya African Democratic Union (KADU) until 1964 and by the populist Kenya People's Union (KPU) from 1966 to university students, local trade unionists, the Luo nation, radical Pan-Africanists operating from Nkrumah's Ghana and the international labor movement. Often an exasperating, cunning debater, he was confident and self-reliant, but so were his many academic and political adversaries. What he did was to sanctify competitive politics as a feature of public life in Kenya, a game one lost or won in the open. The idea of the open society was central to his vision.

For coalitions and political backup, Mboya relied on KANU, of which he was secretary-general. KANU was also his instrument in his Machiavellian quest for power and his shield in the buffeting that his enterprise involved. While Kenyatta reigned over the state, Mboya's political space was the party headquarters, its many manifestoes and electoral statements, and its public retorts and innuendoes against both individual and party opponents. Mboya turned KANU into his machine for visibility, as well as the source of the public authority that the government claimed. The role of the party was a favorite theme in his many lectures and pamphlets. On this score, Mboya enhanced the party system and party rule in Kenya, thereby encouraging competitive intraparty politics (KANU-A and KANU-B) as well as multiparty politics, as KANU battled the opposition in the period 1966–69. Factions and alliances were formed and reformed and coalitions were made and broken. This was Mboya's turf—*siasa*, politics. Yet it did unmake him, finally, through an assassin's bullet on July 5, 1969. A faction within KANU-A, afraid that Mboya might use the system to succeed Kenyatta, organized the fatal shot.

What was his legacy? For Kenya, three layers of his contribution stand out. First, there was the insistence on being a Kenyan, riding high above the ethnic and chauvinistic claims that engaged most of his contemporaries. If new nations are imagined communities, Mboya's career was throughout infused by this imagination. This insistence placed him at odds with the Bonapartist/patrimonial tendencies of the Kenyatta state and also with the recidivist "tribalism" of Kenya's intelligentsia. Second, there was his successful input into institution building: He made Parliament active and relevant, launched constitutional rule in a post–Mau Mau Kenya, and built political organization and clout for his party. Third, there was his practice of leadership, visible and articulate. This practice was informed by a vision, one of the Kenya that might have been, informed by coherent ideas about society and development. To this practice,

Mboya brought style: fast-paced, witty and tenacious to declared principles and platforms. In his region, East Africa, he worked actively for the creation and sustenance of an intellectual community through active engagement in discourses about development and nationhood. Mboya provoked, through his witting alliances with the West, debates about the futures of Pan-Africanism, nonalignment and international labor solidarity, about Africa's affiliations with the development agencies of the West, and about the vicissitudes of continental leadership. As a representation of Africa, Mboya signified youthful ambition.

Did he end in failure? The poetics of his exit suggested so at the time: He did not become president. Yet the painful quest for Kenya's second independence that has been taking place in the country throughout the 1980s, culminating in the open calls for redemocratization of society in the 1990s, signal the need for a revisit to Mboya's imagined Kenya.

BIBLIOGRAPHY

Works by Mboya:

Freedom and After. London: Andre Deutsch, 1963.
The Challenge of Nationhood. London: Andre Deutsch, 1970.

Other Works:

Goldsworthy, David. *Tom Mboya: The Man Kenya Wanted to Forget*. Nairobi: Heine-·
    mann, 1982.
Leys, Colin. *Underdevelopment in Kenya: The Political Economy of Neo-Colonialism*.
    Berkeley: University of California Press, 1974.
Odhiambo, Atieno, and Peter Wanyande. *History and Government of Kenya*. Nairobi:
    Longman Press, 1988.
Schatzberg, Michael G. (ed.). *The Political Economy of Kenya*. New York: Praeger,
    1987.

ATIENO ODHIAMBO

MENGISTU HAILE MARIAM (1936[1939?]–), Vice Chairman, Provisional Military Administrative Council, Chairman, President, People's Republic of Ethiopia, 1974–1991.

In 1974 a military junta overthrew the moribund government of Emperor Haile Selassie* and created the Provisional Military Administrative Council (PMAC), which, in turn, established the People's Democratic Republic of Ethiopia (PDRE) in 1987. Mengistu Haile Mariam has, almost from the beginning, been identified with and has symbolized the best and worst qualities, the triumphs and failures, the hours of glory and moments of shame, of that Ethiopian revolution. Because he was the child of an extremely poor and deprived family, his social and political values and his economic and ethnic background were readily to identify him with the temperament, attitude and goals of the masses.

Unlike his octogenarian imperial predecessor, who had represented only the values of the dominant Amhara nation and an exhausted and corrupt order, the young, dynamic army major from one of the hitherto despised and exploited ethnic groups of southern Ethiopia captured the imagination of a generation of Ethiopians. Later, however, he was considered to have subverted the people's revolution, destroying its message of hope and nullifying its few achievements. He was regarded as the worst of men by a majority that felt betrayed when he failed to restructure the Ethiopian state, to engender the democratic rights of individuals and groups and to lift the country from its socioeconomic morass.

Mengistu played a leading role in all the changes—both progressive and reactionary—that engulfed the country. He is closely identified with the artic-ulation, clarification and implementation of policies that not only constantly changed the nature and purpose of the PMAC but also defined its methods. He also equally influenced the ideological refinement that transformed the revolution from an incoherent and disoriented populism based on an enigmatic slogan, Ethiopia First, through a militant, third-worldish "Ethiopian socialism" to a professed Marxism-Leninism. Accordingly, he alone is commended for the achievements of the revolution and is accused of all its excesses, of the worsening conditions of the people, of the seemingly permanent division among the peoples of the country and the region and of endangering the future of the Ethiopian state.

There is scanty information about Mengistu's early life, and his official bio-graphical data reveal almost nothing. This has led to many rumors and much speculation about his pedigree, his personality and his life-style. He was born probably in 1936, perhaps 1939, in the southwestern town of Jimma, the first of five children of an army sergeant. His mother died when he was very young. He spent most of his young life with his father, a member of an Omotic ethnic group, in Jimma, where he went to school. Thus Mengistu was born outside the milieu that would have enabled him to belong to the elite of the country and to be groomed for leadership. Inevitably, his extreme destitution and his low station shaped his political views and attitudes.

He was forced by hardship to enlist at an early age in the "boys" (juvenile) unit of the army, at half the regular pay, and was transferred to the regular (adult) force at eighteen. He finished ninth grade while in the army, whereupon he became a candidate for officer training at the Holetta Military School. He was commissioned a second lieutenant in 1962 and was immediately assigned to the Ordnance Unit with his father. He was to remain until the revolution in similarly unimpressive posts. In 1965 he was sent to the United States for further training in ordnance at Aberdeen, Maryland. His Foreign Ministry official bi-ographical data mention that he attended the University of Maryland during this brief visit, but this remains unverified. There is nothing in his military record to indicate that he saw action before the revolution or that he was cited for distinguished service. On the contrary, there is evidence that he was repeatedly reprimanded for insubordination, disorderly conduct and slovenliness.

Mengistu's revolutionary past was exaggerated by the government media. However, he is known to have associated with various radical individuals and groups and to have been an active member of a political cell created by junior officers in the Third Army Division in Harrar. As a member of this cell, he travelled to several army camps across the country, secretly agitating the rank and file, denouncing Haile Selassie's government and attempting to prepare for a general uprising.

Although an energetic and committed activist, he was not a revolutionary intellectual with definite philosophical views. It is not at all certain, despite his affectations and official claims, that he was a Marxist-Leninist, but he effectively used that ideology to legitimize his rule, to consolidate power and to vent his animus. On the other hand, Mengistu, like Haile Selassie before him, demonstrated that not only was he a consummate intriguer and skilled manipulator of men and situations, but that he also had an acute sense of timing and an instinct to increase and retain power and to avert disaster. The "creeping," as opposed to the classical coup, that succeeded in overthrowing Haile Selassie was forcefully advocated by him, although it was reputedly the brainchild of his relative and mentor, the éminence grise of the time, Dejazmatch Kebede Tessema.

Mengistu's rise and his consolidation of power are a study in contrast. He was at once cautious and daring. He readily forfeited short-term gains for long-range victories. While he was supportive of friends, he was quick to cut losses and to minimize damage. In April 1974 the Coordinating Committee of the Armed Forces, Police and Territorial Army was created. Mengistu quickly and audaciously manipulated his way to the chairmanship. In September 1974 the PMAC was created. Mengistu correctly assessed that an outsider was preferred for the chairmanship and forcefully led the campaign to install the popular Eritrean army general, Aman Michael Andom, thus securing the first vice chairmanship. After his clash with Aman over the issue of Eritrean autonomy he orchestrated his elimination and execution and then the elevation of an Oromo brigadier, Tafari Banti, to the chairmanship. In February 1977 Mengistu assumed the chairmanship after his daring putsch against Tafari and six of his colleagues who, only a few weeks earlier, had stripped him of meaningful power. Mengistu's rivals were again executed. In three short years an obscure and ungainly "outsider" had, against all odds, become Ethiopia's new head of state and government.

Subsequently, Mengistu initiated and completed several political and legal maneuvers to make himself uncontested leader and absolute dictator. He repeatedly purged the state and party bureaucracies to create both a ruling elite that served his will and a political climate that ensured his pre-eminence. Within a short time he had eliminated or subdued individuals or groups who were actual or potential threats. By 1990 less than a handful of his erstwhile colleagues in the PMAC were in any positions of power. All enjoyed their tenure at Mengistu's pleasure, as evidenced by the sudden fall of Prime Minister Fikre-Selassie Wogderess, a long-time ally. Mengistu assumed the messianic duty of defining the purpose and goal of the revolution, presenting himself as the indispensable revolutionary leader of the masses and the only guarantor of the fragile unity and territorial integrity of the nation. His decisions determined policy, his perceived attitudes and expected reactions influenced bureaucratic decision making, and his pronouncements became the premises for policy analyses.

As Haile Selassie had done, Mengistu set out to create a new ruling elite as soon as he assumed power, and, like him, he pursued an inclusive policy. In spite of official commitment to class struggle, the organs he created, including his clandestine political movement, Abiyotawi Seded (revolutionary flame), the Committee for Organizing the Party of the Working Peoples of Ethiopia (COPWE), the Workers' Party of Ethiopia (WPE) and the state bureaucracy, were all formed by elements other than "leftists," including members of the old ruling classes and political elite. Most members were enlisted from the army. The core of the elite consisted of members of his family, his friends from the Third Army Division or the Holetta Military School and a few members of the PMAC. Each owed his or her position to Mengistu either directly or indirectly and maintained it as long as he or she identified with and was loyal, devoted and obsequious to him. The elite was highly factionalized and struggled for power, privilege and benefits. In what was essentially a patrimonial system, corruption, nepotism and cronyism were inevitable.

Mengistu exercised power and social control through an elaborate system of party and state bureaucracies as well as mass organizations. Theoretically, the WPE was the source of power and the Politburo, as the highest organ of the party, formulated policy and transmitted it for implementation by the party and state bureaucracies and mass organizations. In reality, Mengistu's power was unlimited. He was the party and he was the state. The 1987 constitution legitimized, rationalized and formalized this führerist reality.

Mengistu's leadership style, however, was a tribute to traditional Ethiopian values, rather than to Leninist principles. His political proclivities were molded by values and attitudes emanating from the Byzantine mind-set of feudal Ethiopia. His heroes were the "unifier" emperors, Theodros II and the expansionist Menelik II, rather than the theoretician and party boss Lenin. He sought inspiration more from Ethiopian history than from Marxist theory, hence the "nationalist"/ Marxist paradox and confusion surrounding him. To him, socialism was, in fact, not an end but a means to maintain Greater Ethiopia. This article of faith became the ruthlessly enforced foundation of the new Ethiopian order. It resulted in dire consequences, depriving Ethiopia of realistic leadership and leading to repeated mistakes in policies as well as to brutalities in their execution.

The foreign policy of the country, however, was determined not by ideological considerations and affinities but by the need to obtain armaments to defend a state vulnerable to threats from neighbors and internal upheavals, as witnessed in the war with Somalia (1977), the escalation in 1977 and 1982 of the Eritrean conflict and the proliferation of regional subnational liberation movements from 1975 onwards. Only the Soviet Union was a ready source of aid after 1976. The United States suspended its military assistance program in the early years of the Carter administration due to the new regime's human-rights record and the nationalization without compensation of U.S. companies. Massive Soviet aid and East European, Cuban and South Yemeni military personnel enabled Ethiopia to recover Ogaden Province and rebuff the Tigrean and Eritrean liberation movements in the late 1970s. As a result, Ethiopia's foreign policy grew dependent on the goals and interests of the USSR.

In 1978 Mengistu was also at the pinnacle of domestic power. This was his finest hour. However, victory was short-lived and pyrrhic. The bankruptcy of the military option in resolving political problems became glaringly evident. On the one hand, Eritrea in effect won its struggle for self-determination when units of the Eritrean People's Liberation Front (EPLF) captured Asmara, the Eritrean capital, on May 24, 1991. On the other hand, Mengistu's regime came to a total and inglorious end when the forces of the Ethiopian People's Revolutionary Democratic Front (EPRDF), an umbrella organization representing several opposition fronts and movements, entered Addis Ababa on May 28, 1991, exactly one week after Mengistu fled to Zimbabwe.

Ethiopia's client-patron relationship with the USSR weakened its role in international and regional institutions, its position on major international issues and its relations with other countries. In particular, it caused the drastic erosion of Ethiopia's former prestigious role in African diplomacy and its once-dominant position in the Organization of African Unity (OAU).

Mengistu's regime played a more visible and perhaps more significant role in the liberation struggle in southern Africa by training thousands of Zimbabwean (both Zimbabwe African National Union [ZANU] and Zimbabwe African People's Union [ZAPU]) and Namibian (South West Africa People's Organization [SWAPO]) freedom fighters, by rendering expert advice via the Ethiopian military to these movements, by allowing the wide use by southern African liberation movements of the broadcasting facilities of powerful radio stations and by supplying Soviet weaponry. Yet even these movements have viewed Ethiopia's close association with the Soviet Union with suspicion. The governments of Sudan, Kenya and Djibouti in the region many times were convinced that Ethiopia, until the Gorbachev era, had been a destabilizing agent of the Soviet Union.

Mengistu's domestic policy reflected and suffered from the needs of a militarized state, which undermined the socioeconomic programs, from land reform to accelerated expansion of education, initiated during the early years of the revolution. The land-reform program in its initial stages seemed popular. It was followed by the nationalization of many industries, financial institutions and services and then by a series of two-year development plans, including the Green Campaign, a program to intensify agricultural production. In 1980 the government launched the Ten-Year Perspective Plan for overall development. All these programs were to no avail. Agricultural production, after an initial spurt, steadily deteriorated as the government in villagization and resettlement alienated the peasantry. The state farms became victims of mismanagement, misuse of funds, equipment breakdown and flight of trained manpower. Ethiopia became a net importer of food. The problem was exacerbated in 1984 by a disastrous drought and war. Recurrent famine plagued the countryside in the late 1980s. Ethiopia had to be repeatedly rescued by the international community. The lack of foreign exchange and raw materials and the exodus of experts, compounded by incompetent management, caused most factories to operate at a very low capacity, although labor had been brutalized to docility. Only military production and the operation of allied industries performed efficiently.

Although the policies of the government were purportedly predicated on the needs of the deprived, social services, in fact, were worse than in imperial times. The regime had emphasized and claimed credit for the expansion of education. Facts disprove this. The government's per capita expenditure on education was less than that of the previous regime. After adjustment for inflation, the difference in real terms was larger. A much-vaunted literacy campaign, in spite of early recognition by UNESCO, produced unimpressive results, since the neoliterates have relapsed into their previous condition.

Health, transportation and housing, also slated for improvement, did not fare better. Whatever was achieved in the way of hospitals, roads and buildings was based on the needs of the military and the war effort alone. In fifteen years Mengistu's regime succeeded only in escalating social strife, exacerbating deprivation and rekindling latent hostilities and primordial fears of government. Mengistu will be remembered for the catastrophe that befell the country during his rule, for the barbarity of his methods and for the incompetence and corruption of his regime. He will be remembered by members of the ancien régime as a national aberration—a commoner/outsider who usurped power and, as expected, misused it. To the majority, he will represent the betrayal of a popular revolution.

He will also be remembered for what he failed to do. He might have secured for himself an honorable place in Ethiopian history—even in failure—if he had fought for the message of the revolution. Once he had abandoned it, he could not be but an ignominious failure. Unlike his idol, Theodros II, Mengistu in the end sought refuge outside the country, rather than dying for his beliefs.

Perhaps the beginning of a repudiation of Mengistu's legacy will come as a result of a charter drawn up at the National Conference on Peace and Democracy, convened on July 1–5, 1991, by the EPRDF-controlled transitional government of Ethiopia and attended by at least seventeen national political fronts, movements and groups. The message as well as the spirit of the charter was that of compromise and tolerance, necessary ingredients of a new and possibly democratic Ethiopia of the future.

BIBLIOGRAPHY

Ghebre-Negus, Michael. "Inside the Dergue: Memoirs of an Ex-Member of the Provisional Military Administrative Council of Ethiopia." *Adulis* (1987): special issue.
Giorgis, Dawit Wolde. *Red Tears: Famine, Revolution and War in Ethiopia*. Trenton, N.J.: Red Sea Press, 1987.
Harbeson, John. *The Ethiopian Transformation*. Boulder, Colo.: Westview Press, 1988.
Keller, Edmond J. *Revolutionary Ethiopia: From Empire to People's Republic*. Bloomington: Indiana University Press, 1988.
Lefort, Rene. *Ethiopia: An Heretical Revolution*. London: Zed Press, 1983.

Ministry of Foreign Affairs (Ethiopia). *Short Biographical Sketch of Comrade Chairman Mengistu Haile-Mariam, Chairman of the Provisional Military Administrative Council and the Council of Ministers and Commander-in-Chief of the Revolutionary Army.* Addis Ababa, 1978.

Ottaway, Marina, and David Ottaway. *Ethiopia: Empire in Revolution.* New York: Africana Publishing Company, 1978.

Vivo, Raul Valdes. *Ethiopia's Revolution.* New York: International Publishers, 1978.

AMARE TEKLE

MOBUTU SESE SEKO (1930–   ), Chief of Staff of the Armed Forces, President, Republic of Zaire, 1960–   .

Among Africa's postcolonial autocrats, President Mobutu Sese Seko of Zaire epitomizes the tough, wily, durable opportunist, whose career and the condition of the country he has led since 1960 reflect the tragedy of Africa's decades of "flag independence"—the neocolonial relationship between the state and its citizens and between the state and its foreign patrons. Mobutu was born in the town of Lisala, on the Zaire River, on October 14, 1930. He is a Ngbandi, a member of an ethnic community whose domain lies in the northernmost portion of Equateur Region. His father, Albéric Bemany, was a cook for a colonial magistrate in Lisala. Mobutu has referred frequently both to his father's humble occupation as a cook and to the renown of his father's uncle, a warrior and diviner from the village of Gbadolite, in Mobayl-Mbongo Zone. Mobutu was given the name of his great-uncle, Sese Seko Nkuku wa za Banga ("all-conquering warrior, who goes from triumph to triumph"). When (under his "authenticity" policy) Zairians were obliged to adopt "authentic" names, Mobutu dropped Joseph-Desire and made Sese Seko Nkuku wa za Banga his official postnames.

Mobutu's mother was Marie-Madeleine Yemo. Before marrying Bemany, Yemo had borne four children as one of many spouses of a prominent Ngbandi chief. She followed Bemany to Lisala, then accompanied him first to Mbandaka and then to the colonial capital of Leopoldville (now Kinshasa), where he died in 1938. The widowed Yemo left the capital with her children, first for Mbandaka, then for Gbadolite. Following a conflict with the paternal family, she left Gbadolite with her children. In later years her son would honor "Mama Yemo" by naming Kinshasa's largest hospital after her.

Mobutu, who had completed four years of primary school in Kinshasa, took seven more years to reach the secondary level, moving in and out of schools in Gemena, Libenge and Mbandaka. He had frequent conflicts with the Catholic missionaries whose schools he attended. In 1950, at the age of nineteen, he was definitively expelled. A seven-year disciplinary conscription into the Force Publique (the colonial army) followed. Military service proved crucial in shaping Mobutu's career. Unlike many recruits, he spoke excellent French, which quickly won him a desk job. By November 1950 he was sent to the school for noncommissioned officers in Kanaga. There he came to know many members of the military generation who would assume control of the army after the flight of the Belgian officers in 1960.

In 1952 Mobutu was transferred to army headquarters in Kinshasa. By the time of his discharge in 1956 he had risen to sergeant-major, the highest rank open to Zairians, in the accounting section. He also had begun to write newspaper articles under a pseudonym. Mobutu returned to civilian life just as decolonization began to appear possible. His articles had brought him to the attention of Pierre Davister, a Belgian liberal and editor of the Kinshasa journal *L'Avenir*. At that time a European patron was of enormous benefit to an ambitious Zairian; under Davister's tutelage Mobutu became an editorialist for the new African weekly, *Actualités africaines*. Davister later would provide valuable services by giving favorable coverage to the Mobutu regime as editor of his own Belgian weekly, *Special*.

Mobutu thus acquired visibility among the emergent African elite of Kinshasa. Yet one portal to status in colonial society remained closed to him; recognition as an *évolué* ("civilized" African) depended upon approval by the Catholic church. Denied this recognition, Mobutu refused to perform a Catholic marriage with his wife, boycotted the Catholic newspaper *Courrier d'Afrique,* and aligned himself with the anticlerical milieu.

In 1958 Mobutu was one of many Zairians sent to the Brussels World's Fair as specimens of Belgian colonial achievement. In February 1959 he was able to return to Belgium by securing an internship in the colonial propaganda agency, Inforcongo, as well as a chance to pursue further studies. Residence in Belgium prevented Mobutu from following the path of many of his peers at home, who were building ethnoregional clienteles. This approach was unpromising in any case, since the Ngbandi were a small and peripheral community, and among the Ngala (Lingala-speaking immigrants to Kinshasa) such figures as Jean Bolikango stood in his way. Mobutu pursued another route, as diplomatic, intelligence and financial circles sought clients among the Zairian students and interns in the Belgian capital. He was able to establish a mutually rewarding relationship with various members of the Belgian intelligence community and with American CIA operative Lawrence Devlin.

Fatefully, Mobutu also had met Patrice Lumumba[*] when the latter arrived in Brussels. He allied himself with Lumumba (whose own background inclined him to anticlericalism) when the Mouvement National Congolais (MNC) split into wings identified with Lumumba and Albert Kalonji. By early 1960 Mobutu had been named head of the MNC/L office in Brussels. He attended the Belgo-Zairian political and economic roundtable conferences on independence preparations and returned to Zaire only three weeks before independence, June 30, 1960.

Lumumba, prime minister on the basis of a fragile coalition of many parties, recognized the importance of the military. Retaining for himself the portfolio of defense minister, he made Mobutu secretary of state (deputy minister) for defense on the basis of their presumed friendship, Mobutu's activity in Brussels on behalf of the MNC/L and Mobutu's military experience. When the army mutinied against its Belgian officers, Mobutu was a logical choice to help fill the void. Lumumba named as commander-in-chief a member of his own ethnic group, Victor Lundula, who had served in the army medical corps during World War II and recently had been elected to office in Likasi (Shaba Region). Mobutu was Lumumba's choice as chief of staff.

During the crucial period July–August 1960, Mobutu built up "his" national army by channeling foreign aid to units loyal to him, by exiling unreliable units to remote areas, and by absorbing or dispersing rival armies. He tied individual officers to himself by controlling their promotion and the flow of money for payrolls. Lundula, older and less competitive, apparently did little to prevent this.

After President Joseph Kasavubu dismissed Lumumba as premier on September 5, Lumumba sought to block this action through parliament. Mobutu staged his first coup on September 14. He declared that both Kasavubu and Lumumba had been "neutralized" and on his own authority (but with American backing) installed an interim government, the so-called College of Commissioners, composed primarily of university students and graduates. Lumumba was sent (by Mobutu and others) to secessionist Katanga, where he was subsequently killed.

During the next four years, as weak civilian governments rose and fell in Kinshasa, real power was held behind the scenes by the "Binza Group," named for the prosperous suburban domicile of its members, such as Mobutu, Victor Nendaka of the security police, Albert Ndele of the national bank, and Foreign Minister Justin Bomboko. Starting in 1963, Lumumbist forces launched an insurrection calling for a "second independence" and swept Mobutu's troops before them until they controlled nearly half the country. They were defeated only through the efforts of European mercenaries and Katanga troops, incorporated into the national army when Moise Tshombe, former Katanga premier, became head of the central government. The national army fought well, under the leadership of Mobutu himself, at Kamanyola, near Bukavu. This incident later was incorporated into the mythology of the Mobutu regime.

In 1965, as in 1960, the division of power between president and prime minister led to a stalemate. President Kasavubu was threatening to expel the white mercenaries at a time when their work was not complete and to align the country with progressive forces in Africa. In response, Mobutu again seized power (again with American backing). Unlike the first time, however, Mobutu assumed the presidency, rather than remain behind the scenes. He was elected president in 1970, 1977 and 1984, unopposed.

From 1965 to 1973 Mobutu pursued a state-building strategy, fusing the models of the authoritarian colonial administration and of the postcolonial unitary, nationalist, one-party African state. The security imperative was pursued through the elimination of unreliable military units (including the Katangans and Europeans), the suppression of competing provincial paramilitary forces, the construction of an effective state security agency and the maintenance of linkages with external protectors. He sought enlarged state autonomy by diversifying external patrons (France, China and conservative Arab states, joined by the United States and Belgium) and by chipping away at the entrenched positions of colonial capital while soliciting a multitude of new links to Western multinational corporations and banks. The revenue imperative of the state was met by sharp increases in fiscal impositions on the colonial corporate sector (which previously had been lightly taxed), by a silent perpetuation of the fiscal extraction imposed on the peasant majority and by drawing major new resources from abroad through loans, aid and investments, as well as by mortgaging the rich natural resource base.

To legitimate the new regime, Mobutu and his associates elaborated a new ideology (nationalism became "authenticity," then "Mobutuism") and by weaving together the image of competence of the colonial state with grandiose new development plans. The state was personalized, culminating with the fusion of state and party in the Mouvement Populaire de la Révolution (MPR). To "founder-president" were added ever more extravagant praise-names: "guide of the revolution," "helmsman" (borrowed from Mao Zedong), "mulopwe" (emperor or even god-king) and finally "messiah."

What began as a collegial alliance of the Binza Group, the top military command, some former Lumumbists, and young university graduates, many of them radical, gradually became an assemblage of courtiers doing the bidding of the presidential monarch. Mobutu transformed former colleagues and adversaries into clients. Autonomous power bases of influential First Republic personalities were sapped. Systematic rotation of high office was practiced, and a pool of vacant positions was sustained through the continuous pensioning of former collaborators into lucrative business opportunities. Access to high rank in all state agencies depended upon presidential favor. The sanction for not cooperating in elite circulation was exile or imprisonment on charges of corruption, nepotism or subversion.

Although the security imperative supposedly had been met, new challenges arose in the late 1970s. Shaba (formerly Katanga) was the scene of attempted invasions in March 1977 and May 1978 by the Front de Libération Nationale du Congo (FLNC), directed by a former Katanga police commander, Nathanael Mbumba. In both cases Mobutu's forces were unable to cope with the FLNC challenge, and his external patrons had to rescue him. The 1977 attack was repulsed with the aid of some 1,500 Moroccan troops, airlifted to Zaire by France. In 1978 government forces were initially assisted by French and Belgian paratroops and subsequently by a seven-nation African security force.

The armed forces remained a source of concern to Mobutu. Military coup attempts were reported in 1975, 1978, 1984 and 1987. In each case a purge of high officers followed. These purges, as well as Mobutu's general policy of organizing the security forces like spokes of a wheel with himself at the hub, made it clear that political reliability was given higher priority than military effectiveness.

In addition to armed opposition from the FLNC and Laurent Kabila's Parti de la Révolution Populaire (PRP), Mobutu has faced nonviolent opposition from the Union pour la Démocratie et le Progrès Social (UDPS), headed by his former minister, Tshisekedi wa Mulumba. However, the most persistent and effective opposition has been from the Catholic church, which claims 40 percent of the population as active members. In the early 1970s the church was headed by Joseph Cardinal Malula, and twenty-seven of the forty-six dioceses were headed by Zairian bishops. The Catholic network of schools, clinics and other social services was as large as that of the state and was far more efficiently run. The role of the church thus was pervasive, and its moral credit made it an uncomfortable competitor for the comprehensive allegiance that Mobutu sought.

Initially, the Catholic church had welcomed the new regime. The founding of the MPR led to the first tensions, and in 1969 a conference of bishops privately noted "dictatorial tendencies" in the regime. The following year Cardinal Malula publicly expressed fears regarding the regime's intentions during a mass celebrating the tenth anniversary of independence. In the presence of King Baudouin of Belgium and Mobutu, the cardinal denounced political elites for "a fascination with the triumphant and the superficial, and a hunger for the lavish." To Mobutu, this was an act of lèse-majesté.

Late in 1972 the regime banned all religious broadcasts and dissolved church-sponsored youth movements, arguing that indoctrination of Zairian youth should be an exclusive function of the party. The zenith of this campaign came at the end of 1974 when the religious school network was nationalized and the public celebration of Christmas was banned. Soon thereafter, the regime began to concede tacitly that it had gone too far. By 1976 the school networks were returned to the churches when the state proved unable to operate them effectively. Also by 1976 the Catholic church had re-emerged as the strongest critic of the sociopolitical order. Following fiascoes both domestic ("Zairianization" of the economy) and international (intervention in Angola), a mood of profound demoralization settled over the country. Since that time, church-state relations have been on a seesaw. Mobutu has welcomed the visits of Pope John Paul II, perhaps because they lend a reflected glory to his regime. During the periods of papal visits, church-state relations have been good. At other moments, relations can be strenuous indeed.

Mobutu's Zaire became one of the most heavily indebted African states due to external causes (rising prices of petroleum imports and falling prices of copper exports) and internal ones (the squandering of funds on prestige projects and their diversion into overseas real estate). But under Mobutu's leadership Zaire became a master of "the ritual dance of the debt game." The ritual dance began in 1976, when the first of a long series of economic stabilization programs was adopted under pressure and guidance of the International Monetary Fund (IMF) and other external agencies. Subsequent "Mobutu Plans" were adopted in 1977, 1979, 1981 and 1983. In each instance Zaire entered into a standby or extended fund facility agreement. In line with the IMF's economic orthodoxy, each plan was designed to cut corruption, rationalize and control expenditures, increase tax revenues, limit imports, boost production in all sectors, improve the transportation infrastructure, eliminate arrears on interest payments, make principal payments on time, and generally improve financial management and economic planning. Given the Mobutu regime's record of corruption and mismanagement, even as early as 1976, it is difficult to believe that either Mobutu or the IMF took these goals seriously.

Mobutu continues to extract from the international political-financial system the resources needed to keep his regime afloat. At various points the external sources of funds succeed in narrowing his room to maneuver, but they are unable to impose major reforms. Zaire remains dependent on the international financial institutions, yet to a large extent, Western governments and financial institutions have been ensnared in the relationship and manipulated by Mobutu.

The main characteristics of Mobutu's leadership of Zaire would emphasize the man, the regime and the environment. Mobutu can be seen as a "presidential monarch" and Zaire as an "early modern state." These labels stress state building, one significant dimension of the Zairian political process. In the Second Republic (1972) the regime was found to be "Caesarist." Later it was described as "sultanism, a centralized and most arbitrary form of patrimonialism," and then as "autocratic." Other descriptions of Mobutu include "world-class predator," although perhaps the predators are the international firms and organizations who financed white-elephant projects, such as the Inga Falls scheme, which includes a high dam, a hydroelectric power plant, long-distance power transmission lines and attendant infrastructure. To yet others, Mobutu's regime is neocolonial and Mobutu is "our man in Kinshasa," valid in terms of U.S. backing for Mobutu since 1960. But Mobutu's Zaire remains largely an "unmanageable client state" for the United States in many instances.

Perhaps the best characterization of Mobutu is in the biography entitled *Mobutu, ou l'incarnation du mal zaïrois*. This reverses an expression Mobutu had used in cataloging Zaire's shortcomings. It is typical of Mobutu, however, that even after publication of such a book and others hardly more flattering, he brought back the author Nguza from exile and made him prime minister once again.

In 1990 and 1991 as efforts to democratize authoritarian regimes assumed a certain momentum in a number of African states and social unrest and economic decay proceeded unabated in Zaire, Mobutu successfully continued to manipulate efforts to displace him, distancing himself above the growing political fray. In April 1990 Mobutu lifted a twenty year ban on opposition parties (making an unfulfilled promise to hold elections in 1991). More than eighty political associations were formed, many of which were fronts for pro-Mobutu groups. Calls came for Mobutu's resignation, for an independent commission to draft a new constitution, and for him to return his personal fortune to help repay Zaire's $8.5 billion foreign debt. In May a student protest at the University of Lubumbashi was brutally suppressed by army troops, resulting in an estimated 350 deaths. Higher education throughout the country was in turmoil, barely able to function.

After several postponements, a national conference, purportedly on revising the political structure of the country, opened in Kinshasa in August 1991, attended by 3,450 delegates, many of whom were last-minute arrivals sent by the Mobutu government. The Union for Democracy and Social Progress (UDPS), led by Etienne Tshisekedi wa Mulumba formed the chief opposition group, leading a coalition of opposition parties, the *Union Sacrée*.

Another currency devaluation in August 1991, resulting in price rises for consumers, triggered a mutiny in Kinshasa by an elite parachutist brigade in September, which led to rioting and looting and 250 persons killed. French and Belgian troops were flown in to protect foreign nationals. After publically voiced criticism of his regime abroad, Mobutu appointed Tshisekedi head of a crisis government to manage a transition to a new regime. Shortly thereafter, following a supposed dispute over access to the national bank, Mobutu dismissed Tshisekedi. On November 1, 1991, in the presidential palace Mobutu presided over the installation of the new cabinet and of Mungul Diaka, the new prime minister that he appointed, while Tshisekedi was meeting his parallel, now unofficial cabinet ministers in his private house. Other opposition leaders vainly called for the army to intervene.

On December 4, 1991, Mobutu's seventh term as president came to an end. Characteristically, he refused to step down until a new election was called, but he also refused to name a date.

BIBLIOGRAPHY

Buana Kabue. *Citoyen président: Lettre ouverte au président Mobutu Sese Seko . . . et aux autres*. Paris: Harmattan, 1978.

Callaghy, Thomas M. *The State-Society Struggle: Zaire in Comparative Perspective*. New York: Columbia University Press, 1984.

Chomé, Jules. *L'Ascension de Mobutu: Du sergent Désiré Joseph au général Sese Seko*. Brussels: Editions Complexe, 1974.

———. *Mobutu et la contre-révolution en Afrique*. Waterloo, Belgium: Tiers-Monde et Revolution, 1974.

Jackson, Robert H., and Carl G. Rosberg. *Personal Rule in Black Africa: Prince, Autocrat, Prophet, Tyrant*. Berkeley: University of California Press, 1982.

Lemarchand, René. "Zaire: The Unmanageable Client-State." In René Lemarchand (ed.), *American Policy in Southern Africa: The Stakes and the Stance*. 2nd ed. Washington, D.C.: University Press of America, 1981, 145–64.

Mabaya ma Mbongo. *Le fascisme au Zaïre*. Sartrouville, France: Editions Kolwezi, 1984.

Naipaul, V.S. "A New King for the Congo: Mobutu and the Nihilism of Africa." *New York Review of Books* (June 26, 1975): 19–25.

Nguza Karl I Bond. *Mobutu, ou l'incarnation du mal zaïrois*. London: Rex Collings, 1982.

Nzongola-Ntalaja (ed.). *The Crisis in Zaire: Myths and Realities*. Trenton N.J.: Africa World Press, 1986.

Schatzberg, Michael G. *The Dialectics of Oppression in Zaire*. Bloomington: Indiana University Press, 1988.

Willame, Jean-Claude. *Patrimonialism and Political Change in the Congo.* Stanford, Calif.: Stanford University Press, 1972.

Young, Crawford. *Politics in the Congo.* Princeton, N.J.: Princeton University Press, 1965.

Young, Crawford, and Thomas Turner. *The Rise and Decline of the Zairian State.* Madison: University of Wisconsin Press, 1985.

THOMAS TURNER

DANIEL ARAP MOI (1924–   ), Vice President, President, Republic of Kenya, 1967–   .

Daniel arap Moi's political career has lasted longer and had a greater impact upon modern Kenya than that of anyone else, with the exception of the country's first president, Jomo Kenyatta.* It began in October 1955 when he was appointed by the colonial government to the Legislative Council. It has survived the introduction of democratic elections in 1957, the formation of two rival nationalist parties—KANU (Kenya African National Union) and KADU (Kenya African Democratic Union)—following the first Lancaster House constitutional conference in 1960, the transfer of power in December 1963, the formation of a de facto one-party state in 1969, and Kenyatta's death in August 1978. Arap Moi was the only nominated African legislative councillor who managed to survive the transition to elective politics in 1957. He is one of only five members of Parliament who have been returned at all six general elections since the introduction of universal suffrage in 1963. Since the disbandment of KADU in December 1964, arap Moi has remained at the center of the political stage, serving for fourteen years until August 1978 as minister for home affairs and from January 1967 until Kenyatta's death, eleven years later, as vice president. He has been president of Kenya since August 22, 1978.

A member of the Tugen ethnic group from the Kalenjin peoples of the Rift Valley, Daniel Torotich arap Moi was born September 2, 1924, at Kurieng'wo in Baringo District, the fourth and last child of the senior wife of Kimoi Chebi, a herdsman. He was given the name Torotich, literally "one who embraces cattle." Following the death of his father when he was two, his education at schools of the African Inland Mission (AIM), an American evangelical organization, was financed by his elder brother Tuitoek. At the age of ten he began attending the AIM school at Kabartonjo, twenty-eight miles from his home, where he was taught by Reuben Seroney, the father of his later rival for political leadership of the Kalenjin, J. M. Seroney. On October 20, 1936, he was baptized, taking the name Daniel. Two years later he transfered to the AIM school at Kapsabet, 140 miles away from his home, and then, in 1943–45, to the more advanced government school in the same locality, walking to and from the Tugen hills at the beginning of each term.

Unlike his contemporaries, Shadrack Kimalel, whom arap Moi was to appoint as ambassador to the United Kingdom, and J. M. Seroney, arap Moi did not proceed to the elite Alliance High School but began a teacher-training course at Kapsabet in 1945. After graduating two years later, arap Moi first taught at the

Tambach Government African School before returning to his home district of Baringo as headmaster at Kabarnet Intermediate School in 1948. On passing the London matriculation examination in 1949, arap Moi joined the staff of the Teacher Training College at Tambach, becoming vice principal, where he remained until he was appointed to the Legislative Council in 1955.

As one of the first seven elected African legislative councillors, arap Moi joined his colleagues, such as Tom Mboya* and Oginga Odinga, in campaigning for representative parity with the European settlers. He supported the formation of an African Teachers Union and in 1959 was one of the first prominent African politicians to visit Kenyatta in detention at Lodwar. In January 1960 arap Moi emerged as one of the key supporters of the more moderate nationalist group KADU, along with Ronald Ngala from Coast Province and the Luhya leader, Masinde Muliro. He was elected its national chairman in 1960. Along with his colleagues, he first assumed office in coalition with the moderate settler party, the New Kenya Group, as parliamentary secretary in the Ministry of Education after the 1961 general election. Although KADU urged Kenyatta's immediate release from detention, the party was the strongest among Kenya's smaller and less advanced ethnic groups and favored the introduction of a federal form of government or "Majimbo" constitution, which would have devolved considerable powers, especially in the fields of education, social policy and control of the police, to regional assemblies. Following the formation of a coalition government with KANU in 1962, under the joint leadership of Kenyatta and KADU's Ronald Ngala, arap Moi became the first minister of education and shortly afterwards minister for local government.

Upon KANU's victory in the May 1963 elections and the formation of a KANU-controlled government under Kenyatta's leadership on June 1, 1963, which secured Kenya's independence on December 12, 1963, arap Moi and his colleagues withdrew into opposition, although he was easily re-elected as the KADU member of Parliament for Baringo North. During this period he served as "shadow" minister of agriculture and as first president of the short-lived Rift Valley Region, whose functions the new KANU government quickly abolished.

Within a short period, however, Kenyatta, the new prime minister, began to court the members of the opposition, whose support he needed to reduce the influence of the more radical elements in the ruling party, which were led by Oginga Odinga, the Luo politician, and Bildad Kaggia, who had been one of the key organizers of the Mau Mau rebellion. Kenyatta particularly sought arap Moi's support in order to establish Kikuyu and Kalenjin areas of settlement in northern Nakuru District, which had been part of the European farming area, the "White Highlands." In this area the interests of arap Moi's own Tugen constituency clashed directly with those of the Kikuyu diaspora and threatened not only to disrupt the peaceful allocation of land but also to weaken Kenyatta's own influence over the landless Kikuyu former squatters in northern Nakuru. With the dissolution of KADU one year after independence and the declaration of the Republic of Kenya on December 12, 1964, arap Moi was one of the first members of the former opposition to be invited to join the cabinet as minister for home affairs in control of the police, the prison service and the immigration department.

A loyal, uncontroversial minister, arap Moi was elected KANU's vice president in the Rift Valley Province at the Limuru Conference, following the abolition of the position of party vice president, which had been held by Odinga. Its functions were divided among eight regional vice presidents. Following the resignation of Joe Murumbi, arap Moi was appointed the country's third vice president in January 1967, as Kenyatta attempted to bolster the regime's legitimacy among the non-Kikuyu ethnic groups. Arap Moi's reputation as the longest-serving member of Parliament, former KADU national chairman and most prominent Kalenjin leader in the vital Rift Valley Province, along with his quiet, seemingly unambitious personality, appeared to make him the ideal choice of the Kikuyu clique around President Kenyatta. They were determined to block the rise of the government's most imposing figure, Tom Mboya, a Luo, who since the 1950s had been one of the most influential and articulate Kenyan politicians.

As vice president, arap Moi was also leader of government business in the National Assembly. It was, therefore, his responsibility not only to secure the passage of government legislation, but also to deal with protests of opposition members of Parliament until the Kenya People's Union (KPU) was banned in October 1969 and with the political crises in the assembly that followed the assassinations of Tom Mboya in July 1969 and J. M. Kariuki, the Kikuyu dissident, in March 1975. Following Kariuki's death, arap Moi appeared before a committee of enquiry appointed by the National Assembly, although another prominent cabinet minister, Mbiyu Koinange, and several officials implicated in the death refused to answer questions. During these years arap Moi's reputation rose, and he maintained the confidence of Kenyatta, serving to divert criticism from the clique of Kikuyu politicians, civil servants and businessmen, particularly those from the president's home district of Kiambu, who appeared to dominate the Kenyan state.

After 1975 Kenyatta's health declined as he advanced into his eighties. The network of influential Kiambu Kikuyu grew increasingly concerned about arap Moi's survival as vice president, since under Kenya's constitution he would automatically succeed as acting president for a period of up to ninety days should Kenyatta die. Mbiyu Koinange, minister of state in the Office of the President and Kenyatta's oldest and closest political ally, as well as his brother-in-law, had been reducing the power of the vice president since 1969, taking control of the police and internal security and the immigration department, leaving the Ministry of Home Affairs responsible merely for the operation of the prison system. Eventually, in October 1976 Koinange and the Kiambu Kikuyu clique challenged arap Moi's position in what rapidly became known as "the Change Constitution movement." It was also widely rumored that the movement also intended to secure the appointment of a Kikuyu, preferably from Kiambu, as vice president to prevent the presidency from moving beyond the Chiana River, the northern frontier of Kiambu. Various members of Kenyatta's family and most prominent Kikuyu, Meru and Kamba politicians supported the movement. It was endorsed by the *Standard* newspaper group, which was allied to Kiambu Kikuyu businessmen associated with the Kenyatta family, and the powerful Kikuyu Embu and Meru Association with its varied business and financial interests.

Arap Moi, however, was sustained in office by the attorney general, Charles Njonjo, who himself came from southwest Kiambu, and by Mwai Kibaki, the most prominent politician from Nyeri District in northern Kikuyuland. These two technocrats rallied support for Kenya's future political stability to diversify power and to reduce resentment of Kikuyu power and economic influence in general and of preferential treatment for Kiambu and the close associates of the Kenyatta family in particular. Following Njonjo's intervention in support of arap Moi, endorsed by the president himself at a cabinet meeting in mid-October 1976, the immediate challenge to arap Moi's position abated. Political tension, however, soon grew once more as the first KANU party elections for ten years began in the last months of 1976. It became evident that a faction led by Kenyatta's nephew and personal physician, the former minister of foreign affairs, Njoroge Mungai, would challenge the pro–arap Moi faction for control, sponsoring Taita Towett, another senior Kalenjin politician and cabinet minister from Kericho District, against arap Moi for the new post of KANU vice president. The elections for the national executive, however, had to be cancelled at the last moment, although some delegates had already arrived in Nairobi, when Kenyatta became seriously ill. By this time, however, arap Moi and his supporters, led by the Masai leader, Stanley ole Oloitiptip, G. G. Kariuki, a Kikuyu assistant minister from Laikipia District, and Charles Njonjo, the attorney general, had clearly outmaneuvered Mungai and the remnants of the Change Constitution faction. Even if the elections had been held, arap Moi and his associates would have emerged victorious.

Thwarted by Kenyatta and Njonjo and by arap Moi's quiet but successful courtship of those prominent politicians and district leaders who had been alienated by the antics of the dominant Kiambu faction, the public challenge to arap Moi's position declined. Some prominent Kikuyu, however, financed the development of an elite Anti-Stock Theft Unit under the command of the assistant commissioner of police in the Rift Valley Province, which was intended to assassinate arap Moi, Njonjo and Kibaki, as well as other politicians and civil servants who were known to support a constitutional transfer of power on Kenyatta's death. Upon Kenyatta's sudden death in Mombasa, the constitutional loyalty of the provincial commissioner at the coast and senior figures in the civil service disrupted these plans, enabling arap Moi, who was at his farm near Nakuru, to evade police roadblocks on his way to the State House in Nairobi and to take over the reins of the government before the conspiracy could be effected.

Ensconced in office, arap Moi quickly asserted his authority, as the Change Constitution movement had feared. He was unanimously confirmed as KANU leader and, therefore, as president of the republic on October 6, 1978. Although he retained every member of Kenyatta's cabinet, key individuals were moved to less important departments. In 1980, following the 1979 general election, arap Moi moved against the Kikuyu, Embu and Meru Association, outlawing "tribal" organizations and promoting Kalenjin associates to key positions in the civil service and parastatal organizations. Arap Moi's task was facilitated by a growing conflict between the two most prominent Kikuyu members of his government, vice president Mwai Kibaki and Charles Njonjo, the former attorney general, who resigned from the civil service to become an elected member of Parliament and minister for constitutional and home affairs. While the Kikuyu factions struggled for power, the president skillfully entrenched his supporters in key positions throughout the government machine, the military and the private sector, where many multinational companies were eager to replace Kikuyu representatives of the older order with Kalenjin and Luhya figures close to arap Moi.

These moves to redistribute power and economic opportunities away from Central Province to arap Moi's bailiwicks inevitably aroused considerable opposition. Indeed, virtually every move the president made to consolidate his power alienated influential Kikuyu, who were now increasingly isolated from the rewards of political incorporation: Several Kikuyu-controlled banks and insurance companies experienced acute financial difficulties as the withdrawal of government investment reduced their liquidity. Following the trial of his cousin in 1980 for illegally importing arms, even Njonjo's relations with arap Moi became strained as the president demonstrated determination to free himself from the technocratic factions that had helped him to power.

These tensions came to a head in August 1982 with a failed coup by the lower ranks of the air force. It was widely believed that this attempt pre-empted a more serious Kikuyu challenge to have taken place a week later when arap Moi was out of the country attending a meeting of the Organization of African Unity (OAU). Since 1982 arap Moi has reasserted his power. He broke Njonjo and his supporters in 1983–84; he has attempted to secure legitimacy among the poorer sections of the Kikuyu community by forming an alliance with Kariuki Chotara, a former Mau Mau leader who was KANU chairman in Nakuru until his death in January 1988; and he has reduced Kikuyu power in the military by appointing members of politically marginal ethnic groups to senior command. By skillfully dividing the Kikuyu, revivifying the ruling party KANU since its elections in 1985, asserting control over the party machine and espousing a populist program—Nyayo-ism (the Swahili word for footsteps)—arap Moi has managed to consolidate his position and largely to silence opposition. A few organizations have continued to protest, led by the main Protestant churches in the National Christian Council of Kenya, the Law Society and former politicians.

Two former Kikuyu cabinet ministers and the most prominent Luhya leader have called for greater freedom and multiparty democracy; they have antagonized the KANU hierarchy, resulting in an end to their careers in the National Assembly.

Provided the economy remains buoyant, arap Moi's skills as a manipulator of the clientage politics of the ethnic factionalism should enable him to survive. For over a decade he has presided over the gradual decline of the state apparatus as the system of clientage has come under increasing strains due to demographic pressures. Unlike Kenyatta in the 1960s, arap Moi does not have spare resources of land, investment or employment opportunities, created by the departure of European settlers, to reward ethnic subnationalist leaders. Despite these problems, he has been relatively successful in his attempts to restructure the Kenyan state and to reduce the hegemony of Kikuyu interests. Although arap Moi has little understanding of the complex economic problems of the state and has increasingly intimidated the technocrats in the civil service, many of whom are Kikuyu and who exerted considerable power under Kenyatta, his political survival demonstrates his skills as a political infighter. Indeed, since 1983 he has reified himself above day-to-day factional strife, becoming the focus of political legitimacy and permanence in a rotating system of incorporation and exclusion, in which factional leaders justify their positions in the ruling circle by appealing to the president's support. Under this system only Njonjo has been cast into the political wilderness, whereas other political leaders, who have seemingly been disgraced, have been permitted back into the system when attention has moved elsewhere, with the benign forgiveness of the president. This constantly changing kaleidoscope of political fortunes, whereby no faction or leader is indispensable, but nobody is to be permanently disgraced, provides an effective but static mechanism for distributing patronage and strengthening arap Moi's immediate position. Yet it appears to have stifled political discourse and debate on the country's tremendous economic and demographic problems, repressing opposition.

But by the end of 1991, after resisting domestic opposition and foreign criticism by a combination of defiant words and compliant gestures, Moi announced he would agree to let opposition parties operate and would call elections "soon." Oginga Odinga, a veteran adversary, had formed the National Democratic Party, only to have it declared illegal, but found a home in an opposition movement, Forum for Restoration of Democracy (FORD). The American ambassador to Kenya launched an unprecedented public criticism of human rights abuses of the regime; Moi released jailed dissidents, reinstated tenure for judges, halted summary expulsions of suspected rebels, and arrested a former ally and cabinet minister, Nicholas Biwott, on suspicion of corruption. (It was also widely suspected that Biwott organized the assassination of Robert Ouko, a minister but a critic of corruption.) Nevertheless, not until after a meeting in Paris in November 1991 in which Kenya's twelve international financial donors suspended economic assistance to Kenya did Moi agree to permit opposition parties to operate legally.

BIBLIOGRAPHY

Work by arap Moi:

Kenya African Nationalism: Nyayo Philosophy and Principles. London: Macmillan, 1986.

Other Works:

Gertzel, Cherry. *The Politics of Independent Kenya, 1963–8.* London: Heinemann, 1970.
Karimi, Joseph, and Philip Ochieng. *The Kenyatta Succession.* Nairobi: Transafrica, 1980.
Kenya: The Politics of Repression. London: Zed Press, n.d.
Miller, Norman. *Kenya: The Quest for Prosperity.* Boulder, Colo.: Westview Press, 1984.
Schatzberg, Michael G. (ed.). *The Political Economy of Kenya.* New York: Praeger, 1987.

DAVID THROUP

EDUARDO CHIVAMBO MONDLANE (1920–1969), President of FRE-
LIMO, People's Republic of Mozambique, 1962–1969.

In the scant seven years from his election as first president of the Front for the Liberation of Mozambique (FRELIMO) in 1962 to his assassination in 1969, Eduardo Mondlane crowded in major achievements usually associated only with a long and active lifetime. He founded FRELIMO from three diverse exile organizations and forged them into a unified movement with space for differences of opinion, views and approach, but focused and concentrated on clear common goals, the total liberation of Mozambique from Portuguese colonialism. Under his leadership FRELIMO developed into one of the most successful liberation movements in Africa, ultimately recognized by the Organization of African Unity (OAU) and the United Nations as "the sole legitimate representative of the Mozambican people." He laid the philosophic basis for FRELIMO's approach to the liberation struggle and for social transformation after independence, a legacy that is still a vital part of independent Mozambique today.

Eduardo Chivambo Mondlane was born in 1920 in a small rural village near the town of Manjacaze in the southern district of Gaza, which straddles the basin of the Limpopo River. His father, Nwadjahane Mussengane Mondlane, was regent of a clan of the Tsonga people, called Khambane, and looked after the responsibilities of leadership until a younger cousin would grow old enough to govern. Mondlane's mother, Makungu Muzamusse Bembele, was the last of her husband's three wives, and Eduardo was the last of her children, for his father died before Eduardo was two years old. His father had, in his younger days, fought in the resistance against the Portuguese, and this tradition continued among the Mondlanes.

Mondlane's boyhood was spent looking after sheep, goats and cattle. His mother, grandmother and sisters worked in the fields, breaking off from work to rush back, cook meals and look after the household chores. The younger men in the village came and went, going off to work on the docks at the coast or in the mines of South Africa when the wages melted away, or being pressed into unpaid forced labor by the Portuguese authorities. Mondlane had three older brothers, each destroyed by the colonial system under which they lived and worked: a chest crushed in an accident on the docks, silicosis of the lungs and tuberculosis.

His mother inculcated in him a passionate love for education and a profound belief in the power of education. She urged him to learn all he could of the white man's ways. "It is they," she said, "who hold the secrets of power. You must become master of those secrets and use them to help us all."

At the age of about twelve he went off to school for the first time, walking five miles each way to the rudimentary school in Manjacaze. The teacher knew no Tsonga and little Portuguese. Discipline consisted of continuous beatings. School for him, as he recalled it, was a chaos of thrashings, shouting and hiding under desks and tables. The boys worked for the teacher at manual labor. The lesson was driven home clearly that social justice was not simply a white-black racial issue, but rather an issue of the location and use of power. He shifted to a mission school.

Upon completion of his rudimentary education, Mondlane ran away to the city of Lourenço Marques, got a job scrubbing bandages and linens in the mission hospital there, and talked his way into admission to the mission primary school, working in the headmaster's house in the late afternoons and evenings as a housecleaner, messenger and kitchen boy. He came to know the lush beauty of the European sections of the city and the crowded squalor of the African quarters and experienced the restrictions of movement imposed upon him by the need for Africans to carry identity cards, permits and tax receipts at all times and be able to produce them on demand. At this juncture a Swiss missionary came to regard Mondlane as a young protege who might be groomed for service in the church. When he finished his primary education, Mondlane discovered that under the Portuguese regulatory restrictions he was unable to attend secondary school. Through the American Methodist Episcopal Mission in Khambane, arrangements were made for him to attend a two-year training course in dry-land farming. This agricultural training and experience in working with farmers in Gaza forged an even stronger link between him and the peasants of Mozambique that showed itself clearly in his approach to social reorganization in the liberated zones during the armed struggle for independence.

In 1944, again with mission sponsorship and support, he was able to attend the Douglas Laing Smit Secondary School in Lemana, South Africa. From there he progressed to the Jan Hofmeyr School of Social Work and then matriculated at the University of the Witwatersrand, one of the few South African universities open to black Africans, to study for a degree in the social sciences. At the university an active and popular Mondlane was elected by his fellow students (predominantly white) to represent them on the Student Council and at the National Student Conference.

In the general elections of 1948 the Nationalist Party came to power, and

Prime Minister Daniel Malan began the full and comprehensive implementation of the policy of apartheid. Mondlane's permit to be in South Africa was withdrawn, and in spite of appeals and protests from the students, faculty and administration of the university, he was expelled from the country. The experience in South Africa helped him realize that the liberation struggle was a regional one and that the destiny of Mozambique was inextricably linked to South Africa and the other countries in the region.

Following his expulsion from South Africa, Eduardo Mondlane was put under surveillance and investigation by the Portuguese secret police and security forces, who concluded that he had "been infected with a Communist virus" and that he had "an embryonic spirit of black nationalism which should be uprooted as soon as possible to prevent it from infecting others." The investigation recommended that he be kept under strict surveillance and should be given a scholarship to study in Portugal to keep him away from the African population and to see if he "could be cured of his intellectual and political proclivities."

Mondlane decided at that time that it was important to accept the Portuguese offer in order to get to know the metropole at first hand, learn the language well and avoid direct confrontation with the Portuguese government. He was the first black Mozambican to attend the University of Lisbon, where he came to know several anticolonial nationalists, such as Agostinho Neto* of Angola and Amílcar Cabral* of Guinea-Bissau.

The period in Lisbon, brief as it was, had a great impact on his thinking. In spite of all *luso-tropicalismo* pretensions to the contrary, for the Portuguese, "a black was always a black" and therefore inferior. One could not break the color bar on the strength of education and personal capacities alone. Mondlane came to understand also the nature of the relation between the democratic struggle inside Portugal and that in the colonies. They had to be related and mutually supportive, but the liberation of Africans had to be in their own hands. It could not be subordinated to and subsumed in the overall antifascist struggle in Portugal.

After a year of constant harassment by the secret police in Lisbon and search and seizure raids, Mondlane left Portugal to study in the United States. The Phelps-Stokes Fund in New York arranged a scholarship for him. At the age of thirty-two he entered Oberlin College, graduated with a B.A. in social studies and went on to Northwestern University near Chicago, where he earned both a M.A. and a Ph.D. In the course of his American years Mondlane came to judge Christians and so-called Christian societies by the standards of their own gospel and found them wanting. At a Christian camp where he taught a discussion group on Africa, he met Janet Rae Johnson, a young woman from a white, midwestern, middle-class, church-going family, committed to becoming a lay missionary in Africa. They fell in love and found that their destinies were joined in a common vision of their life's work. They overcame the Johnson family's initial hostility to this interracial friendship, arguing in terms of the family's professed beliefs in Christianity and their ostensible belief in American democracy.

Upon completion of his Ph.D., Mondlane worked for the Trusteeship Commission of the United Nations. He served in the group to oversee the plebiscite in the Cameroons, and then, protected by a UN diplomatic passport, visited Mozambique in 1961. He was overwhelmed by the thousands of people who flocked to see him and hear him speak wherever he went. He was contacted by many involved in the clandestine opposition to the Portuguese in Lourenço Marques. They gathered to hear him in churches, one of the few places in the country where people could still gather and congregate. He was deeply moved by the welcome given not only to him but to his wife and children as well by people everywhere. By the time he took up a teaching appointment at Syracuse University, the attraction of a comfortable academic career dissolved before the opportunity of becoming involved in his people's struggle for liberation. "Even though I love university life," he said, "my life was dedicated to the liberation struggle of my people" (interview with the author, Dar es Salaam, January 28, 1969).

The independence of Tanganyika under the leadership of Julius Nyerere* and discussions with the three diverse, large Mozambican groups in exile led to a meeting in Dar es Salaam at the end of his first academic year at Syracuse. On June 25, 1962, FRELIMO was founded. Eduardo Mondlane was elected its first president by an overwhelming margin. In September of that year FRELIMO held its first congress to confirm the elections and draft the program of the organization. Mondlane returned to Syracuse, but the rapid movement of events caused him to leave the university in February 1963 for East Africa. His family joined him in July.

In the seven years from the birth of FRELIMO to his assassination, Mondlane molded a purposeful and cohesive force out of ethnically, ideologically and personally diverse groups and leaders. It was interesting to note that all the basic difficulties and conflicts in FRELIMO took place outside Mozambique itself—among students in Dar es Salaam and abroad who sought a privileged position for themselves in the liberation struggle and ultimately in independent Mozambique, and in exile-based leadership among FRELIMO representatives in Europe and the United States. In the liberated territories and the contested areas there was no question of the people's acceptance of Mondlane and FRELIMO's leadership. If his social analysis was that of a Marxist, his thinking was permeated with deep democratic beliefs. He had no faith in a top-down revolution, but believed that a truly Mozambican revolution could carve out a vital democratic socialist space. He often spoke against simply imitating models from "outside," no matter how efficient that seemed to be. He argued that the hope for freedom and justice in Mozambique rested upon the capacity of people to choose and implement democratic forms of socialism in the face of pressure from either corporate socialism or state socialism. The latter two tendencies, each in its own way, often became unthinking, unsocial, lacking in compassion and irresponsible. He believed that FRELIMO's role was to empower people to build their own social and economic institutions and to encourage them and assist them in doing so. For Mondlane, Mozambique was to avoid the rigid command economy and the ultimately heartless competitive "free market." The choice for Mozambique, he believed, must not be between bureaucratic collective regimes and democracies mired in capitalism, but between a democratic, bottom-up socialization and corporate, top-down socialization.

Mozambique would have to show what could be done when pressure was brought to bear on capital in the interest of social practice and democratic participation. FRELIMO would constantly have to mobilize people's active consent and would have to avoid that illusion of consent, often sought by corporate socialization, that comes from indifference, passivity and ennui induced by the sense of powerlessness. This meant that constant specific knowledge was needed of the cultural, experiential and existential realities to make democratic socialization more than an ideal.

Mondlane knew that his life was constantly in danger. By late 1968 and certainly in January 1969 he sensed that a violent and early end for himself, but not for the movement, was inevitable. He had attended important solidarity conferences in Cairo and Khartoum and had just spurned an offer from the Portuguese to head an "autonomous Northern Mozambique," which meant recognizing a greater Malawi that would take over some Mozambican territory for an outlet to the sea. He had escaped three assassination attempts. But he felt "at peace," as he put it, with great confidence in the leadership of Samora Machel* and others to continue the armed struggle after he was gone.

Murdered at the peak of his creative political life, Eduardo Mondlane left a legacy that still seeks to play an active role in the shaping of contemporary Mozambique. The process of popular decision making and the goal of social change were central in the internal dispute between "two lines of thought" that took place within FRELIMO just prior to and immediately following the murder of Mondlane. The internal struggle was to determine what FRELIMO was fighting for. A group that formed around Uriah Simango, vice president of FRELIMO, wanted independence without changing the existing social and economic structures. For them, the enemy was the Portuguese, not the system, and the military struggle was of prime importance, not the process of social transformation. The supporters of Mondlane saw the enemy as colonialism and the system that "exploited the peasants." They did not want simply to put Mozambicans into positions then occupied by the Portuguese. For Simango, whites were the enemy. For Mondlane, the system was the problem. Beginning with the second FRELIMO congress in 1968 and reinforced by the election of Samora Machel to the presidency after Mondlane's death, the ideas of social transformation and of the primacy of political change emerged as dominant, and the Simango faction was defeated. Simango quit FRELIMO; his allies defected to the Portuguese. Both became part of that group opposed to FRELIMO and prepared to assist in the creation of the Mozambique National Resistance (RENAMO), which engaged in a brutal war of destabilization only now winding down.

BIBLIOGRAPHY

Work by Mondlane:

The Struggle for Mozambique. With an introduction by Herbert Shore, "Resistance and Revolution in the Life of Eduardo Mondlane." London: Zed Press, 1983.

Other Works:

Bloomfield, Richard (ed.). *Regional Conflict and U.S. Policy: Angola and Mozambique.* Algonac, Mich.: Reference Publications, 1988.
Henriksen, Thomas H. *Mozambique: A History.* London: Collings, 1978.
————. *Revolution and Counterrevolution.* Westport, Conn.: Greenwood Press, 1983.
Houser, George M. *No One Can Stop the Rain.* New York: Pilgrim Press, 1989.
Isaacman, Allen F., and Barbara Isaacman. *Mozambique: From Colonialism to Revolution, 1900–1982.* Boulder, Colo.: Westview Press, 1983.
Munslow, Barry. *Mozambique: The Revolution and Its Origins.* London: Longman, 1983.

HERBERT SHORE

ROBERT GABRIEL MUGABE (1924–   ), Prime Minister, President, Republic of Zimbabwe, 1980–   .

As a teacher, leader of a revolutionary party, pragmatic politician and president of Zimbabwe, Robert Gabriel Mugabe has been at the center of the struggle for majority rule in Southern Africa. Since 1960, when he was reluctantly recruited to give his first political speech at a rally in Highfields, a township of Salisbury (Harare), Robert Mugabe's political agenda has remained remarkably consistent in several areas: antiracism, reconciliation and advocacy of political equality and economic justice.

Born of peasants at Kutama Mission (Jesuit), Zvimba, on February 21, 1924, he was able to qualify as a primary-school teacher in 1941 and taught in Kutama until 1943. Looking for better wages because salaries were under three pounds sterling a month, he then taught for brief periods in several other primary schools. Studying privately for his matriculation certificate, he earned the cherished scholarship to Fort Hare University College in South Africa in 1950. At the university he met members of the Youth League of the African National Congress (ANC), read Marxist literature and talked with South African Communists. However, he said that the most important political influence for him at that time was Mahatma Gandhi.

After earning a B.A. degree, he returned to Southern Rhodesia in 1952 to teach at various schools near Salisbury and Gwelo (Gweru). Earning a bachelor's degree in education by correspondence, he went on to Chalimbana Training College in Northern Rhodesia (Zambia) in 1955, where he met Zambian nationalist leaders. While teaching in Ghana from 1957, just at the time of independence, the young Mugabe turned his attention from his studies to nationalist politics. He said he went as an adventurist; that he wanted to see what it would be like in an independent African state. Once there he began to develop definite ideas, and he accepted the general principles of Marxism. In Ghana he also met his future wife, Sarah (Sally) Heyfron, who later would be arrested and detained for her political activities in Southern Rhodesia.

While on home leave from Ghana in 1960, Mugabe joined in the activities of the National Democratic Party (NDP), and a protest rally changed his mind about returning to Ghana to teach. At the rally demanding the release of recently jailed NDP leaders, Mugabe was asked to speak. Comparisons he tried to make with Ghana as a model did not excite the crowd, but they roared their approval when he said: "The nationalist movement will only succeed if it is based on a blending of all classes. It will be necessary for graduates, lawyers, doctors and others to accept the chosen leadership even if they are not university men." Here was an educated man who could enjoy all the privileges of his rank saying that the people would direct the struggle for majority rule.

Mugabe was elected information and publicity secretary of the NDP and helped to organize the youth wing. As one of the prime organizers against the 1961 constitutional arrangements that allowed Africans only fifteen seats of a sixty-five–member Parliament, he showed his unwillingness to compromise with representative injustice. Because Joshua Nkomo,* leader of the NDP, had accepted the arrangement, this public disagreement between the two was the first of many in their long struggle together. The NDP was banned within a year, but was immediately transformed into the Zimbabwe African People's Union (ZAPU), with Nkomo as head.

Early in 1963 Mugabe and some of his colleagues agreed to begin training a liberation army. Describing the white Rhodesian Front Party as a "bunch of cowboys," Mugabe was charged with sedition, but jumped bail to go to Dar es Salaam in response to a call by Nkomo. President Julius Nyerere* of Tanzania reacted angrily that the Zimbabwean nationalists had not remained inside to organize the resistance. Several in the executive of ZAPU had been criticizing its international appeals in place of internal mobilization and preparation for war; they wrote of their lack of confidence in Nkomo and split to form the Zimbabwe African National Union (ZANU) on August 8, 1963, with Ndabaningi Sithole as the head. As an outspoken critic, Mugabe was elected secretary-general. When ZANU was banned in 1964, he and the other leaders were arrested, and he remained in prison for ten years until November 1974. While in jail, he earned degrees in law and in administration from the University of London and studied as well for a master's degree in law.

In prison Mugabe was named to replace Sithole as head of ZANU, but it took several years before his leadership was fully accepted. When the Front Line States (Angola, Botswana, Mozambique, Tanzania and Zambia) convinced South Africa to force Ian Smith* to send the nationalist leaders to Lusaka to talk about detente (November 1974), the presidents were angry that Mugabe, not Sithole, showed up as head of ZANU. Samora Machel* of Mozambique called the change enacted by the few executive members in prison a coup. Because of the necessity of Front Line support, ZANU subsequently sent Sithole to the detente talks.

ZANU, however, rejected the Front Line presidents' proposal for each party to dissolve into a unity party and refused to disavow the armed struggle. Mugabe led the opposition on both issues, analyzing that the war had not progressed far enough to convince Prime Minister Ian Smith to negotiate majority rule. After a bloody rebellion among the ranks of new recruits (the Nhari rebellion) and the assassination of Herbert Chitepo in Zambia in March 1975, only one member of the military high command escaped detention by the Zambian government. A week later the few remaining members of the Central Committee still free held an emergency meeting in Salisbury. They directed Mugabe and Edgar Tekere to go to Tanzania via Mozambique to attend a meeting of the Organization of African Unity (OAU) Liberation Committee. In a dramatic escape, with the elderly Chief Tangwena leading them on foot through the eastern highlands, the two were able to contact ZANU recruits in Mozambique.

Never making it to Tanzania, Mugabe spent several months in the camps in Mozambique, organizing and training the youth that were pouring over the border. He thus became known as an important leader for the guerrillas. In January 1976 the military wing of ZANU proclaimed Mugabe the undisputed leader of ZANU; the Front Line presidents accepted that conclusion. He was formally elected president of ZANU at the Central Committee meeting held in Chimoio, Mozambique, in September 1977.

Just before the Geneva conference in October 1976, an alliance between ZANU and ZAPU was formed to coordinate the armed struggle and the negotiations. The new alliance, the Patriotic Front, rejected any constitutional scheme that did not allow majority rule. This principle, along with the escalating armed struggle by ZANLA, the ZANU army, led to a number of unsuccessful negotiating conferences. Finally, successes of the guerrilla war persuaded Smith to compromise, and the Front Line States assisted with pressure on Britain to bring Smith to terms. Mugabe and Nkomo led the Patriotic Front's delegation to Lancaster House in London, and the terms for a new constitution for Zimbabwe were accepted in December 1979. Because there were serious compromises about minority privilege (twenty of a hundred seats reserved for whites, who were 3 percent of the population) and land (greatly restricted in its reallocation), Mugabe said that it was the hardest signature he ever had to write.

Having compromised on the constitutional terms (in force for ten years to 1990), he won a resounding political victory in the April 1980 elections. Gaining full political control, ZANU won fifty-seven of the eighty seats for Africans, a clear majority requiring no coalition to rule. Robert Mugabe became the first prime minister of the Republic of Zimbabwe on April 18, 1980.

His immediate broadcast articulated the theme that has lasted throughout his terms in office: reconciliation. Magnanimous in refusing to use his power for revenge after a brutal war, he called on all to build a new Zimbabwe, one that knows no race, color or creed, a Zimbabwe with a single loyalty. Because ZANU and ZAPU never successfully merged their armies during the struggle, the immediate task was to unite them with the enemy, the white Rhodesian forces.

That this inordinate task was done quickly, with little disturbance, shows the depth of his commitment to reconciliation.

The goal of unity was more elusive. Mugabe decided that ZANU would not run for office with ZAPU in the first elections. Nkomo refused the presidency, thinking it too honorific, and became minister of home affairs. However, when arms were found on ZAPU land, ZAPU commanders were detained, and several hundred guerrillas returned to the bush to wage hit-and-run attacks until 1985. Although events of this period are not yet fully documented, it appears that South Africa played more than a minor role in encouraging this response and in arming the dissidents.

After the elections in 1985, in which each leader continued to show over-whelming strength in his own regions but little support outside them, both Mugabe and Nkomo seriously dedicated themselves to unity. The parties were merged by December 1987 under the combined name of ZANU–Patriotic Front. Mugabe became executive president, as the office of prime minister was abol-ished. With a united party for the 1990 elections, Mugabe won 78 percent of the popular vote for president. Mugabe was opposed by Edgar Tekere, former secretary-general of ZANU, whose one-year-old opposition party, the Zimbabwe Unity Movement (ZUM), gained two of three seats won by opposition parties in the accompanying parliamentary elections.

In the first ten years of Zimbabwe's independence, Mugabe has received awards for government policies that promote food production, for example, the Africa Prize for Leadership for the Sustainable End of Hunger. At independence the peasant farmers provided only 8 percent of the marketed production, but their share increased to 64 percent by 1988. Emphasis on improved seeds, transport depots, training of agricultural extension workers, including females, and fair prices encouraged production so that Zimbabwe has become the bread-basket of the region.

Education is also a success story—which has engendered its own problems. Zimbabwe educated more students at the primary-school level in the first six years of independence than the white minority regime did in ninety years of rule. In 1989, four thousand students qualified for admission to the university, which could accept only two thousand. Jobs are available for only one out of six secondary-school graduates. This surfeit of the educated is a "problem" that many African countries would like to have, but it has created a volatile political situation for Zimbabwe.

Health care was a priority for Mugabe, for the government had to resettle over 1.6 million displaced persons. The government reversed the priorities, sending resources to the rural areas to strengthen primary health care, less to urban hospitals for high-tech curative medicine. The program results are as mixed as the difficulties: More people than ever have access to health care in Zimbabwe, but services remain inadequate, from personnel to provisions.

Mugabe has remained steadfastly an internationalist, committing Zimbabwe to a leading role in the region and among the nonaligned countries in fighting economic and political injustice. From 1982 Zimbabwe assisted Mozambique in resisting South African destabilization. By 1989 this was costing U.S.$3 million per week, a drain on a budget for a country that needed more schools and health clinics. Recognizing the contribution of Mozambique to Zimbabwean independence and their mutual concerns, Mugabe stated that the survival of Mozambique is also the survival of Zimbabwe, that the independence of the two countries is intertwined. Mugabe was elected chair of the 101-member Non-Aligned Movement (NAM) in 1986 for three years. His leadership featured priorities to end the arms race, to end intervention in regional disputes, and to call for a just international economic order. At his urging, NAM voted a special southern African liberation fund. In the region, Zimbabwe cooperates as coordinator for agriculture in the Southern African Development Coordination Conference (SADCC) to establish planned and shared development among the ten regional neighbors.

South Africa at first appeared to accept the Mugabe victory in 1980, but then began regular commando raids into Zimbabwe. Attempts were made on Mugabe's life, and brand-new jet fighter planes were blown up on the ground. Commandos assassinated Zimbabwean citizens. South Africa repeatedly sabotaged the Zimbabwean economy, from the refusal to lease twenty-five locomotives needed to move the bumper harvest in 1981 to blowing up storage tanks of oil for Zimbabwe in Beira, Mozambique. Each attack made Mugabe more resolute in committing the military and economic strength of Zimbabwe to the struggle against apartheid. Not able to exercise sanctions against South Africa because of the multiple links between the economies from colonialism, Zimbabwe did cut exports to South Africa in half; at least 30 percent of South African assets in Zimbabwe have been acquired by the government since 1980. Zimbabwe's resolve remained central to regional resistance against South African aggression.

Mugabe refers to himself as a socialist, one concerned with economic equality. Yet the economy of Zimbabwe remains primarily capitalist, as vital mineral production and other industries remain in private hands (65 percent of the corporations were foreign-owned at independence). The state has intervened in some sectors, for example, banks, news media, pharmaceuticals and fertilizers, resulting in criticism of Mugabe from both the left and the right. Those on the left would like to see land reform taken seriously and a national plan for gradual state intervention in the vital industries. They also criticize the rise of a new but small class of wealthy bureaucrats and industrialists, some of whom have been charged with corruption. Mugabe at first investigated cabinet members for selling cars obtained as a government privilege, but then refrained from full prosecution. Those on the right state that restrictions on foreign exchange and prices discourage investment, even with a new and quite open investment code in 1989.

Mugabe has accepted the reality of the inherited capitalist structure and the need for foreign investment, but remains deeply suspicious of foreign domination, a suspicion based not only on the colonial, but also recent, experience.

Despite his personal preference, by the end of 1991, Mugabe's inclinations toward socialism and one party government grew increasingly more difficult to maintain. ZANU's Central Committee had rejected the legalization of a one party system and announced the abandonment of the Marxist-Leninist ideology. Isolated but noisy dissent was voiced by splinter opposition parties and university students. The Zimbabwe government, needing foreign loans in the midst of economic hard times, embraced a Structural Adjustment Program designed by the World Bank and the International Monetary Fund, which would expand free enterprise over a period of five years.

BIBLIOGRAPHY

Works by Mugabe:

Our War of Liberation: Speeches, Articles, Interviews, 1976–1979. Gweru, Zimbabwe: Mambo Press, 1983.
"The Parliament of Zimbabwe and Some Aspects of the Constitution." *Parliamentarian* (January 1984): 1–9.
"The State of the Non-Aligned Movement." *Black Scholar* 18 (March/April 1987): 10–16.
War, Peace and Development in Contemporary Africa. New Delhi: New Delhi Council for Cultural Relations, 1987.
"Struggle for Southern Africa." *Foreign Affairs* 65 (Winter 1987–88): 311–27.
"The World Is One Family." *World Marxist Review* 31 (December 1988): 39–44.

Other Works:

Martin, David, and Phyllis Johnson. *The Struggle for Zimbabwe: The Chimurenga War.* London: Faber and Faber, 1981.
Ranger, Terence. "The Changing of the Old Guard: Robert Mugabe and the Revival of ZANU." *Journal of Southern African Studies* 7 (October 1980): 71–90.
Smiley, Xan. "Zimbabwe, Southern Africa and the Rise of Robert Mugabe." *Foreign Affairs* 58 (Summer 1980): 1060–83.
Smith, David, and Colin Simpson. *Mugabe.* Salisbury [Harare], Zimbabwe: Pioneer Head, 1981.

CAROL B. THOMPSON

YOWERI KAGUTA MUSEVENI (1944–   ), Government Minister, 1979–1980; President, Republic of Uganda, 1986–   .

In January 1986 Yoweri Kaguta Museveni, the leader of a guerrilla army known as the National Resistance Army, carried out a successful military coup that brought him to the helm of the state in Uganda. At the age of forty-two he became the country's seventh executive president since it gained independence from Britain in October 1962, and only the second guerrilla leader in Africa to oust a government since independence (the first having been Hissein Habre of Chad, leader of the Front de Liberation National du Tchad [FROLINAT] guerrilla army, in July 1978 and June 1982). The dramatic assumption of power by Museveni crowned a somewhat checkered political career dating to his student days.

Museveni is a man of political shrewdness and clear military ability. He is an ascetic person who neither smokes nor drinks alcohol. His political philosophy is eclectic: He subscribes to the ideas of Pan-Africanism, African liberation, Marxist socialism and modernization. Intellectually, he has presented his views as clear-cut without dwelling on nuances or subtle alternatives; such an approach to political realities has given him an edge for decisive action.

It was indeed the swiftness of his action that enabled him to capture power in Uganda. Museveni came to power at a time when the country had been beleaguered by crises of leadership, ideology, legitimacy, unity and development. Because of the strength of his personality and the laudable objectives he announced for Uganda, he generated high hopes within and outside Uganda for a new era of peace, respect for human rights and prospects for democracy.

On balance, Museveni's biggest achievements have been in the domain of foreign relations, where he has not only secured for himself a respectable role— in recognition of which African heads of state, for example, appointed him chairman of the Organization of African Unity (OAU) for the year 1990–91— but has also done much to refurbish the hitherto-tarnished image of Uganda with regard to issues of human rights. Thus in foreign affairs Museveni may be described as an astute tactician who has been remarkably successful in cultivating for himself and his government a wide spectrum of support.

In domestic affairs Museveni's record is more mixed. On the credit side, he has brought about a degree of security, observance of human rights and freedom of the press in the southern region, which is the heartland of the country. However, in the northern and eastern regions of the country, insecurity and human-rights abuses—often caused by government troops clashing with rebel groups—have continued to plague the population. Moreover, the government's "pacification" campaigns in these areas have resulted in human suffering and destruction of property.

Of significance also has been the fate of democracy in the country. Although Museveni had championed the cause of democracy when he was a rebel leader, he has so far shelved it while he has been preoccupied with consolidating his power. The mainstay of his government has been the military and not the civil population. In fact, it is clear from many of his speeches and actions that Museveni regards the army as the ultimate institution of state. He has emphasized that the army comes first before other organs of the state, such as Parliament (the legislature) and the judiciary. Because of the importance of the military to his government, he has since 1986 occupied the portfolio of minister of defense. Diversity of political opinions has accordingly been effectively dealt with by him, to the extent that his administration boasts the highest incidence of treason trials in Uganda's history, having held in only five years more than all previous governments combined. Partly because the army has been afforded a disproportionate share of the national budget and partly because the government lacks a viable economic policy, the economy has not performed well under Museveni's rule.

Although any leader must be held responsible both for his or her government's policies and for their impact, many of Museveni's actions have been molded by the historical circumstances of Uganda. In brief, it is a history that has been largely informed by uneven socioeconomic development in different areas of the country, ethnic-generated conflicts, political reliance on the military and dependence on foreign capital for economic development.

Not much is known about Museveni's childhood and the formative influences on his life. Yoweri Kaguta Museveni was born in 1944 in Kyamate, Ankole District, in southwestern Uganda. He was the first child of Amos Kaguta and Esteri Kokudeka. His parents are from the pastoralist (cattle-keeping) Bahima people—a group that is closely related to the Tutsi ethnic group that straddles the border between Rwanda and Uganda. The name Museveni is the indigenous rendering of the English "seven." Apparently, the name Museveni was given to him by his parents in honor of the Seventh Battalion of the King's African Rifles (KAR), the British colonial army in which thousands of Ugandans served during World War II. The name Museveni therefore means "he of the Seventh Battalion."

For his education, Museveni attended Kyamate Primary School, Mbarara Junior High School and Ntare Senior Secondary School; all these schools are located in his home district of Ankole. While at Ntare, Museveni is reported by one of his teachers to have developed a strong affinity for the military and to have been fond of dressing up in military uniforms and of playing the role of a military commander. Museveni was admitted to the University of Dar es Salaam to do a bachelor's degree in economics and political science. His trip to Dar es Salaam was the first time he had left his home area for an extended period.

At Dar es Salaam University—which in the 1960s and 1970s was a hotbed of revolutionary leftist politics—Museveni is not known to have distinguished himself in scholarly work, but he did gain a reputation for his political fervor. To demonstrate his commitment to revolutionary politics, during one vacation Museveni went with a group of students from the university to Mozambique, to the liberated territories held by the Front for the Liberation of Mozambique, (FRELIMO) in its war of independence against Portuguese colonialism. The stint with FRELIMO acquainted Museveni for the first time with guerrilla warfare. The firsthand impression Museveni had of FRELIMO guerrilla operations, together with his experience at Dar es Salaam University, apparently had a profound impact on him, particularly in firming up his political views and tactics. He grew interested in political-military leaders, including Lenin, Mao, Che Guevara, Fidel Castro, Samora Machel,[*] Muammar Qaddafi and Karl von Clausewitz, whom he admired for their qualities in varying degree of disdain for compromise, fanaticism in political ideas and ruthlessness in action.

In 1970 Museveni completed his bachelor's degree at Dar es Salaam and returned to Uganda. He applied to join his country's Foreign Service but was instead recruited by the General Service Intelligence Organization of the government and posted to work in President Milton Obote's[*] office as a research officer. While working for the government intelligence unit, Museveni began to entertain the idea of contesting a seat to Parliament during the general election scheduled to take place in April 1971. But as campaigns were about to get under way, General Idi Amin* overthrew the Uganda People's Congress (UPC) government of Milton Obote on January 25, 1971, and Museveni, together with a host of UPC stalwarts, fled to Tanzania, where Obote had sought political asylum.

The UPC group in exile began to organize for the ouster of the Amin regime. In September 1972 the group—which included Museveni—invaded Uganda through Mbarara, on the premise that the people in Uganda needed only a spark to set off spontaneous rebellions against Amin in the rest of the country. However, the invasion was easily beaten by Amin's forces. The disillusionment that set in among Ugandan exiles after the abortive invasion served to sever the loyalty of some UPC members to their leader, Milton Obote, who was blamed for the fiasco. Museveni was one of those who began to distance himself from Obote in operational matters. It was then that he and his friends formed a guerrilla force called the Front for National Salvation (FRONASA), whose objective was to overthrow Amin's regime. A few Ugandans were recruited into FRONASA and sent for training in Mozambique with FRELIMO, but FRONASA was not a viable guerrilla organization. It had neither a broad sociopolitical constituency nor operational military capacity. Because of the dim prospects that FRONASA would become a political-military force in Uganda, Museveni temporarily left the group and went to work as a teacher at a vocational school in Tanzania, the Moshi Cooperative College. In 1973 he married Janet Kataha, with whom he had four children.

It was not until 1978 that Museveni again emerged on the political scene. At that time, Ugandans in exile were being mobilized to help the Tanzanian army repulse the Ugandan army, which had invaded northern Tanzania on the orders of General Idi Amin. Museveni revived the hitherto-moribund FRONASA in a short space of time. Although FRONASA was not as formidable a force as the UPC Kikosi Maalum (special battalion), the Tanzania Defense Force and the umbrella organization of Ugandans in exile, the Uganda National Liberation Front (UNLF), assigned it the task of fighting against Amin's forces along the western front, while Kikosi Maalum was assigned to the central front. FRONASA was led by Museveni, while Kikosi Maalum was commanded by two colonels. During the military campaign (January to April 1979) Museveni recruited in Ankole over ten thousand people, mostly from the Bahima or Tutsi ethnic groups. They formed the backbone of the Uganda National Liberation Army, as they were incorporated into the national army after the fall of Amin, and later, after 1980, into Museveni's guerrilla force when they deserted from the national army.

When Kampala, the capital city of Uganda, was captured in April 1979 from Amin's forces by the combined forces of Ugandan exiles and Tanzanian troops, Yusufu Lule was sworn in as the new leader of a provisional government. Lule appointed Yoweri Museveni as minister of defense—a strategic position in which he was to oversee the organization of the embryonic national army. Museveni also assumed the position of vice chairman of the Military Commission, which exercised the real power behind the political establishment.

In both these capacities Museveni had the foresight to place his supporters in critical positions within the army; they were the people on whom he would fall back when he failed to win the general election at the end of 1980. In the interim he participated in the ouster of Yusufu Lule in June 1979 and the overthrow of Lule's successor, Godfrey Binaisa, in May 1980. After the removal of Binaisa from the presidency by the Military Commission, the interim government announced that it would conduct general elections to elect members of a National Legislature. In order to prepare for the elections, Museveni and a number of younger-generation Ugandans who had become disillusioned with the two traditional political parties—the Uganda People's Congress (UPC) and the Democratic Party (DP)—recast FRONASA as a political party and named it the Uganda Patriotic Movement (UPM). When elections were held in December 1980, UPM won only 1 out of 126 seats for the National Legislature, while the UPC, led by Obote, gained a majority of seats. Museveni himself was narrowly defeated in his constituency: He polled 12,951 votes, while the UPC candidate obtained 13,015 votes and the DP opponent won with 15,687 votes.

Museveni did not accept the results of the elections, and a few weeks afterwards, on February 6, 1981, he and a number of his supporters went to the bush to embark on a guerrilla campaign against the elected UPC government. The guerrilla group Museveni founded for this purpose was called the Movement for the Struggle for Political Rights (MOSPAR), later renamed the Popular Resistance Army (PRA). PRA merged with another guerrilla group, the Uganda Freedom Fighters, led by Andrew Lutakome Kayiira and Yusufu Lule, to form the National Resistance Army (NRA), with a political wing designated the National Resistance Movement (NRM).

Museveni was determined to gain power by what he termed a "people's war" rather than a military coup, but his guerrilla force lacked the military materiel and financial means to wage the war. In order to get weaponry and money to pursue his guerrilla campaign, on August 26, 1981, Museveni entered into a formal alliance with military groups that had served under Amin—the Uganda National Rescue Front (UNRF) and the Former Ugandan National Army (FUNA). These groups were united in nothing except their antipathy to the UPC government of Obote. The agreement, which called for coordination of war efforts against the government, was facilitated by Colonel Muammar Qaddafi and was signed in Tripoli, Libya. A few months later, on January 7, 1982, Museveni signed in London another agreement with, in addition to the groups already mentioned, the Uganda Freedom Movement (UFM) and ex-president Godfrey Binaisa, despite the fact that he had been at loggerheads with both Binaisa and the UFM prior to the December 1980 elections. Both the Tripoli and London agreements that Museveni signed demonstrate how he would enter into alliances with various groups, notwithstanding ideological differences, in order to further his objectives. Indeed, it was this political shrewdness that was to win for Museveni and the NRA financial backing as well as widespread acclaim from international sources across a wide ideological spectrum.

With the new political and military alliances and with substantial financial support, the position of the NRA was greatly strengthened. In the following three years Museveni stepped up guerrilla operations against the UPC government of Obote. This war of attrition, coupled with the indiscipline and the venality of the government troops and the lack of support for the government among the population in areas where the war was being waged, fatally sapped the capacity of the government and brought about a split within the ranks of the government army. As a result, in July 1985 one faction of the army staged a successful coup against the Obote administration. The Military Council set up to head the new administration immediately called for a negotiated settlement with the NRA and other opposition groups.

At the time of the July coup, Museveni had taken political asylum in Sweden, apparently with little expectation of continuing the campaign against Obote's administration. But the core of his supporters in the bush remained cohesive and continued to command the rank and file—who were otherwise demoralized—urging them on with the idea of the rightness of their struggle. The July coup occurred at a most critical time and offered to Museveni's guerrilla force a window of opportunity. It speaks to the political genius of Museveni that he capitalized on the disarray in the government army and the Military Council to buy time for his forces while he mobilized people and support against the government.

The negotiations between the Military Council and the NRA dragged on for six months in Nairobi, until Museveni signed a peace accord with the Military Council in December 1985. By this time the NRA forces led by Museveni were strong enough to confront the ragtag government troops. This they did, and within one month from the signing of the Nairobi peace accord, on January 25, 1986, Museveni's forces toppled the military junta in Kampala and thus effectively abrogated the accord. Four days later Museveni was sworn in as the new head of state of Uganda.

Since then he has ridden on a wave of acclaim and goodwill on the part of the international community, which sees him as the first of a new breed of leaders in Africa. However, although he has provided the country with strong leadership and enjoys wide support in certain areas of the country, his record on human rights, democratic rule and the economy has left much to be desired. Significantly, although he won the war, after more than five years in power, he still has not yet won peace for the country as a whole. There is no doubt that Museveni is a leader of remarkable political and military acumen, which he has brought to bear in dealing with both friends and opponents and in the way he has often seized opportune moments to further his aims. In 1989 Museveni fulfilled half his promises about returning Uganda to an elected government made on assuming power in 1986: while he extended without election his leadership and that of the NRM to 1995, Ugandans were permitted to elect representatives to the National

Resistance Council (the national assembly) from county and district level bodies, in which political parties were prohibited from actively campaigning on party platforms. Time alone will tell what his ultimate impact on Uganda will be.

BIBLIOGRAPHY

Works by Museveni:

Selected Articles on the Uganda Resistance War. Kampala, Uganda: NRM Publications, 1986.

Other Works:

Bwengye, Francis. *The Price of Freedom*. Baden, Germany: Uganda Human Rights Union, 1988.
Karugire, Samwiri R. *A Political History of Uganda*. London: Heinemann, 1980.
Mamdani, Mahmood. *Imperialism and Fascism in Uganda*. Trenton, N.J.: Africa World Press, 1984.
Omara-Otunnu, Amii. *Politics and the Military in Uganda, 1890–1985*. London: Macmillan, 1987.
Seera-Muwanga, Lance. *Violence in Uganda: What Is Inside Museveni's Uganda*. Vaxjo, Sweden: Vaxjo University Program for Human Rights and Refugee Studies, 1989.

AMII OMARA-OTUNNU

N

ANTONIO AGOSTINHO NETO (1922–1979), President of the People's Republic of Angola, 1975–1979

Agostinho Neto was one of the leading political figures of contemporary Angola. Physician and poet, revolutionary and politician, party leader and president of Angola, Neto was both a man of words and a man of action. He was a pioneering Angolan nationalist leader who was instrumental in the birth and survival of the contemporary phase of Angolan nationalism and who briefly held power as president of the People's Republic of Angola (1975–79). His soft-spoken, reserved, studious character appeared to contradict his personal history as a tough, resilient political infighter, leader of the Marxist-Leninist African nationalist party, the MPLA (Popular Movement for the Liberation of Angola), survivor of the struggle to end Portuguese rule in Angola, and victor in an internationalized civil war.

António Agostinho Neto, second son of a Methodist minister of Mbundu descent, was born near Catete, Angola, on September 17, 1922. Destined to be the most thoroughly educated abroad in both conspiratorial politics and his chosen profession, medicine, of the three main Angolan nationalist leaders who fought to win control of Angola, Neto was one of the rare Africans of his generation who attained the top echelons of Portugal's educational system. Encouraged by his parents and by the Methodist church of Angola, Neto graduated from Salvador Correia High School in Luanda, the capital, in 1944 and served three years in the government health services. After receiving a university scholarship to study in Portugal from the Methodist church in 1947, Neto went to Portugal and entered medical school at the University of Coimbra. Later he transferred to the University of Lisbon.

Neto's years in Portugal (1947–62), including terms of imprisonment by the dictatorship in prisons in Portugal, Angola and Cape Verde Islands (1952, 1955–57 and 1960–62, a total of more than four years in political prisons), transformed his personal, professional and political lives. In his personal life, he met, courted and married a Portuguese woman, Maria Eugénia Da Silva, and began a family. Further defying convention and custom, as well as authority, Neto struggled as a member of a small group of African students to win his medical degree, which he completed finally in 1958, before returning to practice medicine in Angola in December 1959. Contact, friendship and exchange occurred with fellow African students in Lisbon, who included in their select number future leaders of Guinea-Bissau (Amílcar Cabral*), Angola (Mário de Andrade; Lúcio Lara) and Mozambique (Marcelino dos Santos; Eduardo Mondlane*), as well as oppositionist Portuguese students (Mário Soares, future premier and president of the Republic of Portugal).

While in Portugal, Neto, the joiner of proscribed organizations, became a member of MUD-Juventude (the youth wing of the Movement of Democratic Unity), part of the Portuguese opposition to the intransigent dictatorship of Premier Antonio Salazar (1932–68). Neto's long, bitter experience of harassment, arrest and imprisonment under the dictatorship's political police (PIDE) shadowed his years in Portugal. His more than four years spent in prison for his agitation against the dictatorship and its colonial policies began in 1952 with his first arrest and a three-month prison term and ended in March 1962 when he was released from a longer term, his third. In July of that year he escaped police surveillance, went to Morocco and later joined the MPLA headquarters in Kinshasa, Zaire.

While in a PIDE prison during his lonely struggle, Agostinho Neto wrote in one of his revolutionary poems of protest: "I am the Unknown Soldier of Mankind." By mid-1957, however, by means of leftist and humanitarian pressures and publicity, Neto was a well-known political "prisoner of the year" and had been released once again. In the meantime he joined the MPLA, which was founded in Angola in December 1956 by a coalition of forces including members of the Communist Party of Angola (PCA). The MPLA's anticolonial ideology was Marxist-Leninist with Stalinist rhetoric, and its membership was dominated by urban, middle-class intellectuals, former government employees, who were Africans (mainly Mbundu), *mesticos* (mulattos) and whites from the Luanda region. Angolan nationalist politics was riven by bitter rivalries. By the mid-1960s, of dozens of rival groups three distinctly different parties jostled for position in a war against Portuguese rule: the MPLA, the National Front for the Liberation of Angola (FNLA), based largely on rural Bakongo elements, and the National Union for the Total Independence of Angola (UNITA), founded on Ovimbundu groups.

When the Angolan war of anticolonial insurgency broke out on February 4, 1961, with an armed attack on installations in Luanda by MPLA elements, Neto was back in prison in Portugal, following his arrest by PIDE in June 1960 and his imprisonment in Angola. A villagers' protest to call for his release met bloody repression by Portuguese armed forces. The Portuguese defeated early armed uprisings both by MPLA and its rival, the Union of Angolan People

(UPA, later renamed GRAE and then FNLA). The MPLA was struggling to survive.

When he escaped from Portugal in July 1962, Neto joined MPLA headquarters in Kinshasa and was elected president of that organization at the end of the year. Neto's party endured difficult times until the surprising military coup of April 25, 1974, when the Armed Forces Movement in Portugal overthrew the weakened Portuguese dictatorship. Receiving support from the USSR, Cuba and Soviet-bloc states, the MPLA with difficulty pursued the war of insurgency inside Angola. In 1963 MPLA headquarters moved from Kinshasa to Brazzaville, Congo, and in 1969 from Brazzaville to Dar es Salaam, Tanzania. Meanwhile, under Neto's direction, the MPLA opened an eastern front in the vast reaches of eastern Angola after 1966.

During the tough years of armed struggle and exile while directing the MPLA (1962–75), Neto discovered that winning international support for his party and for the cause of liberating Angola stifled his poetic muse. He wrote little poetry between 1962 and 1975, which brought him discouragement. During 1963–68, the rival FNLA, not MPLA, won the favor of the OAU (Organization of African Unity) and even the UN. During 1972–73 the Soviet Union virtually ceased assistance to Neto's party.

The Lisbon military "coup of carnations" of 1974 produced new opportunities for the MPLA, for Neto and for Angola. Unlike the anticolonial wars in Guinea-Bissau and Mozambique, however, the war in Angola had reached a stalemate. While the MPLA had established zones of self-government in eastern Angola, with access from bases in Zambia, neither the MPLA nor its rival parties were close to victory over the Portuguese forces. In the period of transition to de-colonization, Angola's independence prospects were profoundly affected by the revolution and the power struggle of contending forces in Portugal. Despite good intentions and hard work by Portuguese leaders who wished to decolonize Africa peacefully and to prevent a civil war in Angola, Portugal was unable to control the political situation in Angola. A brutal struggle among the MPLA, FNLA and UNITA, with their international backers, devastated the country.

From an initially weak military position, MPLA President Neto entered ne-gotiations to expedite a peaceful transition in Angola. After meeting with rival leaders in Portugal, Neto, Holden Roberto (FNLA), and Jonas Savimbi* (UNITA) signed the ill-fated Treaty of Alvor (January 15, 1975), which established a coalition, transition government and planned for an integrated all-party Angolan army and a free general election to produce a government and independence on November 11, 1975. An escalating, internationalized civil war among the rival parties ensued; much of the Treaty of Alvor became a dead letter. Fighting broke out among the rivals in the spring of 1975. OAU, UN and Portuguese efforts failed to unite the contenders, to stop the fighting or to bring good-faith nego-tiations. Like the war in distant Ethiopia, Cold War shadow boxing was super-imposed upon Angola's internal conflict. Despite the invasion from Namibia of a South African armed force, the MPLA forces held on and were assisted decisively by the USSR, Soviet-bloc states, Cuba, leftist elements in Portugal and the Portuguese Armed Forces Movement; with less conviction and coordination, the FNLA and UNITA were backed by a Vietnam-obsessed United States and by Zaire and South Africa.

Agostinho Neto's personal triumph of a symbolically timed return to Luanda on February 4, 1975, after an absence of nearly twenty-eight years in exile, was short-lived. His party's position in the battle for power was improved when the MPLA in July 1975 took control of Luanda. Internationally supervised elections were not held. The civil war escalated. The remaining Portuguese armed forces withdrew and declared that Portugal's rule was at an end. Power was handed over not to any one party (including the MPLA), but to "the people of Angola."

Agostinho Neto served in the perilous office of president of the People's Republic of Angola from the day Portugal pulled out, November 11, 1975, until his death in Moscow due to cancer on September 10, 1979. His brief but eventful time in power in his native land was fraught with conflict and frustration. While the conventional phase of the internationalized civil war ended in March 1976 with a temporary military victory for MPLA, by 1979 UNITA had revived enough to provide new threats in southern Angola. There was internecine fighting within the MPLA and its administration. In May 1977 Neto's forces crushed a gory military coup attempt led by war hero Nito Alves and his supporters. Angola's economy was in shambles due to the ravages of the civil war—many more persons died than during the colonial war (1961–74)—the cessation of agricultural and industrial production, the critical shortage of skilled workers and managers following the war, the departure during 1974 and 1975 of most of the more than 300,000 Portuguese settlers and the need to address massive public health and social problems amidst large numbers of refugees, wounded, war widows and orphans. Finally, Neto faced the issues of large political and financial debts owed to his armed saviors in Moscow and Havana.

By the time of his death, Neto and his MPLA regime had only begun to deal with these colossal problems. His style of stoical, steady leadership and his commitment to the Soviet Union in important friendship and trade treaties signed in Moscow in 1977 and 1978 had set the tone for policy and action that would follow largely orthodox Marxist-Leninist lines, while attempting to keep the Angolan door open to more Western trade, technical assistance and investment.

In the history of contemporary Angola, Neto must be counted as one of the fathers of independent Angola, a poet-president of his country, after 1975 addressed in Luanda as "comrade president." Despite differences in profession and the manner in which independence was achieved, Neto's literary and political roles may be compared to a degree with those of President Léopold Senghor* of Senegal. Angola's way of entering independence during a full-scale civil war, unique in the annals of modern African independence, provided the tragic backdrop to Neto's short-lived term as political chief of his country. Postwar recovery and a return to normalcy did not occur during his time in office, and Neto's unenviable position at the head of a crippled, divided nation may also be compared with the situations of the harassed leaders of post–World War II France or of the war-ravaged new republics of Eastern and Central Europe in 1919.

Neto's contribution to the movements that fought to win independence from a reluctant Portugal is easier to assess than his role as president of the MPLA-led regime of Angola, which in part was a collective leadership system. As a political infighter, a conspirator and a party thinker, organizer and planner, however, his central role appears to be more decisive. In intraparty factional struggles, as well as in his quest for international support for his party and his country's causes, Neto was above all a supreme survivor with quiet grace and dignity. He never lost heart. It is not coincidental that the word "hope" (*esperança* in Portuguese, also the official language of independent Angola) often appears in his revolutionary poetry and is in the title of his most famous book of poems.

Beside his family, including his widow, Maria Eugénia Neto, at least two key personal legacies will endure: his role in advocating and representing against crushing odds Angolan nationalism and liberation; and his poetry, now translated into many languages. His deceptively simple, free verse continues to have a general, sincere appeal. When the rhetoric of Neto's many MPLA papers and speeches is forgotten, his largely exile-generated poetry, now part of both the political lexicon of Angola and Portugal and of the Angolan literary canon, will live on.

BIBLIOGRAPHY

Work by Agostinho Neto:

Sacred Hope (Sagrada Esperança). Translated from the Portuguese by Marga Holness. Dar es Salaam, Tanzania: Tanzania Publishing House, 1974.

Other Works:

Davidson, Basil. *In the Eye of the Storm: Angola's People*. London: Longman, 1972.
Henderson, Lawrence W. *Angola: Five Centuries of Conflict*. Ithaca, N.Y.: Cornell University Press, 1979.
Khazanov, A. H. *Agostinho Neto*. Translated from the Russian by Cynthia Carlile. Moscow: Progress Publishers, 1986.
Marcum, John A. *The Angolan Revolution*. Vol. 1. *The Anatomy of an Explosion (1950–1962)*. Vol. 2. *Exile Politics and Guerrilla Warfare (1962–1976)*. Cambridge, Mass.: M.I.T. Press, 1969, 1978.
Somerville, Keith. *Angola: Politics, Economics and Society*. London: Frances Pinter, 1986.
Trigo, Salvato (ed.). *A voz igual: Ensaios sobre Agostinho Neto*. Oporto, Portugal: Fundação Eng. António de Almeida, 1989.
Wheeler, Douglas L., and René Pélissier. *Angola*. Westport, Conn.: Greenwood Press, 1978 reprint of 1971 edition.

DOUGLAS L. WHEELER

JOSHUA NKOMO (1917–   ), Nationalist leader, Cabinet Minister, Vice President, Republic of Zimbabwe, 1948–

Joshua Nkomo is known among his supporters as "Father Zimbabwe." From

1948 to 1979 he headed a succession of nationalist parties and guerrilla armies, endeavoring to wrench political power from the white settlers of Southern Rhodesia and their British absentee overlord. He was a member of the team that negotiated independence from Britain in 1979 and was cabinet minister in Zimbabwe's first government. He then spent six years as an object of government denunciation and harassment and re-emerged in 1988 as senior minister in the president's office. He has survived many political struggles and has a long record of nationalist service. What he does not have for all his efforts is the presidency of Zimbabwe. In 1992 Robert Mugabe[*] remained entrenched in that position, and many Nkomo supporters feel that Father Zimbabwe's secondary status is one of the great tragedies of the struggle for Zimbabwe.

"My parents were born when my country was still free," wrote Nkomo in his autobiography, that is, before 1890 when Cecil Rhodes and the Pioneer Column marched from South Africa to an area near present-day Harare. By the time Joshua was born in 1917, his parents had become Christians and were working for the London Missionary Society near Bulawayo, in the part of the country called Matabeleland, after the Ndebele ethnic group. His family avoided the rituals, foods, stimulants and dress of non-Christian villagers, but the adolescent Joshua secretly attended traditional ceremonies with his friends, later drawing connections in his mind between missionaries and the "treaties" European men of God helped to extract from King Lobengula. In what would become characteristic of a pragmatic and reconciliatory style, the adult Nkomo claimed to be a Christian within the framework of belief in the god of traditional African religion.

Nkomo, however, did not always seek middle positions. The Land Apportionment Act forced his family to move several times in the 1930s before finding decent grazing and agricultural areas in the "native reserves." This could have interrupted his education. Yet Joshua trained first at mission school, then at the industrial school, and finally at the South African university. This high-profile education put him into an elite group of educated Africans and a career in the Department of African Affairs at the Rhodesian Railways in Bulawayo. It also made him a likely candidate for leadership positions. In 1948 he assumed the presidency of the African Railway Employees' Association and an early nationalist organization called the Bulawayo African National Congress (BANC). It has been said that the pragmatic Nkomo then became addicted to power and turned his high personal strivings in the direction of political ambition. Nkomo is always quick to deny such accusations and claims that he was insecure about his talents, lacked confidence in early life, always felt that he had to struggle to keep ahead, and had a deep desire to trust in and be trusted by the masses.

Nkomo soon found that he was also a man the white government wanted to court. In 1952 Southern Rhodesia was about to enter the Central African Federation with Northern Rhodesia (Zambia) and Nyasaland (Malawi). Nkomo was invited to represent "the" African position at deliberations in London. The BANC was skeptical of the proposed federation and knew that blacks in other participating territories were gravely concerned that the arrangement could enable Southern Rhodesia to impose its highly racialist society on them. Nkomo attended the meeting in London and spoke eloquently against the federation, bringing attention to himself as spokesperson for the people. Then, arriving in Bulawayo from the second such conference in 1953, Nkomo was caught carrying nationalist literature and turned the occasion of his trial into a defense of black rights in the country. Nkomo claims that his actions accelerated the pace of African opposition to Southern Rhodesian racism and were not personal triumphs.

Nkomo's political career became more uneven and inconsistent, however, as he became more famous. After denouncing the federation, he ran for one of its few African parliamentary seats, claiming that this would show whites that the federation was a farce. He did not win and subsequently opened businesses in auctioning, real estate and insurance. The BANC declined and was galvanized again in 1957, when the more militant City Youth League of Salisbury suggested the joint formation of what was to be the first countrywide nationalist organization, the Southern Rhodesian African National Congress (SRANC). Nkomo was elected to head that organization, less because he was popular with militant members of the Youth League—in fact the opposite seems to have been true— than because he was perceived as a link to educated blacks and their much-needed resources.

Indeed, Nkomo did court support and resources for the organization, mostly outside the country. Between 1957 and 1964 he attended the World Assembly of Youth in India and the All-African People's Conference in Ghana, participated at the United Nations in New York, and contributed to the first meeting of the new Organization of African Unity (OAU). He also cultivated contacts with a variety of states—Nigeria, Guinea, Ethiopia, Tunisia, Cuba, Libya and the Eastern bloc—and with African nationalists such as Gamal Abdul Nasser, Kenneth Kaunda,* Julius Nyerere,* Hastings Banda,* and Kwame Nkrumah.*

Nkomo was in Cairo in 1959 when he learned that the SRANC had been banned and its executive detained. In what became a feature of Nkomo's leadership in the 1960s, at the cusp of reconciliation and ambition, he avoided arrest by going into exile in London, claiming that this move would enable him to publicize the plight of Southern Rhodesian blacks, raise funds, and acquire an attorney to defend his colleagues. When the National Democratic Party (NDP) replaced the SRANC, Nkomo became its secretary for foreign affairs and then its compromise president in absentia. Again he took to the road, joining African nationalists from other colonies in the general effort of the time to negotiate independence for British colonies. Maurice Nyagumbo, a colleague who later broke with Nkomo, credits Nkomo's external missions with making the NDP affluent "in both money and property." Other colleagues began to view his absences as a sign of personal distaste for the hard struggles at home. His popularity, however, held steady among average Africans in Southern Rhodesia—a crowd of thirty thousand gathered to cheer him after one absence of twenty-two months—and there is little doubt that had Nkomo been able to negotiate independence in the early 1960s, some lapses in judgment notwith-standing, he would have emerged as the country's first black head of state.

But the whites in Southern Rhodesia were adamant that independence should come either through the federation, which they controlled, or under a mostly white government at home. They banned the NDP in 1961 (Nkomo was in Dar es Salaam celebrating the independence of Tanganyika) and immediately faced a reconstituted and more militant NDP in the form of the Zimbabwe African People's Union (ZAPU), again under Nkomo's tutelage. This organization stood for independence on the basis of universal adult suffrage and undertook a cam-paign of sabotage to back up its demands. When ZAPU was threatened with banning in 1962, however, Nkomo seemed about to force a confrontation with the Southern Rhodesian government. Instead, after a short detention, he rec-ommended that the ZAPU executive relocate to Dar es Salaam to escape the government's detain-and-rule tactics.

This was the first of three blunders that cost Nkomo his more heroic aspirations. Nkomo gained the approval of other ZAPU executives for the move to Tanzania, but the decision was unpopular among party militants, who grumbled that their leader always sought to operate abroad and was becoming slippery on the issue of what constituted a satisfactory basis for independence (Nkomo had authorized NDP approval for a constitution that would add only fifteen Africans to Parlia-ment, had retracted support only when pressed by party stalwarts, and then had claimed to be a victim of lies). Believing that Nkomo lacked the resolve to face a recalcitrant Southern Rhodesia with armed force, a small group within ZAPU (then called the People's Caretaker Council) tried to unseat Nkomo in 1963. They failed, for reasons of Nkomo's own political maneuvering and timely expulsion from Tanzania, and thereupon took the drastic and unpopular step of breaking the continuous line of Zimbabwean nationalism to form a new party, the Zimbabwe African National Union (ZANU).

For one year members of the two parties denounced and fought each other, and Nkomo's second blunder came in succumbing to the temptation to direct his supporters and resources against ZANU, rather than fight the Rhodesians. ZANU used this misguided priority to good advantage, slowly building popularity on the argument that ZANU was the only party committed to the anticolonial struggle.

In 1964 ZANU was banned, and from that point until the mid-1970s most senior nationalist leaders of both parties, including Nkomo, were detained. This did not stop an armed struggle from developing under the command of two guerrilla forces: Zimbabwe People's Revolutionary Army (ZIPRA) was the So-viet-backed military wing of ZAPU working out of Zambia, and Zimbabwe African National Liberation Army (ZANLA) was the Chinese-backed ZANU army lodged in Mozambique. Nkomo's third blunder came in turning down the Front for the Liberation of Mozambique's (FRELIMO) initial offer of Moz-ambican territory for a ZIPRA staging area, an invitation that carried the belief that ZAPU was the authentic nationalist force in Zimbabwe and that ZANU-

ZANLA was an upstart group. Nkomo vacillated and did not seize the opportunity to place ZIPRA troops in two strategically important locations instead of just one (although ZAPU was immobilized by intraparty disputes and arguably could not accept), and the offer then went to ZANU-ZANLA. As the war unfolded, and particularly once Zambia closed its borders with Southern Rhodesia in 1973, the bulk of the fighting occurred near Mozambique, and ZANLA thereby was in the forefront of the struggle.

The Rhodesian government tried to end the war by seeking separate compromises with each jailed nationalist. Julius Nyerere, president of Tanzania, insisted that ZANU and ZAPU work together against this tactic, and in 1971 the two parties came together to lobby against the latest discriminatory constitution concocted as a basis for independence in Southern Rhodesia. Nkomo then joined other nationalist party leaders at several abortive peace talks and periodically had tête-à-têtes of his own with Rhodesian officials, claiming that he could not bypass opportunities to establish peace through negotiated settlement.

Relations between ZANU and ZAPU never did normalize during the preindependence period. The two parties attended the Lancaster House conference in 1979 and, as an alliance called the Patriotic Front (PF), negotiated a final independence settlement for Zimbabwe. As soon as the signal event was settled, ZANU turned on the party alliance and announced that it would contest the independence elections as ZANU-PF. Nkomo was highly critical of the ZANU decision and felt forced to enter a separate slate of candidates under the party name of PF-ZAPU.

The results of that contest startled observers long familiar with, sympathetic to or confident in the indispensability of Nkomo to Zimbabwean politics. Father Zimbabwe did not emerge as the new executive of the country, nor did PF-ZAPU become a necessary coalition partner with ZANU-PF. Instead, PF-ZAPU won only 24 percent of the common roll votes, which gave it merely twenty seats in a hundred-seat Parliament, while ZANU-PF won 62 percent of the vote and fifty-seven seats (the remaining three "black" seats were won by Abel Muzorewa's United African National Council (UANC), and fifty seats were reserved for the whites). Robert Mugabe became the country's first prime minister.

Nkomo attributed the election upset to campaign activities of ex-ZANLA forces, arguing that they intimidated people and kept them from voting for ZAPU. Reports by Lord Soames, the British overseer for the elections, did not contradict these claims, but neither did they suggest that PF-ZAPU would have won the election in the absence of any voter intimidation. The blunt fact was that ZANU-ZANLA bore more of the fighting during the war, gained widespread attention in doing so, and drew the support of the people in the war zone away from ZAPU.

Prime Minister Mugabe offered Nkomo the position of president of Zimbabwe, but Nkomo declined this ceremonial job and held out for minister of home affairs to ensure, he says, that angry ZIPRA cadres would not sabotage the new government. In mid-1982 a cache of arms was discovered on a ZAPU-affiliated farm. Nkomo said that he knew nothing of this matter and explained that the arms probably had been deposited by demobilizing ZIPRA soldiers who feared that the Rhodesians would try to prevent a peaceful devolution of power to blacks. Mugabe thought otherwise and accused Nkomo and ZAPU of plotting to overthrow the government. He dismissed Nkomo and confiscated his personal property and that of ZAPU, although Nkomo was not charged with any crime. This resulted in ZIPRA desertions from the new national army and the subsequent rise of armed "dissidence" in Matabeleland. In 1983 Mugabe sent a North Korean–trained force into Matabeleland, and Nkomo slipped out of the country (once again) to attack Mugabe's policies from London.

Threatened with expulsion from Parliament for excessive absence, Nkomo returned some months later. ZANU tried to strong-arm him into merging ZAPU with ZANU. Nkomo held out, certain that the 1985 elections would vindicate ZAPU. The result again disappointed him: ZAPU retained strong support in Matabeleland but was not competitive with ZANU among the larger Shona-speaking population. Mugabe then stepped up earlier threats to install a one-party system under ZANU, knowing that this would effectively end Nkomo's political career, and simultaneously attempted to break ZAPU through arrests and alleged torture of party members.

In the waning days of 1987 a grim and defeated Nkomo clasped hands with a triumphant Mugabe and set about to persuade hard-core ZAPU supporters to cooperate with the new unity party of ZANU-PF. Nkomo then became a special senior minister in the Mugabe government, broadly in charge of social-welfare issues under a new presidential system, and has since quietly distinguished himself as an able and loyal minister, an active advocate of land reform and a public servant above reproach. In 1991 he was given the largely honoric post of vice president.

History, it is often remarked, is written by the victors. Until recently the ZANU government and its many chroniclers downplayed all contributions to Zimbabwean independence that Joshua Nkomo and ZAPU made in the years following the ZAPU/ZANU split. Nkomo was characterized as inept, cowardly, authoritarian, a poor loser, a Ndebele tribalist (although he is not technically of the Ndebele ethnic group) and as a man ending his political career as he began it, in compromise, ever concerned to have some power and influence. ZIPRA was accused of fighting the war less impressively than ZANLA and of failing to develop a convincing ideology. The latter charge is ironic, given the degree to which ZANU has backed away from some of its own wartime promises. The negative portrayal of Nkomo conveniently ignores his history as a tireless leader who almost single-handedly put the cause of Zimbabwean nationalism on the international map in the 1960s, and who then maintained the popularity and political dexterity necessary to stay in the limelight long after several other leaders lost heart or were silenced by avenging actions.

Nkomo's pragmatic and ambitious style, however, did falter during the crucial years of the 1960s. First he remained aloof too long—physically and ideolog-ically—from the increasing militancy of his own nationalist movement. Then he seemed too wedded to a reconciliatory style of politics to resist diplomatic methods that increasingly smacked of collaboration with Rhodesia. Perhaps he was also so preoccupied with discrediting ZANU that he failed to correct the perception that ZAPU was losing bite and vision. Once militant initiative passed to ZANU in the 1970s, and especially when areas under ZANLA control became main arenas of combat, Nkomo's luster faded. Even some spectacular ZIPRA achievements in the field failed to win him the coveted pinnacle he dearly sought. His overall efforts, however, did not fail to advance the cause of a free Zimbabwe.

BIBLIOGRAPHY

Work by Nkomo:

Nkomo: The Story of My Life. London: Methuen, 1984.

Other works:

Banana, Canaan S. (ed.). *Turmoil and Tenacity: Zimbabwe, 1890–1990*. Harare, Zim-babwe: College Press, 1990.
Day, John. *International Nationalism: The Extra-Territorial Relations of Southern Rho-desian African Nationalism*. London: Routledge and Kegan Paul, 1967.
Nyagumbo, Maurice. *With the People: An Autobiography from the Zimbabwe Struggle*. London: Allison and Busby, 1980.
Zimbabwe African People's Union. *Zimbabwe: History of the Struggle*. 2nd ed. Cairo: Afro-Asian People's Solidarity Organization, 1972.

CHRISTINE SYLVESTER

KWAME NKRUMAH (1909–1972), Prime Minister, President, Republic of Ghana, 1952–1966.

In an imperfect world, history may ultimately rank Nkrumah as one of Africa's more notable leaders, all of his faults and errors of judgment to the contrary notwithstanding. Against seemingly impossible odds, ahead of the African in-dependence wave, he succeeded in freeing his people from colonial bondage, returning to them the identity denied them by their colonial masters, causing black Africans to be proud once again of their race and cultural heritage. His record of concrete accomplishments, at home and abroad, is impressive. His vision seemed boundless. Once the Gold Coast colony became Ghana—named after an ancient West African kingdom—the newly independent state was to be the base for an all-African renaissance and its beginning. Eventually all of Africa was to be united, under one government, strong enough to rid the continent of all remaining vestiges of economic slavery and exploitation. Unlike so many rulers with comparable power, Nkrumah, considering himself a ''non-denominational Christian and a Marxist,'' steadfastly maintained a profound respect for human life; only one death can be attributed to him and that only indirectly, and he decidedly was not a racist.

Kwame—Saturday's child—was born in Nkroful, Gold Coast, either on September 21 or 28, 1909, or, by his mother's reckoning, three years later; he was baptized Francis Kwame by a Roman Catholic priest. Following elementary school and teacher training, he taught at several Roman Catholic institutions, entertaining briefly the idea of entering the priesthood, and moved to the United States in 1935 for advanced studies. He graduated from Lincoln University, Pennsylvania, with a B.A., and served there as an assistant lecturer in philosophy before being admitted to Lincoln Theological Seminary, enrolling simultaneously for a master's degree at the University of Pennsylvania. He obtained the bachelor of theology from Lincoln in 1942 and the M.S. in education as well as the M.A. in philosophy in 1943 from the University of Pennsylvania, there completing all requirements for the Ph.D. in philosophy except the thesis. His studies also qualified him as a political scientist, and he considered himself such in later years.

During those years, and subsequently while in London, he became "acquainted"—his term—with numerous left-wing organizations of black Africans and West Indians and with Communists. He read Hegel, Marx and Lenin, saying later that their writing "did much to influence me in my revolutionary ideas and activities, and Karl Marx and Lenin particularly impressed me as I felt sure that their philosophy was capable of solving [the problems of colonialism and imperialism]" (Nkrumah, *Ghana* 1957: 45). The writings of Marcus Garvey and W.E.B. Du Bois, and George Padmore* personally, inspired his Pan-Africanism. But he also "gleaned . . . much of value and many ideas" from Mussolini and Hitler, from Cromwell and Napoleon, and from Mahatma Gandhi. While in London, he enrolled at Gray's Inn to study law, attending lectures simultaneously at the London School of Economics. His plans to become a teacher or a lawyer were discarded abruptly with his appointment as secretary of the Organizing Committee for the Fifth Pan-African Congress, followed by appointment as general secretary of the Working Committee of the congress and secretary of the West African Secretariat. In these capacities he met such future African leaders as Nnamdi Azikiwe* and Obafemi Awolowo* of Nigeria, Léopold Senghor* of Senegal, Félix Houphouët-Boigny* of the Ivory Coast and Jomo Kenyatta* of Kenya. A product of the period and a portent of his political style to come was a document drawn up by him, "The Circle." Intended as a guide for a West African students' group, it called for establishment of a Union of West African Socialist Republics; and all members of "The Circle" were pledged to loyalty personally to Nkrumah, who was to be recognized as their undisputed leader. In due course, his leadership talents having come to the attention of nationalists at home, he was invited to become general secretary of the United Gold Coast Convention (UGCC). On December 29, 1947, Nkrumah was formally appointed to that position, and his real career began.

Had his seniors in the movement read "The Circle," they might not have been surprised when soon after his appointment he led a breakaway from the UGCC, founding his own Convention People's Party (CPP) on January 12, 1949. The new party's slogan was Self-government Now, to distinguish it in the public's mind from the more conservative, slow-moving parent organization. There were to be other differences, a commitment to radical socialism, for example. The CPP's strategy and tactics were summarized by "Positive Action," meaning nonviolence coupled with steadily escalating demands for constitutional change, everything pointing to eventual full independence. To him "The Political Kingdom" came first and then "everything else shall be added onto you." But violence could not be prevented, and in 1951 the Colonial Office ordered Nkrumah's arrest and trial—he had briefly been arrested and detained in 1948. As was to be the pattern for so many future Third World leaders, following his conviction, Nkrumah continued to conduct the affairs of his party, including a vigorously fought election campaign, from his prison cell. On February 12, 1951, the CPP having won a stunning victory, the British governor invited the prisoner to become Her Britannic Majesty's Leader of Government Business in the Legislative Assembly dominated by his party. Four months later the first black leader appointed to head a government in the British Empire and Commonwealth returned to his alma mater, Lincoln University, to accept an honorary doctor of laws degree.

Early in 1952 his official title was changed to prime minister. In the following year, by "The Motion of Destiny," Nkrumah moved in the Legislative Assembly that the Gold Coast be granted full independence "at the earliest possible time." After yet another CPP election victory, the British government became convinced that Nkrumah and his party could govern effectively, and that the alternative could be a struggle not worth the effort or the costs. Consequently, the British flag was lowered over the colony on March 6, 1957, and the flag of independent Ghana, with the Black Star at its center, was raised in its place.

Prior to independence, and for a brief period thereafter, Nkrumah worked with the governor and the Colonial Office in something akin to a partnership. As prime minister of a Commonwealth country, he became the first black African member of Her Majesty's Privy Council (eventually to be the queen's first official black guest at Buckingham Palace). That amicable relationship was jolted when it became apparent that certain human-rights safeguards written into a Preventive Detention Act introduced in Ghana one year after independence were not respected in practice. By 1960, after a rigged plebiscite, Ghana was proclaimed a republic, with Nkrumah, now president, replacing the queen as head of state. By then he also had made himself chairman of the CPP for life. Early in 1964, following another in a series of assassination attempts, Ghana was constitutionally declared to be a one-party state. From that point forward, detentions mounted, trusted "Nkrumaists" replaced suspect army officers and trade-union officials, a plan to radicalize higher education was set in motion, and Soviet-bloc academicians, technical experts, including security personnel, were funnelled into the state in greater numbers. Chinese Communist and East European instructors were hired to train selected Ghanaians and other recruits from all parts of the continent in guerrilla warfare and sabotage. The Soviet ambassador became premier foreign advisor to the president.

Early in 1966, facing a crippling economic crisis at home, Nkrumah travelled to Beijing, intending to go on to Hanoi on a peace mission on behalf of Commonwealth prime ministers. By the time his plane landed in Beijing he learned that he had been overthrown by a military coup on February 24, 1966. Granted asylum in Guinea by Sékou Touré,* his partner in the by then defunct "union" between Ghana, Mali and Guinea, he unsuccessfully attempted, by radio appeals and pamphlets, to rally his countrymen to his cause from exile. Eventually, terminally ill, he sought medical aid at a clinic in Bucharest, Rumania. He died there on April 27, 1972. His body was returned to Guinea, to be interred shortly thereafter in Ghana. Thus ended the life and career of Osagyefo (The Redeemer) Dr. Kwame Nkrumah, president of the Republic of Ghana, supreme commander of the armed forces, chairman for life of the Convention People's Party, head of the Order of the Black Star and of the Order of the Volta, holder of the Lenin Peace Prize, chancellor of the University of Ghana and, as shown on Ghanaian coins, "Conditor Ghanaiensis."

Nkrumah's political conduct has been variously interpreted. Some saw in him a power-hungry hypocrite who publicly proclaimed to be committed to scientific socialism while privately enriching himself and his cronies, maintaining all the while a belief in traditional superstition and magic, consulting soothsayers on a regular basis. Some saw him moving his country, by his undeniable charisma and outstanding organizational talent, by means of "benevolent dictatorship," toward some form of parliamentary democracy. Others accepted his posture as a Marxist-Leninist revolutionary. Nkrumah's Ghana did show some concrete manifestations of Marxism, but only some, and even these—especially the way they were applied—no competent Marxist would recognize as such. Some of his closer aides, more or less sincerely, professed to be Marxists, and while he was in power, Accra became a mecca for like-minded free-lancing individuals, mainly from the United States, the West Indies and Great Britain.

Given his commitment to an African renaissance, it was but a question of time before Nkrumah would attempt to replace European-oriented social and political philosophies, including Marxism-Leninism, with his own ideological formulations termed variously "African scientific socialism," "Nkrumaism" or, as advanced in a bizarre, convoluted, surely ghostwritten book, "consciencism." The Kwame Nkrumah Ideological Institute was to be the center of a national as well as Africa-wide training and dissemination program for the new philosophy. All members of the cabinet, as well as key party leaders, were obligated periodically to attend seminars in Nkrumaism at the institute. The faculty included instructors from several East European countries and from the Soviet Union. Among students were expatriates and exiles from countries whose rulers rejected Nkrumah's leadership and from territories yet to be liberated. Following his overthrow, while in exile in Marxist Guinea, he appears to have returned to his earlier Marxist-Leninist preference. Actually, his personal understanding of Marxism, or of political economy in general, was rather shallow and simplistic. Many of his Marxist-sounding writings, when not wholly ghostwritten, were simply adapted from Soviet or Maoist models. Not surprisingly, the nitty-gritty of economics and of public finance, both at the heart of Marxism, were concerns he abhorred. He preferred to busy himself with sweeping foreign policy designs. To an extent, the mismanagement of the national economy reflected Nkrumah's ideological rootlessness.

While the still-viable economy continued to provide the necessary funds, Nkrumah's plan to make Ghana the lodestar of African independence and self-assertion led to remarkable successes. Ghana's Black Star was carried to the far corners of the earth on planes of the new national airline and on ships of the new national shipping company, as well as on the flags raised over rapidly proliferating Ghanaian embassies throughout the world. Educational and health care facilities were expanded significantly. In terms of funds allocated to elementary and higher education and pupils and students in schools, colleges and technical training institutes, and in terms of hospital beds and other medical facilities, his record was initially impressive. So were the numbers of new industrial enterprises launched or in process of formation, pieces of mail transmitted, telephone lines installed and newspapers circulating. Research was pressed to improve for export critical agricultural production, and steps were taken to expand and modernize the economic infrastructure, mainly communication links, roads and ports. The diamond in the crown of Nkrumah's achievements was the Volta River dam and hydroelectric power station, coupled with an aluminum smelter and processing complex, and, to serve it, a greatly expanded port facility.

At the outset of his rule, Ghana could draw on a substantial hard currency reserve. Its raw materials and agricultural products were assured steady markets in the West. At independence Ghana was in relatively better financial shape than was the vastly larger, potentially richer, Belgian Congo or India when it was cut loose from British rule. Nkrumah's decision in the early 1960s to shift much of Ghana's trade from West to East reflected a profound misreading of the true disposition of world economic forces and of the politics driven by them. At the time of his fall, Ghana's per capita income had been reduced. Of some fifty state-owned enterprises, only three showed a profit. International swindlers or self-seeking export-driven foreign corporations had been allowed to fleece Ghana's economy in return for kickbacks to the president or his associates. The technically and economically unfeasible projects thus "financed" wound up as no more than costly white elephants. By 1966 the country's national debt was fifteen times that of five years earlier. The balance of payments was such that many of Nkrumah's ambitious industrialization plans had virtually come to a halt. At the time of his death, the London *Economist* commented that from being the richest country in black Africa at independence, Ghana had become a prime example of what had gone wrong with development on that continent. Or was it, as Nkrumah never ceased to contend, that unless all of Africa was first united, poverty could not be conquered on the continent?

Some successes were scored initially in foreign affairs. A very small colonial backwater was catapulted almost overnight to international prominence. Ghana's diplomatic emissaries, and the president himself, played key roles in West African regional politics, in the Organization of African Unity (OAU)—which came into existence partly through Nkrumah's untiring efforts—within the British-led Commonwealth of Nations, at the United Nations and in the Movement of Non-Aligned States. In the process Nkrumah found himself in the company of the giants of his day as their equal—or so it seemed to him—for example, Tito, Mao Zedong, Nehru and Nasser, among others. The Cold War between East and West created special opportunities for an officially nonaligned country, and Nkrumah found himself courted by both Washington and Moscow.

If a central theme or purpose has to be identified in Nkrumah's management of the polity, it has to be establishment of a personal political machine. Once that was accomplished, executive power was expanded steadily, while legal-constitutional constraints to the machine and to the political corruption on which the machine was based were set aside. As political opposition mounted, a network of informers and an expanded secret service, both accountable to Nkrumah directly, were spread over the country. Although on paper the holder of power in a one-party state, the CPP was reduced to a hollow shell, consigned to serve as an instrument of propaganda, political "education" and mass mobilization for demonstration purposes. The president's executive secretariat, not party headquarters, was the fount of all power in the state. Cronyism replaced the once highly reputed colonial system of public service selection. The president decided personally who was to serve and who was to be dispensed with, justices of the Supreme Court who dared to defy him not excluded.

For several years Nkrumah enjoyed wide popularity, especially among the urban youth, the market women and small farmers. Sections of the populace took pride in their "Show Boy," appreciative that thanks to his leadership at home and initiatives abroad, they were the first black Africans in modern times of whom the world took notice with admiration. Not captivated by him were much of the middle class, university faculty and students, much of the civil service, trade unionists and the British-trained officers in the armed forces and in the police. By the middle of 1965 Nkrumah no longer dared to test his popularity or that of his regime even in a rigged election. When the end came, what British rule had left behind in the way of a political order, a judicial system and the service structure to support these had been dismantled, corrupted or shelved, and nothing but an amateurish, jerry-built political system topped by the personal political machine had been put in their place. All that was swept away by a handful of rebellious officers and troops in the early morning hours of one single day.

While few can quarrel with Nkrumah's concept of a united Africa, execution of his plans left much to be desired. Impatience, suspicion and a measure of arrogance governed his relations with African leaders whose cooperation was not readily forthcoming. At times patronizing, at times outright offensive, Nkrumah eventually alienated almost every African head of state. Training guerrillas for action in member states of the OAU, granting refuge to suspected assassins wanted in neighboring countries, and obliquely expressing approval when Nigeria's Prime Minister Balewa was murdered foreclosed any chance that Nkrumah's leadership would be accepted internationally. Predictably, the grandiose conference hall he ordered constructed to serve as headquarters of an African Union Government in Accra was used exactly once for a meeting of African heads of state, the absence of leaders he had offended marring the occasion.

In his Pan-Africa vision Nkrumah stubbornly ignored internal conditions as well as external ties, commitments, long-standing cultural and historical associations and vital security interests of still-insecure and unstable newly independent countries. Nor did he take into account the strong cross-currents created by the confrontation between the major power blocs. In Nkrumah's world empires would be dismantled by fiery speeches, and a united Africa would be created by quixotic attempts at subversion and insurgency, in the former Belgian Congo, for example, in neighboring French-speaking states or in southern Africa. To him, Africa was a continent seething with revolutionary unrest whose masses impatiently awaited his leadership; only timid, self-seeking rulers stood in the way. Only he knew what needed to be done to free the continent.

The case of Kwame Nkrumah is a prime example of a leader allowing himself to become detached from reality. Once a talented and dedicated person, he let his vision and his ambitions get ahead of his own people, the resources available to him and, in the final analysis, his own abilities. Progressively more isolated and suspicious, inundated by gossip from his army of informers, he increasingly relied on foreign advisors who did not necessarily have Ghana's best interests at heart. Too many of these drew upon experiences, theories and conditions largely, if not wholly, unrelated to those Nkrumah had to address at home and abroad. Regarding his once-closest associates, he seemed unable to distinguish between attachment to the old ways—"colonial mentality," he called it—and wise and timely calls for prudence. Whether just impatient or suspicious, he managed to drive into internal retreat or emigration too many of Ghana's civil servants, lawyers and judges, depriving himself of the services of one of the best-trained civil and legal service corps in British colonial Africa.

Nkrumah appears to have been unable to identify the real obstacles to fulfillment of his dreams. A vain personality bordering on megalomania—he seemed incapable of resisting flattery—inevitably fostered a personality cult. It began with an entirely reasonable campaign to replace the images and vestiges of British colonial rule with appropriate African symbols. It ended with Nkrumah's countenance on stamps and coins and with an imposing statue of himself in the center of the capital. He could not resist being proclaimed "Messiah of Africa" or being described in terms associated with Christ. Doubters, critics or advisors counselling moderation were not tolerated in his government. Consequently, a new ruling class emerged, mediocre and venal sycophants, increasingly drawn from trusted tribal circles, occupying key positions at all levels of government, including, to his ultimate sorrow, the security service charged with surveillance of internal enemies and defense of the regime.

Yet, as his body was brought home, accompanied by a high-level delegation including former associates he had once ordered arrested and jailed, a revival of the Nkrumah cult seemed already under way. Now much larger than life, he seemed to tower high above the little men who followed him. At the time of his burial, an obituary in a Ghanaian newspaper—harking back to a line in a liturgy often sung in his presence—in effect pronounced his epitaph: "And who now doubts that 'Nkrumah Never Dies'?" His last will and testament opened, at the time somewhat grandiloquently, with "I, Kwame Nkrumah of Africa." In years to come, as the blemishes on his record fade with the passage of time, and if the memory of him survives the discrediting of Marxist-Leninist rulers everywhere, Africa may well grant him that distinction, though it may be more a tribute to his dreams and aspirations than to the man.

BIBLIOGRAPHY

Works by Nkrumah:

Ghana: The Autobiography of Kwame Nkrumah. Edinburgh: Nelson, 1957.
I Speak of Freedom: A Statement of African Ideology. New York: Praeger, 1962.
Towards Colonial Freedom: Africa in the Struggle against World Imperialism. London: Heinemann, 1962.
Africa Must Unite. London: Heinemann, 1963.
Consciencism: Philosophy and Ideology for De-Colonization and Development with Particular Reference to the African Revolution. London: Heinemann, 1964.
Neo-Colonialism: The Last Stage of Imperialism. London: Nelson, 1965.
Axioms of Kwame Nkrumah. London: Panaf, 1967.
Challenge of the Congo. New York: International Publishers, 1967.
Voice from Conakry. London: Panaf, 1967.
Dark Days in Ghana. New York: International Publishers, 1968.
Handbook of Revolutionary Warfare. London: Panaf, 1968.
Class Struggle in Africa. London: Panaf, 1970.

Other Works:

Apter, David E. *Ghana in Transition*. Princeton, N.J.: Princeton University Press, 1963.
Bing, Geoffrey. *Reap the Whirlwind: An Account of Kwame Nkrumah's Ghana from 1950 to 1966*. London: MacGibbon and Kee, 1968.
Bretton, Henry L. *The Rise and Fall of Kwame Nkrumah: A Study of Personal Rule in Africa*. New York: Praeger, 1966.
————. "Non-Violent Leadership Response in a Violence-Inducing Setting: The Case of Kwame Nkrumah." In Robert S. Robins (ed.), *Psychopathology and Political Leadership*. New Orleans: Tulane University Press, 1977, 113–50.
Davidson, Basil. *Black Star: A View of the Life and Times of Kwame Nkrumah*. New York: Praeger, 1973.
Jones, Trevor. *Ghana's First Republic, 1960–1966*. London: Methuen, 1976.
Marais, Genoveva. *Kwame Nkrumah As I Knew Him*. Chichester, Eng.: Janay, 1972.
McKown, Robin. *Nkrumah: A Biography*. Garden City, N.Y.: Doubleday, 1973.

Omari, T. Peter. *Kwame Nkrumah: The Anatomy of an African Dictatorship*. New York: Africana Publishing Co., 1970.

HENRY L. BRETTON

SAM NUJOMA (1929–   ), President, South West Africa People's Organization, 1962–   ; President, Republic of Namibia, 1990–   .

Sam Nujoma, the first president of Namibia, led his country to independence in 1990. From 1962 he was head of the South West Africa People's Organization (SWAPO), Namibia's pre-eminent liberation movement. Returning home from long years of exile in 1989, Nujoma joined other leaders of SWAPO in campaigning vigorously for his party in the country's first fully free, national election. The poll, for seats in a seventy-two–member constituent assembly that would write a constitution for Namibia, turned out to be a triumph for SWAPO. In November Nujoma and his colleagues won 57 percent of the total vote (using the proportional-representation method) and forty-one seats in the assembly. The Democratic Turnhalle Alliance (DTA), led by Dirk Mudge, an Afrikaans-speaking white farmer, won twenty-one seats. A small black party, the United Democratic Front (UDF), gained four seats, Action Christian National, a right-wing white party, took three seats, and three black parties won a seat each.

The constituent assembly sat for eighty days between November 1989 and February 1990. Since a two-thirds vote of the whole was required to establish provisions of the new constitutional document, compromise was necessary. Nujoma, whose fiery revolutionary rhetoric had been a staple of his many years in exile, opted in the assembly debates for conciliation. SWAPO moderated its demands in the course of the deliberations of the assembly, dropping any insistence on single-party rule, preventive detention, an all-powerful executive and any radical restructuring of the economy along Marxist lines. Instead, under Nujoma's direction SWAPO accepted the most liberal democratic constitution in Africa. It established a multiparty system, guaranteed fundamental human rights, outlawed discrimination of any kind (including sexual), limited the president to two five-year terms, abolished the death penalty, and enshrined private ownership of property and foreign investment. Schooling was to be compulsory and free. Child labor was abolished.

At the end of the assembly, Nujoma was elected overwhelmingly as Namibia's first president, and he was sworn into office—succeeding South African administrators—by United Nations Secretary-General Javier Pérez de Cuellar on March 21, 1990. The assembly, which was transformed into a lower house of a new bicameral Parliament (one house called the National Assembly and the other the House of Review), limited Nujoma's presidential power to declare states of emergency or martial law. It also provided for impeachment and removal procedures.

Nujoma welcomed the new constitution, with all its limitations on his power and with all its focus on a democratic, nonsocialist state. Looking over his shoulder in February 1990 at South Africa, he suggested that the constitution "might serve as a model for other countries who [were] presently involved in the process of reordering their societies." Such countries might find, he continued, "some positive examples from our humble democratic beginning."

President Nujoma referred both to his fledgling nation and, possibly, to himself. The son of farm workers who lived in Ongandjera, the capital of the Njera section of the Ovambo people, Nujoma was born on May 12, 1929. The Njera were one of the smallest of the seven subethnic groups of Ovambo and among the least prosperous.

Ongandjera lies about fifty miles south of the Kunene River in Namibia's northern savannah region. The Ovambo grow millet, sorghum, melons, beans and pumpkins in a predominantly flat area of occasional flood plains dotted with palm trees. Up to twenty-four inches of rain falls during the African summer, more than on any other part of Namibia. But this has never been a part of the country engaged in cash cropping or in production for export. The Ovambo, however, comprising about half of the population of Namibia, supplied migrant labor to Namibia's copper mine at Tsumeb and its diamond mines in distant Oranjemund.

The Ovambo lived apart from much of the early German colonial settlement and administrative organization of what was the colony of Südwestafrika (1885–1915). The rest of the colony was greatly affected by German depredations and land confiscation. Yet the Ovambo avoided the kinds of modernization that accompanied early colonial intrusions. Nevertheless, Ovamboland presented glorious evangelical opportunities for German and Finnish Lutherans, for British Anglicans, and for German Roman Catholics.

Nujoma, like so many of his politicized contemporaries, was initially schooled by teachers of the Finnish Missionary Society. His years in school were very few, however, and during World War II he left Ovamboland for the home of relatives in Walvis Bay, Namibia's main port city. He may have continued his schooling there, but he was not again under formal instruction until 1949, when he learned English from Anglican missionaries based in Windhoek.

During these years, and until 1957, Nujoma worked for the Namibian section of the South African Railways. First as a sweeper and then as a junior clerk, he saw service throughout what was then called South West Africa. He was dismissed because of union activities. Subsequently he was employed as a clerk in the offices of the Windhoek municipality and as a clerk in a wholesale store.

Nujoma's political awakening took place in the very late 1950s in Windhoek, the territory's capital and indigenous melting pot. One of Namibia's early nationalist movements, the South West Africa National Union (SWANU), organized a mass protest in 1959 against the forced removal of black and brown Namibians from a residential township within Windhoek (the Windhoek Old Location) to the brand-new town of Katutura on the dusty outskirts of the capital. The campaign, in which Nujoma played a charismatic major role, included the boycott of public buses, movie theaters and beer halls. There were frequent demonstrations against the removals and thus against the importation of apartheid into South West Africa. During one of the protests there was a notorious clash with the police in which eleven Namibians were killed, buildings were set on fire, and troubles in Namibia came dramatically to the attention of the world press. Nujoma was jailed for a week.

Two years before, Andimba Toivo ja Toivo and others had formed the Ovambo People's Organization (OPO) as the vanguard political movement of Namibia. After the Katutura protests, with Toivo under house arrest, Nujoma was sent on behalf of OPO to the United Nations. He intended to help make Namibia's plight of more central concern there. In New York, too, along with Mburumba Kerina and other members of SWANU (a mostly Herero organization), Nujoma founded SWAPO. The shift from OPO to SWAPO was clearly essential if the efforts of these young Namibians were not to be derided as merely tribal.

In 1962 Nujoma took control of SWAPO after successfully ousting Kerina. In that year and again in 1964 Nujoma attempted to merge SWANU and SWAPO, but personal and ethnic antagonisms prevented any meaningful compromise on the status of the leadership or the ideological approach of the parties. SWAPO at this time was the more pro-Western of the two organizations; SWANU had begun flirting with Maoist China. As a result of such leanings, the Soviet Union took an interest in Nujoma and SWAPO from about 1964, and Nujoma also began recruiting young Namibians for military training as guerrillas from this period. He and they launched the first, tentative attacks on South West Africa from Zambia in 1966. As a result of these and further incursions in succeeding years, the Organization of African Unity (OAU) in 1968 and the United Nations in 1973 recognized SWAPO as Namibia's sole authentic liberation group.

Nujoma's clear dominance of SWAPO dated from 1969, the time of its last national congress. It also coincided with the intensification of Soviet interest in and military assistance to SWAPO. Nujoma received the Lenin Peace Prize in Moscow in 1968. Nujoma also developed comfortable relations during these years with Sweden, Norway, Algeria and Cuba, and during the 1970s with the former Portuguese colonies of Angola and Mozambique. Although for the decade before independence SWAPO's military bases were in Angola and most of its forays into northern Namibia were launched from southern Angola, Nujoma's home and main center during the 1970s and much of the 1980s was Lusaka, Zambia.

There he presided over SWAPO's sixteen-member national executive and thirty-five-member central committee. Decisions were made by him and his close associates. When they were challenged, as they were by some of his early compatriots in the mid-1970s, Nujoma responded with ruthless authority. In 1976, when guerrillas in their camps accused him and the executive of corruption and inefficiency, Nujoma persuaded the Zambian authorities to arrest the troublemakers and to confine them first in Zambia and then in Tanzania. It was alleged then and in 1989 that many opponents were killed during both the 1970s and 1980s.

As president of Namibia and as guerrilla leader, Nujoma cut an impressive personal figure with his expansive white beard and ready smile. He was described during his long years as exiled national leader as canny, with a keen sense of personal survival. Those from the United States who negotiated with him during the Carter and then the Reagan administrations always commented on his apparently limited grasp of details and disinterest in abstractions, but no one ever faulted his grasp of SWAPO and his direction of his colleagues during the days of the constituent assembly. Details of his private life remain largely undisclosed.

Namibia won its independence less on the battlefield than at the negotiating table. Yet SWAPO was always a guest and never the main protagonist at the table. In the end, during the 1988 mediation that led to the independence of Namibia (and a return to the transitional authority of the United Nations, following a 1978 agreement) as well as the Cuban exodus from Angola, the Soviet Union, Cuba and the United States and, on the other side, South Africa were the key participants. Even so, without Nujoma and SWAPO there would have been no immediate on-the-ground pressure on South Africa throughout the 1970s and 1980s and no nationalist movement to thwart the white Namibian and South African attempts to retain power on the eve of independence.

BIBLIOGRAPHY

Dugard, John. *The South West Africa/Namibia Dispute*. Berkeley: University of California Press, 1973.

DuPisani, André. *SWA/Namibia: The Politics of Continuity and Change*. Johannesburg: J. Ball, 1985.

Green, Reginald H. *Namibia, The Last Colony*. Ed. Kimmo Kiljunen and Marja-Liisa Kiljunen. Harlow, Eng.: Longman, 1981.

Katjavivi, Peter H. *A History of Resistance in Namibia*. London: James Currey, 1988.

Moleah, Alfred T. *Namibia, The Struggle for Liberation*. Wilmington, Del.: Disa Press, 1983.

Rotberg, Robert I. (ed.). *Namibia: Political and Economic Prospects*. Lexington, Mass.: Lexington Books/D.C. Heath, 1983.

Soggot, David. *Namibia: One Violent Heritage*. New York: St. Martin's Press, 1986.

ROBERT I. ROTBERG

JULIUS KAMBARAGE NYERERE (1922–   ), Prime Minister, President, United Republic of Tanzania, 1961–1986.

Outstanding in the pantheon of Africa's independence heroes, Julius Nyerere of Tanzania ranks with the world's major political figures of the post–World War II era. The founding father of his country, the philosopher of *ujamaa* and its ideology of communitarian development, the designer of its political system, and a major actor in Africa's international struggle over continental cooperation and foreign policy nonalignment, Nyerere perdured in power long enough to see all his early policy commitments and some successes severely challenged upon leaving office. One-party democracy, egalitarian socialist progress and national self-reliance, all major themes of Nyerere's political tenure, may now be seen as interlocked phases, rather than the permanent foundations of Tanzania's future development. Yet the legacy of Nyerere's leadership remains firm; it is summed up in his honorific Swahili title *mwalimu* (teacher). Although not immune to the authorization of force in politics, he remained an intellectual—he has translated Shakespeare into Swahili—and a political "prophet" (as he was designated by the authors of an influential comparative study) who continually called ordinary citizens to their better instincts, toward nonracialism, cooperation, a code of moral conduct and social justice. In his later years, despite the failure of his policies of egalitarian socialism and self-reliant development, he departed from active politics as he entered, maintaining a modest life-style, encouraging his supporters and attempting to persuade his critics, secure in the belief that a rational and inclusive political discussion could lead to a better life for all.

Julius Kambarage Nyerere was born in 1922 in the village of Butiama in the Northern Province of what was then Tanganyika, a former German territory mandated by the League of Nations to Great Britain after World War I. He was the son of the fifth wife (of twenty-two) of Chief Burito of the small Zanaki tribe. After baptism as a Roman Catholic and early schooling at the local mission, at age twelve Nyerere was sent to Tabora Government School in western Tanganyika. An excellent student, he went on to Makerere College (at that time the University College of East Africa) in Uganda in 1943 and received a teaching diploma in 1945. At Makerere he founded the Tanganyika African Welfare Association (TAWA) to voice the students' interest in economic and social progress. TAWA later became a branch of the Tanganyika African Association (TAA), an organization mostly of civil servants, which Nyerere joined after he returned to Tabora to pursue his career as a teacher at St. Mary's Roman Catholic Mission Boys School. By 1949 Nyerere decided to continue his studies by taking up a scholarship at Edinburgh University, eventually becoming the first Tanganyikan to graduate from a British university: He received a master's degree in economics and history in 1952. His time in Britain was marked by an expanding awareness of the anticolonial movement through his asociation with other, especially West African, students and with the Fabian Colonial Bureau, a branch of the Fabian Society, which preached non-Marxist socialism and independence for the European colonies. Resuming his teaching career at St. Francis School, Pugu (on the outskirts of Dar es Salaam), upon his return to Tanganyika, within three months Nyerere was elected president of the TAA in 1953. In 1955 Nyerere gave up teaching to become a full-time politician.

On July 7, 1954, TAA had been transformed into the Tanganyikan African National Union (TANU), a territorywide nationalist organization, with a constitution (as Nyerere later recalled) loosely modelled on that of the Convention People's Party of the Gold Coast (Ghana). TANU elected Nyerere president, a post to which he was regularly re-elected—later as chairman of Chama Cha Mapinduzi (CCM), which marked the 1977 unification of TANU with the Afro-Shirazi Party of Zanzibar—until 1987.

TANU's earliest task was popular mobilization through branches throughout the country, but Tanganyika's trust status with the United Nations, inherited from the mandate status under the League of Nations, permitted representations to visiting missions from the UN, an opportunity utilized by TANU in 1954 to press its demand for self-government. With this purpose in mind, Nyerere appeared as a representative of TANU at the UN Trusteeship Council in 1955 and 1956, arguing for a schedule for Tanganyikan independence, much to the annoyance of the British administration. With this intervention, Nyerere established himself as the unchallenged leader of a new mass movement, nonviolent and nonracial, as distinguished from tribal and multiracial associations favored by the British home and territorial governments and most of the small group of territorial settlers; distinguished, as well, from the Mau Mau type of violence exemplified in neighboring Kenya, which the British feared might spread via black nationalism.

Displaying a pragmatism characteristic of his entire political career, Nyerere accepted a nominated position to the Legislative Council of the territory, from which he resigned in 1957 in order to campaign openly for more rapid progress toward self-government. A revealing moment occurred when Nyerere was charged with "sedition" and convicted of libel for an article in the TANU journal, which forced a choice between paying a fine or going to jail (and generating a usable martyrdom). Nyerere paid the fine and continued organizing. Later, in a momentous decision TANU's National Conference was persuaded by Nyerere to participate in, not boycott, the 1958 elections, despite provision for three equal groups of racially defined seats in the legislature. TANU ran its own European and Asian candidates, in addition to its African candidates, and aided by a common electoral roll, it emerged as the largest party represented in the Legislative Council, a result that cast the die for a quick march to independence. The results also vindicated Nyerere's choice of the nonracial middle ground between black "Africanism" and multiracial "partnership" with white settlers. In the election of 1960 TANU won all but one of the legislature's seats. Nyerere became chief minister of the transition government, which gained full independence in December 1961, with Nyerere as prime minister.

Nyerere took over a country regarded as among the most backward of the British dependencies. In 1961 the territorial per capita income was $60 per year, and 3.7 percent of the total land area was recorded as arable. The size of France and Germany combined, Tanganyika had only two major port cities on the Indian Ocean, including the capital of Dar es Salaam, and only two rail lines, essentially serving those ports. It had no manufacturing industries, a few export commodities, such as sisal, tobacco, tea and coffee, and no large deposits of valuable minerals except low-grade coal in an inaccessible part of the country. Poverty, ignorance and disease, which Nyerere would call his prime enemies, were rife.

Nyerere plunged into reorganizing TANU for the task of government by resigning as prime minister to travel the country. The period 1960–61 also saw Nyerere travelling abroad, permitting him to gain recognition as a rising Third World leader whose affable demeanor, persuasive platform performance and record of nonviolent democratic politics made him appear less radical than the

fiery Nasser of Egypt, Nkrumah* of Ghana and Lumumba* of the Congo (Zaire)—
companion African nationalists of the same era. (This marked the commencement
of ''Tanzaphilia,'' which afflicted many Western intellectuals, according to more
critical observers, a condition that lasted through most of Tanzania's first decade.)

In December 1962 Nyerere returned to government as president of the newly
declared republic. In short order he had to confront a revolution in offshore
Zanzibar and a mutiny in his own army. On January 12, 1964, a makeshift attack
on a police armory in Zanzibar Town led to a full-scale uprising of the majority
Afro-Shirazi population against an Arab minority government, which had just
formed a postelection coalition. The hereditary Arab sultanate, recently installed
as a constitutional monarchy by the departing British, was swept away in the
ensuing violence against the Arab and Indian middle class. Order was restored
under the leadership of the Afro-Shirazi Party with the help of three hundred
Tanganyikan policemen.

On January 20, just days after the Zanzibar revolution, elements of the Tanganyika army in Dar es Salaam, disappointed over the slow pace of Africanization
(which had been launched upon independence amid much fanfare in the civil
service), mutinied, imprisoning their British officers. Nyerere hid during rioting
and destruction in Dar es Salaam, but he rallied his supporters after apparently
granting the mutineers' demands and suppressed the mutiny by recalling British
troops. The military was reorganized, subordinated to TANU and removed as a
threat to civilian supremacy, thus saving Tanzania from the fate of many postcolonial African governments. Later in 1964 Nyerere became president of the
United Republic of Tanganyika and Zanzibar, renamed Tanzania later that year.
Zanzibar retains considerable autonomy in the running of its affairs, despite
special arrangements for protecting its interests in the constitutions both of Tanzania and of the CCM.

Although called into question by Nyerere himself (*New York Times*, February
27, 1990), the legitimacy of the one-party system in Africa, and particularly in
Tanzania, as a variation of democracy has been central to Nyerere's thinking
and indeed represents a unique contribution by him to political theory in the
second half of the twentieth century. In 1963 he stated that ''where there is one
party, and that party is identified with the nation as a whole, the foundations of
democracy are firmer than they can ever be where you have two or more parties''
(Nyerere 1963: quoted in Glickman 1967:211). Nyerere's vigorous defense of
the benign monopolitical system was grounded in three arguments: practical,
traditional and instrumental toward development. First, in Tanzania, TANU
could be seen to embody the people's will, as opposition in fact disappeared in
the transition to independence, and serious policy disagreements did not surface
until the 1980s. By 1965 the mechanics of the political system provided for a
party primary selection process and binary electoral competition under the party
umbrella, which allowed for constrained criticism of political performance in
parliamentary elections held every five years. Second, Nyerere claimed that
European dual-party and multiparty systems reflected class and interest differ-

ences that did not apply to African societies. Traditional African decision making supposedly occurred in a consensus fashion in which "people talk until they agree." Finally, the single party would create disincentives for small differences of opinion to escalate into partisan issues; it would also prevent minor cultural ("tribal") differences from forming the basis of potentially deadly political competition. By building a single national policy institution, the national energies could be focused on the primary national goal of development. Nyerere invested much of his own time and energy in party debates and in "safaris" to party/government events around the country to encourage grass-roots participation in party/government affairs; he attempted, as he once put it, "to build a two-way all-weather road" between the people and their leaders. Uncontestably, TANU/CCM accomplished the task of national integration, achieving a national political culture. In this effort it was aided enormously by the spread of Swahili as a lingua franca. Nevertheless, in company with other single-party systems in Africa, even those that eschewed the Marxist-Leninist label, TANU/CCM could not avoid bureaucratic elitism, inefficiency, and divisions over socialist strategy and ethnic favoritism. In his 1990 remarks noted earlier, Nyerere admitted that corruption in Tanzania was "serious" and "commonplace. . . . We are now like the rest of Africa."

In addition to federation with Zanzibar and the establishment of one-party "democracy," Nyerere's major contribution rests with the struggle to implant *ujamaa* (familyhood) socialism as a consequence as well as a strategy of development. Nyerere believed that socialism in general was "an attitude of mind" and that it was mainly about equality. He believed not only that capitalism need not mature as a precursor to socialism, but also that its developmental engine could be captured and strengthened by state direction and regulation, thus avoiding unjust inequalities and leading to the improvement of living conditions for the masses. His first slogan, *uhuru na kazi* (freedom and work), meant starting the development process at the village level, relying on the people's own efforts rather than on grandiose hyperprojects of industrialization. ("Some people reach for the stars; we must reach the village.") Dissatisfied with the relatively slow progress made in the early years of independence—although quite respectable advances in increasing literacy and access to clean water were made—Nyerere promulgated the Arusha Declaration in 1967, which marked a great leap forward toward spurring agricultural production and equalizing services and incomes. The Arusha strategy of development was influenced to some extent by the experience of state-directed socialism in Mao's China, specifically providing for direct government intervention in production and distribution through nationalized "parastatal" enterprises and collectivization of agriculture. It also established the TANU Leadership Code of Conduct, intended to confine politicians, bureaucrats and professionals to an austere noncapitalist style of living in line with that of the ordinary peasant and manual worker.

Ujamaa villages were originally voluntary and built on the idea of agricultural transformation by regrouping scattered peasant homesteads for more efficient sharing of farm equipment and division of labor, and for sharing medical, sanitation and educational services. *Ujamaa* villages sought to attract city folk to rural areas to improve agriculture and contribute to stemming the tide of urbanization. Supposedly, peasants would welcome the prospects for a better life and build on their communal traditions. To encourage *ujamaa* collectivization, self-governing village assemblies were created in 1975 to elect village councils with authority to plan village development. In 1976 independent farmer marketing co-operatives and regional co-op unions were abolished, with *ujamaa* villages assuming the functions of the former co-operatives in dealing with parastatal marketing and distributing units that had replaced the Asian *duka wallahs,* who had served as rural creditors, marketeers and distributors in the past. Despite Nyerere's wish that the government play only a preliminary role to provide the initial assistance and equipment and that the party persuade rather than coerce, farmers had to be forced to cooperate within the new institutions.

This Arusha period of *ujamaa* collectivism carried from 1968 into a second five-year plan, climaxing with forced villagization in 1974–76, a move that shocked many of the democratic socialists among Nyerere's foreign supporters. Some 80 percent of the population, more than thirteen million people, had been grouped together in 7,700 villages, many without adequate planning, yielding many gripes and some hardship. Nyerere admitted in 1991 that agricultural policy and nationalization of enterprises were the two areas of the Arusha Declaration he would have implemented differently. The 1970s saw production drops in agriculture and manufacturing due to failed attempts at diversification, price controls and redistribution of investment and income. The marketing and distribution parastatals failed to provide adequate storage and transport for crops. Urbanization continued apace. What industrialization did continue did not shed its dependence on imported materials. Amidst the turmoil, the government began to implement the decision of 1974 to move the capital from Dar es Salaam to Dodoma in the center of the country. CCM headquarters relocated to Dodoma in 1978.

Nyerere could claim that on social issues, however, his conception of socialism as improvement in the lot of workers and peasants did move closer to realization. In public health, clinics practicing preventive medicine were set up throughout the country, helping to cut in half the infant mortality rates between 1962 and 1984. In addition, the life expectancy of Tanzanians increased from roughly thirty-five to fifty-one years in two decades. In education, Tanzania compares well with other African nations. Primary education is virtually universal, and there has been a vast increase in the number of children of all ages in school. Adult literacy has improved as well, to nearly 90 percent.

Nyerere has also held that while the policies of collectivization of agriculture and nationalization of enterprises could have been improved upon, in the same period of the 1970s Tanzania's economy also suffered an external battering: two successive droughts of unprecedented magnitude, two massive oil price rises, shortfalls in assistance expected from the Arab countries in return for support against Israel, hospitality costs to hundreds of thousands of refugees and exiles from neighboring countries, the breakup of the East African common market and costly disputes with Kenya that closed the border from 1975 to 1983. Only increased foreign borrowing and foreign aid could close the earnings and payments gap. Even the army's welcomed vanquishing of the dictator Idi Amin* in the victorious war with Uganda led in 1979 to material shortages, inflation and an exponential increase in the use of firearms brought back from the war.

By 1986, when Nyerere stepped down as president, the country gave up a six-year struggle against conditions imposed by the International Monetary Fund (IMF) to secure a loan to keep the economy afloat. Support for national self-reliance and the socialist development strategy had shrunk to a group composed of radical academics in the University of Dar es Salaam and left-wing allies on the National Executive of the CCM. The civil service, especially the younger technocrats trained in economics, and most politicians came around to the view that only a return to more private enterprise and more of a market economy could restore economic health. The IMF standby credits in 1986 were $800 million to service the country's $3.7-billion foreign debt (up from debts of $250 million in 1970). Although Nyerere was reluctant to accept help from the IMF and the World Bank due to restrictions imposed on national economic policy, at the end of his presidential tenure it was unavoidable.

In foreign policy Nyerere was outspoken on the world stage for three decades, championing African unity, nonalignment and increased aid from the countries of "the North" within the New International Economic Order. Yet, as in domestic policy, Nyerere's moral reach often exceeded his practical grasp, and he sometimes found his practice contradicting what he had preached. Although a founder of the Organization of African Unity (OAU) and its chairman in 1984–85, he sometimes found himself defying majority OAU opinion, as in recognizing secessionist Biafra in the Nigerian civil war of 1967–70, despite OAU principles maintaining existing territorial boundaries. Although a strong advocate of peaceful settlement of disputes, he found himself at odds at one time or another with all his neighbors and in fact sent troops to the Comoro Islands, to the Seychelles Islands (1979–84), to Mozambique and to Zimbabwe (early 1980s) and finally into Uganda in 1979 in a full-scale war to counter the invasion of Tanzania by Idi Amin. In 1960 Nyerere offered to delay Tanganyika's independence if it would accelerate the pace of decolonization in Kenya and Uganda and bring all three territories to independence as an East African federation. But by 1977, amidst angry disputes over debts and putatively unfair economic tactics between Tanzania and Kenya, the East African Community (a regional association of economic and financial arrangements) passed into oblivion. While Nyerere proclaimed the need for self-reliance in development, by 1965 already 83 percent of the development budget came from foreign grants and loans. By the early 1980s Tanzania found itself the highest per capita recipient of foreign grants and loans on an annual basis in tropical Africa.

Nyerere was known to joke about his moralistic approach to policy. "If I were a Tanzanian voter I sometimes think I would say 'Nyerere for the pulpit, not for President.' " His principled stances sometimes undercut his country's short-term material interests: breaking relations with Britain in 1965 (and losing assistance) when Britain did not suppress Rhodesia's Unilateral Declaration of Independence, or permitting a break with West Germany (and losing its assistance) in the same year over the issue of retaining an East German consulate in Zanzibar, then newly united with Tanganyika. In the case of support for anti-colonial liberation in southern Africa and the end of apartheid in South Africa, Nyerere courted military retaliation and sabotage by his unflinching hospitality to a multiplicity of liberation movements, to the African Liberation Committee of the OAU and to the African Front Line States. Nyerere's Pan-Africanism drew the line at cooperation with dictators; he refused to attend an OAU summit in 1975 chaired by Idi Amin and thwarted the efforts of Muammar Qaddafi to split the OAU ideologically at the summit of 1982.

Although Tanzania's foreign policy of nonalignment was more evenhanded than that of most other Third World countries making the same claim, Nyerere's socialist predilections led him to seek good relations with China and the Soviet Union, as well as with the Scandinavian countries. His personal connections with Britain, especially socialist internationalists there, sustained Tanzania over periods of great differences. He was a favorite target of private and public assistance in the era of President Kennedy in the United States, but Tanzania virtually disappeared as a special case for American foreign policy by the mid-1970s. China financed the Tazara railroad line to Zambia in the late 1960s; the USSR was Tanzania's largest military supplier in the early 1980s; and the Scandinavian countries are the largest aid donors overall to Tanzania. Nyerere has expressed admiration of Cuba's and China's accomplishments, but not of their strategies of revolution or their military intervention in the affairs of other countries.

Although Nyerere himself would probably reject the metaphor as bordering on blasphemy, many Tanzanians would compare his role in the history of his people to the leadership of Moses and Joshua, perhaps all the way to David and Solomon and the post-Solomonic kings. His vision as well as his action led his people to freedom in their own country. He presided over the best and then perhaps the worst years of the new republic. His view shaped the laws by which his people still live, but circumstances conspired to reject his grandest schemes of shared prosperity, social justice and transnational harmony. Like other prophets, his goals were beyond the flawed character and abilities of his followers, for example, when he expected effective cooperation to emerge from collectivization of farming and when he expected skill, devotion, austerity, perseverance and restraint from an expanded public service. Before his retirement from public life Nyerere was asked for what he would like to be remembered. He answered, "For trying."

BIBLIOGRAPHY

Works by Nyerere:

"One Party Government." *Spearhead* (Dar es Salaam) 1 (November 1961): 7–10.
The Second Scramble. Dar es Salaam: Tanganyika Standard, 1962.
Democracy and the Party System. Dar es Salaam: Tanganyika Standard, n.d. [1963].
Principles and Development. Dar es Salaam: Government Printer, 1966.
Freedom and Unity. London: Oxford University Press, 1967.
Socialism and Rural Development. Dar es Salaam: Government Printer, 1967.
Freedom and Socialism. London: Oxford University Press, 1968.
Freedom and Development. London: Oxford University Press, 1973.
The Arusha Declaration Ten Years After. Dar es Salaam: Government Printer, 1977.
Crusade for Liberation. Dar es Salaam: Oxford University Press, 1978.

Other Works:

Bienen, Henry. *Tanzania: Party Transformation and Economic Development*. Princeton,
    N.J.: Princeton University Press, 1970.
Cliffe, Lionel, and John Saul (eds.). *Socialism in Tanzania*. 2 vols. Dar es Salaam: East
    African Publishing House, 1972–73.
Coulson, Andrew. *Tanzania: A Political Economy*. Oxford: Oxford University Press,
    1982.
Duggan, William R., and John R. Civille. *Tanzania and Nyerere: A Study of Ujamaa
    and Nationhood*. New York: Orbis Books, 1976.
Glickman, Harvey. "Dilemmas of Political Theory in African Context: The Ideology of
    Julius Nyerere." In Jeffrey T. Butler and A. A. Castagno (eds.), *Boston University
    Papers on Africa: Transition in African Politics*. New York: Praeger, 1967, 195–
    223.
Hyden, Goran. *Beyond Ujamaa in Tanzania: Underdevelopment and an Uncaptured
    Peasantry*. Berkeley: University of California Press, 1980.
Jackson, Robert H., and Carl G. Rosberg. *Personal Rule in Black Africa: Prince, Au-
    tocrat, Prophet, Tyrant*. Berkeley: University of California Press, 1982.
Liebenow, J. Gus. "Nyerere of Tanzania: The Legend and the Ledger." *UFSI Reports,
    Africa/Middle East*, no. 3 (1987).
Pratt, Cranford. *The Critical Phase in Tanzania, 1945–1968: Nyerere and the Emergence
    of a Socialist Strategy*. Cambridge, Eng.: Cambridge University Press, 1976.
Smith, William Edgett. *We Must Run While They Walk: A Portrait of Africa's Julius
    Nyerere*. New York: Random House, 1971.
Yeager, Rodger. *Tanzania: An African Experiment*. 2nd ed. Boulder, Colo.: Westview
    Press, 1989.

HARVEY GLICKMAN

O

OLUSEGUN OBASANJO (1937–), Head of State, Commander-in-Chief of
the Armed Forces, Federal Republic of Nigeria, 1976–1979.

Olusegun Obasanjo's leadership of his country in a role he did not seek, indeed
never imagined, marked neither the first nor the last time he would find himself
making a critically important contribution to major African events. In 1970, as
the commanding officer of the Third Marine Commando Division, Obasanjo,
then a colonel, was the person to put the formal end to the Nigerian civil war,
accepting the surrender of the Biafran secessionist forces. Moving beyond Nigeria, after handing over its government to civilians in 1979, he became cochairman of the Commonwealth's Eminent Persons Group in 1986, he was central
in fashioning the "negotiating concept" that four years later, as South Africa
moved at last toward genuine democracy, provided a durable starting point for
the process.

From a modest rural background in what is now Nigeria's Ogun State, he had
neither guidance nor assistance as a youngster in fashioning his goals. Only in
1951 did the opportunities a Western education offered come to his farming
father's ears. From then on in Abeokuta, first at Baptist Day School and then
at Baptist Boys High School, education became, as he has said, "a matter of
life and death" to him. His family's slim financial resources depleted by circumstances, he had all-too-typical problems of paying school fees; his educational choices depended more on circumstance than design, though his natural
ability was evident from the start in academic prizes. His success in competitive
examinations, including that to the University of Ibadan in 1957, was not matched
by financial assistance, for there was no advice for successful but impecunious
candidates about potential sources of support.

It was in near desperation, then, that he came upon an advertisement for the
cadetship examination into the Nigerian army. Again successful, but decidedly
seeing the army as an opportunity for further training rather than a military

career, he joined as a cadet officer in 1958. For him, as for many others, the army broadened his sense of his own country, as well as his education and his experience. He chose engineering as his specialization; he attended various military institutions in England and in India. He served as a young officer with the Nigerian contingent of United Nations forces in the Congo (Zaire) in 1961. There he and his close friends began to think seriously about Africa's political problems.

On the eve of Nigeria's first military coup on January 15, 1966, he returned from a stay in India and was in Kaduna. He had no foreknowledge of the plot, despite its having been planned and led by Major Chukwuma Nzeogwu, who had become one of his closest friends through the time they spent and the political discussions they had in the Congo.

As Nigeria's crises of military rule and disunity led events toward the tragedy that was the civil war, Obasanjo could not have anticipated that he would be the one to end it. Nor, having taken the Biafran surrender in January 1970, did he have either ambition for or reason to expect the leadership of his country. With the military government under General Yakubu Gowon[*] first embracing and then retreating from steps toward civilian rule, he found himself appointed early in 1975 to a political post drawing on his technical capabilities: federal commissioner (minister) for works and housing. From that vantage point he saw burgeoning economic opportunities and extravagances, mounting public anger over a feeling of "drift," and the indefinite postponement of a return to democracy.

He would soon find himself again in a key role not of his own design. When a bloodless coup removed General Gowon on July 29, 1975, the colonels who had engineered it selected Obasanjo as chief of staff, Supreme Headquarters, to join Murtala Muhammed as head of state and Yakubu Danjuma as chief of army staff in running the country and the military. The coup makers made their goal clear: to return the country to civilian rule by October 1, 1979.

Chief of staff was a role well suited to Obasanjo. It had substance, allowing him to contribute to steps announced and implemented in the energetic style that came to typify the new head of state and thus the regime, undergirding its popularity. His own energy—of equal magnitude but far less flamboyant—and his insights complemented his colleagues: The regime characterized itself as "low-profile," particularly apt and congenial for him.

By the end of 1975 the domestic goals of the new government and the steps it would take to reach them within four years were clear to all Nigerians. So also was a new assertiveness in foreign policy, resting on Nigeria's economic strength and triggered by inroads on the independence of just-born Angola. With "Africa as its centerpiece," the regime policy would make a special commitment to active involvement in achieving nonracial government in all of southern Africa.

On February 13, 1976, Murtala Muhammed was assassinated in an unsuccessful coup attempt that stunned the country and his colleagues most of all. No one had thought to provide for succession, but in the view of those who had the previous July designated the country's leadership, stability dictated the choice.

Olusegun Obasanjo became head of state and commander-in-chief; he himself said in the title of a memoir about his administration that it was "not my will." This was the first time a man from south and west of the river Niger would lead the country.

Under his leadership one of Africa's most significant attempts to create a stable democratic government after a period of postindependence instability and military rule took place. Then, as since, Nigeria contained a quarter of the population of sub-Saharan Africa. Then, as since, it was capable of providing an economic focus, even a magnet, attracting others, at least potentially, to cooperation beyond arbitrarily drawn colonial boundaries. Then, as since, it had the potential to find accommodations, if not answers, to problems of instability and insecurity.

From the vantage point of Obasanjo's government all that and more—a leading Nigerian role recognized in Africa and beyond—seemed within reach. He and his colleagues in a leadership they always described as collective worked toward those goals in the aftermath of Murtala's assassination. That leadership, and Obasanjo in particular, echoed in their views and their pronouncements assumptions and a vision of another time and place. "I am a systems man," Obasanjo would say and allude to his engineering training. But in planning for the political institutions of Nigeria's future, this translated into a belief that human beings could overcome human foibles: The right institutions, rationally conceived and scrupulously set in place, could and would constrain destructive behavior.

The Nigeria he led was full of optimism; the vision was clear, even if the path to it could not be; no one could then imagine that unbridled energy and ambition would produce some obstacles later confounding those who believed they had anticipated—and institutionally neutralized—the most virulent. Politically, Nigeria remained a federation; its diversity necessitated that. But it could not be the federation of 1960, created more in Britain than in Nigeria, but rather one of more units and thus, it followed, of greater stability. Nor would it be the federation of the previous thirteen years, highly centralized in line with the nature of a military command structure. It allowed room to express diversity by encouraging cross-cutting alliances, shifting according to issues rather than geography or ethnicity or, potentially more destructive, religion. At the same time, it did not allow the kind of "ganging up" that had plagued Nigeria before 1966. Most of all, it maintained Nigeria's unity, assuring that the civil war should not have been fought in vain.

Obasanjo, like every Nigerian leader, had defining attributes that complicated public perceptions of his decisions. As a Christian and a Yoruba, he faced stereotyped expectations, initially that he would favor these interests or those claiming to represent them. These interests, of course, were not monolithic, and Obasanjo, like most of his contemporaries in the military, regarded the army as a national institution and his role in it as a national role. Not trained for politics and not particularly attracted by it or those who practiced it, he managed with considerable skill to be less predictable than many expected and to seek and utilize varied kinds of assistance—from Islamic scholars through traditional rulers—to calm heated public reaction to difficult decisions.

Most important, as the process of political reconstruction played out, and through one challenge after another to it, he was adamant in his determination to see a peaceful and successful handover to civilians. Whatever the criticisms, and in Nigeria they were numerous, he insisted that his administration had not only redeemed the honor of the military but had also seen the country through, as he would put it soon afterwards, the "freest and fairest elections" of the century. With a keener understanding of the country's economy than most heads of state, he sought, despite a dip in the country's oil revenues, to ensure ample foreign exchange reserves for the incoming civilian government, in order to give the new leadership some flexibility. Holding firmly to the view that the quality of civilian government was its only guarantee against future military coups, he left office resolved to offer advice only if and when asked.

Joking about being "unemployed and unemployable," he set out to become a farmer, a decision he had made not only because it interested him. It had become clear to him during his time in office that Nigeria would suffer if it did not rebuild its agricultural base, however its destruction had come about. Furthermore, deploring the prevalent view that farming was what rural, poor, ill-educated people did, he sought to set an example: If a former head of state could farm, everyone could.

Spending most of his time planning and developing his farm, which in time grew into several, he kept a resolutely low profile. Soon, however, he revealed a new dimension. He began writing about the points at which his life and major historical events had intersected and published his account of his role in the civil war and the first of several memoirs dealing with such times. As Nigeria's political and economic circumstances seemed to spiral downward, he began to punctuate his normal silence with occasional if well-publicized criticism, a pattern continued through successive governments.

Meanwhile, however, he was gaining international notice as an African military leader who had not only handed over political power to elected civilians but had then stepped well aside, removing himself from the domestic political stage. As a member of the Palme Commission on Disarmament and Arms Control and a member of the Inter-Action Council of former heads of government, he began to be seen outside Africa as an important figure from the continent, able to contribute ideas and perspectives on a range of global issues.

His nomination by the presidents of Zambia and Zimbabwe to the Commonwealth Eminent Persons Group (EPG), whose 1986 mission proved catalytic in a changing South Africa, allowed him to focus on the issue of apartheid and possibilities for assisting it to its demise, a matter about which he had long felt strong commitment. Under his leadership as cochairman, the EPG played a key role as the first group to engage virtually all major players of all races in its discussions and in mobilizing international pressure on a South African government that had abruptly aborted the effort to start negotiations along virtually agreed-upon lines. The dramatic shift in 1990, with the unbanning of political movements, the release of major political prisoners and the start of broad-based discussion within South Africa about a nonracial democratic political future showed the lasting impact of the EPG and its "negotiating concept."

Increasingly in demand internationally as a spokesman for Africa rather than Nigeria alone, Obasanjo saw as one of Africa's greatest challenges the need to build a reservoir of potential future leaders. With the accelerating pace of change and the increasing global interdependence coinciding with an especially beleaguered period in Africa's recent history, he saw the importance of bringing together, even if only for a few days at a time, those with experience as leaders and some of those at a stage in their careers where pressures allow little time for reflection and interaction. In 1989 he thus started the Africa Leadership Forum, based at his farm in Ota, where periodic thematic conferences draw together people from a range of African countries. The forum has also provided a vehicle for meetings outside Africa where African issues and others impinging on Africa receive attention.

In the decade since leaving power in his own country, Obasanjo has played an increasingly visible role internationally, pursuing a vision in which Africans themselves address Africa's problems in the first instance, stressing his particular concern with greater regional integration. But he also stresses the vital corollary that the industrialized countries of the North, whose politics and economics continue to impinge so forcefully, must not fail to take account of Africa and the views of Africans, even as dramatic changes elsewhere command attention with the approach of the twenty-first century.

BIBLIOGRAPHY

Works by Obasanjo:

My Command: An Account of the Nigerian Civil War, 1967–1970. Ibadan, Nigeria: Heinemann, 1980.
Africa in Perspective: Myths and Realities. New York: Council on Foreign Relations, 1987.
Nzeogwu. Ibadan, Nigeria: Spectrum Books, 1987.
Africa Embattled: Selected Essays on Contemporary African Development. Ibadan, Nigeria: Fountain Publications, 1988.
Constitution for National Integration and Development. Lagos, Nigeria: Friends Foundation Publishers, 1989.
Not My Will. Ibadan, Nigeria: Ibadan University Press, 1990.

Other Works:

Commonwealth Group of Eminent Persons. *Mission to South Africa: The Commonwealth Report.* London: Penguin Books, 1986.
Garba, J. N. *Diplomatic Soldiering: Nigerian Foreign Policy, 1975–1979.* Ibadan, Nigeria: Spectrum Books, 1987.
Okadigbo, Chuba. *Power and Leadership in Nigeria.* Enugu, Nigeria: Fourth Dimension Publishing Co., 1987.

Oluleye, James J. *Military Leadership in Nigeria, 1966–1979*. Ibadan, Nigeria: Ibadan University Press, 1985.

Oyediran, Oyelele (ed.). *Nigerian Government and Politics under Military Rule, 1966–79*. New York: St. Martin's Press, 1979.

JEAN HERSKOVITS

APOLO MILTON OBOTE (1924–   ), Prime Minister, 1962–1971; President, Republic of Uganda, 1980–1985.

Apolo Milton Obote dominated the politics of Uganda for most of the first decade of the country's political independence from British rule, achieved on October 9, 1962. He was overthrown by a military coup d'état in early 1971 but was able to accomplish the rare feat of regaining power in 1980 after the downfall of the bloody regime of Idi Amin.* However, in 1985 he lost power in yet another military coup.

Milton Obote was born in the northern district of Lango in 1924, some twenty-four years after the formal establishment of British colonial rule in what had become the multiethnic and multireligious Protectorate of Uganda. He went to Lira Secondary School in his home district, Gulu High School in Acholi District, also in the northern part of the country, and, later, Busoga College, Mwiri, in the eastern part of the country fifty miles from Kampala, the capital. Eventually, he went on to Makerere College in Kampala, then the most advanced institution of learning in East and central Africa.

Obote did not complete his studies at Makerere, but withdrew after two years of study. He subsequently left the country and went to Kenya, where he worked successively as a laborer, clerk and salesman. He also got involved in trade-union organizing and the activities of the Kenya African Union (KAU), then the foremost African nationalist organization.

He returned to Uganda in 1957 and the next year was selected to represent his home district in the Legislative Council, which had become the central focus for the nationwide independence aspirations of the African political leaders. By that time the forces that were to contribute to instability and violence in the postcolonial phase of Uganda's history had already manifested themselves.

As in most other African colonies, the European colonizers had thrown together diverse cultural, linguistic and political units that had been separate prior to the beginning of the twentieth century. Until its final decade, the colonial regime had had no serious design to amalgamate these units into a viable nation-state. Africans did not start to participate in the Central Legislative Council until after 1945, and then only in a limited way. Otherwise, African political life was restricted to local districts, which were ethnically more or less homogeneous.

To precolonial ethnocultural diversity had been added strong divisions and conflicts stemming from allegiance to the imported Christian denominations of Catholicism and Anglican Protestantism, as well as Islam. These divisions were reflected in the major anticolonial political parties that had arisen in the 1950s and in the quest for the preservation of political and cultural autonomy on the part of the leaders of the most important of the precolonial states, notably the kingdoms of Buganda, Ankole, Bunyoro and Toro. Of these, Buganda was the largest, wealthiest and most central, the location of the capital and other major national institutions, as well as the most assertive in its desire to preserve a high degree of political autonomy or even to secede from the rest of the country.

The oldest and most important of the political parties was the Uganda National Congress (UNC). It represented the most secular and neutralist strand of anti-colonial nationalism. Its major competitor was the Democratic Party (DP). This party was essentially the expression of the frustration of the African Catholic elites who had been subjected to discrimination in the allocation of offices in both the central colonial and African local administrations. Although they out-numbered the Protestants, Catholics were consistently and grossly underrepresented in key positions.

Milton Obote had joined the UNC. Soon after entering the Legislative Council, he showed himself to be an articulate and strong anticolonial nationalist. He later emerged as one of the key figures of the UNC. When the party split into two wings, he became one of the leaders of the dissident faction. When this faction merged with another political party, the Uganda People's Union (UPU) in 1960, to form the Uganda People's Congress (UPC), he became the leader of the new party, which also replaced the UNC as the main rival of the Democratic Party. This marked the beginning of Obote's rapid rise to the pinnacle of power.

In 1961 the British colonial administration organized elections as part of the gradual process of the devolution of political power to Ugandans in preparation for the final grant of independence. The elections were boycotted by most of the electorate in Buganda at the urging of the kingdom's leaders, who were dissatisfied with its proposed status in the prospective independent Uganda. The UPC and the DP defied the boycott and urged their supporters in Buganda to join the rest of the country in going to the polls.

In contrast to the UPC, the DP had a measure of support in Buganda. It therefore turned out to be the beneficiary of the electoral boycott in Buganda, where it won virtually all the seats. With widespread support outside Buganda, the party was able to edge out the UPC and form the transitional government in the period 1961–62. Obote was elected from his home district and became the leader of the opposition.

Following these developments, Obote and the leaders of Buganda—who had also suffered defeat in the sense that an African transitional government had been set up in spite of their electoral boycott—struck a deal that was designed to turn the tables on the DP. The UPC formed an electoral alliance with the Kabaka Yekka ("only the king," KY), a royalist political organization that had been hastily put together by the elders of the Buganda Kingdom and Buganda nationalist politicians. The major aims of the UPC-KY alliance were accomplished in 1962. During the final Constitutional Conference in London that preceded the attainment of independence, Buganda was guaranteed a special position within Uganda, enjoying a federal relationship with the central government, while the other kingdoms and the district of Busoga had a more diluted quasi-federal status. The rest of the country, which constituted the majority of the districts, had direct, unitary relationships with the central government. In the final elections held in 1962, the UPC in alliance with KY, which swept the board in Buganda, dislodged the DP and formed the first government of independent Uganda. Obote became prime minister, and in 1963 the *kabaka* of Buganda became the head of state with the title of president.

On the surface, it looked as if the major threats to Uganda's future political stability were on the way to elimination. However, it was clear that major problems remained. The UPC-KY alliance had been a marriage of convenience. While the leaders of both parties shared the characteristic of being predominantly Protestant, in other respects they stood for different political goals. Obote espoused a neutralist and more egalitarian form of anticolonial nationalism. His party also reflected the opposition and resentments that many politicians from outside Buganda felt toward the latter because of the region's greater advance in socioeconomic terms, the sentiments of ethnic "superiority" toward other groups expressed by the leaders of the kingdom and their social and political conservatism.

From 1962–66 Uganda enjoyed a period of relative political and social stability. Nevertheless, tensions gradually mounted. The UPC-KY alliance was constantly shaken by conflicts between the Buganda government, dominated by the KY, and the national government, dominated by the UPC. Moreover, as Obote managed to entice members of the opposition DP to join his party and government, the alliance became less useful for the UPC, which in turn intensified the conflict between the erstwhile allies. These conflicts inevitably involved the head of state, who was also the *kabaka* of Buganda and de facto leader of the KY party.

The situation was exacerbated by the fact that Obote's dominance of his party had never been total. By 1965 a challenge to his leadership had arisen within the UPC. His opponents, not surprisingly, made common cause with the leaders of Buganda and KY. It was in the subsequent atmosphere of rumors of plots and coups that Obote struck back in February 1966. He arrested five senior ministers of his cabinet who were apparently plotting to depose him, overturned the 1962 constitution and arbitrarily removed the president. In April he introduced a new constitution, assumed the now-strengthened presidency and abolished the semifederal politico-administrative structure.

This putsch was challenged by the *kabaka* of Buganda as well as the Buganda Lukiiko (parliament), which demanded that Obote's government remove itself from Buganda soil. Obote thereupon ordered an attack on the *kabaka's* palace on the grounds that the challenge to his government constituted a rebellion and that arms were allegedly kept in the palace. In the resulting heavy fighting, large numbers of combatants and civilians were killed. Other civilians were killed in different parts of Buganda by soldiers. The *kabaka* survived unscathed and escaped to Britain, where he died in 1969.

Obote had been able to carry out these moves primarily because the military was loyal to him on essentially ethnoregional grounds. By an accident of history, the British colonial administration had traditionally recruited the military from the northern part of the country, which happened to be Obote's own home region.

In 1967 Obote enshrined the results of his coup in a new constitution that was debated in Parliament and the press, but under conditions of extreme fear on the part of opponents who had no chance of effecting any major changes in the draft. One of the most important aspects of the document was the abolition of all the kingdoms. In addition, the term of Parliament, which would have expired in 1967, was extended for another five years. The events of 1966 and 1967 had turned what had been a fairly liberal political system into an authoritarian regime. If he was not to rule merely on the basis of coercion and fear, Obote was bound to look for some alternative basis of legitimacy.

His attempt to resolve this political dilemma took several different forms. First and foremost, he purged the military of anyone suspected of disloyalty and promoted officers deemed loyal, including Idi Amin, who had become army commander. He strengthened the General Service Department, an intelligence unit whose principal domestic task was to ferret out real or suspected dissidents. Buganda was kept under a state of emergency, a legal device under which people could be—and many were—imprisoned without trial or any criminal charges.

Between 1967 and 1971 Obote unsuccessfully sought to find a new basis for political legitimacy through populist rhetoric that revolved around the vague concept of the "common man" and, later on, socialism. Increasing restrictions on the political activities of the opposition and the DP and other groups outside the government culminated in the proscription of all opposition and the decision to declare the UPC the only legal party in 1969.

In the last two years of his regime Obote introduced a new system of parliamentary representation that sought to undermine parochialism by requiring candidates for parliamentary elections to run in four constituencies, one located in each of the four regions of the country. In 1970 he declared the nationalization of a host of foreign-owned enterprises as part of the "Move-to-the-Left" that had been defined as the guiding ideological framework since 1969. In 1968 Obote turned to the reorganization of the party. However, rather than transforming it into a vehicle for genuine participation and choice, he centralized control and reserved to himself the right to appoint key leadership positions. What began to emerge was a personalist, party-state regime.

In spite of surface calm, all was not well. Opposition, especially in Buganda, had gone underground but was implacable and bitter. In December 1969 Obote narrowly escaped death in an assassination attempt at the end of his party's congress in Kampala. Subsequently, a group of people from Buganda was accused and convicted of the attempt.

Obote's first regime was terminated by a coup in January 1971, led by his erstwhile loyal supporter, army commander Idi Amin, while Obote was attending a meeting of heads of Commonwealth states and governments in Singapore. He eventually made his way to Tanzania, where he lived as a guest of the government until 1980. Amin and Obote had fallen out over a host of matters, including Amin's tight control of the military, Obote's desire to promote officers who were loyal to him and independent of Amin and the 1970 assassination of a senior officer for which Amin was suspected to have been responsible.

An attempted invasion by Obote supporters in 1972 was decisively beaten. It was not until 1978, when Amin's troops invaded a portion of Tanzania, that Obote got his chance. As the Tanzanian army prepared for a massive counter-offensive that was clearly designed to remove Amin from office, the government encouraged Ugandan exiles to get together and prepare to take power. Obote did not personally attend the resulting meeting in Tanzania in early 1979 but was represented by a number of delegates. The meeting gave rise to the Uganda National Liberation Front (UNLF), a diverse and far-from-harmonious coalition whose only basis was opposition to the Amin regime.

The conflict-ridden UNLF gave rise to two unstable interim governments following the defeat and flight of Amin and his supporters in April 1979. By June 1980 the pro-Obote faction within the UNLF, which dominated the new army and had been receiving guidance from its leader in Tanzania, was able to defeat its rivals through a military coup. Obote returned to Uganda and plunged into the campaign for elections that had been scheduled for the end of 1980. His supporters controlled the instruments of government, decided on the electoral districts and started the campaign from a strong position.

The pro-Obote interim regime declared the UPC the winner of the December elections. The Commonwealth Election Observer Mission gave a nuanced positive verdict. However, the DP and other UPC opponents, as well as many foreign observers, regarded the results as, at the very least, partly fraudulent. Militant opponents soon started organizing guerrilla warfare.

Obote's second tenure in the Ugandan presidency began in even more inauspicious circumstances than the first. The legitimacy of his regime was questioned by many at home and abroad. Amin had left the economic and social infrastructure in shambles. Law and order was precarious, and many people had access to weapons.

In spite of the difficult circumstances, Obote at first achieved some success in promoting the recovery of the economy. He gradually managed to gain a certain degree of legitimacy abroad. However, as the guerrilla campaign persisted and army counterinsurgency degenerated into massacres, looting and rape, the regime's political position began to weaken. Arbitrary imprisonments became common, and many people, estimated in the hundreds of thousands, died in their homes or in military as well as paramilitary custody.

The end of the second Obote regime, like that of the first, was brought about not by his external enemies but by the military that had upheld him. As a result of ethnic and personal rivalries and dissension, which had been exacerbated by the unsuccessful counterinsurgency operations, the army overthrew Obote in July 1985. Although this time he was in Uganda, he managed to flee and eventually went into exile in Zambia.

Obote's political legacy deserves to be judged at best mixed, but on the whole negative. It is clear that he aspired to create a united Uganda and was concerned to bring about more equal economic and social conditions than prevailed on the eve of the country's independence. However, the alacrity with which he used the police and military to repress his opponents and impose his own vision of the public good gradually made force the final arbiter of political conflict in the country. It is significant that the 1966 putsch started as a strike against the intraparty opposition and only secondarily came to involve the Kingdom of Buganda. Clearly, determination to retain power was as significant as the desire to take advantage of the rupture to impose a more centralized state structure.

Obote can also be faulted for not having taken major steps to reconcile the people of Buganda after he had forced their king into exile and arbitrarily abolished the monarchy. The hostility of such a central part of the country, combined with the evolution of the regime in an authoritarian direction, made the prospects for resolution of the country's underlying political problems even more difficult. Moreover, the absence of any demonstrable basis of political legitimacy encouraged Amin to undertake the 1971 coup that plunged the country into the abyss from which it is still struggling to emerge.

During his second tenure of office, Obote continued to rely on coercive measures to deal with the opposition. Although he was clearly not in complete control of his military and civilian supporters, he did little to curb the repression and atrocities. In fact, he tried to deny or minimize their severity. He also adamantly refused to make any concessions. The abolition of the monarchies and the centralization of government undoubtedly removed a major obstacle to the creation of a more unified state. It is, however, at least arguable that a less violent approach would have spared the country the agony of the last twenty-four years.

BIBLIOGRAPHY

Bwengye, Francis A. W. *The Agony of Uganda: From Idi Amin to Obote.* London: Regency Press, 1985.

Gingyera-Pinychwa, G. G. *Apolo Milton Obote and His Times.* New York: NOK Publishers, 1978.

Gupta, Vijay. *Obote, Second Liberation.* New Delhi: Vikas Publishing House, 1983.

Ibingira, Grace Stuart. *African Upheavals since Independence.* Boulder, Colo.: Westview Press, 1980.

Karugire, Samwiri R. *A Political History of Uganda.* Nairobi: Heinemann Educational Books, 1980.

Kasfir, Nelson. *The Shrinking Political Arena.* Berkeley: University of California Press, 1976.

Mittelman, James H. *Ideology and Politics in Uganda.* Ithaca, N.Y.: Cornell University Press, 1975.

EDWARD KANNYO

P

GEORGE PADMORE (1902[1903]–1959), Pan-African ideologist, advisor, government of Ghana, 1957–1959.

George Padmore, a committed revolutionary intellectual and agitator for the liberation of black people, was a captivating orator and organizer and the architect and mentor of the modern Pan-Africanist movement. Padmore was born in the Aronca District of Tacarigua on the island of Trinidad in the Caribbean to James Hubert Alphonso Nurse and Anna Susanna Symister. His original name was Malcolm Ivan Meredith Nurse.

He received his early education in Trinidad and proceeded to the United States, after he was already married, to receive a university education. He first enrolled at Fisk University, where he studied political science and history, and then at Howard University to study for a degree in law. But his commitment to the "politics of liberation" was much stronger. He abandoned his studies at Howard to devote his life to liberating the black race from colonialism and exploitation.

From those early years in the United States until his death, Padmore remained true to two fundamental commitments: social justice for black people and the liberation and unity of Africa. In the struggle to realize these goals he found a common enemy in imperialism. The first goal took him into the international Communist movement (Comintern), while the second launched him into the leadership of the Pan-Africanist movement. His commitment to these goals was so strong that he broke with the Comintern and justified his fusion of Pan-Africanism with socialism in opposition to communism. His commitment also caused him to adopt the name by which he came to be known: George Padmore.

It was during his Comintern period that he moved to Moscow, having abandoned his university education in 1930. While in Moscow he was assigned as secretary of the Communist International Trades Union Committee of Negro Workers, based in Hamburg, Germany, a section of the Red International of Labor Unions. He became a member of the Moscow City Soviet, though he hardly participated in its deliberations. He lectured regularly at Kutvu University, where the Communist Party of the Soviet Union and the Comintern trained African and Asian students. For about seven years he worked relentlessly for the freedom of the colonial peoples and for the liberty of African-American workers.

For Padmore, adherence to communism was necessary only if it served the goal of emancipating black peoples from colonialism, both internal and external. Accordingly, when the Comintern opposed the nationalist movements in the colonies because they were led by "petty-bourgeois intellectuals" and disbanded the Trades Union Committee of Negro Workers, he broke completely with it. From that encounter he concluded that communism was as much a threat to the colonial peoples of Africa as capitalism; indeed, imperialism was a tendency common to the two rival socioeconomic systems. He reasoned that since both were Euro-centered, they served the interest of Europeans. The future of black people therefore lay in the freedom, unity and progress of Africa.

Padmore did not share the Marcus Garveyist doctrine of Africa for Africans. He remained opposed to both white racism and black chauvinism. He stood for social justice for all. Nonetheless, he had made a decisive shift in the focus of his political activities. He would concentrate on achieving two complementary objectives: first, exposing colonialism especially with regard to Africa, constantly placing it on the political agenda of the imperial powers, and of Great Britain in particular, and agitating for its ultimate solution; and second, fighting communism. The means to achieve these two goals was Pan-African socialism, which was a fusion of what he termed "dynamic nationalism" for the attainment of self-determination, socialism and African unity. The outcome of that metamorphosis was the birth of modern Pan-Africanism.

By 1935 he had left Moscow to live in London, where he could build a network of contacts with the rising generation of African nationalist leaders. Along with Nnamdi Azikiwe[*] and others of the African intelligentsia, whom he had met when studying in the United States, he conferred, debated and planned with most of that generation, either in London or in Paris, and especially with a cross-section of the British left.

In conjunction with members of these groups, as well as other West Indians, including his boyhood friend C. L. R. James, Padmore established a systematic and militant program of anticolonial agitation, propaganda and organization. As "the solitary pamphleteer against colonialism," he used the columns of sympathetic British newspapers of the left to agitate against British colonialism and urge self-determination for the colonial peoples. He denounced the British Empire as "the worst racket yet invented by man" and called for its dissolution. He termed the British government's attempt at reforming colonial rule through the establishment of the Colonial Development and Welfare Fund of 1944 a fraud, designed simply to provide an imperial cover for big colonial corporations in order to continue to dominate the economies of the colonies and reap huge profits, both during and after the war. The harsh manner in which the colonial government handled the strikes in the Copperbelt of Zambia (then Northern Rhodesia) convinced him of the correctness of his indictment. During World War II he also lectured extensively on "the war for freedom and democracy" for all peoples of the world. For him, freedom for the colonial peoples was "the historic prerequisite for the free and voluntary co-operation between all nations and peoples and races."

That period in Britain was the most prolific of his career as the intellectual and ideologue of the Pan-Africanist movement. He was able single-handedly to shape a new political agenda for Pan-Africanism. While previous congresses had concentrated on achieving social justice for black people, freedom for the colonial peoples became the principal agenda of the Pan-Africanist movement from the 1945 Pan-African Conference at Manchester onwards. By the end of the war the shift to Pan-African affairs as the sole focus of his political and intellectual labor had become complete. If the Pan-African Federation (PAF), which he and others formed late in 1944, was the last and most ambitious of the Pan-African bodies he was associated with, then the Pan-African Congress of 1945, which he organized in collaboration with his closest associate, Kwame Nkrumah,* before he left for Ghana, was definitely the most momentous.

World War II was a turning point in Padmore's aggressive anti-imperialist, anticolonial and Pan-Africanist agitations in another respect, namely, the "unprincipled" pronouncements of the imperial powers concerning the African continent. Two episodes of this period were of particular significance. The first was the Roosevelt-Churchill declaration of the Atlantic Charter, in which they trumpeted the inalienable right of all people to self-determination. When the British government denied the applicability of the principles of self-determination to the colonial peoples, Padmore joined African students in England and other militant nationalists in the British colonies to remind the British government that "to condemn the Imperialism of Germany, Japan and Italy while condoning that of Britain would be more than dishonest. All Imperialism is evil." He concluded that the imperial powers were more interested in preserving their colonial possessions than conceding the right of self-determination and democracy as universal rights; that not even the British Left sufficiently appreciated the implications of the war for the liberation of the colonial peoples. The colonial peoples of Africa alone could liberate themselves. They should not count on the support of either the European left or the international working class for their liberation. The second episode was Padmore's discernment of an attempt by the imperialist powers to redivide Africa following the defeat of the fascists. He forecast in 1943 the rise of the United States as the new imperialist nation, competing with Britain and others for spheres of influence in Africa.

Padmore forged a lasting political bond with Kwame Nkrumah that took him to Ghana, where he spent his last years working to implement their vision of Africa's emancipation, unity and socialism; and it was through Nkrumah that Padmore exerted his greatest influence on African and Ghanaian politics. Padmore's contributions may broadly be divided into his ideological influences on

Kwame Nkrumah and Ghanaian domestic policies, and the legacy of struggle for African unity and African socialism. The most casual acquaintance with Padmore's writings, especially that compendium of his writings on socialism and its application to African politics that he drafted in 1959 just before his death, and the writings of Nkrumah on Ghanaian politics and economy provide much evidence of Padmore's influence on Nkrumah's ideological makeup and his political strategies. Other evidence rests on matters such as the role of the party, periodization of the national revolution, the strategy of industrialization and the ideology of the African revolution, all within the context of Ghanaian politics.

Padmore devoted part of his time in Ghana to political work among the Convention People's Party's (CPP) militant wing, the National Association of Socialist Students' Organization (NASSO). Through his leadership the young socialists formulated various party directives, wrote the party's first postindependence constitution and tried to institutionalize Nkrumah's work and thought.

For Padmore, the Ghanaian revolution had two interrelated phases, the national revolution and the economic revolution, the second being dependent upon the first. Padmore called for the "economic counterrevolution." To this end, Padmore and Nkrumah shared a deep antipathy toward African capitalists. Padmore felt that black capitalists are enemies as much as white capitalists. The whole of the economic program was to move away from a trading economy to an industrial economy.

Nkrumah appointed Padmore his adviser on African affairs. Despite hostility from many quarters, Padmore persevered to direct Nkrumah's African policy toward the total emancipation and unity of the continent. Padmore's greatest achievement in this respect was the successful organization of the first meeting of independent African states and the All-African People's Conference, both in Accra, in April and December of 1958, respectively. With these he helped to build a formidable political bridge that led ultimately to the formation of the Organization of African Unity (OAU).

The irony of Padmore's service to Africa and to Ghana is that today he is hardly remembered. Overwhelmed by pervasive poverty and misery, beleaguered by political and economic crises, the continent's peoples and leaders, and this includes the people and leaders of Ghana, have forgotten about this stubborn advocate, ideologue and pamphleteer of Africa's liberation and unity. Ghanaians with whom he struggled for this course, including Nkrumah himself, may yet agree with Nkrumah's epitaph in 1959, that "when the final tale is told the significance of George Padmore's work will be revealed" (quoted in Hooker 1967:140).

BIBLIOGRAPHY

Works by Padmore:

Africa and World Peace. London: Secker and Warburg, 1937.
How Russia Transformed Her Colonial Empire. London: Dobson, 1946.

Africa: Britain's Third Empire. London: Dobson, 1949.
The Gold Coast Revolution. London: Dobson, 1953.
Pan-Africanism or Communism? The Coming Struggle for Africa. London: Dobson, 1956;
    New York: Doubleday Anchor Books, 1972.
How Britain Rules Africa. New York: Negro Universities Press, 1969.

Other Works:

Austin, Dennis. *Politics in Ghana, 1946–1960.* London: Oxford University Press, 1964.
Hooker, James R. *Black Revolutionary.* London: Pall Mall Press, 1967.
Legum, Colin. *Pan-Africanism: A Short Political Guide.* Westport, Conn.: Greenwood
    Press, 1976.

KWAME A. NINSIN

R

JERRY JOHN RAWLINGS (1947–), Chairman of the Armed Forces Revolutionary Council, 1979; Chairman of the Provisional National Defense Council and Head of State, Republic of Ghana, 1981–

Jerry John Rawlings is the first of a new, postindependence generation of African leadership. In 1979, at the age of thirty-one, he emerged from virtual anonymity to lead a populist revolt aimed at unseating the political and military establishment that had ruled Ghana in the postwar period. Although he withdrew from the political arena within less than four months, his absence was temporary. On December 31, 1981, he led a second successful military coup and has served as the Ghanaian head of state ever since.

Jerry Rawlings exemplifies both the alienation and the frustration that permeated the African continent in the 1980s as well as the ongoing quest for economic and political rehabilitation. The transformation of Jerry Rawlings from a revolutionary protester into a political leader coincided with the revamping of the Ghanaian political economy. His brand of responsible radicalism, with all its ambiguities, has introduced a new model of leadership into contemporary African politics.

Jerry John Rawlings, Jr., was born in Accra on June 22, 1947 to John Jerry Rawlings, a Scot, and Victoria Abbotoi, a catering officer from Dzelikope, near Keta in the Volta region. He received his primary education in Accra and then proceeded to Achimota, Ghana's premier secondary school. At Achimota he first became sensitized to politics, openly expressing his concerns over the social inequities that began to emerge during the Kwame Nkrumah[*] years. Upon graduation in 1966, despite his mother's opposition, he decided to join the Ghana air force, thus wedding an elite education with a military career. He enlisted as a flight cadet at the Takoradi Air Force Station in August 1967 and received training there and at the Military Academy and Training School at Teshie. He was commissioned as a pilot officer in January 1969, winning the Speed Bird

Trophy as the best flight cadet in his graduating class. In 1971 Jerry Rawlings was promoted to the rank of flight officer. In 1978 he attained the rank of flight-lieutenant and was attached to the Jet Squadron of the Air Force Station, Accra. Married to Nana Konadu Agyeman, a member of the Asante royal family and an old classmate from Achimota, he was known as an accomplished swimmer, deep-sea diver, horseman and polo player.

Flight-Lieutenant Jerry Rawlings first gained headlines after he was arrested for leading an abortive coup d'état on May 15, 1979. At the subsequent public treason trial, which opened on May 28, 1979, the prosecution highlighted Rawlings's concern for the underdog and his dissatisfaction with the corrupt practices of the military leadership of the Supreme Military Council (SMC) under I. K. Acheampong and, later, Fred Akuffo. The objectives of the attempted coup—the eradication of economic mismanagement and social injustice and the rehabilitation of the tarnished image of the military—were given widespread coverage in the press. When the trial resumed several days later, the courtroom was packed with supporters who found in Jerry Rawlings the spokesperson for their growing misery and discontent.

Early in the morning of June 4, 1979, Rawlings was freed from prison by a group of junior officers and soldiers of other ranks, whom he led in a successful coup that brought an end to the seven-year rule of the SMC. The June 4 uprising was carried out in the long Ghanaian tradition of popular revolts against oppressive, autocratic and exploitative rule. Jerry Rawlings and the members of the newly formed Armed Forces Revolutionary Council (AFRC), like the traditional *asafo* companies in the precolonial period and, like Nkrumah's "youngmen" during decolonization, came to personify the quest of the common man for a modicum of justice and dignity. Rawlings, with a certain naivete, assumed the mantle of the moral crusader who would stamp out elite abuses and insert a new standard of honesty and probity into the public realm.

The June 4 insurrection was a turning point in Ghanaian history. Within a few days of the coup, all living leaders of the country (Acheampong, Akuffo and A. A. Afrifa), together with the top officeholders of the defunct SMC, were brought to trial and summarily executed. The AFRC then turned its attention to a housecleaning operation; charges were brought against senior government officials in an effort to rid the bureaucracy of those deemed responsible for the rapid economic deterioration of the late 1970s. Soldiers hounded traders and entrepreneurs suspected of illicit practices (generally referred to as *kalabule*), bringing them before hastily assembled public tribunals for swift trial. The climate of economic uncertainty prevalent at the time was compounded by a growing feeling of personal insecurity.

From the outset, however, the leaders of the June 4 uprising had no intention of staying in office. Jerry Rawlings, as promised, oversaw the scheduled elections for a return to civilian rule and duly transferred power to Hilla Limann as first president of the Third Republic on September 24, 1979. Nevertheless, the activities of the AFRC had given vent to an intense popular disaffection from government and served notice that the actions of any future leadership would be closely monitored by the army rank and file and by "J.J.," who emerged as the charismatic and dynamic mouthpiece of populist sentiments.

Jerry Rawlings's return to the barracks was short-lived. In late November 1979, barely two months after the handover of power, he was summarily retired from the armed forces by President Limann. This action inadvertently paved the way for the systematic political education of Jerry Rawlings. During the brief civilian interlude between 1979 and the end of 1981 he developed strong ties with a core group of radical intellectuals, professionals and army officers with whom he conducted extensive political discussions, and who were later to constitute the initial backbone of his government. Rawlings expanded his organizational base, heading several revolutionary groups, including the June Fourth Movement, the New Democratic Movement and the Kwame Nkrumah Revolutionary Guards, and lending active support to the socialist student movement and radical trade unionists. He travelled extensively in West Africa, visiting Libya twice, establishing a close relationship with Muammar Qaddafi. Throughout this period he spoke out on various political topics, building up a broad constituency, gradually evolving a detailed political program.

Jerry Rawlings returned to power on December 31, 1981 in a military coup that was prompted not only by a tangible deterioration in economic and social conditions and increased corruption in the ruling party, but also by the constant harassment of Rawlings and his cohorts by the Ghanaian security services. The second Rawlings takeover differed from the first in that its leader intended from the outset to assume power and, via the Provisional National Defense Council (PNDC), to substantially alter the tenor and direction of Ghanaian politics.

The PNDC under Jerry Rawlings is on the verge of becoming the longest-lasting government in independent Ghana. During almost a decade in office it has undergone three distinct phases. The first, the radical populist stage of PNDC rule, began on December 31, 1981, and continued until mid-1983. The main theme of the early period of rule was the total social and political transformation of Ghana. Jerry Rawlings, in the name of anti-imperialism and anticolonialism, sought to govern Ghana by effectively handing over power to the people. He constructed a series of revolutionary institutions, including People's Defense Committees (PDCs), Worker's Defense Committees (WDCs), Interim Management Committees and Public Tribunals, whose task was to eliminate elite privilege and monitor official conduct. With the support of radical urban groups (students, unionists and rank-and-file soldiers), he launched a campaign against professionals and politicians—substantially contributing to a massive brain drain from the country—and imposed wage and price controls in an effort to mitigate the effects of rampant inflation.

These policies intensified the level of officially sanctioned violence (culminating in the murder of four high court justices in the summer of 1982) and significantly exacerbated social tensions on a class basis. As civil liberties were abused and coercion became commonplace, external relations shifted. Rawlings encouraged the development of strong ties with Libya and Cuba, further contributing to the image of Rawlings's Ghana as an emerging model of revolutionary populism in Africa.

Radical rhetoric was not accompanied, however, by substantial improvements in the economic sphere. By mid-1983 Ghana had lost most of its skilled manpower, production rates were at an all-time low, and drought conditions threatened to decimate an already-impoverished population. In these circumstances Jerry Rawlings accepted the conditions imposed by the International Monetary Fund (IMF), approving a stabilization and structural adjustment regimen drafted by his secretary of finance, Kwesi Botchwey. The adoption of the Economic Recovery Program (ERP) coincided with an attenuation of radical rhetoric and with a renewed stress on productivity, discipline and self-reliance. Rawlings justified the shift in terms of the need for a "common-sense revolution," one that shunned civil confusion in favor of careful planning, efficiency and responsible leadership.

The second stage of the PNDC, devoted to economic reconstruction, coincided with the transformation of Rawlings from prophet to government leader. During this period the PNDC, under his aegis, underwent a process of civilianization. A Council of Secretaries (cabinet) was created, and a chairman of the Council of Secretaries (prime minister) was appointed. The revolutionary institutional structures of the first PNDC were totally revamped: Committees for the Defense of the Revolution replaced the PDCs and WDCs, the centrality of the bureaucracy was reaffirmed, a call was issued for Ghanaians abroad to return to the country, and pacts were established with key sectors of the population, including chiefs, traders and entrepreneurs. These measures inevitably eroded the urban support base of the first PNDC (workers, students and the radical intelligentsia), who charged Rawlings with betraying the revolution, without attracting the active backing of the middle class, which remained wary of the PNDC's ongoing commitment to revolutionary objectives.

Rawlings succeeded in surviving the critical years between 1983 and 1987 through the careful utilization of a combination of autocratic techniques and corporatist strategies, coupled with palpable economic achievements. The steps initiated under the ERP increased the flow of basic commodities, improved the country's infrastructure, and contributed to a rise in productivity (especially in the agricultural sector). The shifting terms of trade between the rural and urban areas enhanced Rawlings's popularity in the countryside, while highlighting the precarious basis of his authority in the politically sensitive major cities.

The third phase of PNDC rule, commencing in 1987, has concentrated on the quest for regime legitimacy. On the fifth anniversary of the December 31 revolution, Rawlings announced his intention of holding district assembly elections to begin the process of civilianization and democratization. The promulgation of the "Blue Book" on local government reform paved the way for three rounds of district assembly elections in late 1988 and early 1989. Participation rates in the voting exercise, which provided Rawlings with much-needed backing in the rural areas, were the highest in the history of local elections in the country. The ballot, however, accentuated the tenuous nature of regime support in critical urban circles and exacerbated the call for a return to civilian rule at the national level as well. By the beginning of 1990s some of the adverse social effects of the structural adjustment program had become evident. While the World Bank and the IMF claimed success in reversing the downhill slide of Ghana's economy in the decade of the 1980s, the PNDC and its leader were faced, once again, with a series of political decisions that would directly affect the stability of the government and the political fortune of Jerry Rawlings himself. In 1990 and 1991 the country was led through a national political dialogue in regional forums, supervised by the National Commission for Democracy and the Ministry of Local Government, culminating in a consultative constitutional assembly. The PNDC announced a transition to multiparty politics but did not lift the ban on opposition parties. New opposition groups, such as the Movement for Freedom and Justice (MFJ) and the Movement for Multiparty Democracy (MMD), as well as the Ghana Bar Association, the National Union of Ghanaian Students and the Trade Union Council, emerged to criticize the government.

Rawlings has progressed during the course of his political career from the spokesperson of popular discontent to the prophet of a new Ghana, and from there to cautious reformer and ultimately to uncertain head of state. His political survival has depended on his capacity both to transform his leadership style and to maintain an image of honesty, dedication and commitment to justice. Jerry Rawlings has been able to adjust his policies because he brings to his leadership tasks an astute mind capable of absorbing nuances in conditions and options, a highly independent disposition that reduces his long-term dependence on advisors and colleagues, and an ingrained pragmatism and piecemeal approach to the solution of problems. He has been able to retain an image of reformer and champion of the underdog primarily because of his acknowledged charisma, his personal honesty, his principled stance on basic issues and his capacity to keep his overall political objectives at the forefront of his pronouncements and actions.

Rawlings came to power at a critical moment in Ghanaian history. While he bears direct responsibility for the turmoil that engulfed the country in the early part of the 1980s, he has also played a central role in the process of political and economic resuscitation. The remolding of Ghana has paralleled the maturation of Jerry Rawlings as leader. But his legacy to Ghana is mixed: He sanctioned violence and institutionalized coercion in the name of social justice; he also encouraged the reversal of the urban-based political bias of the postcolonial generation he ousted. Rawlings has not yet, however, been able to achieve his declared mission of reconstructing Ghanaian society, not only because the contents of his program remain vague and the organizational instruments he has created are weak, but also because he is as much a product of the country he governs as he is a source of its reordering. Jerry Rawlings is still the enigmatic embodiment of the anger, the aspirations, the uncertainties, the capabilities and the potential vision of a new independent leadership generation in Africa.

BIBLIOGRAPHY

Agyeman-Duah, Baffou. "Ghana, 1982–6: The Politics of the PNDC." *Journal of Modern African Studies* 25 (1987): 613–42.
Chazan, Naomi. *An Anatomy of Ghanaian Politics: Managing Political Recession, 1969–1982*. Boulder, Colo.: Westview Press, 1983.
Ninsin, Kwame. "Ghanaian Politics after 1981: Revolution or Evolution?" *Canadian Journal of African Studies* 22 (1988): 137–39.
Okeke, Barbara. *4 June: A Revolution Betrayed*. Enugu, Nigeria: Ikenga Publishers, 1982.
Owusu, Maxwell. "Rebellion, Revolution and Tradition: Reinterpreting Coups in Ghana." *Comparative Studies in Society and History* 31 (1989): 372–97.
Pellow, Deborah, and Naomi Chazan. *Ghana: Coping with Uncertainty*. Boulder, Colo.: Westview Press, 1986.
Ray, Donald I. *Ghana: Politics, Economics and Society*. London: Frances Pinter, 1986.
NAOMI CHAZAN

S

THOMAS SANKARA (1949–1987), Prime Minister, 1983; Head of the National Council of the Revolution, President of Burkina Faso, (formerly Republic of Upper Volta), 1983–1987.

Prior to the rule of Thomas Sankara, Upper Volta was identified with crushing poverty, uninspiring leadership and doomed development prospects. During Sankara's four-year rule, the name of the country was changed to Burkina Faso. Poverty was attacked with a rare combination of revolutionary zeal and pragmatism. The vision he instilled in leadership brought hope to the country's development prospects. However, the qualities that characterized Sankara's rule dissolved with his assassination in a counterrevolutionary coup in 1987.

Thomas Sankara adopted unorthodox operating procedures. Where others had failed to take steps in tackling the needs of the masses, he identified with populist demands. Where others maintained an unquestioned allegiance with former colonial masters, he was critical of exploitation from within and imperialism from abroad. Sankara's leadership style made many foreigners and peers across Africa uncomfortable, but it offered hope and admiration to the unprivileged majority on the continent and in the African diaspora.

Sankara never received formal political training. He rose only to the rank of captain as a military officer. He was born in Yako, a small town in the northwest of Upper Volta, on December 21, 1949. The third of ten children born to the humble family of Joseph and Margaret Sankara, the young Thomas lived in many cities, accompanying his father, who worked as a part-time worker for the postal services, to Gaoua and Ouagadougou, the country's capital. He later attended secondary school in Lycée Ouezzin Coulibaly in Bobo-Dioulasso and obtained a school diploma, the *brevet*. These varied travel experiences exposed the young Sankara to early traces of poverty, exploitation, inequality and racial discrimination, which were to become preoccupations of his regime.

In 1966 Sankara enrolled in the military preparatory school in Ouagadougou, graduating after three years. In 1970 he entered the military academy in Antsirabe, Madagascar, and gained a classic formative experience in the protests and strikes that led to the establishment of a revolutionary government there in 1972. From Madagascar, Sankara went to France, where he attended parachute training sessions and accumulated knowledge of ideological and revolutionary activity by close identification with left-wing activities of other students from Upper Volta, which was regarded with suspicion, given his military background. Sankara's early leadership was established during the first border war between Mali and Upper Volta, December 1974 to January 1975. As commander of his forces, he accepted the capitulation of Malian troops by surrender rather than bloodshed, considering the war to be unjust and unnecessary. In 1976 Sankara was appointed commander of the National Training Center for Commandos in Po in south central Upper Volta, near the Ghana border. While attending another training session at the parachute school in Rabat, Morocco, in 1978, Thomas Sankara met fellow officer Blaise Compaore for the first time. Both men remained friends until the crisis leading to Sankara's assassination in October 1987.

The Lamizana regime in Upper Volta was overthrown by Colonel Saye Zerbo in 1980. Sankara reluctantly joined the Saye Zerbo government in 1981 as secretary of information. (He was replaced by Compaore at his former position at Po.) Both Sankara and Compaore were arrested after they resigned from their government posts and from the ruling military body. Although both officers did not participate in the November 1982 coup that established the regime of Jean-Baptiste Ouedraogo, Sankara was appointed prime minister of the new government in January 1983.

As prime minister, Sankara upstaged the head of state largely because of his clear personal engagement with the needs of the majority of the people. This led to a coup attempt inspired by Ouedraogo, in which Sankara was arrested and imprisoned. His other colleagues, including Compaore, evaded arrest. They later organized the resistance and popular protest against the coup that led to Sankara's release from jail in May. He remained under house arrest until a decisive coup d'état, spearheaded by Compaore, overthrew the Ouedraogo regime. A ruling National Council of the Revolution (CNR) was established, and Thomas Sankara was released from house arrest to be made head of state on August 4, 1983.

The revolutionary government of August 1983 was a military junta made up of four officers, including Sankara and Compaore. In this quadripartite arrangement the more charismatic Sankara was the leader and popular figure. Similar to other military-ruled African countries, the former Upper Volta did not officially embrace multipartyism. However, unlike other African countries, it was rich in the variety of political organizations within the military, labor and student ranks, in which citizens openly espoused leftist doctrines. Many of these organizations were also represented in the CNR, presided over by Thomas Sankara. In a bid to defactionalize the country's politics and popularize the revolution, Sankara created Committees for the Defense of the Revolution (CDRs) across the country.

The CDRs were to serve as guarantors of the people's sovereignty in the exercise of revolutionary power. They were also his direct link with the masses in the arduous task of social, political and economic transformation.

In 1984, at the first anniversary of the revolutionary regime's accession to power, Sankara announced the change of the country's name from Upper Volta to Burkina Faso, a combination of words from the Jula and Moore languages meaning "land of upright men." Underlying this simple change of name was the profound need for change in the collective vision of a people. Many significant innovations in the lives of the Burkinabe people were initiated by Sankara.

On the social level, he took a passionate interest in the emancipation of the Burkinabe women from toil and oppression. He appointed four female members of government, set out an elaborate plan to combat prostitution, and announced special days when men did housework in place of women. As a convinced revolutionary, identifying with the working class and peasants, he decreed a year-long suspension of all residential rents and began a housing-construction project in 1985. He forced members of the state bourgeoisie to take pay cuts and used the collected funds to construct village schools and health care centers through indigenous effort. Under his four-year rule the literacy rate increased from 12 to 23 percent.

He waged successive battles against massive corruption, bureaucratic irresponsibility and the embezzlement of public funds. Government ministers were obliged to declare their assets before revolutionary tribunals in a bid to ascertain their financial health. To promote greater political accountability and demonstrate grass-roots experience, the cabinet was dissolved annually and its members forced to supervise development projects in rural areas. They were returned to the government only after a satisfactory performance in these community projects.

Sankara believed that despite the natural and historic conditions that condemned his country to economic backwardness, some degree of progress could be achieved through hard work and economic discipline. Consequently, he led the people of his country in collective construction projects like dams, farm-to-market roads and railroads. He also encouraged the planting of trees to combat deforestation. He imposed a rigorous two-meal-a-day plan and decreed the use of small quantities of water per day for every Burkinabe. In addition, Burkinabe officials and diplomats were subjected to meager allowances on missions abroad. It was the determination of the Sankara government to make elites and masses live according to the realities of the country. Sankara himself faithfully manifested this design in many ways: He never owned a house of his own; he considered it imprudent for his country to own a presidential plane; he dressed mostly in military attire or in locally produced material; and he had only a musical instrument, the guitar, as his most costly asset.

Sankara's love for simplicity, hard work, sacrifice and revolutionary dedication was not shared to the same degree by all Burkinabes. In 1984, fifteen hundred degree-holding teachers who organized a strike instigated by the Voltaic Progressive Front were fired. Leading members of the Confederation of Trade Unions, who espoused Soviet-style Marxism and provoked the revolutionary government, were jailed. Also, civil servants were fearful of a proposed regulation that would evaluate their official performance on the basis of skills exhibited in mandatory, bi-weekly, collective sports, authorized by the revolutionary government.

Domestic opposition and revolutionary fatigue of the elites were not the only problems Sankara faced. His fervent anti-imperialism taught him that his regime was doomed to destruction by the activities of reactionary African governments and Western powers. For this reason, he cultivated good relations with other revolutionary governments in Africa and paid friendly visits to Cuba, Nicaragua, China and the Soviet Union.

Suspicion and allegations of plots throughout Sankara's leadership characterized relations between Burkina Faso and its southwestern neighbor, Côte d'Ivoire. Border warfare with Mali, the neighbor to the northwest, broke out again on December 25, 1985. Furthermore, Sankara antagonized both countries when he tried and jailed a high-ranking official of Malian and Ivorian origin for mismanagement of the subregion's economic cooperation organization. In other capitals of the subregion it was feared that the revolutionary precedents created by Jerry Rawlings* in Ghana, followed by Sankara in Burkina Faso, could be imitated by other low-ranking military officials and lead to the overthrow of their governments.

Sankara made news in other ways beyond the West African subregion. He was friendly with Libya without yielding to Qaddafi's dictates. He was critical of France and its multinational transport companies, which refused to carry his country's exports for sale overseas. At least once in his four-year rule he shunned participation in the Franco-African summit, which was growing in stature at the expense of the Organization of African Unity (OAU). During a visit by the French president to Burkina Faso in 1986, he ignored diplomatic decorum and openly criticized French ties to the apartheid regime of South Africa.

On the global scene, Sankara played to the international audience. Before the thirty-ninth session of the United Nations General Assembly, he not only defined the contours of the Burkinabe revolution, but he spoke on behalf of the great disinherited people of the world, including women and mothers, children, artists and those living in ghettos. It was his conviction that his country was the quintessence of these misfortunes and a painful synthesis of all of humanity's suffering. Sankara became the first African head of state to visit and speak to a crowd in Harlem, the black ghetto in New York, in October 1984. In the course of his four-year tenure, he hosted international conferences for women, artists and the antiapartheid movement.

By mid-1987, while Sankara was acclaimed abroad as a statesman and hero of populist dimensions, his hold on power at home was under challenge. Fears of outside machinations to topple him, coupled with internal dissatisfaction with the growing hardships of the revolution, occupied him continuously. But his final undoing came in the intimate circle of the ruling junta. Rumors of dissension between the leading members of the revolutionary government multiplied but were never substantiated. Antirevolutionary tracts indiscriminately attacking the junta, including Sankara, began to appear in Ouagadougou by September 1987. Although Sankara publicly denied any disagreement, he had quickly been reduced to a minority within the ruling junta by October. It was in this atmosphere of fear and threats that Compaore ordered his troops into a counterrevolutionary palace coup that ended in the assassination of Thomas Sankara on October 15, 1987. He was buried unceremoniously in an unmarked grave in the capital city. There have been no official or reliable accounts of the events leading to Sankara's death. However, it is assumed that domestic wrangling and foreign involvement both played a role in ending the Sankara regime.

To justify the overthrow, the thirty-eight-year-old leader was accused of personalizing power and of dispensing a kind of mystical autocracy characterized by renegade tendencies and paranoia. Sankara's violent elimination from the political scene sent shock waves across the African continent and the revolutionary world. He had spoken with almost prophetic accuracy about his life and his ties with Compaore. He never claimed perfection in leadership nor excellence in governance. He recognized the multiple setbacks of the revolution but also believed that some victories had been won. The victories, however, could not transform Burkina Faso from a 'Fourth World' country to a haven of wealth in four years, but they seemed to have given hope to many. The revolution itself and the hopes it awakened followed Sankara to his grave.

Blaise Compaore, who replaced him as head of state, continued to face problems not unconnected with the Sankara tragedy. No matter how the future of the country unfolds, Sankara takes a legitimate place in the exclusive ranks of the prodigious young leadership to have emerged from Africa. However, interpreting Sankara's place in history also requires connecting it with Compaore. It was Compaore who organized the revolt that brought Sankara to power and Compaore who engineered the bloody assassination that toppled Sankara from leadership.

Unlike Africa's early revolutionary heroes, such as Patrice Lumumba[*] and Amílcar Cabral,[*] who diligently inspired revolution but never fully gained power to practice it, Sankara was unique in that he preached revolution, put it into practice, and was consumed by it. The greatest irony of the Sankara legacy was that perhaps the kind of simplicity, pragmatism and discipline that African leadership so badly needs was provided only to one of its poorest countries and only for a short period of time.

BIBLIOGRAPHY

Work by Sankara:

Thomas Sankara Speaks: The Burkina Faso Revolution, 1983–87. New York: Pathfinder, 1988.

Other Works:

Andriamirado, Sennen. *Sankara, le rebelle*. Paris: Jeune Afrique Livres, 1987.
Ziegler, Jean. *Sankara: Un nouveau pouvoir africain*. Lausanne, Switzerland: Editions
       Pierre Marcel Favre, 1986.

                                                                    H. MBELLA MOKEBA

JONAS MALHEIRO SAVIMBI (1934–   ), President, National Union for the
Total Independence of Angola (UNITA), People's Republic of Angola, 1966–.

For a quarter century Jonas Savimbi was instrumental in Angola's transition
from colonial possession to independent state. Since 1975, however, the guerrilla
army commanded by Savimbi has effectively prevented Angola from realizing
its enormous economic potential. Savimbi, once denounced as a "tool of Western
imperialists," a "puppet of South African racists" and "Africa's enemy number
one," has staged a political comeback that may enable UNITA to compete in
free, fair, multiparty elections. It would not be unexpected if UNITA, dominated
by the charismatic Savimbi, drew a significant percentage of the vote.

Jonas Malheiro Savimbi was born in Munhango, Angola, on August 3, 1934.
He is the son of Loth Malheiro Savimbi and Helena Mbundu Savimbi. Loth
Savimbi was employed by the Benguela Railroad. His son, Jonas, educated by
Protestant missionary schools, received in 1958 a scholarship to finish high school
and begin university study in Portugal. Already active in the Angolan anticolonial
struggle, Savimbi continued his clandestine political activities in Portugal, drawing the attention of the Portuguese secret police, the International Police for
Defense of the State (PIDE). After three detentions, Savimbi fled Portugal for
Switzerland, where he studied medicine for two years at Fribourg University
and later enrolled at Lausanne University. In July 1965 he graduated with honors
in political science and juridical sciences.

The Angolan national liberation struggle against Portuguese colonialism faced
a dilemma common throughout sub-Saharan Africa. Efforts toward freedom were
being channeled along the major Angolan ethnic groupings. The three major
ethnic groups in Angola, Ovimbundu (37 percent), Luanda-Mbundu (25 percent)
and Bakongo (13 percent), comprised 75 percent of the population. Historical
differences among the many peoples who comprise Angola were exacerbated by
Portuguese colonial policies.

While fulfilling his academic requirements, Savimbi, an Ovimbundu, explored
methods to best participate in the liberation struggle. He contacted representatives
of the Popular Movement for the Liberation of Angola (MPLA) and the Union
of Angolan People (UPA). On the advice of Tom Mboya[*] and Jomo Kenyatta[*]
of Kenya, Savimbi opted to join UPA in 1961. Appointed secretary-general, he
began intensive diplomatic efforts to win recognition of UPA by African states.
He also played a prominent role in the coalition of UPA and the Angolan
Democratic Party (PDA) to form the National Front for the Liberation of Angola
(FNLA).

Despite his efforts on behalf of FNLA and Angolan nationalism, Savimbi grew disenchanted with the one-dimensional character of the movement. On July 6, 1964, at an Organization of African Unity (OAU) conference in Cairo, Savimbi resigned from FNLA. He maintained that the Angolan liberation struggle must have not only a military component, but a socioeconomic one as well. Savimbi was also critical of Bakongo domination of FNLA, President Holden Roberto's lavish life-style in exile, and the unwillingness of both MPLA and FNLA to cooperate in the struggle against Portugal.

In collaboration with other disillusioned Angolan exiles, Savimbi promulgated the Manifesto of Friends of Angola (Amangola). The document, citing the failures of MPLA and FNLA, invited all Angolans to participate and assist in a new strategy for Angolan liberation. Savimbi travelled to the Soviet Union, East Germany, Algeria, Egypt, Czechoslovakia and Hungary searching for international support. The only positive response came from the People's Republic of China. In January 1965 Savimbi and eleven other Angolans journeyed to China to receive military training at the Nanking Military Academy. Returning from China, this cadre of nationalists infiltrated into Angola through Zambia. At Muangai, in the eastern province of Moxico, the founding congress of UNITA was conducted in March 1966. UNITA, a multiethnic organization, became the third major Angolan national liberation movement.

UNITA guerrillas began attacking economic targets, including the Benguela Railroad. The rail line was vital, not only for Portuguese/Angolan interests, but for Zambia and Zaire too. In 1967 Savimbi again left the bush to seek international support. On his return to Angola, Zambian officials arrested him. The Portuguese government had employed diplomatic, economic and even military threats to coerce Zambian authorities to ban UNITA activities. Rather than deliver Savimbi to Portuguese military authorities, Zambian president Kenneth Kaunda* deported him to Cairo. For one year Savimbi remained in Egypt. Finally, in July 1968 he clandestinely crossed the Zambia/Angola border, returning to UNITA forces. From that time until the Armed Forces Movement (AFM) coup in Portugal, Savimbi did not leave the Angolan bush. Instead, he implemented the tenets of Maoist liberation thought. UNITA conducted not only extensive guerrilla action against Portuguese military forces, but also engaged in propaganda efforts to develop a politically educated peasantry. UNITA's political orientation featured socialism with respect for ethnic cultural heritage. Savimbi acknowledged that UNITA could not militarily defeat Portugal; therefore, it became crucial to ensure that the peasants in UNITA operational areas embraced the insurgents and their goals. Such support would be vital if the Portuguese were to negotiate a political settlement to the stalemated war. Unfortunately, the military wings of MPLA, FNLA and UNITA spent as much time battling one another as fighting the Portuguese forces.

The 1974 coup by the Armed Forces Movement (AFM) in the Portuguese military in Lisbon caught all three Angolan liberation movements by surprise. After thirteen years of armed rebellion the insurgents were no closer to victory than when the insurgency had begun in 1961. It took a revolution in Portugal to end colonial domination of Angola. The Portuguese negotiated with the three most prominent Angolan forces, and during the course of three peace conferences Portugal agreed to free Angola in November 1975. At the conference in Alvor, the most important groups, MPLA, FNLA, and UNITA, agreed to establish a tripartite government and a national army and conduct free elections for a constituent assembly.

Under such a scenario, UNITA would have fared quite well, based upon the success of its Maoist philosophy: to provide economic gratification and political indoctrination. UNITA had spent the previous eight years employing its military wing to build political/economic support. Of the three liberation organizations, UNITA was probably the best prepared to take advantage of a peaceful transition to independence.

The liberation groups massed in Luanda, the capital, but personal, ideological and ethnic conflicts quickly arose. MPLA forcibly expelled FNLA and UNITA from the capital and declared the People's Republic of Angola on November 11, 1975. UNITA and FNLA launched a brief, but bitter, civil war. MPLA, along with twelve thousand Cuban combat troops and $200 million worth of Soviet military equipment decimated FNLA and drove UNITA back into the bush to continue its low-intensity guerrilla war.

Savimbi was frustrated that the Alvor agreement had collapsed. He quickly regrouped UNITA forces and began what he labelled the Third War of National Liberation (the first was the struggle against Portugal; the second was the 1975–76 civil war). The insurgents continued to employ Maoist military tactics, but Savimbi redefined his political message. Portuguese colonialism was replaced by Soviet/Cuban social imperialism.

The term "Negritude" perhaps best describes the political philosophy of UNITA. Savimbi adapted Negritude, originally conceived by Léopold Senghor* of Senegal, to the Angolan experience. Negritude proposed government by consensus and compromise, exultation in African culture, recognition of the importance of ethnic groupings and belief that Pan-Africanism is an unrealistic goal that should be replaced by cooperation between independent nations.

Placed in the Angolan context, Negritude is an indictment of MPLA rule. According to the UNITA leader, MPLA does not govern by consensus or compromise, nor does it value the various ethnic groups that comprise the Angolan people; the MPLA leadership is dominated by *assimilados* and *mesticos*, while the President, Jose Eduardo dos Santos, is of São Toméan descent; Angolan culture has been emasculated by the socialist dogma of MPLA; and, finally, Pan-Africanism betrayed UNITA's cause by refusing to negotiate an end to the civil war.

This eclectic approach to Angolan politics was troublesome to potential supporters. Savimbi had attempted to obtain support from the Soviet Union, the East European countries, China and the United States. During the civil war and after, UNITA accepted South African aid. The UNITA–South African relationship made suspect the insurgents' goal of free, fair elections in Angola.

The South African Defense Forces (SADF) had entered the Angolan civil war to stymie the Leninist-oriented MPLA and its Cuban/Soviet benefactors. As global public opinion condemned the South African endeavor, in effect sanctioning the Cuban/Soviet intervention, the SADF withdrew to bordering Namibia (then South West Africa). In fulfillment of its socialist obligations, MPLA allowed the South West Africa People's Organization (SWAPO) to establish bases in Angola from which to launch guerrilla forays against South African interests in Namibia. As well, after the 1976 turmoil in South Africa, MPLA allowed the African National Congress (ANC) to establish "safe havens" within Angolan territory. Between 1976 and 1988 the SADF conducted a series of raids against ANC and SWAPO bases. These raids had the ancillary effect of punishing Angolan economic and military installations, Cuban troops and Soviet advisors. Because UNITA's strength was in southern Angola, and since the guerrilla war focused upon MPLA and Cuban/Soviet support for the regime, a marriage of convenience between UNITA and South Africa was undertaken. While militarily sound, this tacit alliance was detrimental to Savimbi's revolutionary credentials, not only in Africa, but around the world.

In order to protect Angola from South African incursions, Cuba increased its troop strength to sixty thousand by 1988. The Soviet Union delivered one billion dollars per annum of military materiel between 1980 and 1990. The consequence of this massive display of support by South Africa, Cuba and the Soviet Union was to inhibit any attempt at reconciliation by the warring parties.

In 1985 and 1987 MPLA/Cuban forces launched huge compaigns to capture UNITA's provisional capital, Jamba, in southeastern Angola. In each case South African ground troops intervened to turn the tide in favor of UNITA. This further hampered Savimbi's efforts to portray UNITA as an independent political and military organization.

The long-running, low-intensity civil war prevented Angola's economic recovery. Over the course of the 1980s both UNITA and MPLA came to the gradual realization that neither could decisively conclude the civil war. The Angolan government was seeking Western economic, technological and monetary support. Western business interests promised an impressive array of aid, but only if the civil war got resolved. Consequently, by 1988 MPLA realized that some accommodation would have to be reached with Savimbi. Savimbi, on the other hand, spent the decade searching for a viable alternative to South African military sponsorship. The United States, through the implementation of the Reagan Doctrine, began in 1985, steadily and in escalating amounts, to provide UNITA with an alternative source of military provisions.

In 1988 South Africa, Angola, Cuba and the United States initiated the "four-party" talks toward resolving the Cuban presence in Angola and South African control of Namibia. UNITA, SWAPO and the Soviet Union were observers to the negotiations, which in December 1988 led to an agreement (the Brazzaville Accord) stipulating that all Cuban troops would be withdrawn from Angola by July 1, 1991, while South Africa would grant independence to Namibia by

November 1, 1989. Additionally, the SADF had previously ended all assistance to UNITA on September 1, 1988.

For the first time both MPLA and UNITA found themselves without any major foreign patron. The Soviet Union, bowing to domestic economic pressure, and Cuba, through treaty, were easing their commitment to MPLA. South Africa, enjoying newfound international respectability, refused to intervene on UNITA's behalf. In January 1989 MPLA hard-liners launched another military offensive against the UNITA stronghold of Jamba. After some initial setbacks, UNITA was able to repel the MPLA forces, inflicting heavy casualties. The stage was set for genuine negotiations between the two warring parties. Those negotiations began in April 1990; thirteen months later MPLA and UNITA tentatively agreed to a cease-fire and a date for free, multiparty elections.

For the last twenty-five years Jonas Savimbi has been in the Angolan bush, fighting first Portuguese colonialism and since 1975 the one-party minority rule of MPLA. Despite facing thousands of Cuban troops equipped with Soviet weaponry, Savimbi's forces not only protected their guerrilla bases, but spread the conflict throughout the country.

Savimbi has been the unquestioned leader of UNITA. He serves as president and commander-in-chief of the armed forces. In a land dominated for centuries by ethnic conflict, Jonas Savimbi is the foremost representative of Ovimbundu nationalism. His ideology provides the political direction of the movement, his charisma keeps the organization unified, and his leadership has placed UNITA in a position to enter the mainstream of Angolan politics.

UNITA has survived because it is more than a military force. Under Savimbi's leadership the organization drafted economic recovery proposals, political reorganization strategies and foreign-policy themes and initiatives. Because UNITA stressed political, economic, cultural and military matters, Savimbi is better prepared to participate in the rebuilding of Angolan society than most insurgent leaders who can lead the revolution, but lack the necessary skills to govern.

Savimbi has consistently called for free, fair elections to decide the political future of the nation. He has promised that UNITA will abide by the results of such elections. Despite an early flirtation with other ideologies, Savimbi has been consistent in his appeal for democracy in Angola. In discussing the application of Chinese communism to Angola, Savimbi once said, "From Mao I learned how to fight a guerrilla war. I also learned how not to run a country" (Savimbi *Policy Review* 1986:19).

The UNITA leader has been constant in that belief during a period when Western governments were reluctantly willing to accept Leninist-style dictatorships in sub-Saharan Africa. He is one of the few African leaders to challenge the notion that Western or Eastern political structures and economic development strategies are superior to traditional African modes of government. Socialism has not fared well on the African continent. In rejecting alien political ideologies, Savimbi has promised to tap the historical legacy of Angolan pride, ethnic achievements and cultural diversity.

BIBLIOGRAPHY

Works by Savimbi:

Angola. Lisbon: Agencia Portuguesa de Revistas, 1979.
Quando a terra a voltar a sorrir um dia. Lisbon: Perspectivas & Realidades, 1985.
Por um futuro melhor. Lisbon: Nova Nordica, 1986.
"The War Against Soviet Imperialism." *Policy Review* no.35 (winter 1986): 18–24.

Other Works:

Bridgland, Fred. *Jonas Savimbi: A Key to Africa*. New York: Paragon House, 1987.
Gibson, Richard. *African Liberation Movements: Contemporary Struggles against White
    Minority Rule*. London: Oxford University Press, 1972.
Marcum, John. *The Angolan Revolution*. Vol. 2, *Exile Politics and Guerrilla Warfare
    (1962–1976)*. Cambridge, Mass.: M.I.T. Press, 1978.

                                                        W. MARTIN JAMES

HAILE SELASSIE (1892–1975), Regent, King, Emperor of Ethiopia, 1916–
1974.

In a political career spanning half a century, Haile Selassie presided over the
transition of Ethiopia from a feudal country into a more centralized and bureaucratic one, more modern, but also suffering from all the weaknesses afflicting
contemporary African states. With him, the Ethiopian monarchy reached the
apex of its power and then disappeared.

Haile Selassie's accomplishments as the leader of this transition spanning fifty
years were considerable, but his reputation went even further, taking on an
almost legendary quality. As an exiled monarch asking the League of Nations
for help against the Italian invasion of Ethiopia in 1936, he became a symbol
of the smaller countries left defenseless against fascist aggression by the lack of
resolve of the European powers. In the early 1960s, as head of the oldest
independent African country, he became the symbol of the rebirth of the continent. Across the world in the Caribbean, Haile Selassie—Ras Tafari before he
became emperor—was made the object of veneration by a religious sect naming
itself after him, the Rastafarians.

Haile Selassie was born Tafari Makonnen in 1892. His father was a cousin
and confidant of Emperor Menelik, who had served as envoy to Europe and
governor of Harar Province. Tafari was singled out early for leadership positions.
In 1910, after his father's death, he became governor of Harar Province. By the
time Emperor Menelik died, Tafari had already established himself as a strong
contender for the throne, both because of his political ability and because he
could claim descent, through a long line of ancestors, from King Solomon and
the Queen of Sheba. But the succession was a protracted and complex process.
Totally incapacitated since 1909, Menelik died in 1913, leaving as heir a young
grandson, Lij Eyasu, who never succeeded in consolidating his power. After
three years of intrigue, Lij Eyasu was ousted. Empress Zewditu, Menelik's
daughter, succeeded him on the throne, and Ras Tafari became regent in 1916.

Tafari had received a traditional upbringing, with minimal exposure to Western education, although he was fluent in French. Nevertheless, he was considered a modernizer at court. As governor of Harar he had sought to improve the administration, register land, and promote economic activity.

As regent, however, Tafari found himself hemmed in by powerful personalities, particularly the minister of war and the head of the Coptic church, and could not assert his power immediately. For ten years he maneuvered and waited. His opportunity came in 1926, with the death of the powerful minister, Fitwarari Hapta Giorgis. Tafari strengthened his position by taking control of Hapta Giorgis's army and land. Two years later he prevailed upon the empress to bestow upon him the title of *negus*—king.

Empress Zewditu died in 1930, and Tafari was crowned emperor under the name of Haile Selassie I. The long battle for the throne was over. The battle for control over the country was just beginning. The centrifugal power of the regional dynasties and the provincial nobility has always been strong in Ethiopia. The long years of uncertainty between the death of Menelik and the rise of Haile Selassie had only increased it. As an ambitious ruler, determined to consolidate his position, Haile Selassie was bound to clash eventually with the regional potentates. He started centralizing power in his own hands after the coronation, but the process was cut short by the Italian invasion in 1935.

As emperor, Haile Selassie confirmed his reputation as a modernizer. He opened a few schools and sent many young Ethiopians to study abroad. He also undertook to form and train a standing modern army to replace the feudal armies raised by the nobility in time of war. To this end, he recruited Belgian instructors to organize the Imperial Guard and Swiss officers to train the personal army he still controlled in Harar Province. He invited a Swedish mission to open the first military school at Holeta.

Nevertheless, Haile Selassie remained a traditional ruler. Innovation was in the service of goals he shared with all his predecessors, that of strengthening of Ethiopia vis-à-vis external enemies and the emperor vis-à-vis internal ones. The nature of power and political control were not expected to change. The promulgation of a constitution in 1931 made this clear. It created a bicameral parliament, with a senate appointed by the emperor from among the nobility and a lower house nominated by the senate. But the parliament functioned only as a consultative council and had practically ceased to exist by the time of the Italian invasion.

When Italy, which already had colonies in Eritrea and Somalia, invaded Ethiopia in 1935, the feudal armies were levied, but in vain. After participating in the initial resistance, Haile Selassie went into exile in Britain. His appearance at the League of Nations to denounce the invasion and plead for help acquired a symbolic meaning. It was long remembered by people who knew nothing about Ethiopia. At home, however, he was criticized for abandoning the country.

The Italian occupation came to an end in 1941 when a British expedition from the Sudan joined forces with the Ethiopian bands fighting the occupation. Haile

Selassie was reinstated on the throne despite some resistance to his return. In Tigrai Province a rebellion was suppressed with British help. During the following thirty years Haile Selassie undertook a series of reforms that changed the character of Ethiopia irrevocably.

He continued the modernization of the army, originally with British, French and Swedish help. After 1952, when the United Nations gave the former Italian colony of Eritrea to Ethiopia in a federal arrangement, the United States became the major provider of both military and economic aid. In return, the United States received a base near Asmara, Kagnew Station, which was used until 1977 as a communications center. By 1974 the Ethiopian military numbered about forty thousand men, and the feudal armies faded into memory.

A second task to which Haile Selassie dedicated much effort was the expansion of education. A university college was opened in Addis Ababa in 1951. It later became Haile Selassie I University. Primary and secondary schools were opened all over the country, and more students were sent abroad. Ethiopia continued to have one of the highest illiteracy rates in the world, but the students grew numerous enough to constitute a political force, extremely vocal and critical of the regime.

Haile Selassie also reorganized the administration, particularly in the provinces. This was not only an attempt to improve efficiency, but also a maneuver to strengthen his power to the detriment of the provincial nobility. Provincial governors and administrators continued to be drawn heavily from the ranks of the nobility, but they were no longer sent to their home areas, in order to deprive them of an independent power base. They had no financial autonomy, and they were forbidden to collect taxes other than those imposed by the central government. This protected Ethiopians from the extortions of greedy officials, but it also made the officials totally dependent on Addis Ababa. The result was increasing centralization and the virtual disappearance of the provincial nobility as a political force capable of challenging the emperor.

By 1960 Haile Selassie had greatly weakened his traditional enemies, but he was being challenged by new ones. An attempted military coup, which won much support among the students, was launched while the emperor was out of the country on a state visit. Although it was suppressed in a few days by loyal troops, it pointed to the source of challenge to the emperor in the future—the military and the educated elite dissatisfied with the pace of change.

In the early 1960s Haile Selassie became an important participant in the international politics of independent Africa. The Organization of African Unity (OAU) was set up in 1963 with headquarters in Addis Ababa. Haile Selassie was responsible for the inclusion in the organization's charter of a clause committing all African countries to respect the borders established by the colonial powers. While promptly accepted by African governments fearful of opening the Pandora's box of border disputes, the clause directly served the interests of Ethiopia, since it denied legitimacy and African support to the Somali attempts to annex the Ogaden region.

Despite the popularity he enjoyed abroad as the dean of African leaders, in the 1960s Haile Selassie faced growing political challenges at home. Student unrest increased. The decision to dissolve the federation with Eritrea in 1962, reducing the autonomous region to a province without special status, triggered a guerrilla movement there that continued to gather support despite the attempt to suppress it militarily.

In 1972 Haile Selassie celebrated his eightieth birthday. The event focused attention on the issue of succession, adding a climate of uncertainty to the other problems. The emperor had no obvious heir. Relations between him and Crown Prince Asfa Wossen had been strained ever since the latter had agreed, under duress, to read the proclamation deposing the emperor during the 1960 coup. Never a very forceful personality, Asfa Wossen had been incapacitated by a stroke. It was generally assumed that the death of Haile Selassie would create great uncertainty, but the crisis occurred earlier.

In 1973 a drought hit the northern regions of Ethiopia. Instead of mounting a relief effort, the government pretended that nothing was wrong. Eventually the extent of the tragedy became public. The attempted cover-up disgusted the educated elite and the urban population in general. Adding to the emperor's difficulties, a series of strikes by workers and mutinies by army units occurred in early 1974. The emperor's attempt to save his own position by dismissing the cabinet failed. In June 1974 a military council seized de facto power.

Increasingly powerless and isolated, the emperor saw his ministers and generals arrested one by one throughout the summer. He was finally deposed on September 12, 1974, unceremoniously driven away from the palace in a small Volkswagen in the early morning hours, and imprisoned at army headquarters. He died there in 1975. The circumstances of his death remain unclear. Officially, he died of old age and complications from prostate surgery. But rumors persisted in Addis Ababa that his death was not due to natural causes. It is unlikely that the truth will ever be established.

Haile Selassie is a figure of enormous importance in Ethiopian history, although his role changed greatly from period to period. If he had passed from the political scene with the Italian invasion of 1935, he would be remembered as a strong but essentially traditional emperor who continued his immediate predecessors' policy of strengthening personal power and introducing a number of innovations into the country—education, telecommunications, better roads and the rudiments of modern technology.

If he had been deposed in the 1960 coup, he would probably be remembered as a modernizer, determined to move the country from feudalism into the contemporary world, eventually falling victim to his own reforms. While there was no hint of democratic ideals in Haile Selassie's attitude—the 1955 constitution provided for the election of the lower chamber of parliament but did not circumscribe the emperor's own power—he was creating the beginnings of modern bureaucratic administration in Ethiopia. Furthermore, education was expanding rapidly, agricultural production was increasing, and some industry was developing. Haile Selassie demonstrated not only great ability as a politician, successfully maneuvering for several decades in the thicket of Ethiopian politics, but also qualities of leadership. He had a vision of the future of Ethiopia, that of an eighteenth-century enlightened monarch, not that of a twentieth-century leader. Yet at the time such a vision put him ahead of most of his contemporaries in Ethiopia.

But Haile Selassie departed from the scene in 1974. By this time other aspects of his historical role, and particularly its limitations, had become evident. Haile Selassie's reforms and his struggle to increase his own power had destroyed the old political system without creating a viable new one. The old empire was based on a complex social and political system in which many had a stake. The system was not democratic, or just by contemporary standards, but it managed to tie together emperor, aristocracy, provincial nobility, church and peasants in a web of interdependence. Reforms after 1941 weakened that system. Its last moment of vitality probably occurred in the reaction to the attempted coup in 1960.

Haile Selassie failed to create a new system with a reach comparable to the old empire. Expansion of his power narrowed its base. By the end of his reign, as the 1974 coup demonstrated, the regime was supported only by a rudimentary administration and by the military. Few others had a stake in it. When the military withdrew its support from the emperor, there was nothing left. Haile Selassie ended his reign not as a traditional monarch whose anachronistic regime was destroyed by the inexorable march of history, but as a contemporary African authoritarian leader who remained in power because of the support of the army. The traditional empire was destroyed by Haile Selassie. Haile Selassie was destroyed by the army, like innumerable other contemporary African heads of state.

BIBLIOGRAPHY

Work by Selassie:

The Autobiography of Haile Selassie I. Vol. 1, *My Life and Ethiopia's Progress, 1892–1937*. London: Oxford University Press, 1976.

Other Works:

Clapham, Christopher. *Haile-Selassie's Government*. London: Longman, 1969.
Gilkes, Patrick. *The Dying Lion*. London: Friedmann, 1975.
Greenfield, Richard. *Ethiopia: A New Political History*. London: Pall Mall Press, 1965.
Perham, Margery. *The Government of Ethiopia*. 2nd ed. Evanston, Ill: Northwestern University Press, 1969.
Spencer, John H. *Ethiopia at Bay: A Personal Account of the Haile Sellassie Years*. Algonac, Mich.: Reference Publications, 1984.

MARINA OTTAWAY

LEOPOLD SEDAR SENGHOR (1906–   ), President, Republic of Senegal, 1960–1980.

Like the vast majority of Senegalese of his generation, Léopold Sédar Senghor was born a French subject. Unlike the *citoyens,* those born in the four coastal cities of Dakar, Gorée, Rufisque and Saint Louis, the *sujets* enjoyed none of the political rights of French citizens. Yet via the path of a Catholic education, Senghor went on to achieve fame in France as a poet and writer and then to become a major political figure in France and in post–World War II French West Africa. At independence he became the first president of the Republic of Senegal, a post he would hold for two decades. On December 31, 1980, Senghor resigned the presidency, thus becoming the first elected African head of state to voluntarily turn over power to a successor. In retirement he has maintained a remarkable distance from politics, choosing instead to return to a literary career that was crowned by his 1984 election to the French Academy, making him the first black member of that most exclusive of European institutions.

Senghor's tenure as president was marked by a series of paradoxes. A devout Roman Catholic, he led a predominantly Muslim country with the support of the Muslim religious elite, who more than once rallied to his side in a dispute with a Muslim rival. While he was himself the model of the ''assimilated'' African, the black Frenchman, Senghor's political support came principally from among the rural population least touched by the influence of French culture. While by education and temperament he is very much the intellectual theoretician, he proved to be highly skilled at the practice of politics as the art of the possible.

Senghor was born in 1906 in the coastal of Joal, where his father was a successful merchant. Baptized a Catholic, he was sent as a child to Catholic mission schools in Joal and nearby Ngasobil. At sixteen, initially hoping to become a Catholic priest and teacher, he went to Dakar to continue his education. In recognition of his success there, Senghor received a rare partial scholarship to pursue his literary studies in France. Thus in 1928, at the age of twenty-two, he left Dakar for Paris, where, over the course of the next thirty years, he was to establish himself first as a poet and teacher, then as a politician and statesman.

The literary and cultural movements with which Senghor became involved during his student days in Paris influenced his philosophical development and laid the intellectual foundations that were to shape his approach to politics throughout his career. The most significant of these movements was Negritude. In 1929, shortly after his arrival in Paris, Senghor befriended the Martiniquais poet, Aimé Césaire. Together the two men formed the core of a group of black writers and intellectuals whose common insistence that the West acknowledge the unique contributions of the black race to human civilization gave birth to Negritude. In the famous essay *Black Orpheus,* Jean-Paul Sartre described Negritude as ''an anti-racist racism,'' and much has been written in attempting to understand and define its many aspects. Senghor's interpretation in particular has been frequently maligned by critics who have pointed to the potentially dangerous implications of its insistence on racial distinctiveness. Yet Senghor has consistently defended Negritude, and in both his poetry and his politics it has occupied a central position in his career.

Senghor's studies in Paris culminated in 1935 when he became the first African to receive the prestigious degree of *agrégation* in French grammar. Although he could have returned to a position of some importance in Senegal—he was offered a post as head of French West Africa's school system—he chose instead to remain in France, take a teaching position in a *lycée*, and continue his studies and literary endeavors.

The onset of World War II temporarily disrupted these activities. As a naturalized French citizen—a prerequisite status for the *agrégation*—Senghor was called to military service at the outbreak of hostilities. In June 1940 he was captured by the Germans, subsequently spending almost two years as a prisoner of war. Upon his release he returned to his teaching post and his writing and participated in the anti-Nazi Resistance, once hiding a Jewish woman and her child in his apartment. His academic career reached its peak in 1944 when he was appointed to the chair in African languages and civilizations, previously held by the noted Africanist Maurice Delafosse, at the Ecole Nationale de la France d'Outre-mer.

Senghor's entry into politics came in 1945 with his appointment by General de Gaulle to the commission charged with studying the issue of colonial representation in the new constitution for the Fourth Republic. His acceptance signaled a break with his earlier refusal of direct political involvement. Later he also accepted an offer from Lamine Guèye, Senegal's elder statesman and long-time representative of the *citoyens* to the French Assembly, to join him on the Socialist Section Francaise de l'International Ouvriére (SFIO) ticket as the candidate for the newly created seat representing the formerly disenfranchised *sujets*. Senghor quickly proved himself a skilled politician, forging the alliances with the rural elite—most notably the *marabouts*, powerful leaders of the Muslim Sufi orders—that were to constitute his base of support throughout his political career.

The ticket won easily, and Senghor's political star rose rapidly. In 1948, confident of his power base, he broke with Lamine Guèye and the Socialists to found his own party, the Senegalese Democratic Bloc (BDS). Given the gradual postwar extension of the franchise in France's African territories, by 1951 the balance of votes lay with rural Senegal. In that year Senghor's BDS defeated Lamine Guèye to take both of Senegal's seats in the French Assembly.

In 1948, at the beginning of his political career, Senghor began his reading of the Jesuit philosopher, Pierre Teilhard de Chardin. From him Senghor adopted the idea of the complementarity of races. Building on his conception of Negritude, Senghor articulated a vision of what he named *la civilization de l'universel*. Each race, each people, Senghor believed, has a unique contribution to offer to the construction of this new "universal civilization." To do so, each must first ground itself firmly in its own tradition and culture—as Negritude does for the black race—while also adopting the best of what other cultures can offer. The future, Senghor insisted, lies in this great mixing of civilizations. For the rest of his political career and beyond, Senghor has clung to this vision of universal civilization; the term appears as a leitmotif through all his writings, and its logic has never been far in the background in his political battles.

Throughout the short-lived Fourth Republic (1946–58) and in the struggles to write a constitution for the Fifth Republic, Senghor was to play a central role in French politics, notably in the controversies surrounding the redefinition of the relationship between the African territories and the metropole. In the complex politics of shifting alliances of that period, conceptions of the status of colonial territories changed rapidly as pressures for decolonization increased. During this time Senghor served as a vocal and eloquent spokesperson for a variety of federal and confederal arrangements with France, before eventually supporting ''independence in interdependence.'' Displaying the political skills that marked his career, he adapted quickly to political outcomes, even when he had initially and vocally opposed them.

Throughout this period Senghor's politics reflected his cultural theories. He campaigned relentlessly for arrangements that would recognize and maintain the separate identity of black Africa—hence, for example, his critique of Socialist support for the policy of assimilation whereby Africans were to achieve political equality as French citizens by adopting French culture. At the same time he battled furiously, down to the moment of independence, to maintain the political unity of the French Empire and especially of French West Africa. Senghor envisioned these territories, secure in their Negritude, united as equals with France in the construction of universal civilization. He thus loudly denounced the *Loi-Cadre* (the framework law) of 1956, which expanded the powers of the individual territories of French West Africa at the expense of the interterritorial government, as an attempt to ''balkanize'' and thus weaken Africa. Following the collapse of the Fourth Republic and the 1958 referendum on the French Community that effectively destroyed the colonial federation of French West Africa, Senghor struggled to maintain unity among the territories. The short-lived Mali Federation uniting Senegal and the French Soudan represented the last such effort. With its collapse in August 1960, the balkanization that Senghor had so long feared became reality.

Senghor wasted no time in redirecting his energies to the task of governing a newly independent Senegal. His first decade in office was marked by struggles to consolidate both his personal power and the position of his party, renamed the Senegalese Progressive Union (UPS). The first serious threat to Senghor's position came in 1962. The sharing of executive power foreseen by the Senegalese constitution quickly led to tensions between Senghor and Prime Minister Mamadou Dia, Senghor's long-time collaborator from the early days of the BDS. Responding to accusations that Dia was moving to consolidate power in his own hands, Senghor reacted quickly and forcefully to thwart what he described as an attempted coup d'état. Thanks in part to the support of the conservative *marabouts* against his Muslim—but more ''radical''—rival, Senghor emerged victorious. Dia was imprisoned, his partisans in the government were ousted, and the constitution was modified to consolidate executive power in the hands of a strong president.

Faced with periodic protests, strikes and occasional violence from students and workers in urban areas, where his support had always been weakest, Senghor gradually eliminated his main opposition. Although he protested his distaste for the excessively authoritarian notion of a single party, claiming instead to seek a "unified party," by 1968 Senegal was de facto, if not de jure, a single-party state. Preferring co-optation to overt repression, Senghor held out the carrots of ministerial portfolios and ambassadorships to his principal rivals in exchange for adherence to the UPS. Yet faced with resistance, he did not hesitate to use sticks; the difficulties of the Marxist African Independence Party (PAI), which found itself banned for most of Senghor's presidency, provides the most notable example. Thus in contrast to the violence that marked Senghor's contested re-election in 1963, the elections of 1968 and 1973, in which neither he nor the UPS faced any opponent, were uneventful.

In 1970 Senghor began his cautious relaxation of the political system with the re-establishment of the office of prime minister and his naming of Abdou Diouf, a young technocrat, to fill it. With the UPS machine firmly in place, Senghor agreed in 1974 to recognize an opposition party, the Senegalese Democratic Party (PDS), under the direction of Abdoulaye Wade. Finally, in 1976 the constitution itself was amended to dictate a three-party system and to prescribe each party's ideology. The UPS, renamed the Socialist Party (PS), reserved for itself the centrist "socialist and democratic" position, leaving space to the right for a "liberal" (i.e., capitalist) party and to the left for a "Marxist-Leninist or Communist" one.

The opening of the system permitted Senghor (with the help of François Mitterrand and the French Socialists) to gain his party's admission to the Socialist International. In keeping with his vision of building a universal civilization, Senghor assigned great importance to the development of such international connections throughout his presidency. Although careful never to endanger his close ties with France, Senghor courted relations with a wide range of countries. Thus Senegal maintained a position of leadership among the "moderate" states in the Organization of African Unity (OAU) and in the nonaligned movement. Building on the predominance of Islam in Senegal, Senghor also sought political and economic ties with the more conservative countries in the Arab world, as well as with the shah's Iran.

But the area in which Senghor invested the most energy, and on which he staked much of his prestige, was the development of connections with the Francophone world. Given the importance he assigned to language and culture, Senghor envisaged a community of nations united in their use of the French language as a crucial building block in the development of universal civilization. Although the institution of the French-language commonwealth that Senghor sought never became a reality, the continued cooperation of many Francophone countries in diverse aspects of the international arena must in large part be credited to his efforts.

As befitted the primary spokesman for Negritude, Senghor placed great emphasis on African culture and arts throughout his presidency. Perhaps the moment of crowning glory of his administration was the international success of the 1966 Festival of Negro Arts held in Dakar. In Senghor's Senegal cultural and artistic institutions could count on presidential patronage, but only at the price of presidential tutelage. Senghor frequently became personally involved in literary and artistic debates, and innumerable scholarly books published under his tenure appeared with a preface by the president himself. Ever the pedagogue, Senghor's tendency was to lecture and instruct, and he demonstrated little patience with those unwilling to assimilate his lessons. Never particularly popular among the urban population, Senghor's leadership style proved particularly distasteful to students and intellectuals who resented the implicit condescension, and the University of Dakar was regularly the source of protests, strikes and, when allowed, electoral opposition.

Moreover, as the economic situation in rural Senegal deteriorated in the late 1960s and early 1970s, Senghor found support eroding in his traditional stronghold. The version of African socialism that he attempted to implement following independence—a mixture of modern economic planning and technical knowledge with supposedly traditional African values of cooperation and community—did not achieve the desired economic results. Natural conditions such as drought, and unfavorable developments in the world economy, along with ill-conceived policies and an inefficient bureaucracy, worked against Senghor's efforts to improve the economy. The economic situation of rural Senegal degenerated steadily.

When Senghor resigned from the presidency at the end of 1980, he left his hand-picked successor, Abdou Diouf, an ambiguous legacy. The country remained miserably poor; real per capita income had actually declined over the course of Senghor's presidency, and given a bureaucracy bogged down in a system of patronage, clan politics and corruption, there was little prospect for improvement in the 1980s. In addition, the maintenance of close ties with France and the ever-increasing reliance on Western economic aid left Senegal in a position that defined the very paradigm of a neocolonial state of dependency and underdevelopment.

Yet in contrast with its neighbors, Senegal could point to some striking successes. The state remained firmly in the hands of a civilian and secular government, which enjoyed enough popular support to withstand at least partially free elections. At a time when most regimes on the continent were consolidating one-party rule, Senegal was allowing opposition parties to organize and contest elections. Relative freedom of speech and of the press were real rights enjoyed by the Senegalese. Heir to this situation, Abdou Diouf was faced with the task of remedying the economic failures while maintaining and advancing the successes of Senghor's reign.

Statesman and skilled politician, but also teacher, poet, philosopher and cultural theoretician, Senghor exemplifies the practice of intellectual leadership. His dogged pursuit of visionary goals and his constant elaboration of theoretical bases to support them blinded him at times to his limitations and rendered him intolerant of his critics. Yet this same vision also guided his policies and circumscribed his exercise of power, keeping him from the excesses of authoritarianism all too frequent in the region. Senghor's visionary, intellectual leadership has left its mark on Senegal. In the decade since his departure from office Senegal has continued—for better and for worse—to evolve along the lines of the economic and political trends of his administration. Barring an unlikely revolutionary restructuring of the Senegalese state, Léopold Sédar Senghor's imprint will certainly continue to influence the theory and practice of Senegalese politics for the foreseeable future.

BIBLIOGRAPHY

Works by Senghor:

Pierre Teilhard de Chardin et la politique africaine. Paris: Editions du Seuil, 1962.
On African Socialism. New York: Praeger, 1964
La Poésie de l'action: Conversations avec Mohamed Aziza. Paris: Stock, 1980.
Ce que je crois: Négritude, francité, et civilisation de l'universel. Paris: Bernard Grasset, 1988.
A series of volumes of Senghor's collected speeches and essays has also been published by Editions du Seuil:
    Liberté I: Négritude et humanisme. (1964).
    Liberté II: Nation et voie africaine du socialisme. (1971).
    Liberté III: Négritude et civilisation de l'universel. (1977).
    Liberté IV: Socialisme et planification. (1983).

Other Works:

Foltz, William J. *From French West Africa to the Mali Federation.* New Haven, Conn.: Yale University Press, 1965.
Hesseling, Gerti. *Histoire politique du Sénégal: Institutions, droit et société.* Paris: Karthala, 1985.
Hymans, Jacques Louis. *Léopold Sédar Senghor: An Intellectual Biography.* Edinburgh: Edinburgh University Press, 1971.
Markovitz, Irving Leonard. *Léopold Sédar Senghor and the Politics of Négritude.* New York: Atheneum, 1969.
Vaillant, Janet G. *Black, French and African: A Life of Léopold Sédar Senghor.* Cambridge, Mass.: Harvard University Press, 1990.
Zuccarelli, François. *La Vie politique sénégalaise (1940–1988).* Paris: CHEAM, 1988.

LEONARDO A. VILLALON

IAN DOUGLAS SMITH (1919–   ), Prime Minister, Republic of Rhodesia (now Zimbabwe), 1964–1979.

Ian Douglas Smith was the last prime minister of white-ruled Rhodesia (earlier known as Southern Rhodesia, now Zimbabwe). Smith was born in Selukwe, a small mining township in Rhodesia, son of Jock Smith, a Scottish pioneer and cattle farmer. He was educated at Rhodes University, Grahamstown, South Africa, where he took a bachelor of commerce degree. During World War II he served in the Royal Air Force as a combat pilot and squadron leader. He was shot down over Italy and for a time fought with Italian partisans behind the German lines. After the war he married a young widow, Janet Duvenage, née Watts. The couple took up farming. Smith also went into politics. In 1948 he was elected to the Legislative Assembly, where he represented the Liberal Party, the right-wing opposition to the ruling United Party (later the Federal Party) headed by Sir Godfrey Huggins (later Lord Malvern).

In 1953 Southern Rhodesia joined the short-lived Federation of Rhodesia and Nyasaland (dissolved in 1963). The federal project was supported by Rhodesian merchants and manufacturers who looked to the creation of a wider market, and by British imperialists who regarded the federation as a last bastion that would hold its own, both against Afrikaner nationalism in South Africa and black nationalism of the Gold Coast (Ghanaian) variety. By contrast, the federation met with hostility not only from black nationalists, but also from the less prosperous whites—small farmers, artisans and clerks—Smith's subsequent constituency. Smith gave tepid support to the federation on the grounds that it would prevent the emergence of a "black Communist" state on Southern Rhodesia's northern border. In 1953 he joined Huggins's Federal Party and for a time served as his party's chief whip in the federal Parliament.

The federation, however, soon tottered. The ruling party's position became even more difficult as Sir Edgar Whitehead, the Southern Rhodesian premier, negotiated in 1961 a new constitution that would have opened the way to the slow advancement of Africans toward a parliamentary majority. Smith opposed this constitution, as did the African nationalists; in 1961 he resigned from the Federal Party, and in 1962 he played a major part in creating a new right-wing party, the Rhodesian Front.

In 1962 the Rhodesian Front gained a decisive electoral victory, and Smith took office, first as deputy prime minister and minister of treasury under Winston Field, a fellow farmer, and from 1964 as prime minister. In 1965 Smith issued Rhodesia's Unilateral Declaration of Independence (UDI), putatively severing residual British authority in defiance of the British Labour government. Within the context of Rhodesian Front politics, Smith pursued a centrist course. In 1968 he successfully rid himself of the right-wing opposition within his own cabinet. At the same time, the Union Jack was hauled down and replaced by a flag of green and white, Rhodesia's rugby colors—this in a land of loyalists. In 1969 a new constitution went onto effect that in the long run could have secured parity of parliamentary representation for whites and blacks, in itself a striking retreat from UDI's original objective. In 1970 Rhodesia officially became a republic, but was officially recognized by no other country.

In theory, Smith's UDI should have been a nine days' wonder. British Prime Minister Harold Wilson in 1966 predicted that the rebellion might end "within a matter of weeks rather than months." Experts writing for journals such as the London *Economist* and the *New York Times* were equally confident of Rhodesia's early collapse. Smith, a backwoods farmer, and his "Cowboy Cabinet" were widely adjudged unfit to run a state—an assumption that paralleled Smith's own beliefs concerning the Africans' presumed incapacity for self-government. The rebel state was subjected to international sanctions. Rhodesia soon had to cope with guerrilla warfare initiated by the Zimbabwe African National Union (ZANU) and the Zimbabwe African People's Union (ZAPU), later precariously united in the Patriotic Front. There was unremitting hostility from the UN, the Organization of African Unity (OAU) and Great Britain. But despite the destruction wrought by a sustained and bloody civil war, the Rhodesian economy proved far more resilient than Rhodesia's critics had anticipated. The farming industry diversified. New import-substitution industries came into existence. Between 1966 and 1975 the gross domestic product went up from RH $688.5 million to RH $1.9 billion.

Smith stood for the Rhodesia of small townships and scattered farms built of red brick, covered by corrugated iron roofs, with wide verandas and color splashes of poinsettias and jacarandas. But he was saved for a while by the new Rhodesia of business and finance, which had largely voted against Smith in politics. There were other ironies. War had the unintended effect of speeding African advancement in industry and the army. The military recruited an ever-increasing number of Africans; the army ceased to be a largely white force; Africans in the end secured commissions as officers—a state of affairs unthinkable in the Rhodesia in which Smith had been born. There were successive talks with the British, held during the 1960s on the British warships *Tiger* and *Fearless*. But Smith mistakenly believed at first that his position was strong enough for a settlement largely on his own terms.

From the mid-1970s, however, UDI became increasingly less workable. In 1974 the Portuguese colonial empire collapsed. A new front then opened along the Rhodesian-Mozambique border, in addition to the northern front along the Zambian frontier, and the Rhodesian army was increasingly overstretched. Whereas Smith had increasingly placed reliance on traditional chiefs, the guerrillas gained support among the mass of the African population. Above all, South Africa, tired of bearing an ever-growing fiscal and diplomatic burden, withdrew its military and financial support—an eventuality that Smith had not foreseen. Attempts at a direct settlement between Smith and Joshua Nkomo,* leader of ZAPU, collapsed. Under pressure from South Africa, the United States and Great Britain, Smith in 1976 made what was, on the face of it, an astonishing volte-face. He agreed to African majority rule two years after the establishment of an interim government.

The composition of such a government, however, led to further controversy. Failing to reach agreement with the British and the African guerrilla forces, Smith in 1978 arrived at a so-called internal settlement with African moderates headed by Bishop Abel Muzorewa. In 1979 Muzorewa became prime minister, with Smith as minister without portfolio, in effect a leading policy maker. The Muzorewa government gained a striking electoral victory, but the guerrillas would not participate, and the Muzorewa government could neither end the war nor gain international recognition.

After lengthy negotiations at Lancaster House between the British, the guerrilla movements and the Muzorewa government, a new agreement was reached. In 1980 Robert Mugabe* gained for ZANU a decisive electoral victory. Zimbabwe attained independence under a compromise constitution that preserved white property rights. Smith—unlike many white hard-liners, and also unlike some self-described white radicals—remained in his native country. He had no wish to end his days as one of those Rhodesian expatriates in South Africa (known as "when-we's" for their assumed proclivity for initiating all reminiscences with that particular phrase). Instead, he continued in the new Parliament, where he represented a small European group without significance, the Conservative Alliance, last sprig of the Rhodesian Front.

Smith ran Rhodesia for fifteen years, providing a remarkable example of political longevity. He was not imaginative. Challenging the Organization of African Unity, the Commonwealth and the United Nations seemed to him of small concern. He thought little of the domestic white opposition, the "Queen's men." (In fact, the main white opposition within Rhodesia derived from the churches.) He never questioned the rightness of UDI. Both the civil service and the military followed his lead, and the High Court of Rhodesia recognized the legality of his government.

Smith was an uncomplicated person. He was honest according to his own lights. He looked at Africans from a rural employer's standpoint. His farm provided a dispensary, a schoolroom for the laborers' children, reasonable wages—and that was that. Among whites, Smith was the very opposite of a charismatic leader. Tall and athletic, he was a dull speaker, lacking flamboyance and unsmiling (war wounds had stiffened his facial muscles). But he was the first Rhodesian prime minister actually born in Rhodesia; he spoke English with a clipped South African accent. He represented the new class of "improving" farmers—no longer backwoodsmen, but trained in agricultural colleges, engineering schools or universities. A Calvinist, he spoke for those white Rhodesians who stood aloof from that traditional local establishment that had centered on the Anglican cathedral and the Salisbury Club, linked to England.

Smith's politics were those of a small-scale electorate, mainly though not entirely white, based on a property-weighted, not a mass, franchise. It was in the politics of tea parties, "socials" and public meetings held in school halls that Smith excelled. Smith also moved easily among senior Rhodesian civil servants and parliamentarians—men usually with a background similar to his own, mostly born in small towns, educated at provincial colleges, proud of their wartime commissions earned in technical arms or colonial or county regiments. Such people had nothing in common with the new African leaders, with former Oxford dons turned politicians, or with Tory grandees, with whom they had to negotiate. In a wider sense, UDI signified not merely the white Rhodesians' rejection of African political claims, but also a breakdown in that tacit partnership that had linked the old Rhodesian elite with the traditional British Tory establishment.

In the international arena Smith's case found few takers—comparatively few even on the right. (Smith himself equally disliked the pro-Nazi right, the ultrareligious right and the anti-Semitic right, just as he had little time for intellectuals.) Smith's position was also unacceptable to Afrikaner theoreticians of apartheid. In Britain Smith had a following among conservatives of Margaret Thatcher's persuasion. But even Margaret Thatcher was dissuaded from recognizing the Muzorewa government in which Smith participated, partly on the grounds that recognition would rend the Commonwealth.

There was no touch of corruption to Smith—his worst enemies never accused him of making money on the sly. He was dour and unyielding; his policy led to a sustained and bloody civil war. But he was neither a fanatical nor a cruel man. (Robert Mugabe, for instance, and other African internees in Rhodesian detention camps were able to complete degrees by correspondence course.) Smith was no outstanding strategist. Yet he was the only Western prime minister who had himself fought for a time as a guerrilla, and he had some understanding of the way in which the civilian and military war effort should be coordinated. But Smith and his advisors resisted the temptation of using the civil service and the economy as instruments of political patronage. As Jeffrey Herbst, an American academic, put it later:

> Zimbabwe achieved independence with a stronger economy than most other African countries, due to the advances made by previous regimes, as well as the import substitution drive induced by sanctions; manufacturing accounted for twenty-four percent of the gross national product in 1980. . . . perhaps most importantly, the agricultural, manufacturing and mining sectors were staffed by highly competent citizens who had demonstrated their versatility in responding to earlier crises. (*Journal of Modern African Studies* 27, no. 1 1989:69)

Even from a purely white perspective, UDI turned out to be a mistake. Sir Edgar Whitehead later estimated that his own (1961) constitution would have led to an African majority by 1977. If Whitehead was correct, Smith's political stubbornness merely delayed the changeover for three years. But as a Rhodesian white might have put it, they had an incredibly strong collective, emotional feeling that the whole world seemed to be ganging up on them, conspiring to do them down. Whether they were right or wrong, that is how they saw it. They acted as a group, emotionally and perhaps irrationally. Smith could not resist this current; had he done so, he would have been replaced, as he had dislodged his predecessor.

The final settlement reached in 1980 represented Smith's political demise. By that time the Front Line States were tired of a war that had imposed heavy sacrifices on Mozambique and Zambia, who had sheltered and supported the guerrillas at much cost to themselves. South Africa and Britain alike were ready for a settlement. So was the rebel Joshua Nkomo. So was Ian Smith's treasurer and deputy; so was the Rhodesian commander-in-chief. Smith's war had reached a stalemate, in which neither could the Rhodesian armed forces win nor could the guerrillas defeat the Rhodesian army.

In social terms the 1980 settlement did not, however, represent a total defeat for the cause that Smith had represented. The settlement was a compromise that reflected the precarious military balance of power at the time. The new government abandoned much of the hard-line Marxist-Leninist ideology that had filled the pages of ZANU and ZAPU publications during the war. Mugabe confiscated no white farms and even pledged to honor all debts incurred by the Smith government, except those relating to arms purchases. When asked by a Swedish television interviewer why his government had not placed Smith and others on trial for treason, as ZANU had vowed to do, he answered, "We did not win a military victory, otherwise we would have done so. We reached a political settlement . . . a compromise."

Mugabe remained true to his word, even in his personal dealings with Smith. In 1985 Smith was subjected to parliamentary censure for making on British television "statements derogatory to the Government and the African people." But the government made no attempt to harm either Smith's person, his farm or his pension rights. No African ever desired to settle a personal score with the fallen minister. In a sense, Smith and his kind had become part of the new Zimbabwe.

BIBLIOGRAPHY

Berlyn, Phillippa. *The Quiet Man: A Biography of the Hon. Ian Douglas Smith, I.D.* Salisbury (Harare), Zimbabwe: M. O. Collins, 1978.
Bowman, Larry W. *Politics in Rhodesia.* Cambridge, Mass.: Harvard University Press, 1973.
Gann, L. H., and Thomas H. Henriksen. *The Struggle for Zimbabwe: Battle in the Bush.* New York: Praeger, 1981.
Good, Robert C. *U.D.I.: The International Politics of the Rhodesian Rebellion.* Princeton, N.J.: Princeton University Press, 1973.
Joyce, Peter. *Anatomy of a Rebel: Smith of Rhodesia, A Biography.* Salisbury (Harare), Zimbabwe: Graham Publishing, 1974.
Mugabe, Robert. *Our War of Liberation.* Gweru, Zimbabwe: Mambo Press, 1983.
White, Matthew C. *Smith of Rhodesia.* Cape Town: Dan Nelson, 1978.
Young, Kenneth. *Rhodesia and Independence.* London: J. M. Dent, 1969.

L. H. GANN

MANGALISO ROBERT SOBUKWE (1924–1978), President, Pan-Africanist Congress, Republic of South Africa, 1959–1960.

Robert Sobukwe's restricted life under apartheid and his brief career of protest and inspiration for militant antiapartheid politics represent a leadership loss for the South African people, but also a contribution to the vision of equality that must undergird a future South Africa. Mangaliso Robert Sobukwe was born in Graaff-Rienet in the Eastern Cape in 1924. After graduating from Healdtown High School, he commenced studies at Fort Hare University College. A person of great intellectual ability, Sobukwe was also politically active in the African National Congress (ANC) Youth League, formed as a pressure group within the ANC in 1943. Among the members of the ANC Youth League (ANCYL) were

Nelson Mandela,* Oliver Tambo and Jordan Ngubane. The most dynamic and articulate among them was Anton Muziwakhe Lembede, a self-educated intellectual of humble peasant origins.

Lembede was the ideologue of the ANCYL. The teachings of Lembede had a strong influence on Sobukwe, as evidenced by his address to the Fort Hare graduating class in 1949, which earned him distinction among his peers. Sobukwe bitterly attacked the paternalism of the white authorities, pointing out that despite Fort Hare's predominantly African student population, the faculty was predominantly white. The curriculum was deficient, the absence of an African studies program being most conspicuous. Sobukwe spoke of the rebirth of Africa. To him, education meant service to Africa. In his view Fort Hare had to be to the Africans what the Universities of Stellenbosch and Pretoria were to the Afrikaners. The Afrikaans-language universities were the cradles of Afrikaner thought, culture, values, political philosophy and activism.

After graduation from Fort Hare, Sobukwe was appointed to a teaching post at Standerton in the Transvaal. The conditions of his employment prohibited political activity; while adopting a low profile, he was a frequent anonymous contributor to the *Africanist*. He was dismissed from his teaching post for participating in the ANC's Defiance Campaign of 1952 but was later reinstated. In 1954 he accepted a position at the University of Witwatersrand as an instructor in African languages.

The decade of the 1950s was a decade of political mobilization, as the National Party government that came to power in 1948 consolidated Afrikaner rule and enforced its policies of racial apartheid. Coupled with the rigid separation of the races was a system of draconian legislation to suppress dissent. The Suppression of Communism Act of 1950 was used not only to outlaw the Communist Party, but also to restrict individual ANC leaders and activists.

The "Africanists" within the ANC were critical of the multiracial alliances fashioned by the ANC with the South African Indian Congress and the white Congress of Democrats. They believed that this was a deviation from the ANC's 1949 Program of Action, which advocated African nationalism. They also believed that the multiracial alliances diluted African nationalism. As far as the Africanists were concerned, the indigenous Africans alone should struggle against the regime. The "coloreds" were regarded as Africans; whites and Indians were regarded as "foreign minorities."

In the face of state repression, the ANC called off the Defiance Campaign. The leaders prepared for a Congress of the People at Kliptown in 1955, at which the Freedom Charter was adopted. Thereafter, the ANC came under attack from the state, which charged some 156 ANC members with treason, and from the Africanists, who objected to the preamble of the Freedom Charter. The preamble stated: "South Africa belongs to all who live in it, both black and white." The Africanists contended that the country belonged to the indigenous Africans. The ensuing ideological struggle led to a split and the formation of the Pan-Africanist Congress (PAC) in 1959.

Sobukwe, who was elected the first president of the PAC, was its most eloquent spokesperson and added intellectual depth to the new organization's platform. He proclaimed:

> [The PAC aims] politically, at government of the Africans, by the Africans, for the Africans, with everybody who owes his only loyalty to Africa and who is prepared to accept the democratic rule of an African majority being regarded as an African. We guarantee no minority rights, because we think in terms of individuals, not groups. (*Speeches* 1980:20)

He repeated the Africanists' criticisms of the role of white liberals and Communists: Whites benefited materially from the status quo and could not identify completely with the Africans' cause. He stated that the PAC's ultimate political objective was the creation of an "Africanist socialist democracy," without clearly defining the concept. Sobukwe analyzed the relationship between Western imperialism and white minority rule, arguing that the latter was the watchdog of the former's interests. Yet he stated that the PAC aspired to democracy as known in the West.

Later he praised the People's Republic of China, claiming that development under that country's centralized economy had outstripped development in India. Clearly influenced by Kwame Nkrumah,[*] under whose leadership Ghana achieved independence from Britain in 1957, Sobukwe foresaw the creation of "the United States of Africa" and remained committed to the ideal of Pan-Africanism.

Another strong influence on Sobukwe was the Trinidadian George Padmore,[*] who became disillusioned with communism. In his book *Pan-Africanism or Communism?* Padmore advocated the establishment of a united Africa as a bloc between capitalism and communism. Sobukwe emphasized the need for Africans to accept the best from both East and West. Sobukwe was aware that his new organization was competing with an old established organization for the hearts and minds of the African masses. For that reason he identified with Nkrumah and other nationalist leaders in Africa who were leading their countries to independence. He accused the ANC leadership of cowardice, of hiding behind the masses.

Sobukwe announced two PAC campaigns, beginning with the Status Campaign, in which the African majority were urged to assert their "African personality." This campaign was abandoned without explanation. Instead, the normally cautious Sobukwe abided by a decision of the PAC National Executive Committee to launch a Positive Action Campaign, the first action of which was to be a campaign against the hated Pass Laws. While critical of the ANC's Defiance Campaign, the PAC nevertheless embarked upon a campaign that was no different in strategy and tactics. There were two reasons for the haste: PAC's potential sponsors in Ghana had suggested that the organization undertake a spectacular confrontation against apartheid; and second, the PAC decided to preempt the ANC, which planned a similar campaign somewhat later.

Sobukwe led the PAC in its first and only campaign against the Pass Laws in

March 1960. Intended as a nonviolent demonstration, in which Africans would march to police stations to surrender themselves for arrest for refusing to carry passes, the protest resulted in the shootings at Sharpeville and the subsequent banning of the ANC and the PAC. Although the apartheid regime survived, Sharpeville was a watershed in the liberation struggle. International condemnation of the Pretoria regime and the flight of capital created a crisis of confidence among whites. Sharpeville convinced many Africans of the ineffectiveness of nonviolent resistance.

Sobukwe was sentenced to three years imprisonment on Robben Island for his role in the Anti-Pass Campaign. His statement during his trial, that he refused to plead on the ground that he did not recognize the authority of the court, was subsequently emulated by other political leaders. Upon completion of his sentence, he was detained annually by a special act of Parliament known as the "Sobukwe Clause" of the General Laws Amendment Act. He was finally released in 1969 and immediately restricted to the diamond-mining town of Kimberley in the northern Cape Province, where he practiced law.

Sobukwe was offered a professorship at the University of Wisconsin and applied to leave the country on a one-way exit permit. The home affairs minister granted him an exit permit, but the justice minister refused to relax his restriction order to allow him to travel outside the Kimberley magistrate district to the airport. A South African journalist, Patrick Lawrence, wrote about Sobukwe while he was under restriction:

> There is a gentleness about him, not the gentleness of the meek, but that of a man who knows he does not have to shout. Within and beyond it are a passionate conviction and an iron will. . . . Though he is a man of great intellectual vigor, the bedrock of his strength is faith—belief in the slow but inexorable advance of African Nationalism—confidence in the future buttressed by a particular view of the past. His continued commitment to Pan-Africanism, even after all these years of isolation and political quarantine, have been acknowledged by some of his staunchest political enemies. (Quoted in *Speeches* 1980:3)

In the years before his death, even though he could not be quoted in South Africa, Sobukwe's interviews with foreign reporters provided some measure of his intellectual depth and political acumen. He acknowledged that he had erred in 1960 in setting a timetable for revolution. He recognized the setback the resistance suffered as a result of the post-Sharpeville repression. Sobukwe also recognized the qualitative growth in the resistance: He pointed out that whereas the older generation "was often forced to give up," the younger movements that emerged in the late 1960s forged ahead despite the regime's repressive measures. His assessment of the 1976 Soweto students' uprising was that at Sharpeville blacks overcame the fear of going to jail, and at Soweto they overcame the fear of the gun, and that since the liberation movements also had access to guns—which they did not have in 1960—confrontation was inevitable.

Sobukwe cautioned against the limited reforms initiated by the government of Prime Minister Vorster, arguing that they were designed to maintain white supremacy. Similarly, he criticized Gatsha Buthelezi[*] and other "Bantustan" leaders for having accepted short-term gain at the expense of the long-term goal of the liberation struggle, which was complete equality for all South Africans. Even in his criticisms of the Bantustan leaders, however, he distinguished between the Transkeian Bantustan leaders—Kaiser and George Matanzima—and Gatsha Buthelezi. Sobukwe believed that the Transkeian and other Bantustan leaders were consolidating tribal unity within specific rural areas, which, though unacceptable, was less dangerous than the tribal unity being pursued by Buthelezi in the urban as well as the rural areas.

While Sobukwe remained under restriction in South Africa, the PAC in exile was weakened by perennial power struggles and corruption. As a result, the PAC lost influence and support in South Africa and internationally to a point where the Organization of African Unity (OAU) questioned whether the movement deserved continued recognition and support. Despite the PAC's disintegration, Sobukwe's prestige remained high, and even his political rivals respected his integrity.

Sobukwe inspired an entire generation of South Africans. He restored confidence in the ability of Africans to lead the resistance and challenge the regime. Significantly, criticisms of inferior education during his 1949 graduation address were echoed by another young leader, Onkgopotse Tiro, in 1972 during a graduation ceremony at the segregated University of the North. Like Sobukwe, Tiro believed that unless the students' education equipped them to serve Africa, such education was useless, and Tiro's expulsion by the university authorities sparked a nationwide black student protest.

Although the black consciousness movement (BCM) that emerged in the post-Sharpeville period was not created by the ANC or PAC, it was ideologically close to the PAC and to Sobukwe's views on the role of whites in the liberal struggle. The importance of psychological liberation, noncollaboration with the regime, universal suffrage and majority rule were further developed by Steve Biko,[*] Tiro and other young BCM leaders.

Sobukwe died of cancer in February 1978. During the funeral in Graaff-Rienet, Gatsha Buthelezi was intercepted and rebuffed by BCM activists who announced the formation of the Azanian People's Organization (AZAPO) to replace the seventeen organizations recently outlawed by the Pretoria regime, yet another branch of the tree planted by Robert Sobukwe.

BIBLIOGRAPHY

Works by Sobukwe:

Speeches of Mangaliso Sobukwe. New York: PAC Observer Mission to the United Nations, 1980.

Other Works:

Gerhart, Gail M. *Black Power in South Africa*. Berkeley: University of California Press, 1978.

Lodge, Tom. *Black Politics in South Africa since 1945*. London: Longman, 1983.

Meli, Francis. *South Africa Belongs to Us*. Harare, Zimbabwe: Zimbabwe Publishing House, 1988.

Motlhabi, M. *The Theory and Practice of Black Resistance to Apartheid*. Johannesburg: Skotaville, 1984.

Ngubane, Jordan K. *An African Explains Apartheid*. New York: Praeger, 1963.

Nkosi, Lewis. "Robert Sobukwe: An Assessment." *Africa Report* 7, no. 4 (April 1962):7–9.

No Sizwe. *One Azania, One Nation*. London: Zed Books, 1979.

Pogrund, Benjamin. *How Can Man Die Better. Sobukwe and Apartheid*. New Brunswick, N.J.: Rutgers University Press, 1991.

HENRY E. ISAACS

SIAKA PROBYN STEVENS (1905–1988), Prime Minister, 1967, 1968–1971; President, Republic of Sierra Leone, 1971–85.

Trade unionist, appointed member of the Protectorate Assembly, elected member of the Legislative Council, member of Parliament, mayor of Freetown, leader of the opposition, prime minister, president—Siaka Stevens was a major force in Sierra Leone politics for almost fifty years. He gained national recognition in the 1940s as a successful trade-union organizer. By the 1960s his image took on almost legendary proportions as populist, nationalist and master politician.

Stevens was head of government for seventeen years. His ascent to the prime ministership in 1967 remains today among a small number in Africa in which the electoral process brought the leader of the opposition party to power. By the mid-1970s the myths and the populism were somewhat tarnished by the failures of his economic policies and the growing web of personal power and corruption. Yet to the end he was an astute politician, managing to survive or outwit his opponents, and remaining a hero for many Sierra Leoneans long after he left the political state. His retirement from the presidency in 1985 was also among an equally modest number of transitions in which the succession process was orderly and peaceful.

Siaka P. Stevens was born in 1905 in Moyamba in a humble setting. He regarded himself as a model of the diversity of Sierra Leone with a Limba father from the North, a mother from the Gallinas in the South, and the strong Creole influences of the family with whom he lived and worked while going to school in Freetown. Stevens was influenced by Islam on his mother's side, and on his father's by Christianity. His father served in the West African Frontier Forces and later became a trader like his mother. Siaka Stevens completed his formal education at the Albert Academy. In 1947 he arrived in England to spend a little more than a year learning about trade-union operation and studying industrial relations at Ruskin College, Oxford. Siaka Stevens's first job was in the Sierra Leone police (he rose to the rank of sergeant). He later worked for the Sierra Leone Development Company (DELCO) at a variety of jobs, including telephone operator and station master. It was his work at DELCO that led Stevens into politics, first as a union organizer, later as cofounder of the United Mine Workers

Union, in an environment in which employers and colonial officials were hostile, wages and benefits low, and labor plentiful. His prominence in the labor movement led to his appointment to the Protectorate Assembly in 1946.

Britain had divided Sierra Leone into a colony and a protectorate. The colony was an extension of the territory on the peninsula on which the original settlement of the "Land of Freedom" had been established as a home for former slaves and people of African descent in 1787. These settlers became the dominant African political force in Sierra Leone, although not a majority of its population. The rest of Sierra Leone was referred to as the protectorate, with British control exercised primarily through chiefs and colonial officials. Siaka Stevens was among a small group of educated protectorate Africans who began to push for equal political rights for the protectorate. The 1951 colonial constitution reflected these efforts, making major concessions in the direction of equality between the colony and the protectorate. Building on these new opportunities, Milton Margai (who later became the nation's first prime minister), Siaka Stevens, and several others formed the Sierra Leone People's Party (SLPP) in 1951. It quickly became the major political party in the country, ending the dominant position of colony Creoles and setting the stage for the integration of colony and protectorate. Stevens was among those elected in 1951 to the Legislative Assembly and was named minister of lands, mines and labor in 1952. During the 1950s Sierra Leone developed an active multiparty system. In the 1957 elections, for example, six parties put up 122 candidates for the thirty-nine seats. By 1960 Britain was ready to discuss independence. Among those participating in the negotiations in London was Siaka Stevens. Complaining about the mutual defense pact and the lack of new elections before independence, he refused to sign the agreement.

Returning to Sierra Leone, Stevens held a number of mass meetings based around a loose coalition called the Elections before Independence Movement that was soon transformed into a political party, the All Peoples Congress (APC) in 1960. It appealed particularly to northerners and easterners who felt that their regions had been neglected, but attracted a broad base of support throughout the country. The APC was soon the only significant political opposition to the SLPP. In the 1962 national elections the APC won sixteen contested seats to twenty-eight for the SLPP. Stevens represented Freetown West II; he also became mayor of Freetown and leader of the opposition in Parliament. This began a period of intense political competition between the SLPP and the APC.

Support for the SLPP government waned in the mid-1960s as the popularity of Stevens and the APC grew. When elections were announced for 1967, Stevens and the APC mounted an extensive campaign. The APC won thirty-two of sixty-six seats, compared to twenty-eight for the SLPP. It gained the support of enough Independents to give it a majority. The governor general called upon Stevens to form a government. He was sworn in as prime minister on March 22, 1967, to widespread rejoicing.

The celebrations were short-lived when elements of the army and police staged a coup with the encouragement of the former prime minister, Albert Margai.

Resentment over the coup was widespread among supporters of both parties, and violent clashes between citizens and the military left several dead and scores injured. The military government was never able to gain popular support or legitimacy. In April 1968 warrant officers, privates and others in the army, working closely with leaders of the APC outside the country, brought military rule to an end.

On April 26, 1968, after a triumphal return to Sierra Leone, Siaka Stevens was once again sworn in as prime minister. In announcing his cabinet, Stevens made a gesture toward unity by including several prominent SLPP leaders. The APC majority in Parliament was increased as a result of by-elections in 1968. Its control of Parliament was virtually uncontested in 1973 after the SLPP withdrew from the campaign, complaining about violence and intimidation. In 1977 the APC had all but the fifteen seats won by the SLPP in an election again marred by violence. One year later a new constitution establishing a one-party state was approved by Parliament and then by a national referendum. It was now the law of the land that Sierra Leone was a one-party state, and thus the remaining SLPP legislators were forced to join the APC or lose their seats.

In 1980 Siaka Stevens became chairman of the Organization of African Unity (OAU), hosting the meetings in Freetown. Stevens was also instrumental in establishing a loose federation of Liberia and Sierra Leone in 1973 called the Mono River Union, joined by Guinea in 1979.

The 1970s and 1980s brought serious economic problems to most of Africa, and Sierra Leone was no exception. During the 1970s Sierra Leone managed to weather the crisis, but the 1980s proved disastrous for the economy and the people. Stevens's popularity plummeted. In 1985 he stepped aside as president, keeping his position as head of the APC, but passing the presidency to his successor, Joseph Saidu Momoh.

The legacy of Siaka Stevens as a political leader contains paradoxes and dualities. On the one hand, he was a charismatic leader, a man of the people, a champion of justice, a nationalist, a concerned and generous advocate of the poor and a brilliant tactician. Yet there was another side that could be corrupt, venal and destructive. Much of the success of the APC in opposition was attributable to Stevens's dynamism and personal political skills. He seemed to personify the needs and demands of ordinary people yet he was larger than life— a phenomenal campaigner, storyteller, nationalist and populist wrapped into one. He attracted peasants, intellectuals, workers and many former supporters of the SLPP. He also had a skillful and dedicated leadership core around him.

When Stevens returned to power in 1968 after the countercoup, the prospects for Sierra Leone looked bright. Expectations for change were widespread, and there seemed to be broad grass-roots support for the government. The APC recruited talented professionals to its ranks, the judiciary had proven its loyalty to the rule of law even under duress, the military was back in the barracks, and the press was again alive and active.

The organizational genius of Siaka Stevens became clear during this period.

He rewarded his loyal associates and followers and kept in close contact with the people of Sierra Leone through frequent trips, speeches and an "open-door" policy. There were always large crowds of people waiting to see him at State House, and most of them did. He was generous with this time and judicious in spreading his help (be it rice, cash or a scholarship) to individuals from all parts of the country.

Stevens had an uncanny ability to manipulate even his closest supporters and in doing so increasingly centralized and personalized power. This was facilitated by a civil service already weakened by his predecessor, the increasing dependence of chiefs on the government for income and authority, and the fact that the government was the major employer and provider of services. While there were still autonomous centers of power in Sierra Leone, including professionals, students, workers, business groups and traditional associations, by the late 1960s most of them were supporters of Stevens and the APC. By the time some had second thoughts, Stevens was effectively in control. His initial successes were based on persuasion, charm and careful planning to consolidate support. By the 1970s no major decision and no important appointment, not even the installation of a chief, occurred without his approval.

What had started out as an effort to ensure the return of civilian rule in Sierra Leone in 1968 became one of Siaka Stevens's major failures, introducing new elements of violence that were soon out of control. The APC had mobilized, trained and armed a large number of its militants in Guinea in 1967–68. These supporters had quietly returned to Sierra Leone before the countercoup to join in that effort if necessary. Since the countercoup went smoothly, their arms and fighting skills were not needed, but they needed to be rewarded. In the end, their leaders received major party or government jobs, some of the militants became the base for a new security unit designed as a check on the army, and others were recruited by politicians as bodyguards. In the long run, they provided the basis for what was to become a period of increasing violence and thuggery on a grand scale. While not under Stevens's personal direction, the growing violence was an unintended consequence of both the nature of the return of the APC and the patronage system Stevens developed.

One of the ironies of Siaka Stevens's rule was that the man who so successfully led the fight against the one-party state as leader of the opposition was to be responsible for introducing it in 1978 when APC control was in jeopardy. The champion of multiparty competition was then to dismiss it as "an open invitation to anarchy and disunity."

It was also during Stevens's leadership that a once-thriving Sierra Leonean business community (going back to the 1870s for the Creoles and long before that for the traders) was almost totally decimated as a consequence of state intervention in its access to capital, licenses and markets. It was replaced by Afro-Lebanese, Asians and other foreigners. The indigenous population could not compete in a system in which these opportunities were bought and sold, though in the end they paid the higher prices exacted. Another of the ironies of

Stevens's career was that the man who promised to break the foreign diamond monopoly in 1967, opening up opportunities for Sierra Leoneans, facilitated the diversion of most diamond profits primarily to Lebanese and other "strangers," with less and less income accruing to either the government or the people of Sierra Leone.

Perhaps the most difficult problem created by the personalization and centralization of political power was what was seen by many of its proponents as its major virtue—the focusing of power in the hands of Siaka Stevens. This fostered a lack of responsibility within a bureaucracy that had once been relatively honest and efficient. It led ministers and high government officials to try to make as much money as possible while in positions of authority and created a growing climate of cynicism and despair among a citizenry that had once been trusting and proud. One of Siaka Stevens's major accomplishments was almost twenty years of political integration and stability. Stevens understood how to build and maintain coalitions across ethnic, class and religious lines. But the personalization of power that resulted weakened the ability of Sierra Leoneans to economically respond to both opportunities and challenges.

Although Stevens's political skills staved off public disapproval long after it might have undermined others, discontent became increasingly visible in 1980. He was not unaware of these currents. Stevens was officially seventy-five years old. Although remarkably energetic and in good health, he was concerned about the erosion of his popularity, several abortive coups, and growing opposition both inside and outside the APC. The strategy Stevens adopted in the short run proved once more his political genius—letting it be known that there would be competitive elections some time in the not-too-distant future within the context of the one-party state. The first hints of competitive elections had the effect of mobilizing almost all political elites and their supporters, effectively diverting even Stevens's most successful critics. The campaign lasted almost two years for the candidates and thousands of their supporters, serving an important legitimizing function for Stevens, the APC and the government at a critical moment.

During this period Stevens began to orchestrate his retirement from office. Like many of his previous moves, this too was carefully crafted and executed. Stevens was able to manipulate the succession process in the midst of the loss of much of his popularity, growing hostility and grave economic and security problems. The process of centralization and personalization carried out by Stevens over the previous seventeen years left him in control of both party and government plus extensive patron-client networks he had built over the years. The ambiguity he created over the process of succession made it difficult to criticize lest that seem self-serving. Throughout this period Stevens skillfully played potential candidates against each other while seeming to support them all, evaluating their potential, and finding most of them wanting.

Stevens's choice, Major General Momoh, seemed a brilliant move in a situation in which other contenders had deficiencies, not only in failing to suit Stevens's personal preferences and needs, but also in the view of much of the rest of the elite and interested public. They were relieved to have the issue settled. Momoh had eleven years of parliamentary experience as an appointed member. He was also a northerner, a loyal officer and a popular person in his own right, yet not mired in party intrigue. Stevens thought that he would maintain control as head of the party. Momoh enhanced his status as heir apparent by insisting on taking the presidential election seriously, even though there was no opposition. He toured the country and met the people. On November 28, 1985, the succession process was completed, with Siaka Stevens handing over the symbols of office to Joseph Momoh in a ceremony in Parliament.

The transfer of power was not in the long run to be one of Siaka Stevens's successes in political leadership. President Momoh had his own agenda, which included greater public participation, economic reform and the establishment of a "new order" of justice and accountability. Siaka Stevens and much of the old guard of the APC were alarmed at the changes. By mid-1986 there was open hostility between the two camps, with Stevens eventually involved in an unsuccessful move to have the party remove Momoh. In March 1987 there was a coup attempt in which a number of members and supporters of the old guard were implicated.

Siaka Stevens bequeathed to Momoh a legacy of economic disintegration, corruption, violence and mismanagement. President Momoh attacked these problems with great energy and vigor at the outset, but the deterioration continued and his government seemed to falter, whether because the situation was already beyond remedy or because the legacy was too entrenched for Momoh to alter. Ironically, by the time of Stevens's death on May 28, 1988, his reputation with the public was rising, and his coffin was followed by crowds lamenting his departure and shouting his virtues.

BIBLIOGRAPHY

Work by Stevens:

What Life Has Taught Me: The Autobiography of His Excellency Dr. Siaka Stevens, President of Sierra Leone. London: Kensal Press, 1984.

Other Works:

Cartwright, John R. *Politics in Sierra Leone, 1947–67.* Toronto: University of Toronto Press, 1970.
Cox, Thomas. *Civil-Military Relations in Sierra Leone: A Case Study of African Soldiers in Politics.* Cambridge, Mass.: Harvard University Press, 1976.
Hayward, Fred M. "Political Leadership, Power and the State: Generalizations from the Case of Sierra Leone." *African Studies Review* 27 (1984): 19–39.
Hayward, Fred M., and Jimmy Kandeh. "Perspectives on Twenty-five Years of Elections in Sierra Leone." In Fred M. Hayward (ed.), *Elections in Independent Africa.* Boulder, Colo.: Westview Press, 1987.
Kilson, Martin. *Political Change in a West African State.* Cambridge, Mass.: Harvard University Press, 1966.

FRED M. HAYWARD

T

DIALLO TELLI (BOUBACAR TELLI DIALLO) (1925–1977) Diplomat, Secretary-General of the Organization of African Unity, 1958–1972; Minister, Republic of Guinea, 1972–1976.

A major figure in African diplomacy during the early years of postcolonial independence, Boubacar Telli Diallo was a superb representative of the generation of highly trained administrators who assumed responsibility for public affairs during a time of great political turbulence. He was a leader in articulating African interests in the global arena during the era of intense Cold War competition over the Third World. Diallo entered public service at a time when it could be a dangerous profession and ultimately gave his life for his ideals.

As a nationalist, Diallo Telli (as he was generally known in public life) entered the diplomatic service of Guinea in 1958 when his country burst into world prominence by alone seizing an opportunity for independence that no one had anticipated. As a Pan-Africanist, he took on the immensely delicate task of shepherding the Organization of African Unity (OAU) through its formative years, laying the foundations for a key continental institution. Unity has been one of the goals of many African political leaders; Telli's efforts were instrumental in leading African governments to construct a framework for the achievement of that common goal. Like Dag Hammarskjold, who held a similar role at the United Nations in the 1950s, Diallo was often at the center of controversy, but he earned himself a place among the founders of the modern inter-African diplomatic system.

Boubacar Telli Diallo was born in the village of Porédaka in the Fouta Djalon region of Guinea, the son of Diallo Mody Kindi and Diallo Kadidiatou. His father had a small herd of livestock but also a dubious reputation as a cattle thief. It was his mother, Kadidiatou, who saw to it that little Telli was sent to Quranic school and then to the colonial elementary school. Telli grew up in the heart of the Peul (or Fulbe) country before going off to Conakry at about the age of fifteen to continue his studies. A talented student, he went on to the Ecole Normale William Ponty in Senegal, well known as the training ground of the African administrative elite of French West Africa since the early twentieth century. In fact, the Diallo family's means were so modest that he was unable to complete his degree there; instead he entered directly into the colonial administration at the age of twenty-one in 1946.

The postwar environment of the newly baptized French Union was propitious for unusually gifted young Africans. Under a special provision for early-career civil servants, Diallo was awarded a scholarship to the Lycée of Dakar, where he earned the French baccalaureate degree. This in turn opened the doors of the French university. In Paris he completed a degree in law and economics and passed the entrance examination to the prestigious Ecole Nationale de la France d'Outre-mer (ENFOM, the National School of Overseas France, once named the Colonial School). Admission to ENFOM, rare for anyone actually from the colonies, guaranteed the young Guinean a comfortable career in the French civil service; at the same time student life in Paris also exposed Diallo to the rising nationalist consciousness of African intellectuals like Alioune Diop, the founder of the influential journal *Présence Africaine*. Thoroughly versed in Western thought, yet intensely loyal to his Muslim and African roots, he harbored a deep conviction in the African future to be shaped by his generation.

Upon graduation as a magistrate from ENFOM, Diallo was posted to the judicial system in Thiès (Senegal) in 1954. Within a year he was summoned to Dakar to enter the administration of Bernard Cornut-Gentille, high commissioner of French West Africa (AOF), the eight-territory federation that spanned the region from Mauritania to Benin (then Dahomey). Here as a young administrator, Diallo first met the firebrand politician and future president of Guinea, Ahmed Sékou Touré,* who would never quite trust the French-trained civil servant from the Guinean hinterland. Leader of the Democratic Party of Guinea (PDG), Sékou Touré represented Guinea in the Grand Council of the AOF, a regional assembly that acquired some legislative power upon passage of the 1956 *Loi-Cadre* (enabling or framework law) that introduced several provisions of local self-governance into the French colonies. Diallo was nominated in 1957 to serve as secretary-general of this council. Thus became intertwined the careers of two vastly different political leaders, the trade unionist and the magistrate, the national demagogue and the international diplomat, an ill-starred collaboration destined to end in tragedy.

In his work with the regional council, Diallo encountered the full roster of Francophone Africa's future leaders: Léopold Senghor,* Félix Houphouët-Boigny,* Hamani Diori, Modibo Keita* and numerous others. The *Loi-Cadre*, a response to pressures for decolonization, proved to be but the first in a series of rapid steps by which power devolved upon the colonial territories. In 1958 a political crisis stemming from France's war in Algeria brought General Charles de Gaulle to power, who directed that the black African colonies should vote upon their future association with France. As a civil servant, Diallo took no public position on the referendum of September 1958, in which all but his native Guinea voted in favor of continued confederation with France. Without hesitation, Diallo made his first major political decision, namely to enter the public service of the newly independent state of Guinea.

Sékou Touré promptly named him his personal emissary in the campaign that stood above all others for the fledgling state: the battle for diplomatic recognition and admission to the United Nations over the opposition of France, which in a fit of pique sought to isolate the renegade republic. His very first mission presaged his future role in inter-African diplomacy as he accompanied Sékou Touré to Ghana, the other vanguard state in West Africa. From Accra the emissary went on to London, Washington and finally New York to line up support for immediate entry of Guinea into the world body. For a host of reasons, not the least of which was an imminent debate on the Algerian question in the General Assembly, France sought to delay UN recognition of the new state as long as possible. The newly minted diplomat argued Guinea's case with the tact and persuasion necessary to complete his mission successfully. Forthwith he became Guinea's permanent representative to the United Nations, and on December 13, 1958, he cast its first vote on a resolution that condemned the policy of France in Algeria. From this baptism under fire Diallo Telli emerged as one of Africa's most eloquent spokespersons for the liberation and development of the continent.

Over the following five and a half years he served in New York or as ambassador in Washington, and occasionally as both. He distinguished himself as a leader of the African group at the United Nations. His oft-impassioned anti-imperialist oratory caught the attention of the U.S. representative to the UN, Adlai Stevenson, who once observed that Diallo and his delegation sounded like "worse S.O.B.'s than the Russians" (his fiery speeches and activism also won him the nickname "Diablo"). These gibes, however, were essentially marks of respect, and in 1963 the member states elected Diallo chair of the UN Special Committee against Apartheid. Despite his ardent representation of Guinea's worldview at the UN, he was nonetheless always suspected among radicals in Conakry of being secretly pro-Western.

Diallo Telli was present at the founding conference of the OAU in 1963; he was chair of one of the two drafting committees that prepared the documents for the meeting of heads of state. A year later he was elected the first secretary-general of the organization by twenty-three votes to ten cast for Emile Zinsou of Dahomey. The latter was the candidate of several conservative Francophone states—including Senegal, Cameroon, Madagascar, Gabon, Chad and Dahomey—that were wary of a Guinean at the helm of the inter-African organization. Telli's greatest political challenge would be to steer the organization across the rifts that divided radical, moderate and conservative regimes in the quest for African unity. In 1968 he was re-elected, the only secretary-general to date to serve two terms of office. During these eight years he presided over an inherently fragile and divided institution, forging it into an instrument of creative diplomacy.

After his extended sojourns in New York and Addis Ababa (seat of the OAU), Diallo Telli returned to his homeland in 1972 to become minister of justice. He was aware that this might be an imprudent move, for Sékou Touré had become a dictator haunted by the fear of subversion. Trusting, no doubt, that his international reputation would protect him from harm, Telli took his place in the Guinean government as the atmosphere of suspicion and distrust grew more oppressive. During the summer of 1976 Touré announced to all who might believe it that he had uncovered a Peul conspiracy to overthrow his rule. Telli was arrested, imprisoned in the notorious Camp Boiro, and cruelly starved to death—to become the most illustrious martyr of a bold vision that turned into a grim nightmare.

Leadership is an especially elusive quality in the context of an international organization. The states that are members of international institutions jealously guard their sovereignty and pursue their national interests inside the parameters of the organization that they themselves have created. The administrative head of such an organization must serve many—and contradictory—masters, while also serving the higher goals to which the organization is dedicated. As one of Diallo Telli's successors, the Togolese statesman Edem Kodjo, has put it, the powers of the secretary-general "are hallowed in ambiguity . . . . At once everything and nothing, the Secretary-General . . . is merely what [the states] want him to be . . . but also what he decides to be." He must, according to Kodjo, give spirit, direction, energy, and initiative, and "navigate across the reefs and breakers, all this without 'making waves' " (Jouve 1984: vi). In truth, Diallo Telli was not one not to make waves, but he did chart a course that saved the OAU from the ever-present threat of shipwreck.

During his stint in Addis Ababa he organized the secretariat and recruited a dedicated multinational staff. He wrestled with material problems and cajoled the member states to meet their financial obligations to the organization, which often operated on a shoestring. He succeeded in incorporating certain pre-existing organs under the authority of the OAU. Each year he learned to work with a different head of state (Nasser, Nkrumah,* Haile Selassie,* Mobutu,* Boumediene, Ahidjo* and others) in the position of annual chairman of the OAU, coordinating his responsibilities with theirs. Much as was the case at the UN during the Hammarskjold years, when the motto became "Let Dag do it," a spirit took hold at the OAU to "let Telli do it."

The diplomatic chores that Telli took on were often imposing. One of the most difficult occurred at the beginning of his tenure, the political crisis that broke out in the Congo (now Zaire) in 1964 when Moise Tshombe, the erstwhile secessionist leader of Katanga Province, returned from exile to become prime minister. Facing an insurrection in the eastern provinces of the country, Tshombe called in foreign mercenary soldiers to quell the uprising. Numerous African governments that had long deplored Tshombe's role in the demise of Patrice Lumumba* called an extraordinary session of the Council of Ministers of the OAU to deal with the crisis. Over several months of heated arguments and complex negotiations, punctuated by a joint Belgian-American military intervention, Diallo Telli sought to affirm the primacy of the inter-African organization in resolving the dispute. Although the OAU was severely buffeted by the divisions among pro- and anti-Tshombe governments, the secretary-general would eventually stress in his report to the 1965 summit meeting that the UN Security Council by its resolution of December 30, 1964, had "for the first time . . . turned voluntarily to a regional organization to solve a problem falling within its jurisdiction . . . of crucial importance and gravity for world peace."

Among the other crucial matters in which Diallo exercised diplomatic leadership were the Nigerian civil war, Rhodesia's Unilateral Declaration of Independence, the role of Africa in the Arab-Israeli dispute, tensions stemming from charges of Ghanaian subversion during the Nkrumah era, and the host of issues concerning the Portuguese colonies and South Africa. Less earthshaking, but no less challenging, was his obligation to mediate disputes that involved Guinea and various of its neighbors, including Côte d'Ivoire, Ghana and Senegal, at one time or another. Throughout 1965 and again in 1966, the disputes surrounding Zaire and Ghana raised serious doubts over the very question of whether the annual summit meeting would be held. At each obstacle in the path of continental cooperation, the magistrate-turned-statesman exercised his skills as mediator and facilitator to help the states to find a solution.

Diallo Telli's great accomplishment was to operationalize one of Africa's dearest collective aspirations. He succeeded in institutionalizing practices of regular consultation and deliberation that made the OAU into an indispensable instrument of continental diplomacy. To be sure, "unity" in the full sense of the term is still more myth than reality in Africa; but myths serve to inspire heroic goals that raise nations' sights. At its tenth-anniversary celebration in 1973, the OAU sought to bestow upon Diallo Telli its medal of "Hero of Africa" for his contributions to Pan-African cooperation. Ominously, the ruler of Guinea forbade his departure to Addis Ababa to receive the prize. In retrospect, it was evident that Diallo's final heroism was his fateful decision to return to his troubled land in 1972.

Had he done otherwise, Diallo Telli might one day have become secretary-general of the United Nations. He gave thought to posing his candidacy in 1971, and in 1976 his name circulated in the corridors as a possible African-sponsored successor to Kurt Waldheim. There is no reason to believe that he would not have done honor to Africa in that role. Diallo Telli once remarked of his eight strenuous years running the OAU, "I have the feeling of being the geometric center of all the [continent's] discontents, but also of all its potentialities." His leadership during the formative years of Africa's continental organization did indeed place the Guinean statesman at the center of a tumultuous era in African history. As competing visions of Africa's destiny swirled around his office and his person, Diallo Telli bargained and brokered among states in order to maximize Africans' potential for progress through international cooperation. His public career, cut short by a nationalist revolution gone awry, was an act of faith in Africa's potentialities.

BIBLIOGRAPHY

Attwood, William. *The Reds and the Blacks*. New York: Harper and Row, 1967.
Diallo, Amadou. *La mort de Diallo Telli*. Paris: Karthala, 1983.
Kodjo, Edem. "Preface." In Edmond Jouve, *L'Organisation de l'Unité Africaine*. Paris: Presses Universitaires de France, 1984.
Lewin, André. *Diallo Telli: Le tragique destin d'un grand africain*. Paris: Jeune Afrique Livres, 1990.
Wolfers, Michael. *Politics in the Organization of African Unity*. London: Methuen, 1976.

ROBERT MORTIMER

AHMED SEKOU TOURE (1922–1984), President, Republic of Guinea, 1958– 1984.

Sékou Touré was a courageous fighter and defender of dignity, independence and freedom for Africa, its peoples and its causes. He identified, more than any other contemporary leader, with the desires and aspirations of African nationalists during the struggle for independence in the late 1950s and early 1960s. Yet by the end of his twenty-six–year reign he had become one of Africa's most oppressive and brutal rulers in domestic affairs and had managed to shift from radical to moderate positions in international affairs.

Ahmed Sékou Touré was born at Faranah, Upper Guinea, on January 9, 1922. His parents were peasants with a clan kinship to Samory Touré, a nineteenth-century resister of some renown to the French occupation. A Muslim, Touré's early education took place at a Quranic and elementary school in Faranah before he attended the George Poiret Technical School in Conakry, the capital city of Guinea. He was later expelled from boarding school for his activity in a food strike. Thus ended his formal schooling. This had a tremendous influence on the ways he was to react to contemporary African intellectuals who had gone into higher education at African and European universities.

At age eighteen in 1940 Ahmed Sékou worked as a clerk at the Compagnie Française du Niger, a subsidiary of Unilever, the international trading and manufacturing company. In 1941 he passed a competitive exam to become a clerk of financial services in post and telecommunications. By the end of World War II, through hard work and organizing skills, he positioned himself as the Secretary-General in the Guinea and French West Africa trade union, Confédération Générale du Travail (CGT). In 1946 the World Peace Council at its second congress elected him a member of the Council for Africa. In 1952 he took over from Amara Soumah the leadership of the Democratic Party of Guinea (PDG). In 1953 he was elected territorial counsellor of Beylà.

Elected mayor of Conakry in 1955, he was also elected a year later deputy for French Guinea in the French National Assembly. In 1957, when his party, the PDG, had won fifty-seven of the sixty seats in the newly established Guinean Territorial Assembly, Touré was the undisputed leader of Guinea. The party grass-roots organizations had capitalized on popular discontent and aspirations for advancement. The party asserted notions of equality, pride and dignity, and support for the liberation of youth, women and captives from the traditionally oppressive order of elders and chiefs. The PDG in its early years called for emancipation for workers from colonial and mercantile companies. This platform was influenced by the Marxist leanings of the Groupe d'Etudes Communistes. Touré, who became the vice-president of the Government of Guinea under self-rule (*Loi-Cadre*, 1957), used his powers astutely by abolishing traditional chief-taincies, by establishing democratically elected village councils, and by pursuing a policy of radical Africanization, which later, however, lowered educational standards.

Virtually completely ruled by a single party under Sékou Touré, Guinea gained its independence from France in 1958. French Prime Minister Charles de Gaulle offered the French African territories south of the Sahara the choice in a refer-endum between limited self-determination within the French Community and complete international sovereignty. Guinea alone chose independence by saying no to de Gaulle, "preferring poverty in freedom to riches in slavery," as Touré put it. (Guinea's move to independence would be followed two years later by the majority of French colonial territories in Africa). In 1958 the French admin-istration was abruptly withdrawn, literally taking every piece of equipment that was portable.

President Touré turned to the USSR and enjoyed a honeymoon period with radicalism between 1958 and 1961. Guinea's economic and cultural relations with Eastern European countries blossomed. But in the midst of a teachers' strike in 1961 Touré expelled the Soviet ambassador for allegedly consorting with Touré's opponents in the powerful teachers' trade union. By 1961 Touré had began to pursue an opportunistic policy of nonalignment, assuming leadership among the emerging nations of the Third World, beginning with the Non-aligned Conference in Belgrade, Yugoslavia, in 1960.

Sékou Touré flirted for a time with the idea of a union between his Guinea, Modibo Keita's* Mali and Kwame Nkrumah's* Ghana and was an enthusiastic supporter of the "Casablanca Group" of supposedly nonaligned African coun-tries in the early 1960s. Pan-African conferences and aspirations also were featured in the early years of foreign policy of the newly independent Guinea. But after 1964 Touré grew increasingly preoccupied with his own problems and with protecting himself and his regime against real and imaginary threats both from within the country and without.

Touré's objective was the creation of a people's democracy, a one-party state based on African socialism. The roots of this African socialism à la Sékou Touré were to be discovered first in the egalitarian character of the African society; second, in the communal ownership of land; and third, in the extensive network of social obligations. This nationalist interpretation of what he called an African "communocratic" system underlay Guinea's agricultural collectivization schemes. By denying the existence of any class struggle in the tradition of the African communal system as well as in preindependence Guinea, an integrated unity was created among the state, the bureaucracy and the party that enabled the PDG to dominate the state politically, economically and administratively. By 1964, however, Touré proclaimed the existence of a class struggle. The PDG in any case provided governmental structures down to the grass-roots level and was directly involved in trade, agriculture and industrial production. Single-party dominance, fashionable in African independence movements in the 1960s, enabled Touré and his successive governments to perpetuate his regime for twenty-six years. But the putative achievement of economic prosperity, individual liberty, administrative efficiency, honesty and equitable distribution of political power, economic goods and incomes fell far short of expectations whipped up by the PDG.

Touré and his team of advisors in the 1960s (led by a French professor, Charles Bettelheim) stressed internal development in an independent Guinea with a democratic, popular and egalitarian power base. Banks, currency, credit channels and trade were brought under state control. In that centrally planned economy, economic surplus was to be mobilized for development, which was to promote capital formation and accumulation, rather than consumption. In order to encourage innovation, self-confidence and commitment to progress, the team sought to adapt the social relations of production and the cultural notions of passivity, leisure orientation, superstition and myth to the scientific objectives of development.

The Guinean constitution, drawn up to the taste of Sékou Touré in 1958, theoretically guaranteed democracy through the checks and balances of the legislative and judicial branches of government. However, the supremacy of the PDG was in conflict with constitutional directives. Appointments to the higher levels of the civil service and discussion of key issues were mainly handled by members of the PDG Political Bureau or the Executive Committee of the PDG Congress. "Democratic centralism" informed the exercise of all political, legislative, judicial and administrative functions by the single party.

Some power was given to more than fifty thousand local party committees, the Pouvoirs Révolutionnaires Locaux (PRLs). About 347,000 local leaders staffed these committees. By adding 177 regional executive committees, staffed by 2,125 party leaders, Guinea under Touré's PDG had one elected official for every eleven persons. Adherence to the party was compulsory. The party conducted marriages, granted divorces and distributed material provisions. This popular participation assured a semblance of democratic functioning, but it was mainly a controlling mechanism. Most decisions were made by the Political Bureau of the PDG and, above all, by Sékou Touré himself.

As a result of internal political crises, Guinea ended a brief experiment with private trading (1958–64). In the aftermath of the coup in 1966 in Ghana against President Kwame Nkrumah and that in 1968 in Mali against President Modibo Keita, a "Cultural Revolution" was installed as policy by the PDG in its eighth party Congress. The PDG called for the people's militia to reinforce ideological training in light of what was seen as an encircling plot. Touré grew more intolerant, vindictive and paranoid. His reactions to a succession of coup attempts, real or alleged, led to purges of party ranks and the state apparatus. On November 22, 1970, opposition Guinean exiles, backed by the Portuguese navy, invaded Conakry in a spillover tactic in the antiguerilla war in neighboring Portuguese Guinea. The invasion backfired, with the result that Touré intensified his campaign against potential opponents within the PDG. Arrests and public hangings abounded. Thousands of political prisoners were tortured; hundreds were condemned to death by starvation, including many international figures, such as Keita Fodebà, the founding Director of the Ballets Africains, Karim Bangoura, former ambassador to the United States, and the former secretary-general of the Organization of African Unity (OAU), Diallo Telli.*

While Touré's rhetoric grew more Marxist-Leninist from the mid-1960s to the mid-1970s, in practice his nationalist beliefs prevailed over his commitment to socialism. Touré strongly believed that Guineans, unlike himself, who had succeeded in the Western educational system had sold their African souls. He thus waged a personal war against Guinean intellectuals, which he connected to his policy of "Cultural Revolution." Touré also believed that any good militant could accomplish what he, a self-made man, had done. As a result, Touré promoted political appointees without administrative qualifications. While he was impressed by political fervor, he practiced opportunism as well. He directed state affairs and managed Guinea's economy largely by trial and error. He regularly moved high-level government workers among different positions, fearing networks of plotters or empire builders. The frequent cycles of repression served increasingly to concentrate power in the hands of Touré and his close associates, particularly his family. By the mid-1970s Touré's clan in government included Ismael Touré, minister of development and housing; Moussa Diakite, minister of the environment, married to the half sister of Touré's wife; Abraham Kabassan Keita, minister of public works, married to a cousin of Diakite; Mamadi Keita, minister of education, related through an uncle who married Sékou Touré's mother-in-law; Commandant Siaka Touré, a cousin, head of the Secret Service; Abdoulàye Touré, minister of foreign affairs and co-operation, a cousin; Sékou Chefic, minister of the interior, brother-in-law of the president; and other relatives, such as Mamadou Lamine Touré, governor of the Central Bank of Guinea; Amara Touré, federal secretary of the PDG's Faranah branch; Manourou Touré, an ex-ambassador; and Mandju Touré another ex-ambassador. These family members and their associates used their government posts to acquire massive illicit earnings. Although the PDG retained control of Guinea, it was no longer the mass party of its earlier years. A class of nouveaux riches emerged inside party ranks and at the higher levels of the bureaucracy.

The atmosphere of terror and oppression was exacerbated by a series of failures of economic and social development plans. The PDG ideology from the late 1960s served survival more than the management of the national economy. Centralization, party control at regional and local levels, and loss of foreign economic investment resulted in a sharp drop in output of most sectors of the economy. In the 1970s the limitations of the newly created local and nonconvertible currency led to financial speculation, stagnating agricultural production and an acute shortage of food and consumer goods. Schools deteriorated drastically as a result of Africanization programs initiated in African languages without pilot experimentation. Smuggling of cash crops (bananas, coffee and palm kernels) and imported consumer goods out of Guinea increased enormously. Produce was sold in neighboring countries where higher prices could be obtained or exchanged for goods that were unavailable in Guinea. The government imposed a production tax that reduced independent producers' market incentives. Rapid monetary expansion and a decline in quantity of goods and services marketable through authorized commercial channels created shortages. Prices of rice, vegetable oil and sugar skyrocketed. Substitutes could not be imported due to a shortage of foreign exchange. The attempt to manage the economy through state enterprises saw almost all of them operating at a loss. The government's solution, to engage either in domestic borrowing or carry losses against foreign earnings, resulted in chronic inflation and a continuing balance-of-payments deficit.

After 1974, however, the process of development was no longer based on internal development (African socialism) but rather on reformist options. The first option was mineral exports; the second was increased exports and a growth of import-substituting industries; the third—and least likely—was industrialization through building infrastructure, such as railroads and dams. Unfortunately, surpluses for reinvestment, technical know-how and necessary entrepreneurial skills were all depleted. Corruption, profiteering, black marketing and bureaucratic red tape were rife. Compared to neighboring countries, there was little or no capital formation, and there were severely inadequate levels of household consumption, agricultural production, and industrial growth. By the early 1980s the government's economic policy was reduced to renting mineral concessions to foreign companies. Perhaps a million people had fled the country.

Sékou Touré died in 1984. He bequeathed Guinea uncertainty, powerlessness, and economic insecurity. General Lansanà Conté overthrew the successor government to Sékou Touré in a nonviolent military coup a week after Touré's national burial. This new government adopted liberal economic reforms and submitted a new constitution to a popular referendum. It was accepted by an overwhelming majority of 98 percent, ending almost thirty years of authoritarianism and decay.

BIBLIOGRAPHY

Works by Touré:

L'Action politique du Parti démocratique de Guinée. Paris: Présence Africaine, 1959.
L'Expérience guinéenne et unité africaine. Paris: Présence Africaine, 1959.
The Political Action of the Democratic Party of Guinea for the Emancipation of Guinean Youth. Cairo: S.O.P. Press, 1962.
The Doctrine and Methods of the Democratic Party of Guinea. Conakry: Government Printer, 1963.
Guinean Revolution and Social Progress. Cairo: S.O.P. Press, 1963.

"Révolution Démocratique Africaine." *Revue Mensuelle du P.D.G.*, no. 1 (January 1966): whole issue.
L'Afrique et la révolution. Paris: Présence Africaine, 1967.
Défendre la révolution. Conakry: Imprimerie Patrice Lumumba, 1969.

Other Works:

Adamolekun, Ladipo. *Sékou Touré's Guinea: An Experiment in Nation-Building.* London: Methuen, 1976.
Benôt, Yves. *Indépendances africaines: Idéologies et realités.* Paris: François Maspero, 1975.
Camara, Sylvain Soriba. *La Guinée sans la France.* Paris: Presses de la Fondation Nationale des Sciences Politiques, 1976.
Diallo, Alpha Abdoulaye. *La Vérité du ministre: Dix ans dans les geôles de Sékou Touré.* Paris: Calmann-Lévy, 1985.
Morrow, John H. *First American Ambassador to Guinea.* New Brunswick, N.J.: Rutgers University Press, 1967.
Riviere, Claude. *Guinea: The Mobilization of a People.* Ithaca, N.Y.: Cornell University Press, 1977.
Suret-Canale, Jean. *La République de Guinée.* Paris: Editions Sociales, 1970.
Wallerstein, Immanuel. "L'Ideologie du PDG." *Présence Africaine*, no. 40 (ler trimestre, 1962): 35–41.
Yansané, Aguibou Y. *Decolonization in West Africa States with French Colonial Legacy, Comparison and Contrast: Development in Guinea, the Ivory Coast and Senegal, 1945–1980.* Cambridge, Mass.: Schenkman Publishing Company, 1984.

AGUIBOU Y. YANSANE

WILLIAM VACANARAT SHADRACH TUBMAN (1895–1971), President, Republic of Liberia, 1944–1971.

Perhaps the last of the repatriate hegemonic leaders, William V. S. Tubman came to power at a time when Liberia was poised for social reconciliation domestically and for the international challenges of postwar restructuring, particularly the decolonization of Africa. During a presidency extending over a quarter of a century, he presided over a significant state-sponsored assimilation of indigenous Liberians into the repatriate-dominated body politic and concerted his efforts with an emerging conservative leadership in Africa to blunt the effects of the radical Pan-African nationalism that was led by Kwame Nkrumah[*] of Ghana. Under Tubman Liberia registered almost three decades of social peace and material development, but at a cost that was to become apparent only after his passing.

Known widely as a man of grace, charisma and political savvy, Tubman was above all a father figure in the traditional African sense, who employed the goodwill generated from his national "unification" policy and the material benefits that came from his "open-door" economic policy to build a political machine that made him perhaps the most powerful president in Liberian history. This was made possible by his usurpation of the country's political system, as he followed a pattern first set in motion not by Edwin Barclay, his immediate predecessor, but by Arthur Barclay, who was president from 1904 to 1912. It was a pattern of strengthening the presidency at the expense of the legislature and the judiciary. Tubman so perfected the pattern that a legacy of personal dictatorship became a prominent feature of his rule.

Tubman was born November 29, 1895, at Harper, Maryland County, Liberia. His parents were descendants of repatriates from the state of Georgia in the United States, and it was among the Grebo peoples in southeastern Liberia that Tubman was born and nurtured. His father, Alexander Tubman, had been a member of the Liberian House of Representatives and, for a time, the Speaker. William's formal education began in 1903 at the government elementary school in Harper. He later attended a Methodist missionary establishment in the same area and received the equivalent of a high-school education by 1913. The remainder of his formal education was conducted through an apprenticeship system under which he studied law, eventually qualifying for admission to the bar of Maryland County.

Education had prepared him for possible participation in the leadership of the developing settler state. Development in nineteenth- and early twentieth-century Liberia meant influence by the Christianizing and "civilizing" ethos that suffused the American missionary movement then shaping the Liberian national character. That movement only dimly perceived, and the Liberian leadership inadequately addressed, how the New World seeds of repatriates and their ethos and institutions would take root in the soil of indigenous African peoples. Tubman's forebears had to confront this challenge, as did Tubman as president.

Tubman's public career, which spanned more than half a century, began with his appointment in 1916 as recorder of the monthly and probate court of Harper, Maryland County. He next held the position of collector of internal revenues for Maryland County. In 1919 he became county attorney.

The practice of law was interspersed with public engagements; private practice was concomitantly pursued with public service. He was able to build a reputation as a selfless public defender with an affable and sensitive personality. It was his apparent desire to do good that led him to the defense of a notorious relative, Vice President Allen N. Yancy, who was implicated in the forced-labor scandal that wracked Liberia in the 1930s and led to the resignations of both the president and the vice president of the county.

At the age of twenty-eight Tubman was elected a senator from his home county, but he resigned his seat in 1931 because of the controversy surrounding his association with the disgraced former vice president, as well as his alleged complicity in the scandal involving charges of forced labor and slavery. In his own defense some thirty years later, Tubman dismissed the charge against him of kidnapping as mere allegation, pointing out that several of the indigenous chiefs interviewed by the Commission of the League of Nations had simply stated that as their lawyer he "did not manifest due diligence and act squarely with them in their matter." Unlike other senators, Tubman was exonerated, but he resigned his seat in 1931 nevertheless.

When Tubman sought later to regain his seat, some Marylanders tried to stop him, but his supporters fought back. Tubman eventually prevailed, returning to the Senate in 1934. Less than three years later he accepted an appointment to the Supreme Court as associate justice. His career on the high court lasted for six years. Then came his bid for the presidency of the nation.

As his administration came to a close in 1943, President Edwin J. Barclay (1930–44) was still seeking to restore public order following the forced-labor scandal that led to his predecessor's resignation and brought him to the presidency. Barclay's regime was widely viewed as dictatorial, repressive and narrow. The economic takeoff anticipated with the 1926 introduction of the Firestone Rubber Company was far from realized, although the country's international reputation seemed restored and a significant alignment with American efforts in World War II was under way.

The race for the presidency, which had significance for national unity issues later, saw the emergence of an opposition candidate, James F. Cooper of the Democratic Party. But the leading contenders, Associate Justice Tubman and Secretary of State Clarence L. Simpson, were from the ruling True Whig Party (TWP). It was a foregone conclusion that the TWP nominee would be the next president. Simpson, who was of mixed repatriate/Vai descent, was persuaded to accept nomination for vice president. Despite a strongly contested election in 1943, the expected TWP victory materialized and the Tubman presidency was launched.

For the next three decades Tubman dominated the Liberian political scene. In 1959 he initiated the idea of the Association of African States, on which the Organization of African Unity (OAU) was eventually built. He was elected to the presidency for six successive terms (1943, 1952, 1956, 1960, 1964, and 1968). The twenty-seven–year period divides into three categories: The first was the new-departure period (1944–55), when successful efforts were made to replace elements of the old inner core of leaders with repatriate and indigenous individuals personally and politically loyal to Tubman. The second period (1955–68) not only consolidated the gains of a decade and employed the benefits from unprecedented foreign investment to attempt modernization of the country's economic and social institutions, it also carried Liberia to the center of the African international stage, as the process of organizing African unity gained momentum. The period ended, domestically, with a political crisis, the treason trial of the Vai/Liberian diplomat, Ambassador Henry Boima Fahnbulleh, which *Jeune Afrique* aptly characterized as the trial of the Liberian regime itself. The final period of "retrenchment," 1968 to Tubman's death in 1971, witnessed diminishing returns in many areas and reflected a regime then striving simply to survive.

At the outset Tubman attempted the initial implementation of his declared policies of the pursuit of national unity and foreign-induced economic development on the home front, as well as an affinity with the Western world on international issues. Although committed to the view of the state that had traditionally been projected by the repatriate leadership, Tubman's objectives included a more vigorous assimilation of the indigenous population into the repatriate-dominated state structure. Regarding a critique in 1946 of a Liberian "governing class," Tubman remarked that had it not been for the "intrepidity of the forebears of this 'governing class' there would have been no nation," and what became Liberia would have been swallowed up by one or more European powers.

Tubman single-mindedly built a personal political following among both repatriate and indigenous Liberians. Through patronage, by which he removed the distinction between public and private resources, he "made" men, established alliances with prominent elements of the old order, and extended his clientele to include large numbers of indigenes in the hinterland and in urban areas.

But Tubman's leadership was also resisted. From the traditional "feuding" among the repatriate core elite, under Tubman there emerged perhaps the first sharp differences, involving questions such as how much foreign investment was appropriate and how far to pursue assimilation, as well as the perennial "native problem." Some people were also concerned about the developing "cult of the presidency," as Tubman unrelentingly pursued personal power. Tubman's response was swift and decisive. Emergency powers were sought to deal with "Communist" influences in the 1950s. Indigenous Liberians were reminded that they had never had it so good and that loyalty to him was the only assurance of steady sociopolitical progress. The opposition, he averred, was angry with him because "they cannot treat you as they did before."

Serious open opposition to Tubman materialized in 1955 when former President Edwin Barclay ran in the May election. Barclay's Independent True Whig Party charged that the Tubman administration had seen "the structure of public morality, financial integrity, and social welfare being ruthlessly torn down." Tubman remained in firm control, winning the election and the subsequent legal challenges. Barclay died within the year, and with him went the manifestations of direct opposition.

It was Tubman's policy of an "open door" to foreign investors for the exploitation of Liberia's resources that provided the motor force for the economic gains of this period. At least twelve foreign concessions in iron ore, rubber and timber were granted, with aggregate investment of $500 million. These concessions to private companies were crucial in national economic stimulation in the short run, but before long they became enclave industries unlinked to the rest of the economy. From a small base, spectacular growth rates during the decade preceding 1961 reflected the pervasive effects of considerable investment. Nevertheless, Liberia demonstrated what has been termed "growth without development."

Externally stimulated massive economic activity mobilized great numbers of Liberians for work in the mines and cities and on plantations. The distribution of the accrued benefits was skewed, tending to follow the traditional core/periphery pattern. The leading politicians became the leading businessmen. Tubman himself acquired sizeable rubber estates, owning 1,600 acres.

Intense economic activity created the need for more modern political institutions. In 1963 the nation's political subdivisions were rearranged in an effort to bring the hinterland provinces on a political par with the coastal counties. Four new hinterland counties were added to the original five coastal ones. This move was in reality an effort at controlled representation, for the majority of the population was in the newly created hinterland counties, but that was not reflected in the legislature. In effect the action represented the removal of legal barriers to integration. The restrictive national "expressive symbols" and other social barriers were not immediately affected. The initiative, though timely, was clearly a conservative political reformation.

Tubman took his conservative instinct to the continental politics of organizing African unity. Years before Kwame Nkrumah appeared on the African stage, Liberia provided support for African nationalist causes by offering material assistance and travel documents to Hastings Banda,* Joshua Nkomo,* Herbert Chitepo and other political activists of the 1950s. Nkrumah's appearance on the scene with his message of radical nationalism impelled Tubman into more vigorous action, with the support of the United States in the throes of the Cold War. When Nkrumah in Ghana, Nasser in Egypt, Touré* in Guinea, and others in Africa's "radical states" of the late 1950s vituperated against the "colonialists, neocolonialists and imperialist stooges," Tubman absorbed the insults, consulted with a steadily increasing majority of like-minded states (the "Brazzaville Twelve" and Nigeria, for example) and intensified his contacts with the West. The truly landmark gatherings in Saniquellie (Liberia) in 1959, Monrovia in 1961, and Addis Ababa in 1963 each carried the imprimatur of African conservatives.

The interactive politics of Africa that resulted in the OAU were joined by fallout from domestic developments in raising difficult questions for the Tubman regime during its period of consolidation. The president's political base had been strengthened among repatriates and broadened among the indigenes. This had even wider implications when seen in the context of an emerging Africa with egalitarian and socialist principles. In this light, Tubman's initiation of such things as the ballot for women and indigenous Liberians in 1946, accelerating foreign investment, and realigning the national administrative structure cannot be seen as ends in themselves, but as means to ends that deviated from the needs of his political machine.

When the effects began to be felt, when the "momentum of modernization" was taking its course, and when the politics of African decolonization began to impact Liberia, Tubman sought to contain the unsettling occurrences. To the emerging opposition, consisting in part of indigenes dissatisfied with the slow progress opportunistically allowed them, but composed largely of youthful Liberians disillusioned and embittered by political cynicism and hypocrisy, Tubman's response was a reign of political terror. Several coup plots were concocted by the regime between 1963 and 1968, culminating in a flurry of activities associated with the treason trial of Ambassador Fahnbulleh.

The last years of the Tubman administration were marked by economic stagnation and political retrenchment. The regime, faced with economic recession and fiscal stringency, had to take austerity measures that created discontent at various levels of the populace. Economic discontent led to an increasingly assertive opposition, the latter forced to operate clandestinely. The insecurity engendered for the regime led it to expand the size, budget and influence of its security forces. Amidst this atmosphere Tubman died suddenly, following surgery in London, on July 23, 1971.

Tubman had made modest progress with his twin policies of national unification and the open door to foreign investment. But the measure of social peace and economic growth achieved soon buckled under the strain of the momentum of modernization and Tubman's dictatorial inclinations. The conservative instincts that he brought to the task of organizing African unity also prevented him from seeing beyond the needs of his political self-perpetuation. Although he was able to carry Liberia modestly forward in the earlier years of his presidency, he left in the end a legacy of personal dictatorship that remains to plague Liberia.

BIBLIOGRAPHY

Works by Tubman:

President William V. S. Tubman of Liberia Speaks. Ed. Reginald E. Townsend. Monrovia, Liberia: Consolidated Publications, 1959.
The Official Papers of William V. S. Tubman, President of the Republic of Liberia. Ed. Reginald E. Townsend and Abeodu Jones. London: Longmans, 1968.

Other Works:

Clapham, Christopher. *Liberia and Sierra Leone: An Essay in Comparative Politics*. London: Cambridge University Press, 1976.
Dunn, D. Elwood, and S. Byron Tarr. *Liberia: A National Polity in Transition*. Metuchen, N.J.: Scarecrow Press, 1988.
Liebenow, J. Gus. *Liberia: The Quest for Democracy*. Bloomington: Indiana University Press, 1987.
Smith, Robert A. *William V. S. Tubman: The Life and Work of an African Statesman*. Monrovia, Liberia: Providence Publications, 1966.

D. ELWOOD DUNN

DESMOND MPILO TUTU (1931–   ), Anglican Bishop of Johannesburg, 1985–1986; Archbishop of Cape Town, Republic of South Africa, 1986–   ; Nobel Peace Prize, 1984.

By the 1980s Desmond Mpilo Tutu was one of the best-known black South African opponents of apartheid, second only in domestic stature and international celebrity to the imprisoned African National Congress (ANC) leader, Nelson Mandela.* Yet Tutu does not consider himself a politician and has never joined a political organization. As a churchman, though, he commands formidable institutional power. From 1986 head of the Anglican Church of South Africa, he ministers to a community of two million Christians, more than 80 percent of them black. Holding senior positions within the church since 1972, he became a national figure through his eloquent championship of the cause of the school-children in the 1976 rebellion.

Tutu was born in Klerksdorp, seventy miles west of Johannesburg, in 1931, the son of a Methodist elementary school teacher. In 1943 the family moved to Johannesburg, settling in Sophiatown. Tutu's secondary education was inter-rupted for two years by tuberculosis. He was treated between 1945 and 1947 in the Community of the Resurrection's hospital, where he met the English cleric, Father Trevor Huddleston, whom Tutu later acknowledged as the greatest single influence on his life. He was impressed initially by the courtesy the priest showed Tutu's mother, the first time he witnessed a white man doffing his hat to an African woman. Even so, the priesthood was not Tutu's first choice of a career. Giving up an early ambition to study medicine—his family could not afford the fees—he attended a government training college between 1951 and 1953, and in his first year as a high-school teacher he completed a correspondence B.A. He married his wife, Leah, in 1955.

In 1959 the government subjected African secondary schools to a "Bantu education" syllabus. Tutu resigned from Krugersdrop's Muncieville High School and enrolled at St. Peter's Theological College in Johannesburg. He was ordained in 1961 and served a congregation in Benoni Location. Considered by the fathers at St. Peter's as one of their brightest proteges ever, Tutu received Community of the Resurection sponsorship to undertake more advanced theological studies at the University of London between 1962 and 1966. He accompanied his studies with work as a curate in several middle-class parishes outside London ("Bletch-ingly fell in love with the Tutus," his biographer [Du Boulay, 1988:68] was informed in 1987) and obtained an M.A. in 1966. For the next five years he lectured in theology, first at the Alice Theological Seminary (when he was also appointed chaplain to the University of Fort Hare) and later at the University of Lesotho. Between 1972 and 1975 he returned to Britain, helping to administer the World Council of Churches' Theological Education Fund. His subsequent ascent within the church in the province of South Africa was meteoric: dean of Johannesburg in 1975; bishop of Lesotho between 1976 and 1978; secretary-general of the ecumenical South African Council of Churches from 1978 to 1985; bishop of Johannesburg in February 1985; enthronement as archbishop of Cape Town on September 7, 1986. In 1984 he was awarded the Nobel Peace Price, the most prestigious of a series of tributes that have included over two dozen honorary doctorates. In 1985 the London *Sunday Times* conducted a survey in which black South Africans were asked, "Who would make the best President for South Africa?" Tutu polled 24 percent of the vote, bettered only by Nelson Mandela.

Tutu's rise within the Anglican hierarchy was partly the consequence of the church's reorientation during the 1980s to the needs of its predominantly black congregation, but even within a less sympathetic institutional environment he might well have distinguished himself as a substantial theologian, adept administrator and inspirational preacher. The foundations of his political popularity, though, are more complicated. Certainly, circumstances favored him; in the mid-1970s, when he first emerged as a black spokesperson, the number of professionally prominent Africans was so tiny that the compulsions upon them to become public notables were very strong, especially after the beginning of the uprising in 1976. In the absence of mass-based organizations, compelling and talented individuals could exercise a considerable political influence through the popular press, itself in the late 1970s increasingly anxious to identify eloquent and "authentic" black voices. Even so, Tutu's intellectual and rhetorical gifts made him exceptional among the older generation of post-Soweto leadership. Well before the schoolchildren's protest, Tutu's sermons were politically messianic. Although he was ultimately uneasy with many of the more uncompromising tenets of Third World "theology of the oppressed," Tutu's religious faith expressed itself in a vocabulary that could resonate powerfully among black-conscious intellectuals. In 1978, for example, Tutu preached of

> a God who is the God of the Exodus, the liberation God who is encountered in
> the Bible for the first time as a liberator striding forth with outstretched arms to
> liberate the rabble of slaves, to turn them into people for his possession, for the
> sake of all his creation. (Tutu 1983:50)

The last clause is the key to the meaning of the passage, for Tutu's central theme in much of his writing and oratory has been the necessity for racial harmony: one section of the community cannot be truly free while another is denied that freedom.

Notwithstanding his often-militant terminology, Tutu has distinguished himself as a black leader by the extent to which he has directed his arguments and oratory at a white South African audience, whether from the pulpit, in university assembly halls, in newspapers and magazines or in public statements. The tone of such exhortations could be surprisingly conciliatory, as on the occasion in May 1976 when he wrote a letter to Prime Minister John Vorster, reminding him of an earlier incident in which Vorster had interceded to give Tutu a passport, warning him that "unless something drastic is done very soon the bloodshed and violence are going to happen," and appealing "in deep humility" to his emotions as "a loving and caring father and husband, a doting grandfather" (Tutu 1983:32, 28).

Tutu's discourse balances exhortations to different constituencies through its calculated ambiguity. It is a verbal ambiguity rather than a moral inconsistency, though, characterized by a language that can capture the bitter anguish of black South Africans and yet reflect Tutu's essential gentleness. In 1979, while visiting Denmark, he condemned the Danish purchase of South African coal. After his subsequent refusal to retract the statement during an interview with the minister of justice, his passport was confiscated. From that point he became popularly identified with the advocacy of sanctions, though until 1986 he was always careful to qualify his endorsement of such measures. In January 1985 he suggested that foreign companies should attach reformist conditions to their investments for the next eighteen months. At the end of the year he set an April 1986 deadline for sanctions unless the government began to dismantle apartheid, lift the emergency, and open negotiations with jailed black leaders. In April 1986 he urged sanctions without any further conditions and continued to do so, even using the forum supplied by the ceremony in which he was installed as archbishop. For Tutu, sanctions were the most potent alternative measure to violence; in his defense of his conduct in Denmark he observed that "if we cannot consider all peaceful means then people are in effect saying that there are no peaceful means."

It was Tutu's political moderation that made him such an effective exponent of sanctions. For Western governments his voice was difficult to disregard, representing, as it seemed to, mainstream currents in black South African opinion. He was a principal force in creating the public pressures that prompted the United States and European governments to adopt a program of limited sanctions. Tutu's aversion to violence was heartfelt. It was a personal attitude, though, and it did not lead him to take up a position hostile to the ANC. Disavowing a principled pacifism, he could be contemptuous of conservative critics of the congress's guerrillas: "Why do you all suddenly become pacifist, when it comes to freedom for blacks?" If sanctions failed, he noted in Toronto in July 1986, the "church would have no alternative but to say it would be justified to use violence." He himself, though, "could not pick up a gun and fight."

Despite the subtleties of his position, Tutu was conspicuous in his efforts to check the more cruel extremes of activist behavior during the 1985–86 township insurrection. Outspokenly hostile to "necklacing" (a gruesome form of execution), on one occasion at a crowded meeting in Duduza, Transvaal, he risked the wrath of the "comrades" to hustle into safety a suspected informer about to be set alight. During the unrest his main contribution to events was as a peacemaker. At one time he dissuaded a furious gathering from embarking on what would have been a bloodily contested march on a police station in Alexandra, Johannesburg; at another point he negotiated a cease-fire in the murderous strife between the United Democratic Front (UDF) adherents and police-backed "witdoekes" (vigilantes) at Crossroads squatter camp.

By 1986, though he remained popular, his authority as a leader was being questioned increasingly by young people. This was especially evident after the failure of his efforts to negotiate a police standoff in the embattled township of Alexandra. In any case, with the emergence of structured mass organizations such as the UDF, the influence of independent figures like Tutu lessened considerably. Conversely, in 1988, after two years of emergency rule, in which political organizations were severely weakened, the archbishop was once again in the forefront of black resistance, leading a symbolic march of 150 priests on Parliament to challenge restrictions on demonstrations. The following year Tutu was a highly visible presence in the Defiance Campaign in which the church network was one of the principal sources of institutional support.

There are three dimensions to Tutu's significance as a leader. First is the part
he played in shifting the church establishment toward a more politically assertive
posture. To be sure, he was hardly the first South African clergyman to express
disenchantment with "churches that merely pass pious resolutions," but Tutu's
contribution in helping to develop an activist program of social commitment for
the churches was a very substantial one, particularly during his tenure as secretary-general of the South African Council of Churches (SACC). From the late
1970s the SACC became a vital force in the reconstruction of civil society
proceeding at that time. Its downtown offices in Johannesburg accommodated a
multitude of welfare agencies, civil-liberties groups, advice offices, educational
projects and cultural activities. The council funded newspapers, looked after
prisoners' families, administered scholarships, sponsored films and perfor-
mances, supported voluntary associations, arranged legal defense, and established a network of rural field officers. Ninety percent of the SACC's funding
came from American and European churches; when Tutu assumed control, its
internal affairs were in disarray. Tutu presided over an administrative housecleaning, while simultaneously engaging in a spirited defense of the council,
which was under investigation for subversion by the government-appointed Eloff
Commission. "Our God," Tutu informed the Commissioners,

> cares that children starve in resettlement camps . . . that people die mysteriously in
> detention. He is concerned that people are condemned to a twilight existence as
> non-persons by an arbitrary bureaucratic act of banning without giving them the
> opportunity to reply to charges brought against them. (Du Boulay 1983:155)

Tutu's second achievement was in communicating a set of political aspirations
across an extraordinarily broad social spectrum. Even though he became the
frequent object of caricature and derision among white press pundits, his wit,
gaiety and eloquence could charm as frequently as outrage. But more important,
for South African whites he personalized black politics and made them familiar
and impossible to ignore. This was partly a function of the moral forcefulness
of much of his language, which often highlighted the paradoxical and absurd in
South African social arrangements: "We cannot allow ourselves to accept as
normal what is abnormal." The simplicity of his political creed could also be
disarming; Tutu's political vision may have been susceptible to charges of naivete
but never to accusations of malice. Winding up an article spelling out his antipathy to capitalism (heavily influenced by E. F. Schumacher's *Small Is Beau-
tiful*), he wrote in 1980:

> The key notion in my philosophy is sharing, which goes together with compassion
> and gentleness, underlining that people and not things matter. I am opposed to the
> stultifying and excessive individualism that characterizes our day and against which
> modern youth is revolting. There is a search for viable community, which gives
> a sense of belonging without suffocating one's personhood. (Tutu *Frontline*
> 1980:32)

Finally, along with other black leaders, Tutu's personality gave to black South Africans an assertive and attractive social identity that was a key ingredient in inspiring the public identification with the antiapartheid cause in North Atlantic countries during the 1980s. More than any other South African politician, Tutu had mastered the skills of reaching an audience through the media. As the *Financial Mail* sourly commented on the eve of his enthronement: "Tutu will be preaching to those who respond to him best—foreign television viewers." On television, especially, Tutu's humor could arouse the affections of millions, as during his first ceremonial address as archbishop, in which he began with the words: "Brother . . . er, primates, . . . a somewhat unfortunate name that" (Du Boulay 1988:258). In making people smile, Tutu appealed to their emotions in a much more effective fashion than merely by playing upon their consciences.

BIBLIOGRAPHY

Works by Tutu:

"Capitalism: Plastic Surgery Can't Change Its Ugly Face." *Frontline* (September 1980): 30–32.
"Nightmarish Fears." In Mothobi Mutloatse (ed.), *Forced Landing*. Johannesburg: Ravan Press, 1980.
Hope and Suffering. Johannesburg: Skotaville, 1983.

Other Works:

Du Boulay, Shirley. *Tutu: Voice of the Voiceless*. London: Hodder and Stoughton, 1988.
Jordan, Phyllis. "Bishop Tutu: A Profile." *Sechaba* (December 1984): 16–18.
Lodge, Tom. *Black Politics in South Africa since 1945*. New York: Longman, 1983.
Murray, Martin J. *South Africa: Time of Agony, Time of Destiny, the Upsurge of Popular Protest*. London: Verso, 1987.
Nolutshungu, Sam C. *Changing South Africa: Political Considerations*. New York: Africana Publishing Co., 1982.

TOM LODGE

V

HENDRIK FRENSCH VERWOERD (1901–1966), Prime Minister, Republic of South Africa, 1958–1966.

Hendrik Verwoerd was the major architect of South Africa's apartheid policy. He was born in Amsterdam, the Netherlands, to parents whose sympathy for the Boers in the Anglo-Boer War (1899–1902) and whose interest in missionary work led them to emigrate to the Cape Colony in 1903. Verwoerd received his initial education in English, first in Cape Town and subsequently in Bulawayo, in what was then Southern Rhodesia. The family returned to the Orange Free State in 1917 when Verwoerd completed his school education.

Thereafter he went to Stellenbosch University, a stronghold of Afrikaner nationalism, where he achieved outstanding academic results. He was awarded a doctorate in psychology in 1924 and was appointed a lecturer. After a period of study in Germany and the United States, Verwoerd returned to Stellenbosch in 1928 to take up the chair of applied psychology. In 1932 he was appointed professor of sociology and social work.

Verwoerd had shown political inclinations from an early age, his fiery zeal for Afrikaner nationalism having been kindled both by his family and by the British colonial environments in which he spent much of his youth. At Stellenbosch he was active in student politics, becoming chairman of the elected Student Council in 1923. A contemporary recorded that even in his student days Verwoerd had set his sights on becoming prime minister.

Verwoerd achieved national prominence in 1934 through his active involvement in the organization of a national conference convened to consider the "poor white" problem: nearly 25 percent of Afrikaners had been found by the Carnegie Commission in 1932 to be "very poor." Verwoerd's promise as an intellectual propagandist for Afrikaner nationalism was soon noticed by leading figures in the "Purified" National Party—the extreme wing led by D. F. Malan, who had refused to follow General J. B. Hertzog into the fusion in 1934 of the National

Party with Jan Smuts's South African Party. Like most radical younger Nationalists, Verwoerd sided with Malan, and he had little hesitation in accepting Malan's invitation to become editor of a newspaper, *Die Transvaler*, which was intended to become the mouthpiece of "purified nationalism" in the north.

Verwoerd's editorship began in October 1937 and ended in 1948, when he entered Parliament. By ordinary journalistic criteria Verwoerd was not a successful editor. His newspaper was a party organ that propagated a fiery brand of republicanism, often to the discomfiture of the more moderate Cape leadership of the party. Verwoerd's extremism led him perilously close to apparent support of the Nazis after 1939, and in 1941 he lost a libel action against an English newspaper that claimed that he was a propagandist for the German cause. Despite his anti-Semitism and his collaboration in the drafting of an authoritarian republican constitution in which English was relegated to a subordinate status, Verwoerd explicitly rejected National Socialism. His newspaper repeatedly attacked the neo-Nazi *Ossewabrandwag* during the war years.

In 1937 Verwoerd became a member of the Broederbond, an elite, secret society that was committed to furthering nationalist aims. He became a member of its executive council in 1940 and remained an active member for the rest of his life.

Verwoerd contested a parliamentary seat in the 1948 elections, but was narrowly defeated. As a reward for his services the National Party elected him to the Senate, where he rapidly rose to the party leadership. In October 1950 he was made minister of native affairs, a portfolio that he was to occupy until he became prime minister in 1958.

Verwoerd brought to his portfolio both zeal and ruthlessness. The premise of his thinking was the traditional segregationist proposition that if races mixed in "intermingled communities" (his phrase), competition and conflict would occur. Africans would increasingly demand equality, including the franchise. "Mixed development," he insisted, would lead to a severe clash of interests and ultimately to misery for all. Policy, therefore, must plan for divergent or separate development. Verwoerd never deviated from this view, and he delighted in offering detailed accounts of strife in multiethnic societies. He regarded the failure of racial "partnership" in the Central African Federation to the north as vindication of his views.

Verwoerd developed his policies on the basis of this premise with a remorseless logic that inspired his admirers and bemused his parliamentary opponents. If the premise was valid, then there could be no cogent objection to the hardship that was inflicted on apartheid's victims. The outcry that Verwoerd's social engineering occasioned never daunted him. He possessed an overbearing self-confidence and a total conviction about the correctness of his plans. He once told a journalist, "No, I do not have the nagging doubt of wondering whether, perhaps, I am wrong." Verwoerd intended to entrench apartheid so deeply into society that whatever government might subsequently come to power, it would be unable to reverse what he had done.

In the early years of apartheid some of the more idealistic proponents of racial separation maintained that only total separation could have a morally defensible basis. Opposition politicians played on business's and agriculture's fears that apartheid would deprive them of labor. As minister, Verwoerd was at pains to insist that National Party policy did not aim at total separation. It was, he argued, a long-term ideal, but it was impossible to implement immediately.

Central to Verwoerd's policy was his view that the number of "detribalized" Africans in the white areas (which constituted 87 percent of the country) should be frozen, while further influx should be limited to migrant labor that would oscillate between the homelands and the white areas. In 1950 he estimated that just over one-third of the African population resided in, or had roots in, the homelands, the remainder being in the urban areas and in the white-owned agricultural areas. He believed that only a segment of the urban African population was fully urbanized and "detribalized."

Verwoerd adopted drastic means to achieve his aims. The Pass Laws, known officially as influx control, were tightened up and extended to apply to women as well; African property rights in urban areas were abolished; new townships were sited as far from white areas as possible; severe restrictions were imposed on African traders; sub-economic housing schemes were terminated; plans were made to enforce "ethnic grouping" in African townships; and instructions were given that the future expansion of African secondary and tertiary education should take place in the homelands.

Underlying these draconian measures was Verwoerd's insistence that urban Africans were "temporary sojourners" (the official description). Africans in the white areas could not expect to enjoy any rights in those areas; they could enjoy rights only in the homelands. Accordingly, Verwoerd sought unsuccessfully to revitalize the links between urban Africans and their homelands. He believed that the wider application of the migratory labor system would also serve to ensure that such links were maintained.

Verwoerd's grandiose schemes did not go unchallenged even in the cabinet. In 1953 he proposed that a total prohibition should be imposed on the entry of Africans into the Witwatersrand area, particularly Johannesburg. Other ministers protested; Verwoerd was forced to drop the proposal. He was more successful in declaring the Western Cape a "Colored labor preference area" in 1955. The intention was to keep the African population in this region as low as possible by insisting that Colored (mixed-race) people be given preferential treatment in the labor market.

The counterpart of these schemes was Verwoerd's plan to develop the homelands as areas in which the different African ethnolinguistic groups could enjoy unhindered development as "nations." Beginning in 1951 he attempted to reinvigorate tribal forms of government, insisting that chiefs were the "natural" leaders of their people and that tribal government was essentially democratic. The implementation of this scheme, in terms of the Bantu Authorities Act, was pursued with vigor, resulting in serious conflict in several homelands. In 1950

Verwoerd's predecessor had appointed a commission, under Professor F. R. Tomlinson, to investigate the socioeconomic development of the homelands. The exhaustive report was finally published in 1956. Verwoerd had never been enthusiastic about the commission, since he had not appointed it himself, and he proceeded to reject some of its major recommendations. In particular, the commission had recommended that white capital be permitted to finance development in the homelands. Verwoerd flatly refused to allow this, telling Parliament that it would mean "a gradual penetration of whites into the Bantu areas instead of the present gradual withdrawal." In other words, apartheid would be subverted. A contemporary has alleged that Verwoerd told his caucus that white capital should be kept out because, inter alia, "it would keep the Jews out."

Arguably Verwoerd's most devastating impact was on African education. The Bantu Education Act of 1953 centralized control of education in Verwoerd's ministry and sought to align it with the overall aims of apartheid. Verwoerd had been dissatisfied with the previous system, which was largely under missionary control. It produced, he maintained, "black Englishmen," that is, Africans who had been deracinated and, consequently, demanded equal rights with whites in a common society. In a Senate speech in 1954 he outlined how in future African education should have its roots entirely in the homelands:

> The Bantu must be guided to serve his own community in all respects. There is no place for him in the European [white] community above the level of certain forms of labor. Within his own community, however, all doors are open. For that reason it is of no avail for him to receive a training which has as its aim absorption in the European community while he cannot and will not be absorbed there. (Varwoerd Speaks: Speeches, 1948–1966:83)

The new system plunged African education into a crisis from which it has not yet recovered. It also made African schools a political battlefield, a situation that remained in the 1970s and 1980s, when alienated and embittered African pupils often justified their rebellious activities by quoting Verwoerd's 1954 speech.

Verwoerd's long tenure as minister of native affairs made him the cutting edge of apartheid. Although he was a relatively junior minister, his prominence enabled him to defeat his more senior rivals after two ballots in the National Party caucus's election for the leadership when J. G. Strijdom died in 1958. This was the first time that the party's leadership had been decided by ballot, and a large minority preferred either of the other two rivals. Moreover, only three members of the cabinet were said to have supported Verwoerd.

Election as *hoofleier* (leader-in-chief) of the party meant automatically that Verwoerd became prime minister. He immediately began to prepare the ground for realizing his life's ambition—making South Africa a republic. In calling for a referendum among white voters (including those in Namibia), Verwoerd took a calculated risk because he could not be certain that he would gain a majority.

The referendum was held in October 1960, and in a 90 percent poll a narrow majority (74,000) brought victory to the republican cause. Verwoerd had always wanted a republic outside the Commonwealth, but, probably in the hope of obtaining at least some English-speaking support, he had undertaken to apply for continued membership. Faced with considerable hostility at the Commonwealth Conference in London in March 1961, Verwoerd avoided the ignominy of having the application refused by withdrawing it. He returned to a hero's welcome from his supporters in South Africa, telling them that "the present Commonwealth with its majority of non-European nations is a different Commonwealth to the one we wished to be a member of."

The Sharpeville episode in March 1960, when sixty-seven protesting Africans were killed, had heightened South Africa's isolation. Indeed, British Prime Minister Harold Macmillan had warned Verwoerd of increasing Western disfavor in the "winds of change" speech delivered in Cape Town a few weeks before. Withdrawal from the Commonwealth and mounting criticism of South Africa's rule in Namibia contributed further to the internationalization of the apartheid issue. Verwoerd remained undeterred, even defiant. Macmillan was firmly, though politely, rebuffed, and the world was told not to interfere in South Africa's domestic affairs.

The defiance, however, concealed an underlying recognition that the ideological legitimation of racial policy had to be adapted to meet the changing circumstances in the world. Verwoerd's predecessor Strijdom used the crude term *baasskap* (mastership) to characterize his policies, assuming that racial domination was the natural order of things. Verwoerd sought a more subtle justification that avoided such blatant racism. He acknowledged wishing that the old order could continue, but given the changes in the modern world and the rapid decline of colonial empires, "the old traditional policy of the White man as the ruler over the Bantu, who had no rights at all, could not continue."

After 1959 Verwoerd acknowledged that homelands could, if their level of development warranted it, become sovereign, independent states, linked to the Republic in a common market or commonwealth. Political independence could go hand in hand with economic interdependence. Africans from the homelands could continue to work in "white" South Africa, but their status would be like that of *Gastarbeiters*, foreign migrant laborers, who worked in the economies of Western Europe. He tried increasingly to portray South Africa as resembling other colonial powers who were gradually shedding their colonies.

Verwoerd was at the height of his power when he was assassinated by a deranged messenger on the floor of the House of Assembly on September 6, 1966. He had miraculously survived an earlier assassination attempt in 1960; many of his admirers had interpreted this sheer good luck as providential protection.

By the time of his death, Verwoerd had brought Afrikaner nationalism to the zenith of its strength. The elections of 1966 put the National Party in an unassailable position, and, for the first time, substantial numbers of English-speaking whites supported it. Afrikanerdom has never been a monolithic entity, but under Verwoerd it reached an unprecedented degree of solidarity. Partly this was attributable to the sheer dominating force and charismatic quality of his leadership. He appeared to have all the answers, and it was said that he thought for the entire cabinet.

Partly, though, Verwoerd's dominance was achieved by simple intimidation. He was a fundamentally autocratic man who brooked no opposition from within the ranks of Afrikanerdom. Dissident clergy, intellectuals, writers and others, including a solitary member of his caucus who opposed Verwoerd on a particular issue, were slapped down and effectively excommunicated, often with severe social consequences. His dictatorial methods and often-arbitrary actions bred a dangerous degree of subservience within his party and its support base. Shock at the tragic manner of his death was combined with some measure of relief.

He treated his parliamentary opponents with a correctness that barely concealed his disdain, while he despised the more radical African politicians who operated in the extraparliamentary arena. In Verwoerd's view African nationalists were the dupes of communism, agitators who stirred up otherwise contented people. He had no hesitation in banning the African National Congress and the Pan-Africanist Congress in the aftermath of Sharpeville, and he fully supported his minister of justice, B. J. Vorster, in a ruthless campaign to eliminate them completely.

None of Verwoerd's successors has attained a comparable measure of control. Vorster (1966–78), P. W. Botha* (1978–89), and F. W. de Klerk* (1989–   ) have had to cope with an increasingly fractured Afrikanerdom. Botha lost the support of at least one-third of all Afrikaners, while it is highly doubtful that in 1992 de Klerk enjoys majority support among Afrikaners. Each successor chipped away at the apartheid edifice. Vorster abandoned Verwoerd's fantastic projection that by 1978 the flow of Africans from the homelands to the "white" areas would reverse itself, and he obliquely recognized that urban Africans were not "temporary sojourners"; Botha recognized that all races were entitled to a common South African citizenship; and de Klerk presides over the final dissolution of the entire apartheid system.

The Verwoerdian mind-set, however, lives on in the minds of a substantial number of whites. The policy of the principal opposition party, the Conservatives, is based squarely on Verwoerd's thinking, and his widow, Betsy Verwoerd, has been prominently associated with it. At least two of Verwoerd's seven children, as well as his son-in-law, Professor Carel Boshoff, are leading figures in current efforts to establish a "white state." The Conservative Party and other ultraright organizations are a formidable threat to the National Party's reform initiatives begun in 1990.

Verwoerd's legacy lives on also in the deplorable state of African education and, more generally, in the unstable and dislocated conditions of the big urban townships. Verwoerd's policies consciously sought to institutionalize insecurity among urban Africans, and although all of the main elements of those policies have been abolished, stability has so far eluded these communities. There are an estimated three million young Africans, collectively referred to as "the lost generation,'' who are unemployed, ill educated, and prone to anomic violence. They are apartheid's most damning legacy. Verwoerd must bear much of the responsibility for them.

The "showpiece" of apartheid, independent homelands, is in tatters. Three of the four ostensibly independent states have indicated a strong desire for reincorporation with the Republic. None of the others shows any wish for independence. In 1990 South Africa began the enormous task of establishing a democratic order. The most difficult obstacle to overcome will be transcending the legacy of hatred and alienation to which Verwoerd so greatly contributed.

BIBLIOGRAPHY

Works by Verwoerd:

Verwoerd Speaks: Speeches, 1948–1966. Ed. A. N. Pelzer. Johannesburg: APB Publishers, 1966.

Other Works:

Adam, Heribert, and Hermann Giliomee. *Ethnic Power Mobilized: Can South Africa Change?* New Haven, Conn.: Yale University Press, 1979.
Botha, Jan. *Verwoerd Is Dead*. Cape Town: Books of Africa, 1967.
De Klerk, Willem A. *The Puritans in Africa: A Story of Afrikanerdom*. London: Rex Collings, 1975.
Hepple, Alexander. *Verwoerd*. Harmondsworth, Eng.: Penguin Books, 1967.
Hill, Christopher R. *Bantustans: The Fragmentation of South Africa*. London: Oxford University Press, 1964.
Kenney, Henry. *Architect of Apartheid: H. F. Verwoerd, an Appraisal*. Johannesburg: Jonathan Ball, 1980.
O'Meara, Dan. *Volkskapitalisme: Class, Capital and Ideology in the Development of Afrikaner Nationalism, 1934–1948*. Cambridge, Eng.: Cambridge University Press, 1983.
Pienaar, S., and Anthony Sampson. *South Africa: Two Views of Separate Development*. London: Oxford University Press, 1960.

DAVID WELSH

LISTING OF SUBJECTS
BY COUNTRY

GUINEA-BISSAU
    Amílcar Cabral
KENYA
    Jomo Kenyatta
    Tom Mboya
    Daniel arap Moi
LIBERIA
    Samuel Kanyon Doe
    William Vacanarat Shadrach Tubman
MALAWI
    Hastings Kamuzu Banda
MALI
    Modibo Keita
MOZAMBIQUE
    Samora Machel
    Eduardo Chivambo Mondlane
NAMIBIA
    Sam Nujoma
NIGERIA
    Obafemi Awolowo
    Nnamdi Azikiwe
    Ahmadu Bello
    Yakubu Gowon
    Olusegun Obasanjo
SENEGAL
    Léopold Sédar Senghor
SIERRA LEONE
    Siaka Probyn Stevens
SOMALIA
    Muhammad Siyaad Barre
SOUTH AFRICA
    Stephen Bantu Biko
    Pieter Willem Botha
    Mangosuthu Gatsha Buthelezi
    Frederik Willem de Klerk
    Albert John Luthuli
    Nelson Rolihlahla Mandela
    Mangaliso Robert Sobukwe

CHRONOLOGY

1892   July: Birth of Haile Selassie of Ethiopia.

1895   November: Birth of William V. S. Tubman of Liberia.

1897   Birth of Jomo Kenyatta of Kenya.

1898   Birth of Albert J. Luthuli of South Africa.

        May: Birth of Hastings Kamuzu Banda of Malawi.

1901   September: Birth of Hendrik F. Verwoerd of South Africa.

1902   Birth of George Padmore of Ghana.

        Birth of Sylvanus Olympio of Togo.

1903   March: British occupy Sokoto Caliphate in Northern Nigeria.

1904   November: Birth of Nnamdi Azikiwe of Nigeria.

1905   August: Birth of Siaka P. Stevens of Sierra Leone.

        October: Birth of Félix Houphouët-Boigny of Côte d'Ivoire.

1906   October: Birth of Léopold Sédar Senghor of Senegal.

1909   March: Birth of Obafemi Awolowo of Nigeria.

        September: Birth of Kwame Nkrumah of Ghana.

1910   Birth of Ahmadu Bello of Nigeria.

        May: Union of South Africa established.

1912   January: African National Congress founded (as South African National Native Congress) in South Africa.

1914   Federation of colonial entities under British rule and governorship of Frederick (Lord) Lugard in Nigeria.

1915   May: Birth of Modibo Keita of Mali.

1916   January: Birth of Pieter W. Botha of South Africa.

1917   June: Birth of Joshua Nkomo of Zimbabwe.

1918   Birth of Nelson Mandela of South Africa.

1919   April: Birth of Ian D. Smith of Zimbabwe.

         Birth of Muhammad Siyaad Barre of Somalia.

1920   Birth of Eduardo C. Mondlane of Mozambique.

1921   July: Birth of Sir Seretse Khama of Botswana.

1922   January: Birth of Sékou Touré of Guinea (Conakry).

         March: Birth of Julius K. Nyerere of Tanzania.

         September: Birth of A. Agostinho Neto of Angola.

1924   February: Birth of Robert G. Mugabe of Zimbabwe.

         April: Birth of Kenneth Kaunda of Zambia.

         Birth of Amílcar Cabral of Guinea-Bissau.

         May: Birth of Sir Dawda K. Jawara of The Gambia.

         Birth of Milton Obote of Uganda.

         August: Birth of Ahmadou Ahidjo of Cameroon.

         September: Birth of Daniel arap Moi of Kenya.

         December: Birth of Robert Sobukwe of South Africa.

1925   Birth of Idi Amin of Uganda.

         Birth of Diallo Telli of Guinea (Conakry).

         July: Birth of Patrice Lumumba of Zaire.

         July: Birth of Quett Masire of Botswana.

1928   August: Birth of Gatsha Buthelezi of South Africa.

1929   May: Birth of Sam Nujoma of Namibia.

1930   August: Birth of Tom Mboya of Kenya.

         October: Birth of Mobutu Sese Seko of Zaire.

         November: Haile Selassie crowned emperor of Ethiopia.

1931   Birth of Desmond Tutu of South Africa.

         William Tubman resigns Senate seat in Liberia amidst allegations of involve-
         ment in forced-labor scandal.

1933   September: Birth of Samora Machel of Mozambique.

1934   August: Birth of Jonas M. Savimbi of Angola.

         October: Birth of Yakubu Gowon of Nigeria.

1935   October: Italy invades Ethiopia.

         Birth of Gnassingbe Eyadema of Togo.

1936   Birth of Mengistu Haile Mariam of Ethiopia.

         March: Birth of F. W. de Klerk of South Africa.

1937   Birth of Olusegun Obasanjo of Nigeria.

1941   May: Haile Selassie returns to Addis Ababa after defeat of Italian forces and
         liberation of Ethiopia by British troops.

1943   May: William V. S. Tubman elected president of Liberia for the first of six
         consecutive terms of office.

1944   January: Brazzaville Conference of political leaders of Free France and French colonial officials; recognition of African participation in constituent assembly of post–World War II France and African representation in the French parliament.

Birth of Yoweri Museveni of Uganda.

Nnamdi Azikiwe joins with Herbert Macaulay to found the National Council of Nigeria and the Cameroons in Nigeria.

Eliud Mathu appointed first African member of colonial legislature of Kenya.

1945   April–June: United Nations Charter written. Sub-Saharan African independent states of Liberia, Ethiopia and South Africa are founder-members of the UN.

May: End of World War II in Europe.

October: Pan-African Congress held at Manchester, England. George Padmore and Kwame Nkrumah among the organizers. Jomo Kenyatta and W.E.B. Du Bois in attendance.

November: African representatives, including Félix Houphouët-Boigny and Léopold S. Senghor, elected to French Constituent Assembly in Paris.

1946   March: New constitution for the Gold Coast, which becomes the first British colony in Africa to have an African majority in its legislative council.

April: French abolish forced labor in French West African colonies.

June: Loi Lamine Guèye extends French citizenship to all inhabitants of French overseas territories.

September: Jomo Kenyatta returns to Kenya after fifteen years abroad.

October: Inauguration of the constitution of the Fourth Republic of France; Africans represented in French parliamentary institutions based on limited franchise; African colonial territorial assemblies achieve limited powers.

October: Congress of (French) African Deputies meets in Bamako, Soudan. Rassemblement Démocratique Africain (RDA) established as a union of several parties in French West Africa by Félix Houphouët-Boigny, Modibo Keita and others.

December: UN rejects proposal of South Africa to incorporate South West Africa (former of League of Nations Mandate to South Africa) into Union.

December: Birth of Steve Biko of South Africa.

1947   January: New constitution makes Nigeria "self-governing" with an African majority in the legislative council and in the regional Houses of Assembly.

January: South Africa declines to place South West Africa under UN trusteeship.

April: Nationalist uprising in Madagascar against French rule; French troops intervene; nearly 50,000 people killed.

June: Birth of Jerry J. Rawlings of Ghana.

June: Jomo Kenyatta elected president of Kenya African Union.

1948   January: Somali Youth League clashes with government supporters.

February: Boycott of European goods and riots in the Gold Coast (now Ghana), in part led by Kwame Nkrumah and the United Gold Coast Convention. Twenty-nine protesters killed.

April: East African Central Legislature meets under British sponsorship in Nairobi, Kenya.

May: National Party wins South African general election on platform of implementing a policy of apartheid.

November: Bloc Démocratique Sénegalais founded by Léopold S. Senghor. General strike in Zanzibar.

1949   January: Convention People's Party (CPP) founded in the Gold Coast by Kwame Nkrumah.

Victoria Falls Conference in favor of federation of Rhodesia and Nyasaland; African opposition to proposed federation.

Industrial disturbances at Enugu colliery and riots in Southern Nigeria.

June: Seretse Khama proclaimed chief of the Bangwato, but barred from returning to the Bechuanaland Protectorate (now Botswana) due to marriage to a white woman.

December: Birth of Thomas Sankara of Burkina Faso.

December: UN puts Italian Somaliland under trust status, administered by Italy.

1950   April: Britain returns former Italian Somaliland and joins it to former British Somaliland as a United Nations trust territory of Somalia, administered by Italy, for ten years.

May: Birth of Samuel Doe of Liberia.

October: Hendrik Verwoerd becomes minister of native affairs in South African cabinet with plans to accelerate apartheid legislation.

December: Apartheid laws passed in South Africa: Immorality Act, Population Registration Act, Suppression of Communism Act, Group Areas Act.

December: World Court rules that South West Africa is under United Nations trusteeship. South Africa refuses to accept trust status for South West Africa.

Félix Houphouët-Boigny elected deputy from Côte d'Ivoire to the French parliament.

Action Group formed in Nigeria, led by Obafemi Awolowo.

1951   February: CPP wins general election in Gold Coast (Ghana); Nkrumah emerges from jail to become leader of government business in the Legislative Assembly.

October: Sierra Leone People's Party (SLPP) founded.

November: Second Victoria Falls Conference results in the British government's acceptance of the idea of a federation of the Rhodesias and Nyasaland.

December: Municipal elections in the Belgian Congo; local African parties participate.

1952   March: Kwame Nkrumah becomes prime minister of the Gold Coast.

September: United Nations terminates its administration of Eritrea, permitting absorption into Ethiopia in a federated status as an autonomous province.

Defiance Campaign against apartheid Pass Laws launched by African National Congress (ANC) in South Africa; Albert Luthuli elected president of the ANC.

October: Emergency declared by Kenya government to combat Mau Mau uprising.

1953   Emergency powers introduced by the South African government against passive resistance; new racial laws introduced: Reservations of Separate Amenities Act, Public Safety Act, Criminal Law Amendment Act, Bantu Education Act.

April: Jomo Kenyatta and five others convicted of managing Mau Mau in Kenya.

October: Central African Federation of Rhodesia and Nyasaland created (lasts until 1963).

1954   April: Federal system of government formalized by proposed constitution in Nigeria.

June: Convention People's Party (CPP) wins general election in the Gold Coast, and Britain promises independence.

July: Tanganyika African National Union (TANU) formed with Julius Nyerere as president.

October: Ahmadu Bello named premier of Northern Region of colonial Federation of Nigeria.

1955   April: Bandung Conference in Indonesia attended by representatives of many African nationalist parties.

May: Rebellion launched in French Trust Territory of Cameroun by Union des Populations du Cameroun (UPC). UPC banned; thousands killed over several years.

June: Multiracial Congress of the People adopts the Freedom Charter in South Africa.

November: Right to vote granted in Ethiopia.

1956   February: End of "Cape colored" voting rights in South Africa.

February: Félix Houphouët-Boigny of Côte d'Ivoire appointed minister in French cabinet.

June: *Loi-Cadre* (enabling or framework law), introduced in the French parliament (inaugurated in 1957), provides for greater local autonomy in Francophone Africa (except Algeria), including enhanced powers for territorial assemblies, direct universal suffrage and a single electoral college for territorial and French national elections.

Modibo Keita, deputy from French Soudan, elected vice president of the French National Assembly.

African miners strike in Northern Rhodesian Copperbelt; state of emergency declared.

September: Amílcar Cabral founds the African Party for the Independence of Guinea and Cape Verde (PAIGC).

December: Popular Movement for the Liberation of Angola (MPLA) founded.

December: Start of the treason trial in South Africa (lasts until 1961).

1957   March: Gold Coast becomes independent (united with former British Togoland) as Ghana, with Kwame Nkrumah as prime minister; he thus becomes the first black African member of the Privy Council of Great Britain.

March: Sékou Touré, with his Democratic Party of Guinea (PDG) winner of the territorial elections in French Guinea, takes office as vice president of the Government Council.

May: Houphouët-Boigny becomes president of the Grand Council of French West Africa.

May: Constitutional conference for Nigeria; offer of regional self-government; Eastern and Western regions become self-governing.

May: Sierra Leone People's Party (SLPP) wins general election in Sierra Leone under new constitution with ministerial government.

1958   April: Hendrik Verwoerd wins leadership of National Party; becomes prime minister of South Africa.

April: Conference of Independent African States, Accra, Ghana. Eight states invited, three from Africa south of the Sahara, South Africa excluded.

May: Crisis in Algeria leads to the fall of the French government, return of Gen. Charles de Gaulle as leader.

July: Hastings Banda returns to Nyasaland (now Malawi).

September: Tanganyika African National Union (TANU) candidates, led by Julius Nyerere, sweep multiracial elections for legislature in Tanganyika.

September: Referendum on the relationship of Francophone territories with France. Premier de Gaulle advocates internal autonomy for French overseas territories within a new French "Community." Guinea, led by Sékou Touré, votes no; other French territories assent to new relationship with France.

October: Guinea declares independence with Sékou Touré as president; all other French African territories remain within French Community.

December: All-African People's Conference in Accra, Ghana; Tom Mboya is chairman. Kwame Nkrumah, Patrice Lumumba, Joshua Nkomo and other African political party leaders in attendance.

December: Self-government for French Cameroun, with Ahmadou Ahidjo as premier.

1959   January: Riots in Belgian Congo.

February: State of emergency declared in Southern Rhodesia; disturbances in Northern Rhodesia and Nyasaland.

March: State of emergency declared in Nyasaland; Hastings Banda imprisoned.

March: Northern Region of Nigeria becomes self-governing.

April: South West African People's Organization (SWAPO) founded by Sam Nujoma and Jacob Kuhangua.

May: Ghana-Guinea "union" declared by presidents Nkrumah and Touré, with invitation to all independent African states to join.

July: Saniquellie (Liberia) Meeting of presidents Nkrumah of Ghana, Tubman of Liberia and Touré of Guinea recommends a "Community of Independent African States."

October: Dawda Jawara forms People's Progressive Party in The Gambia.

December: Senegal and Soudan demand independence, an end to the constitutional relationship within the French Community.

December: Robert Sobukwe becomes president of the Pan-Africanist Congress, formed in April, at its first national conference in Johannesburg, South Africa, after a split with the African National Congress over the primacy of nonracialism in the struggle against apartheid.

Death of George Padmore.

1960   January: Cameroon achieves independence from French trusteeship under the United Nations.

February: Prime Minister Harold Macmillan of Great Britain warns South Africa of "winds of change" in speech in Cape Town.

March: Uganda People's Congress formed; headed by Milton Obote.

March: Pan-Africanist Congress, led by Robert Sobukwe, organizes demonstrations against Pass Laws in South Africa. In Sharpeville and Langa sixty-seven Africans are killed by the South African police.

April: Togo becomes independent.

May: Ahmadou Ahidjo becomes president of Cameroon.

June–August: Most member states of the French Community in Africa become independent.

June: Senegal and Soudan achieve independence from France as the Mali Federation. Léopold Sédar Senghor becomes president, Modibo Keita becomes premier of the federation.

June: Congo (later Zaire) becomes independent; Patrice Lumumba is prime minister.

July: Force Publique mutinies in the Congo; Belgian troops intervene; Katanga Province (later Shaba) secedes. Multination force organized by the United Nations sent into the Congo.

July: Ghana becomes a republic; Kwame Nkrumah is president.

July: Somalia achieves independence as a unitary state, composed of the former Italian Trust Territory joined to former British Somaliland, which achieved independence in June.

August–September: Mali Federation dissolves. Modibo Keita, expelled from Dakar, becomes president of the former Soudan entity, retaining the name Mali. Senghor remains as president of Senègal.

September: Prime Minister Lumumba dismissed by President Joseph Kasavubu in the Congo; military coup led by Col. Mobutu takes over the government, now run by a College of Commissioners.

September: TANU wins preindependence election in Tanganyika (later Tanzania), and Julius Nyerere becomes chief minister.

October: Federation of Nigeria becomes an independent state within the British Commonwealth.

October: Restricted-franchise referendum narrowly approves republic status for South Africa.

November: Nnamdi Azikiwe becomes governor-general of Nigeria.

November: Félix Houphouët-Boigny becomes president of Côte d'Ivoire.

December: Coup attempt foiled against Emperor Haile Selassie of Ethiopia.

December: Brazzaville Conference of independent Francophone African states, attended by heads of newly independent governments, pledge economic and political co-operation. Presidents Senghor, Ahidjo and Houphouët-Boigny, among others, in attendance.

1961   January: Ousted Prime Minister Patrice Lumumba killed while in military custody in Katanga (Shaba).

January: Casablanca Conference of heads of independent African states includes presidents Nkrumah of Ghana, Keita of Mali and Touré of Guinea. Other leaders in attendance from North African countries. Regarded as a "radical" grouping.

February: Uprising in Luanda begins rebellion in Angola against the Portuguese.

February: Referendum in British Trust Territory of Cameroons results in Northern Cameroons voting to join Nigeria, Southern Cameroons voting to join former French Cameroun, now independent.

March: South Africa leaves the Commonwealth and becomes a republic.

April: Sierra Leone becomes an independent state within the Commonwealth.

April: Jomo Kenyatta released from prison in Kenya, released from full detention in August.

May: Monrovia Conference of African States, President W. V. S. Tubman presiding, includes the heads or representatives of the sub-Saharan Francophone independent African governments (Houphouët-Boigny, Senghor, Ahidjo and others, except for the divided government of the Congo), and Nigeria, Somalia, Sierra Leone and three North African states. Regarded as a "conservative" grouping.

August: General election in Nyasaland won by Malawi Congress Party, led by Hastings Banda.

September: UN forces defeat Katanga secessionist forces in the Congo and gain cease-fire.

October: Federal Republic of Cameroon formed, with Ahmadou Ahidjo as federal president, and with a vice president and premier of West Cameroon State as well as a premier of East Cameroon.

December: Albert J. Luthuli is awarded the Nobel Peace Prize for 1960.

December: Tanganyika (later Tanzania) gains independence, with Julius Nyerere as prime minister.

December: Zimbabwe African People's Union (ZAPU) founded, successor to the banned National Democratic Party; Joshua Nkomo is president.

1962   April: Milton Obote becomes prime minister of Uganda.

June: Front for the Liberation of Mozambique (FRELIMO) formed, uniting three anticolonial movements. Eduardo C. Mondlane becomes president.

July: Trust Territory of Ruanda-Urundi gains independence from Belgium as Republic of Rwanda and Kingdom of Burundi.

October: Trial, conviction and sentencing of Nelson Mandela to prison in Robben Island, South Africa.

October: African majority control in Northern Rhodesia legislature for the first time, in a coalition government led by Kenneth Kaunda.

Ethiopia dissolves federal arrangement with Eritrea. Beginning of Eritrean guerrilla opposition.

October: Uganda achieves independence.

December: President Léopold S. Senghor ousts and jails Prime Minister Mamadou Dia in Senegal, changes the constitution to consolidate executive power.

Sam Nujoma elected president of South West Africa People's Organization (SWAPO).

December: Tanganyika becomes a republic, Julius Nyerere becomes president almost a year after resigning as prime minister to devote his attention to party development.

1963   January: Official end of Katanga secession in the Congo.

January: Assassination of President Sylvanus Olympio of Togo.

February: Hastings Banda becomes prime minister of Nyasaland (later Malawi), as country achieves internal self-government.

General Law Amendment Act passed to give South African government wide powers of arrest.

May: Summit conference of leaders of African states, Addis Ababa, Ethiopia, including Haile Selassie, William V. S. Tubman and Félix Houphouët-Boigny. Organization of African Unity (OAU) established and charter approved by thirty African heads of state in Addis Ababa.

May: Modibo Keita of Mali receives Lenin Peace Prize.

August: Founding of Zimbabwe African National Union; Robert Mugabe is secretary-general.

October: Uganda becomes a republic with Sir Frederick Mutesa, the *kabaka* (king) of Buganda, as president.

October: Nnamdi Azikwe becomes president of the Federal Republic of Nigeria.

December: Final dissolution of the Central African Federation (Northern and Southern Rhodesia and Nyasaland).

December: Independence for Kenya with Jomo Kenyatta as prime minister.

December: Zanzibar becomes an independent state within the Commonwealth.

1964   Ghana declared officially a one-party state.

Massacre of Tutsi in Rwanda.

January: Revolution in Zanzibar; the sultan is overthrown and A. A. Karume becomes president.

January: Army mutinies in Kenya, Tanganyika and Uganda; British troops called in to help restore order.

February: French troops intervene to reverse the overthrow of President Leon M'Ba of Gabon.

April: Tanganyika and Zanzibar agree to union, with Julius Nyerere as president of the United Republic.

April: Ian Douglas Smith becomes prime minister of Rhodesia (Zimbabwe).

June: Rivonia sabotage trial in South Africa; conviction of eight defendants, including Nelson Mandela, who is resentenced, to life imprisonment.

July: Diallo Telli elected the first secretary-general of the Organization of African Unity (OAU).

July: Moise Tshombe, former head of Katanga secessionist government, becomes president of the Congo. Revolts in several Congo provinces; Belgian paratroops land at Stanleyville (Lumumbashi) and elsewhere to rescue Europeans.

July: Malawi becomes an independent state within the Commonwealth.

September: FRELIMO begins armed struggle against Portuguese in Mozambique.

October: Independence for Northern Rhodesia, renamed Zambia, as a republic within the Commonwealth. Kenneth Kaunda becomes president.

Rhodesia government bans ZANU, imprisons Robert Mugabe.

December: Kenya becomes a republic with Jomo Kenyatta as president.

1965 February: Organization Commune Africaine et Malagach (OCAM) formed at conference of heads of state of Francophone African countries at Nouakchott, Mauritania.

February: Independence for The Gambia. Dawda Jawara named prime minister.

Chinese premier Chou En-lai visits Tanzania.

July: One-party system officially adopted in Tanzania. Parliamentary elections to offer choice between two TANU candidates.

November: Prime Minister Ian Smith promulgates Rhodesia's Unilateral Declaration of Independence (UDI) from Britain; UN Security Council votes an embargo on Rhodesia.

November: Gen. Mobutu Sese Seko dismisses civilian government, takes over as president in the Congo (Zaire).

1966 Commonwealth Conference at Lagos.

January: Military coups in Upper Volta (Burkina Faso) and Central African Republic.

January: Military coup in Nigeria led by Igbo officers. Federal Prime Minister Tafewa Balewa and Northern Region Premier Ahmadu Bello killed.

February: Military coup overthrows Kwame Nkrumah and his government in Ghana. Nkrumah granted asylum in Guinea.

February–May: Government crisis in Uganda: Milton Obote arrests five members of his cabinet; assumes full powers of government; later takes position of president of Uganda with a new centralized constitution. Encountering resistance from the Baganda supporters of the former president, Obote orders the seizure of the *kabaka's* palace in Kampala. Heavy fighting ensues; the *kabaka* escapes to Britain.

July: Malawi declared a republic; Hastings Banda becomes president.

July: Lt. Col. Yakubu Gowon ousts Gen. Aguiyi-Ironsi as head of military government of Nigeria.

September: Botswana becomes an independent republic within the Commonwealth, with Seretse Khama as president; Khama awarded a knighthood by the British government.

September: Assassination of Prime Minister Hendrik Verwoerd in South Africa.

Union Minière du Haut-Katanga taken over by Congo government.

Jonas Savimbi becomes president of UNITA.

1967 January: Military coup in Togo.

February: Arusha Declaration, outlining the aims of *ujamaa* socialism, issued in Tanzania by President Julius Nyerere.

March: Siaka Stevens becomes prime minister of Sierra Leone after All Peoples Congress (APC) opposition wins election. Army and police stage coup, supported by ousted Sierra Leone People's Party. Military government set up.

April: Lt. Col. Gnassingbe Eyadema assumes full power in Togo, dismisses Committee of National Reconciliation and becomes president.

May: Secession of Eastern Region of Nigeria as independent Republic of Biafra and the beginning of civil war in Nigeria (to 1970).

Uprising in eastern and northern Congo ended by foreign mercenaries employed by Gen. Mobutu's central government.

June: East African Community established by Kenya, Tanzania and Uganda.

July: Death of Albert John Luthuli of South Africa.

1968 March: Start of armed rebellion against the Rhodesian government, led by the guerrilla forces of Joshua Nkomo's Zimbabwe African People's Union (ZAPU) and Robert Mugabe's Zimbabwe African National Union (ZANU).

Malawi establishes diplomatic relations with South Africa.

April: Tanzania, Ivory Coast and two other African states recognize Biafran independence.

April: Noncommissioned officers oust military government in Sierra Leone; Siaka Stevens returns as prime minister of civilian government.

May: Sam Nujoma receives Lenin Peace Prize.

September: Swaziland, the last British colonial territory in Africa, becomes an independent state within the Commonwealth.

October: Equatorial Guinea becomes independent of Spain.

November: Military coup in Mali ousts President Modibo Keita. Moussa Traore takes over.

November: "Cultural Revolution" declared by Sékou Touré in Guinea.

December: Black university students form the South African Students' Organization under the leadership of Steve Biko.

1969   February: Assassination of Eduardo C. Mondlane.

June: Sir Humphrey Gibbs, the last British governor of Rhodesia, resigns. Restricted-franchise referendum approves a republican constitution, severing all ties with Britain.

July: Assassination of Tom Mboya in Kenya.

September: General election in Ghana returns Kofi Busia as prime minister, restoring civilian government after three years of military rule.

October: Serious political disturbances in western Kenya; opposition party Kenya People's Union (KPU) banned.

Ghana expels thousands of aliens.

November: Maj. Gen. Muhammad Siyaad Barre takes over as president of the Supreme Revolutionary Council of Somalia after a coup overthrows civilian government, which was unable to agree on a successor to the assassinated president.

December: Attempted assassination of Milton Obote in Uganda.

1970   January: End of the Nigerian civil war; a reduced Biafra surrenders; secessionist leader C. O. Ojukwu flees.

February: President Léopold S. Senghor promulgates changes in the Senegalese constitution to re-create the office of prime minister.

March: Rhodesia declared a republic, officially recognized by no country, although Portugal and South Africa keep their consulates open.

April: Sir Dawda Kairaba Jawara becomes president of the Republic of The Gambia.

May: President Milton Obote introduces the "Common Man's Charter" in Uganda.

May: Samora Machel takes over as head of FRELIMO as well as leader of guerrilla forces in Mozambique fighting against the Portuguese.

October: Construction of Tanzam (later Tazara) railway from Dar es Salaam to the Zambian Copperbelt officially starts; built with Chinese aid after the World Bank and Western countries refuse.

November: Portuguese commandos, mercenary troops and Guinean exiles repulsed in an attempted seaborne landing in Conakry, Guinea.

December: State of emergency declared by Ethiopian government in Eritrea.

1971   January: Gen. Idi Amin leads military coup that overthrows President Obote of Uganda.

April: Sierra Leone becomes a republic; Siaka Stevens sworn in as president.

July: Death of President William V. S. Tubman of Liberia; Vice President William Tolbert succeeds him.

July: Hastings K. Banda sworn in as president for life in Malawi.

August: President Banda of Malawi makes a state visit to South Africa and becomes the first black African head of state to do so; Ivory Coast delegation also visits South Africa.

October: Congo renamed Zaire.

1972   January: Army coup in Ghana: Gen. I. K. Acheampong overthrows civilian government of Prime Minister Kofi A. Busia.

January: Pearce Commission in Rhodesia reports an overwhelming no by African population to settlement proposals.

March: Serious drought in Sahelian region, continuing into 1974.

April: Assassination of A. A. Karume, head of Zanzibar government, federated within Tanzania.

April: Death of Kwame Nkrumah.

May: Hutu rising in Burundi suppressed with great loss of life.

May: Military coup in Madagascar.

June: Cameroon abolishes federation, becomes a unitary state, Ahmadou Ahidjo as president.

August: President Idi Amin begins to expel Asians from Uganda.

November: "African authenticity" campaign launched by President Mobutu in Zaire.

December: United National Independence Party named only legal party in Zambia.

1973   January: Rhodesian border closed by President Kaunda of Zambia.

January: Assassination of Amílcar Cabral.

January: Widespread strikes by black workers in South Africa.

African Games at Lagos.

Prime Minister Smith of Rhodesia begins talks with African nationalists in an attempt to find some form of internal settlement.

Oil crisis brings great increase in prices for African states.

Widespread famine revealed in Ethiopia.

PAIGC declares independence for Guinea-Bissau and Cape Verde, having liberated most of the territory.

1974   April: Coup in Lisbon by army officers disillusioned with the African wars brings down the Caetano regime in Portugal and begins the process of decolonization of the Portuguese empire in Africa.

Opposition party recognized in Senegal.

June: Emperor Haile Selassie of Ethiopia loses control of his government to a military council.

September: Emperor Haile Selassie officially deposed by military coup. Provisional Military Administrative Council (PMAC) established to rule the country.

September: Portugal recognizes the independence of Guinea-Bissau and Cape Verde. Peace accord signed and transitional government led by Samora Machel established in Mozambique.

December: Mengistu Haile Mariam becomes president of Ethiopia.

1975   Lomé Agreement signed between European Economic Community (EEC) and thirty-seven African states.

Economic Community of West African States (ECOWAS) treaty signed by fifteen states.

Haile Selassie dies in Ethiopian military prison.

January: Alvor Accords signed between the Portuguese government and the three major rival liberation movements in Angola to end the fighting and co-operate in the transition to full independence.

June: Mozambique gains independence from Portugal. Samora Machel becomes president.

July: Formal independence from Portugal for Cape Verde Islands and São Tomé and Príncipe.

July: Coup removes Maj. Gen. Yakubu Gowon as head of state in Nigeria. Gen. Murtala Muhammed named head of state, with Lt. Gen. Olusegun Obasanjo one of two partners running the government, pledged to return to civilian rule in October 1979.

August: Portuguese government resumes administration in Angola as internal peace agreement breaks down.

November: Angola gains independence from Portugal under MPLA government with A. Agostinho Neto as president. Civil war intensifies. Cuban troops, with USSR military assistance, support MPLA government. U.S. covert assistance goes to opposition fighting MPLA. South African troops invade Angola from Namibia in support of Jonas Savimbi and UNITA.

Tanzam railway officially opened between Zambia and Tanzania.

Four "Front Line" presidents at Quilemane pledge support for the Zimbabwe National Liberation Army.

1976   February: Gen. Murtala Muhammed, Gowon's successor, assassinated in Lagos, Nigeria. Lt. Gen. Olusegun Obasanjo takes over as head of Nigerian military regime.

June: Riots in Soweto, South Africa.

September: Ian Smith accepts principle of black majority rule as a basis for negotiations to end guerrilla war in Rhodesia (Zimbabwe).

October: South Africa declares "Bantustan" entity Transkei as independent state.

"Palace coup" in Addis Ababa.

Senegalese constitution revised to countenance a three-party system, with ideologies ranging from left to right. The ruling party of Senegal, renamed the Socialist Party (PS), led by President Léopold S. Senghor, is recognized as centrist and social democratic and is admitted into the Socialist International.

Gatsha Buthelezi takes over as chief minister of KwaZulu in South Africa; he is also head of Inkatha cultural organization.

December: Jean Bedel Bokassa crowned emperor of Central African Empire.

1977   February: Mengistu Haile Mariam becomes chairman of PMAC, ruling military junta of Ethiopia, upon assassination of Gen. Tafari Banti. Widespread purge of leadership commences.

February: MPLA government of People's Republic of Angola declares victory in civil war and is recognized by most African states.

March: Mozambique signs Treaty of Friendship and Co-Operation with USSR.

March: Invasion of Shaba Province, Zaire, by Katangese rebel exiles from Angola.

June: Djibouti becomes an independent state; final withdrawal of France from African territory.

June: Somali-supported forces invade Ogaden; serious fighting in the region. Cuban aid to Ethiopia in the war. Soviets desert Somali clients and support Ethiopia. Somalia expels Soviet advisors and breaks diplomatic relations with Cuba.

June: Death of Modibo Keita.

August: South Africa denies nuclear test despite alleged evidence of satellite photos.

September: Death of Steve Biko in police custody in South Africa.

Death of Diallo Telli in prison in Guinea.

Constituent Assembly meets in Nigeria in preparation for a return to civilian government.

P. W. Botha elected leader of the National Party in South Africa and takes over as prime minister.

November: UN votes arms embargo against South Africa.

TANU merges with the Afro-Shirazi Party of Zanzibar to form Chama Cha Mapinduzi (CCM), creating one ruling party for the United Republic of Tanzania.

1978   February: Death of Robert Sobukwe.

March: Internal agreement in Rhodesia; transitional government formed.

March: Somali forces defeated by Ethiopia in Ogaden war.

May: Ethiopia steps up its attacks on rebel Eritrean nationalist forces.

New constitution in Sierra Leone declaring a one-party state wins approval in national referendum.

Reconciliation of Guinea with France.

August: Death of Jomo Kenyatta, succeeded as president of Kenya by Vice President Daniel arap Moi.

September: B. J. Vorster resigns as prime minister of South Africa, undermined by ''Muldergate'' scandal; succeeded by P. W. Botha.

December: Ugandan invasion of Kagera salient in northwest Tanzania.

December: South Africa agrees to UN plan for independence for Namibia.

1979   January: Tanzanian troops, with support of former president Milton Obote of Uganda and Ugandan National Liberation Front, invade Uganda.

April: President Idi Amin of Uganda defeated by invading Tanzanian army and Ugandan exile force. Amin flees to Saudi Arabia. Yusufu Lule named head of provisional government, with Yoweri Musaveni as minister of defense.

May: Arrest of Flight-Lieutenant Jerry J. Rawlings in abortive coup against I. K. Acheampong's military regime in Ghana.

June: Junior officers free Flight-Lieutenant Jerry Rawlings from jail while on trial. He leads a coup in Ghana that overthrows the government of Gen. I. K. Acheampong. Armed Forces Revolutionary Council takes over; three former heads of state executed.

September: Death of A. Agostinho Neto in Moscow while president of Angola.

September: J. E. dos Santos becomes president of Angola.

September: Emperor Bokassa overthrown and Central African Republic re-established.

September: Military regime of J. J. Rawlings permits elections for new civilian government in Ghana. Hilla Limann becomes president of Ghana's Third Republic.

October: Military government of Gen. Olusegun Obasanjo steps down; Nigeria holds elections in a return to civilian rule.

October: Lt. Col. T. O. Nguema Mbasogo takes over as president of Equatorial Guinea.

December: Lancaster House agreement in London on a settlement for Zimbabwe; the country reverts to British rule for a transitional period.

1980   April: Elections in Zimbabwe result in overwhelming victory for ZANU-PF party. Robert Mugabe becomes prime minister of the Republic of Zimbabwe.

April: President Tolbert of Liberia killed in military coup led by Sgt. Samuel Doe and junior army officers.

May: Military coup overthrows President Godfrey Binaisa in Uganda. Paul Mwanga takes over as head of state.

July: Death of Sir Seretse Khama, president of Botswana. Vice President Quett Masire succeeds him.

Military coup in Guinea-Bissau separates Guinea from Cape Verde.

November: President Sangoule Lamizana of Upper Volta (now Burkina Faso) overthrown by military coup. Col. Saye Zerbo takes over.

November: President Luis Cabral of Guinea-Bissau overthrown by military coup. Gen. J. Bernardo Vieira becomes head of state.

December: Milton Obote elected president of Uganda.

December: Libyan forces enter civil war in Chad to help President Goukouni Oueddei.

December: Léopold Sédar Senghor resigns from the presidency of Senegal. Abdou Diouf succeeds him.

1981   January: One thousand killed in riots involving members of a radical Islamic sect in Kano, Northern Nigeria.

February: ZAPU supporters of Joshua Nkomo defeated by Zimbabwe troops loyal to Prime Minister Mugabe.

February: Yoweri Musaveni launches guerrilla war against new Obote government in Uganda.

August: South African army invades Angola, attacking SWAPO guerrilla bases.

November: Libyan forces withdraw from Chad. Troops loyal to President Oueddei attack Sudanese border town in retaliation for alleged Sudanese invasion.

December: Flight-Lieutenant Jerry John Rawlings overthrows the government of Ghana and becomes head of state. People's Tribunals replace courts.

1982   February: Dissidents connected to exiled Tanzanians hijack an airplane in Tanzania, demanding resignation of President Julius Nyerere. They surrender and are allowed to flee the country.

February: The OAU announces the withdrawal of its peacekeeping force in Chad by June 30 unless a cease-fire is negotiated to end the fighting.

August: Junior officers in the Kenya air force fail in an attempted coup against the government of President Daniel arap Moi. After looting and arrests in Nairobi, Moi announces the disbanding of the air force.

October: Rebel leader Hissein Habre becomes president of Chad.

November: Ahmadou Ahidjo resigns from the presidency of Cameroon. Paul Biya succeeds him.

November: Military coup in Upper Volta (now Burkina Faso); Jean-Baptiste Ouedraogo takes over.

1983   January: Nigeria expels noncitizens as economy declines after oil prices plunge.

January: Capt. Thomas Sankara becomes prime minister of Upper Volta (Burkina Faso).

May: South African planes bomb suspected ANC guerrilla camps in Mozambique in retaliation for a car bombing that killed twelve people in Pretoria.

July: United States announces aid to government of Hissein Habre in Chad fighting Libyan-backed supporters of former government.

August: Thomas Sankara, released from house arrest, becomes head of state of Upper Volta (Burkina Faso) after military colleagues overthrow Ouedraogo government.

August: Former President Ahidjo of Cameroon implicated in antigovernment plot.

December: In a bloodless coup Maj. Gen. Muhammad Buhari overthrows the government of President Shehu Shagari of Nigeria. The constitution of the republic is suspended and political parties are banned.

1984   Bishop Desmond Tutu is awarded the Nobel Peace Prize.

Death of Sékou Touré.

Pieter W. Botha becomes state president of South Africa.

March: South Africa signs nonaggression pact, the Nkomati Accord, with Mozambique, requiring the expulsion of ANC guerrillas from Mozambique.

April: Coup fails in Cameroon; rebels drawn from supporters of former President Ahidjo.

Former President Léopold Senghor of Senegal elected to the French Academy.

August: Prime Minister Mugabe calls for a one-party state in Zimbabwe.

August: Upper Volta renamed Burkina Faso.

August: United States criticizes the Uganda government of Milton Obote for human-rights abuses.

October: Drought and famine in Ethiopia. Massive food relief organized internationally.

November: South Africa installs new constitution with an executive presidency and a tricameral parliament that includes chambers with limited powers for "coloreds" and Asians, but still excludes blacks from voting and from representation.

December: Growing protests in the United States over the "constructive engagement" policy of the Reagan administration toward South Africa and the slow pace of apartheid reform.

1985   February: Antiapartheid protests and violence grow in South Africa.

June: U.S. Congress passes Comprehensive Anti-Apartheid Bill, which authorizes sanctions against South Africa. President Reagan vetoes it.

July: South Africa declares state of emergency.

July: Robert Gabriel Mugabe becomes president of Zimbabwe.

July: Milton Obote's regime in Uganda ended by a military coup led by Tito Okello.

July: International "Live-Aid" concert raises $70 million to alleviate starvation in Africa.

July: UN World Conference on Women in Nairobi, Kenya.

August: President Pieter Botha of South Africa rejects further reform of apartheid.

August: Maj. Gen. Buhari ousted by Maj. Gen. Ibrahim Babangida in internal shake-up in Nigerian military government.

October: Samuel Doe elected president of Liberia amid charges of fraud at the polls.

November: President Siaka Stevens of Sierra Leone leaves office, succeeded by the recently elected Joseph S. Momoh.

November: Ali Hassan Mwinyi elected to succeed President Julius Nyerere of Tanzania.

December: Border war between Mali and Burkina Faso.

1986 January: Samuel Kanyon Doe sworn in as president of Liberia.

January: Julius Kambarage Nyerere steps down as president of Tanzania.

January: Yoweri Museveni, head of the National Resistance Army, seizes power in Uganda, becomes president.

January–February: Jonas Savimbi, UNITA rebel leader in Angola, requests greater U.S. aid in war against MPLA government. United States continues covert assistance.

March, May: Commonwealth Eminent Persons Group, cochaired by Gen. Olusegun Obasanjo of Nigeria, visits South Africa, fails to persuade government on apartheid reform.

May: South African military units raid alleged guerrilla bases in Zambia, Botswana and Zimbabwe.

June: Two months after rescinding the emergency in South Africa, President Botha reimposes it. Violence increases.

August: Britain agrees to limited sanctions against South Africa. Six other Commonwealth nations approve broader sanctions.

September: Desmond Tutu enthroned as Anglican archbishop of Cape Town.

October: President Samora Machel of Mozambique killed in a plane crash in South Africa en route to Mozambiqe.

December: Riots in the Copperbelt of Zambia over food price rises. President Kaunda cancels price changes.

1987 February: Ethiopia approves a new constitution, which provides for a civilian one-party government, led by the Workers Party, headed by Mengistu Haile Mariam.

April: Thousands of black workers in South Africa strike in sympathy with black transport union's stoppage. Violence and mass arrests.

May: National Party parliamentary majority slightly increased in limited-franchise elections.

May: Obafemi Awolowo dies in Nigeria.

July: 386 civilians reportedly killed in one incident by RENAMO rebels in Mozambique.

October: Assassination of Thomas Sankara in Burkina Faso.

Julius Nyerere steps down as chairman of CCM after thirty-three consecutive years as party leader in pre- and postindependence Tanzania.

1988 Cuban troop strength in Angola reaches 60,000.

May: Death of Siaka P. Stevens of Sierra Leone.

June: Two million black workers strike in South Africa, the largest strike in the country's history.

August: Truce declared in civil war in Angola. South Africa and Cuba begin military withdrawal.

September: Thousands killed in ethnic violence in Burundi.

October: Libya ends state of war with Chad. OAU to settle disputed border territory.

December: Conclusion of the Brazzaville Accord, an international agreement involving all parties connected to the Angolan conflict, agrees to the independence of Namibia, the end of the civil war in Angola, and the complete withdrawal of all foreign troops.

1989   Africa Leadership Forum founded, headed by Olusegun Obasanjo, former Nigerian head of state.

February: Botha resigns as National Party leader after suffering stroke, but retains state presidency of South Africa. F. W. de Klerk chosen to succeed Botha as party leader.

July: Nelson Mandela meets secretly with President P. W. Botha of South Africa.

August/September: P. W. Botha resigns presidency of South Africa. F. W. de Klerk appointed acting president, then elected president.

October: De Klerk government frees eight imprisoned black political leaders.

November: Ahmadou Ahidjo, former president of Cameroon, dies.

November: Opening of constituent assembly to write a constitution for Namibia.

December: Rebel attacks begin civil war in Liberia.

1990   February: ANC unbanned in South Africa. Nelson Mandela released from prison.

March: Namibia independent. Sam Nujoma becomes president.

April: President Mobutu in Zaire lifts the ban on opposition parties.

June: Franco-African Summit meeting at La Baule, France. Francophone African countries urged by the French government to move toward democracy.

June: South Africa lifts state of emergency for the whole country except Natal Province. Nelson Mandela tours United States and Europe.

June: Cameroon government endorses multi-partyism.

July: Ghana launches a national dialogue, consisting of "District Assemblies and the Evolving Democratic Process," supervised by the National Commission for Democracy and the Ministry of Local Government.

September: President Samuel Doe captured and killed by rebels as bloody civil war nears an end in Liberia.

September/October: Gabon's first multi-party legislative elections in 22 years sees 75 parties competing. President Omar Bongo and ruling PDG victorious, despite selective invalidations and alleged fraud.

October: Anti-government demonstrations in Togo. President Gnassingbe Eyadema appoints a constitutional commission to prepare for a multi-party system.

September: President Kaunda, calling for a new constitution, announces that Zambia will eliminate all obstacles to multi-party elections for president and parliament.

October: National conference in Burkina Faso presents draft constitution to President Blaise Compaore to permit multi-party system.

October/November: Competitive multi-party presidential and parliamentary elections in Côte d'Ivoire. President Houphouët-Boigny and PDCI victorious.

November: State of emergency in South Africa ends for the whole country.

December: Zambia legalizes opposition parties, ending the one-party system in place since 1972.

1991   January: Regime of President Siyaad Barre collapses as rebels enter the capital of Somalia. Barre flees.

January: President Robert Mugabe announces abandonment of effort to make Zimbabwe a one-party state.

January: Multi-party election in Cape Verde ousts the PAIGC government.

February: Formal legal segregation requirements of the Group Areas Act, the Registration of Population Act, and the Land Act repealed in South Africa.

March: Opposition wins presidency in contested election in Sao Tome and Principe.

March: In Benin's first presidential election in 21 years, caretaker Prime Minister Nicephore Soglo defeats recently ousted President Mathieu Kerekou.

March: Pro-democracy groups force the resignation of Mali's president, Moussa Traore, after 200 people are killed in violent protests.

May: Mengistu Haile-Mariam's regime in Ethiopia collapses, as rebels enter the capital and Mengistu flees the country.

May: Agreement between MPLA and UNITA on a cease-fire in Angola and future multi-party elections for a new government.

May: PNDC government in Ghana announces a transition to multiparty politics but continues the ban on political parties.

June: National conference in Congo-Brazzaville drastically reduces power of President Denis Sassou-Nguesso, forcing constitutional reconstruction, and schedules competitive elections for 1992.

July/August: Togo convenes national conference, creates transitional government with Kokou Koffigah as prime minister, and schedules competitive elections for 1992.

August: Military mutiny in Kinshasa, Zaire, triggers rioting, looting; 250 persons killed. French and Belgian troops arrive to protect foreign nationals. President Mobutu appoints Etienne Tshisekedi wa Mulumba, leader of the coalition Union Sacrée, head of a crisis government.

September: President Kenneth Kaunda dissolves the Zambian parliament, allowing the 27-year-old state of emergency to expire, and schedules competitive, multi-party elections for parliament and presidency to take place in two months.

October/November: Opposition party, the Movement for Multiparty Democracy, and presidential candidate Frederick Chiluba win overwhelming election victory over incumbent UNIP and over President Kaunda. Chiluba inaugurated second president of Zambia as Kaunda retires.

November: President Mobutu in Zaire invests new cabinet and new prime minister, Mungul Diaka, replacing dismissed prime minister, Etienne Tshisekedi, who refuses to resign.

December: President Moi agrees to allow opposition parties to operate in Kenya.

December: Togolese army dismisses transitional government.

BIBLIOGRAPHICAL NOTE

Readers interested in further information on the life and times of the subjects of the profiles in this volume are referred to the brief bibliography at the end of each entry. Readers wishing to pursue the analysis of leadership in Africa south of the Sahara are referred to the brief bibliography at the end of the Introduction. Below is a short supplemental bibliography of other works dealing with political elites and broad political trends in Africa south of the Sahara since 1945.

Austin, Dennis. *Politics in Africa*. Hanover, N.H.: University Press of New England, 1978.

Baum, Edward, and Felix Gagliano. *Chief Executives in Black Africa and Southeast Asia*. Athens, Ohio: Ohio University Center for International Studies, 1976.

Baynham, Simon (ed.). *Military Power and Politics in Black Africa*. London: Croom Helm, 1986.

Bienen, Henry. *Armies and Parties in Africa*. New York: Africana Publishing Co., 1978.

Bretton, Henry L. *Power and Politics in Africa*. Chicago: Aldine, 1973.

Butler, Jeffrey, and A. A. Castagno (eds.). *Boston University Papers on Africa: Transition in African Politics*. New York: Praeger, 1967.

Carter, Gwendolen M. (ed.). *African One-Party States*. Ithaca, N.Y.: Cornell University Press, 1962.

————— (ed.). *National Unity and Regionalism in Eight African States*. Ithaca, N.Y.: Cornell University Press, 1966.

Carter, Gwendolyn M., and Patrick O. O'Meara (eds.). *African Independence: The First Twenty-five Years*. Bloomington: Indiana University Press, 1985.

Chabal, Patrick (ed.). *Political Domination in Africa: Reflections on the Limits of Power*. London: Cambridge University Press, 1986.

Coleman, James Smoot. *Nigeria: Background to Nationalism*. Berkeley: University of California Press, 1958.

Coleman, James Smoot, and Carl G. Rosberg (eds.). *Political Parties and National Integration in Tropical Africa*. Berkeley: University of California Press, 1964.

Collier, Ruth Berins. *Regimes in Tropical Africa: Changing Forms of Supremacy, 1945–1975*. Berkeley: University of California Press, 1982.

Decalo, Samuel. *Coups and Army Rule in Africa: Studies in Military Style*. New Haven, Conn.: Yale University Press, 1976.

Diamond, Larry, Juan J. Linz, and Seymour Martin Lipset (eds.). *Democracy in Developing Countries*. Vol. 2, *Africa*. Boulder, Colo.: Lynne Rienner Publishers, 1988.

Doro, Marion E., and Newell M. Stultz (eds.). *Governing in Black Africa*. Englewood Cliffs, N. J.: Prentice-Hall, 1970.

Duignan, Peter, and Robert H. Jackson (eds.). *Politics and Government in African States, 1960–85*. London: Croom Helm, 1986.

Dunn, John (ed.). *West African States: Failure and Promise: A Study in Comparative Politics*. Cambridge, Eng.: Cambridge University Press, 1978.

Emerson, Rupert, and Martin Kilson (eds.). *The Political Awakening of Africa*. Englewood Cliffs, N. J.: Prentice-Hall, 1965.

First, Ruth. *The Barrel of a Gun: Political Power in Africa and the Coup d'Etat*. Harmondsworth, Eng.: Penguin Books, 1970.

Friedland, William H., and Carl G. Rosberg (eds.). *African Socialism*. Stanford, Calif.: Stanford University Press, 1964.

Glickman, Harvey (ed.). *The Crisis and Challenge of African Development*. Westport, Conn.: Greenwood Press, 1988.

Harbeson, John (ed.). *The Military in African Politics*. New York: Praeger, 1987.

Hayward, Fred M. (ed.). *Elections in Independent Africa*. Boulder, Colo.: Westview Press, 1987.

Hodgkin, Thomas L. *Nationalism in Colonial Africa*. London: Frederick Muller, 1956.

———. *African Political Parties*. Harmondsworth, Eng.: Penguin Books, 1961.

Lee, J. M. *African Armies and Civil Order*. London: Chatto and Windus, 1969.

Legum, Colin. *Pan-Africanism: A Short Political Guide*. Westport, Conn.: Greenwood Press, 1976.

Lemarchand, René (ed.). *African Kingships in Perspective*. London: Frank Cass, 1977.

Lloyd, Peter C. (ed.). *The New Elites of Tropical Africa*. London: Oxford University Press, 1966.

Mackenzie, W.J.M., and Kenneth E. Robinson (eds.). *Five Elections in Africa: A Group of Electoral Studies*. Oxford: Clarendon Press, 1960.

Markovitz, Irving Leonard. *Power and Class in Africa*. Englewood Cliffs, N.J.: Prentice-Hall, 1977.

Mazrui, Ali A. *On Heroes and Uhuru-Worship*. Harlow, Eng.: Longman, 1967.

———. *Political Values and the Educated Class in Africa*. London: Heinemann, 1978.

———. *The Africans: A Triple Heritage*. Boston: Little, Brown, 1986.

Mazrui, Ali A., and Michael Tidy. *Nationalism and New States in Africa*. London: Heinemann Educational Books, 1984.

Morgenthau, Ruth Schachter. *Political Parties in French-Speaking West Africa*. Oxford: Clarendon Press, 1964.

Mowoe, Isaac James (ed.). *The Performance of Soldiers as Governors: African Politics and the African Military*. Washington, D.C.: University Press of America, 1980.

O'Brien, Donal B. Cruise, John Dunn, and Richard Rathbone (eds.). *Contemporary West African States*. Cambridge, Eng.: Cambridge University Press, 1989.

Ottaway, David, and Marina Ottaway. *Afrocommunism*. New York: Africana Publishing Co., 1981.

Rodney, Walter. *How Europe Underdeveloped Africa*. Dar es Salaam, Tanzania: Tanzania Publishing House, 1972.

Rosberg, Carl G., and Thomas M. Callaghy (eds.). *Socialism in Sub-Saharan Africa: A New Assessment*. Berkeley: Institute of International Studies, University of California, 1979.

Rothchild, Donald, and Naomi Chazan (eds.). *The Precarious Balance: State and Society in Africa*. Boulder, Colo.: Westview Press, 1988.

Sandbrook, Richard. *The Politics of Africa's Economic Stagnation*. Cambridge, Eng.: Cambridge University Press, 1985.

Selassie, Berekat Habte. *The Executive in African Governments*. London: Heinemann, 1974.

Sklar, Richard L. *Nigerian Political Parties: Power in an Emergent African Nation*. Princeton, N.J.: Princeton University Press, 1963, 1970; New York and Enugu: NOK Publishers International, 1983.

———. *Democracy in Africa*. Presidential address to the 25th annual meeting of the African Studies Association, Washington, D.C., November 5, 1982. Los Angeles: African Studies Center, University of California, Los Angeles, 1982.

Wallerstein, Immanuel M. *Africa, the Politics of Independence: An Interpretation of Modern African History*. New York: Vintage Books, 1961.

———. *Africa: The Politics of Unity*. New York: Random House, 1967.

Welch, Claude E. (ed.). *Soldier and State in Africa*. Evanston, Ill.: Northwestern University Press, 1970.

Wiseman, John A. *Democracy in Black Africa: Survival and Revival*. New York: Paragon House, 1990.

Young, Crawford. *Ideology and Development in Africa*. New Haven, Conn.: Yale University Press, 1982.

Zolberg, Aristide R. *Creating Political Order: The Party-States of West Africa*. Chicago: Rand McNally and Co., 1966.

INDEX

Boldface page numbers indicate location of entries.

CONTRIBUTORS

C. WILLIAM ALLEN received a Ph.D. in mass communications from Syracuse University while on leave from the University of Liberia, Department of Communications. He was the first Editor-in-Chief of the independent daily *Footprints Today* and is the author of a novel, *An Obituary for Hawa Barchue*. Dr. Allen has also served in the Department of Agriculture of Liberia.

CHOOLWE BEYANI is on leave from the post of Assistant Professor of History in the University of Zambia. He holds a B.A. and a diploma in international law from the University of Zambia and a M.Phil. from Columbia University, where he is now pursuing a Ph.D. in history.

HENRY L. BRETTON taught political science at the University of Michigan from 1951 to 1969. He served as Distinguished Professor at the State University of New York, Brockport, from 1969 to 1985, and as Emeritus Professor from 1985. He has also served as a Visiting Professor at the Universities of Ghana (Legon) and East Africa (Nairobi), and at universities in Europe. He has published numerous books, articles and chapters in books on African politics and comparative government. His works include *Power and Stability in Nigeria* (1962) and *Power and Politics in Africa* (1973).

PATRICK CHABAL teaches the history, politics and literature of Africa at King's College, University of London, with a specialty in the Portuguese-speaking African countries. He holds a B.A. in political science from Harvard, a Master's in international affairs with certificate in African studies from Columbia University and a Ph.D. in African history and politics from Cambridge University. Among his publications are *Amílcar Cabral* (1983) and *Political Domination in Africa* (1986).

NAOMI CHAZAN is Professor of Political Science at the Hebrew University of Jerusalem, where she also chairs the Department of African Studies and is senior research fellow at the Harry S. Truman Institute for the Advancement of Peace. She has written numerous works on Ghanaian and comparative politics. Her recent books include *Politics and Society in Contemporary Africa* (with Robert Mortimer, John Ravenhill and Donald Rothchild, 1988) and *The Precarious Balance: State and Society in Africa* (edited with Donald Rothchild, 1988).

SAMUEL DECALO obtained his B.A. at Ottawa University, Canada, and his M.A. and Ph.D. in political science at the University of Pennsylvania. He has been affiliated with several institutions in the United States, most recently Emory University, as well as the University of Botswana in Africa. He is currently at the University of Natal, South Africa. He is the author of many books and numerous articles. His most recent work is *Psychoses of Power: African Personal Dictatorships* (1989).

MARK DELANCEY is Professor of Government and International Studies and Director of Graduate Studies for International Studies at the University of South Carolina, Columbia. A former Fulbright Professor in Cameroon, he is the author of many articles and two books: *Cameroon: Dependence and Independence* (1989) and *Historical Dictionary of Cameroon,* with H. Mbella Mokeba (1990). He is also editor of the *African Studies Review*, associate editor of the *African Book Publishing Record* and editor of *Handbook of Political Science Research on Sub-Saharan Africa: Trends from the 1960s to the 1990s*, Greenwood Press (1992).

D. ELWOOD DUNN is Associate Professor of Political Science at the University of the South in Tennessee and editor of the *Liberian Studies Journal*. He holds a B.A. from Cuttington University College, Liberia, and a Ph.D. in international studies from American University, Washington, D.C. He has taught at Seton Hall University and served in the cabinet of the government of Liberia. His books include *The Foreign Policy of Liberia During the Tubman Era, 1944–1971* (1985) and *Liberia: A National Polity in Transition* (with S. B. Tarr) (1988).

PETER P. EKEH was head of the Department of Political Science at the University of Ibadan, Nigeria, for a number of years. He has also served as Chairman of the Ibadan University Press, Cadbury Visiting Fellow at the University of Birmingham, England, and Fellow at the Woodrow Wilson International Center, Washington, D.C. His work has appeared in journals of African studies and comparative sociology. Currently he is Professor in the Department of African American Studies of the State University of New York at Buffalo.

ROBERT FATTON, JR., is an Associate Professor in the Department of Government and Foreign Affairs at the University of Virginia. He is also the Associate Director for Curriculum at the Carter G. Woodson Institute for Afro-American and African Studies. He is the author of two books and numerous articles, including *Black Consciousness in South Africa: The Dialectics of Ideological Resistance to White Supremacy* (1986) and *The Making of a Liberal Democracy: Senegal's Passive Revolution, 1975–1985* (1987).

L. H. GANN was born in Germany and obtained his doctorate in modern history at Oxford University. He spent eleven years in Zambia and Zimbabwe as a historian with the Rhodes-Livingstone Institute (now the Institute for Social Research at the University of Zambia) and as archivist and editor at the National Archives of Rhodesia and Nyasaland (now the Zimbabwe National Archives). He is now Senior Fellow at the Hoover Institution, Stanford University. He has written extensively on colonialism and white settlement in Africa, including *A History of Northern Rhodesia: Early Days to 1953* (1964); *A History of Southern Rhodesia: Early Days to 1934* (1965), and *Huggins of Rhodesia: The Man and His Country* (with Michael Gelfand) (1964).

DEON GELDENHUYS is a Professor in the Department of Political Science at the Rand Afrikaans University in Johannesburg, South Africa. He holds a Ph.D. from Cambridge University in England and has been a von Humboldt Fellow in Germany. His publications include *The Diplomacy of Isolation: South African Foreign Policy Making* (1984) and *Isolated States: A Comparative Analysis* (1990).

HARVEY GLICKMAN is Professor of Political Science at Haverford College, Pennsylvania, editor of *Issue: A Journal of Opinion* of the African Studies Association of the United States, and editor of this biographical dictionary. He is the author of a number of articles on Tanzanian politics and on politics in Eastern and Southern Africa. His most recent books include *The Crisis and Challenge of African Development* (1988) and *Toward Peace and Security in Southern Africa* (1990).

FRED M. HAYWARD is Professor of Political Science at the University of Wisconsin, Madison, and former Chairman of the African Studies Program and the Political Science Department. He received his Ph.D. from Princeton University and has taught at the University of Ghana and Fourah Bay College in Freetown, Sierra Leone. His many published works on Africa include studies of national integration, political participation and political leadership, including editing and contributing to *Elections in Independent Africa* (1987).

JEAN HERSKOVITS is Professor of African History at the State University of New York, Purchase. She has been writing, teaching and consulting about sub-

Saharan Africa and U.S. relations with Africa since 1960. Her Oxford D.Phil. thesis was published as *A Preface to Modern Nigeria* (1965). Her recent research on South Africa and its neighbors and U.S. policy toward Africa has appeared in major foreign-policy journals.

RICHARD HODDER-WILLIAMS holds a personal chair in Politics at the University of Bristol, England. Educated at Oxford University, he has taught in Zimbabwe, Kenya, Malawi and South Africa and as a Visiting Professor at the University of California, Berkeley. He was founding coeditor of the *Journal of Southern African Studies* and has served as editor of *African Affairs*, the journal of the Royal African Society. He is the author of *White Farmers in Rhodesia, 1890–1965: The History of the Marandellas District* (1983), *Conflict in Zimbabwe: The Matabeleland Problem* (1983) and *An Introduction to the Politics of Tropical Africa* (1984), as well as numerous articles and parts of books.

JOHN D. HOLM teaches political science at Cleveland State University, Ohio. He has written about rural development, citizen participation and voting behavior in Botswana. Most recently he has been analyzing the emergence of democratic practice in Botswana since independence.

HERBERT M. HOWE received his B.S., M.A., and Ph.D. from Wisconsin, the Fletcher School, and Harvard, respectively. He was a free-lance journalist in southern Africa for the *Philadelphia Inquirer* and worked as an analyst of southern African affairs for the Library of Congress, Washington, D.C. He has taught at Georgetown University since 1984, where he is the Director of African Studies and Research Professor of African Politics.

PASCAL JAMES IMPERATO lived and worked in Mali from 1966 to 1972, organizing and directing public health and development programs. A physician and specialist in tropical medicine and public health, he formerly served as Commissioner of Health of New York City and Chairman of the Board of Directors of the New York City Health and Hospitals Corporation. He is currently Professor and Chairman of the Department of Preventive Medicine and Community Health at the State University of New York, College of Medicine, in New York City. His books include *A Wind in Africa: A Story of Modern Medicine in Mali* (1975) and *African Folk Medicine: Practices and Beliefs of the Bambara and Other Peoples* (1977).

HENRY E. ISAACS has a law degree from Victoria University, New Zealand, and a bachelor's degree from the University of the Western Cape, South Africa. He has also been a research associate at American universities. From 1979–82 he was Director of Foreign Affairs and Representative at the UN for the Pan-Africanist Congress of South Africa. He is the author of *Struggles within Struggle: An Inside View of the PAC of South Africa* (1985). Formerly head of African

Research and Communications, Inc., Washington, D.C., he is now a business consultant in South Africa.

EHIEDU E. G. IWERIEBOR has a B.A. and M.A. in history from the University of Ibadan, Nigeria, and a Certificate in African Studies, M.Phil. and Ph.D. in history from Columbia University. He has taught at the University of Ilorin, Nigeria, and at Rutgers University, New Jersey. He has published in scholarly journals and has contributed to major Nigerian newspapers.

W. MARTIN JAMES is Associate Professor of Political Science at Henderson State University in Arkadelphia, Arkansas. He has travelled throughout southern Africa and written extensively on the region. His latest book is *A Political History of the Civil War in Angola, 1974–1990* (1991).

SHERIDAN JOHNS is Associate Professor of Political Science at Duke University, Durham, North Carolina. He has taught at the Universities of Zambia and Zimbabwe and published many articles on South Africa and southern Africa. His recent books are *Mandela, Tambo and the African National Congress: Forty-One Years of Struggle against Apartheid, 1948–1989*, coedited with R. Hunt Davis, Jr. (1991), and *From Protest to Challenge: A Documentary History of African Politics*, Volume 1, *Protest and Hope, 1882–1934* (1972, 1987).

EDWARD KANNYO obtained his B.A. at Makerere University, Uganda, and his Ph.D. in political science at Yale University. Currently Assistant Professor of Political Science in Wells College, Aurora, New York, he has served as Visiting Assistant Professor in Political Science at UCLA and at Kalamazoo College, Michigan, and as Administrative Officer and Consultant on Human Rights at the United Nations, the Lawyers Committee for Human Rights and the U.S. Committee for Refugees.

A.H.M. KIRK-GREENE is Lecturer in the Modern History of Africa at Oxford University and a Fellow of St. Antony's College. He lived in Northern Nigeria from 1950 to 1965, first as a colonial administrator and then as a professor at the Ahmadu Bello University. He is the author of numerous books and articles on Nigerian history and politics.

HENNIE KOTZE is Professor and Head of the Department of Political Science at Stellenbosch University in South Africa. He was educated at Stellenbosch, Manchester and Rand Afrikaans universities. He has written widely on South African politics with a primary interest in comparative political behavior.

BARBARA LEWIS has taught African and comparative politics at Rutgers University since completing her doctorate in political science at Northwestern University. Her research in Côte d'Ivoire since 1970 includes studies of the

Truckers Association, policy and credit among Abidjan's market women, fertility and employment in Abidjan, the women's wing of the Ivoirian ruling party, agricultural policy and economic restructuring, and farming households' responses to price changes. Her monograph, *Ivory Coast: Mired Miracle,* is forthcoming.

TOM LODGE returned to the Department of Political Studies at the University of the Witwatersrand in Johannesburg, South Africa, in 1991, after directing the Africa Program at the Social Science Research Council in New York for three years. Born in Britain, he was educated there and in Nigeria and Malaysia, receiving a B.A., B.Phil. and Ph.D. from the University of York. He is the author of *Black Politics in South Africa since 1945* (1983) and editor of *Ideology and Resistance in Settler Societies* (1986).

KENNETH MENKHAUS is Assistant Professor of Political Science at the American University in Cairo, Egypt. He received a Fulbright-Hays doctoral dissertation grant to conduct field research in rural Somalia in 1987–88. His publications on Somalia include *Somalia: An Annotated Bibliography* (1988) (coauthored with Mark W. Delancey, Sheila Elliot, December Green, Mohammed Haji Moqtar and Peter J. Schraeder) and a forthcoming book on the role of the state in rural society in southern Somalia.

H. MBELLA MOKEBA holds a Ph.D. in international studies from the University of South Carolina and a graduate diploma in integration studies from the Europa Institut in the University of the Saar in West Germany, as well as a licence and maitrise in history from the University of Yaounde in Cameroon. As Acting Assistant Professor at Louisiana State University in Baton Rouge, he teaches in international and comparative politics. He is coauthor with Mark DeLancey of *Historical Dictionary of Cameroon* (1990).

ROBERT MORTIMER is Professor of Political Science at Haverford College in Pennsylvania. He has taught, lectured or conducted research in several countries in French-speaking Africa, as well as in the Maghreb, most recently as Fulbright Professor at the Université Cheikh Anta Diop in Dakar, Senegal, in 1991–92. He has served on the editorial board of the *African Studies Review.* His books include *Politics and Society in Contemporary Africa* (with Naomi Chazan, John Ravenhill and Donald Rothchild, 1988, 1992) and *The Third World Coalition in International Politics* (1984).

KWAME A. NINSIN obtained the B.A. degree in political science and history with honors from the University of Ghana. A Fulbright-Hays scholarship permitted completion of a Ph.D. in political science at Boston University in 1976. He is currently Senior Lecturer and former Chairman of the Department of Political Science, University of Ghana, Legon. He has written and published extensively on Ghanaian politics, including the forthcoming *The Informal Sector in Ghana's Political Economy*.

SULAYMAN S. NYANG is the Chairman of the African Studies Department, Howard University, Washington, D.C. He received his B.A. from Hampton University and his M.A. and Ph.D. in government from the University of Virginia. He has published a number of scholarly and journalistic articles on The Gambia after completing his doctoral dissertation on "Political Parties and National Integration in The Gambia."

ATIENO ODHIAMBO received a B.A. in history with honors from Makerere University, Uganda, in 1970 and a Ph.D. from the University of Nairobi in 1973. He has taught at Nairobi, Stanford and Johns Hopkins universities. His books include *The Paradox of Collaboration and Other Essays* (1974); *Siasa: Politics and Nationalism in East Africa* (1981); and *Democratic Theory and Practice in Africa* (1988) (coedited with Walter O. Oyugi, Michael Chege and Afrifa K. Gitonga). He is currently Professor of History at Rice University, Houston, Texas.

AMII OMARA-OTUNNU is Assistant Professor of History at the University of Connecticut. He was educated at Makerere University, Harvard, the London School of Economics and Oxford University, and he has taught at Oxford and the University of Massachusetts, Boston. He is the author of *Politics and the Military in Uganda, 1890–1985* (1987) and articles on Uganda history and politics.

MARINA OTTAWAY taught and carried out research at the University of Addis Ababa, Ethiopia, 1974–77, and is now working in South Africa. She was an Associate Professor in the School of International Service at American University and an Adjunct Professor at the Johns Hopkins School of Advanced International Studies, Washington, D.C. Her published works include *Soviet and American Influence on the Horn of Africa* (1981), *Ethiopia: Empire in Revolution* (1978) and *Afrocommunism* (1981, 1986). The last two books were coauthored with David Ottaway.

JACK PARSON is Professor of Political Science at the College of Charleston, South Carolina. He taught at the University of Botswana from 1973 to 1978 and held Fulbright research grants in Botswana during 1984/85 and 1990. He is the author of *Botswana: Liberal Democracy and the Labor Reserve in Southern Africa* (1984), editor of and contributor to *Succession to High Office in Botswana* (1990), and has published numerous articles on the political economy of change in Botswana.

NEIL PARSONS is a free-lance academic and writer presently living in London. After serving as a teacher in Botswana and then as a graduate student in African studies at Edinburgh University, he taught history at the Universities of Zambia and Swaziland and engaged in educational research at the University of Botswana. He has authored four history textbooks for African schools and contributed to scholarly works, such as *The Roots of Rural Poverty in Central and Southern Africa* (1977), which he edited with Robin Palmer, and *Succession to High Office in Botswana* (1990), edited by Jack Parson.

CARL G. ROSBERG is Professor and former Chairman of the Department of Political Science and former Director of the Institute of International Studies at the University of California, Berkeley. He has taught in the University of East Africa and was Chairman of the Department of Political Science at the University of Dar es Salaam from 1967 to 1969. Among his publications are *The Kenyatta Election: Kenya, 1960–61,* with George Bennett (1961); *The Myth of "Mau Mau,"* with John Nottingham (1966); and *Personal Rule in Black Africa,* with Robert Jackson (1982).

ROBERT I. ROTBERG is President of Lafayette College, Pennsylvania, and was Academic Vice President, Tufts University, Massachusetts. For many years he was Professor of Political Science and History at the Massachusetts Institute of Technology. He is the author of many books and articles; his most recent book is *The Founder: Cecil Rhodes and the Pursuit of Power* (1988).

ROBERT SCHRIRE is Professor of Political Studies at the University of Cape Town and Director of the Institute for the Study of Public Policy. Educated at the University of Cape Town, Columbia University and the University of California, he has lectured at many American universities and is an African Associate at Johns Hopkins University. He is the author/editor of several books, including *Critical Choices for Africa* (1990).

HERBERT SHORE is Professor and Associate Dean, the School of Theater, University of Southern California, Los Angeles. His work on southern Africa has been supported by numerous fellowships and grants. In 1989 he was awarded the Medal of Bagamoyo by the Assembly of the Republic of Mozambique. Author, dramatist, poet and theater director, he is at present completing books on the life and legacy of Eduardo Mondlane and on the struggle for freedom in Mozambique.

RICHARD L. SKLAR is Professor of Political Science at the University of California, Los Angeles, and a former President of the African Studies Association (United States). His publications include *Nigerian Political Parties* (1963, 1970, 1983), *Corporate Power in an African State* (1975) and *African Politics and Problems in Development* (with C. S. Whitaker, 1991). He has taught at the University of Zambia, Makerere University College and the University of Zimbabwe.

NEWELL M. STULTZ is Professor of Political Science at Brown University. He has held teaching and/or research appointments at Northwestern University, Rhodes University in South Africa, the University of South Africa, Yale University and Connecticut College. He edited (with Marion Doro) *Governing in Black Africa* (1970, revised 1986) and is the author of *Transkei's Half Loaf: Race Separatism in South Africa* (1979) and *South Africa: An Annotated Bibliography with Analytic Introductions* (1989).

CHRISTINE SYLVESTER is Associate Professor of Political Science at Northern Arizona University and was formerly a Visiting Fellow at St. Antony's College, Oxford. Her works on Zimbabwean political economy, feminist theory and international relations have appeared in many scholarly journals. She is the author of *Zimbabwe: The Terrain of Contradictory Development* (1991). She is now writing a book on women, production and power in Zimbabwe.

AMARE TEKLE is Associate Professor and Program Chair of Political Science at Morris Brown College in Atlanta, Georgia. He received a Ph.D. from the Graduate School of International Studies, University of Denver, and has held posts as Head of the Bureau of Sanctions and Decolonization at the Organization of African Unity in Addis Ababa, as Director-General of the Ministry of Finance of Ethiopia and as senior officer in the Ministry of Foreign Affairs of Ethiopia. He has published many articles on politics in Ethiopia and in the Horn of Africa.

CAROL B. THOMPSON, Associate Professor of Political Science at the University of Southern California in Los Angeles, has published two books on the southern African region, the most recent being *Harvests under Fire: Regional Coordination for Food Security* (1991). She is a former editor of the *African Studies Review*. Her current research includes a cross-regional comparison of economic cooperation in Central America and southern Africa.

DAVID THROUP holds an undergraduate degree in history from Sidney Sussex College, Cambridge, and a master's degree in politics from the London School of Economics and Political Science. After teaching in Kenya, he returned to Cambridge for his doctorate in Kenyan history in 1983. In research and teaching capacities he has visited at Magdalene College, Cambridge, at the University of Virginia, at the Johns Hopkins School of Advanced International Studies, and at Northeastern University, Boston. Since 1988 he has been Lecturer in the Department of Politics, University of Keele, Staffordshire, England.

WILLIAM TORDOFF was educated at Cambridge, Manchester, and London universities. He holds a Chair in Political Science at the University of Manchester, where he served also as Dean of the Faculty of Economic and Social Studies. He has taught at the University of Ghana, University College of Dar es Salaam, the University of Zambia and the University of California, Los Angeles. His books include *Ashanti under the Prempehs, 1888–1935* (1965); *Government and Politics in Tanzania* (1967); and *Government and Politics in Africa* (1984). He is editor and coauthor of *Politics in Zambia* (1974) and *Administration in Zambia* (1980) and joint author of *Third World Politics* (1988).

THOMAS TURNER holds a Ph.D. in political science from the University of Wisconsin, Madison. He is Professor of Political Science and Director of the International Studies Program at Wheeling Jesuit College, Wheeling, West Virginia. He is the author of numerous articles on the history and politics of Zaire and is coauthor, with Crawford Young, of *The Rise and Decline of the Zairian State* (1985).

LEONARDO A. VILLALON received a Ph.D. from the Department of Government, University of Texas at Austin, completing a dissertation, "Islam and the State in West Africa: Disciples and Citizens in Fatick, Senegal," based on field work in Senegal, 1988–89. He teaches political science at the University of Kansas, Lawrence.

HERBERT F. WEISS is Professor of Political Science at Brooklyn College, City University of New York. He is also associated with the Institute of African Studies, Columbia University. He is the author of *Political Protest in the Congo* (1967) and other works dealing with protest movements in pre- and postindependence Zaire. During his early field research he was helped personally by Patrice Lumumba.

DAVID WELSH is Professor of Southern African Studies in the Political Studies Department, University of Cape Town, and was educated at the Universities of Cape Town and Oxford. He has also taught at Columbia University and the School of Advanced International Studies, Johns Hopkins University, where he is an Africa Associate. He has written two books, *The Roots of Segregation* (1971) and (with F. van Zyl Slabbert) *South Africa's Options* (1979). A third book, *Twentieth Century South African Politics*, is in process of completion. In addition, he has written approximately eighty articles, papers and chapters in books.

DOUGLAS L. WHEELER is Professor of History at the University of New Hampshire and editor of the *Portuguese Studies Review*. He has published widely in journals of Africana and historical studies; his books include *Angola* (with René Pélissier, 1971), *Republican Portugal* (1978), *In Search of Modern Portugal* (coedited with L. S. Graham, 1983) and *A Ditadura Militar Portuguesa 1926–1933* (1988). He is completing a volume on Portugal in World War II and producing a documentary film on the life of Aristides de Sousa Mendes, a Portuguese diplomat and "hero of conscience" of that period.

AGUIBOU Y. YANSANE is Professor of International Relations and Ethnic Studies at San Francisco State University, California. He was educated in Guinea and completed a Ph.D. at Stanford University, where he was also Research Associate in African Studies. He has taught at the University of California, Berkeley, San Jose State University and the University of Ibadan, Nigeria. He has published two books: *Decolonization and Dependency: Problems of Development of African Societies* (1980) and *Decolonization in West African States with French Colonial Legacy, Comparison and Contrast: Development in Guinea, the Ivory Coast and Senegal, 1945–1980* (1984), as well as articles in journals and books on dependency relations of African countries.

WILLIAM B. YOUNG is a former U.S. Foreign Service Officer. His African posts were Côte d'Ivoire and Togo; he headed the Research Division on West and Central Africa of the U.S. Department of State from 1971 to 1975. He maintains an interest in African affairs and does consulting work in the Washington, D.C. area.

About the Editor

HARVEY GLICKMAN is Professor of Political Science at Haverford College in Pennsylvania, where he is now Coordinator of the Bryn Mawr–Haverford Peace Studies program. He has degrees from Princeton University and Harvard University; he has studied also at Oxford University and the London School of Economics; and he has taught at Harvard, Princeton, Hebrew University in Jerusalem, Israel, University College, Dar es Salaam (now Dar es Salaam University) in Tanzania, the University of Cape Town, South Africa, the University of Pennsylvania, the University of California at Berkeley, and Lincoln University in Pennyslvania. He has written numerous articles on African politics and has consulted for the Rand Corporation, the U.S. Department of State, the U.S. Agency for International Development and the U.S. Defense Intelligence College. His books include *The Problem of Internal Security in Britain* (with H. H. Wilson); *The Crisis and Challenge of African Development* (editor and coauthor); and *Toward Peace and Security in Southern Africa* (editor and coauthor). He has served as Secretary of the American Political Science Association and book review editor of *Africa Report* and now serves as editor of *Issue: A Journal of Opinion*, a semiannual publication of the African Studies Association.